RADAR
REFLECTIONS

THE SECRET LIFE OF AIR FORCE RADAR MECHANICS IN WORLD WAR TWO

By the same author

Pathfinder Cranswick

The Powerless Ones: Gliding in Peace & War

The Starkey Sacrifice: The Allied Bombing of Le Portel, 1943

Beam Bombers: The Secret War of No 109 Squadron

RADAR
REFLECTIONS

THE SECRET LIFE OF AIR FORCE RADAR MECHANICS IN WORLD WAR TWO

MICHAEL CUMMING

RADAR ASSOCIATES

Published by:
Radar Associates
11303 – 11th. Street, S. W.
Calgary, Alberta, Canada, T2W 2N8

Distributed in Canada by:
Bunker To Bunker Publishing
4520 Crowchild Trail S. W.
Calgary, Alberta, Canada, T2T 5J4

ISBN
1-894255-10-0

Canadian Cataloguing in Publication Data

Cumming, Michael
Radar Reflections:

Includes bibliographical references and index.
ISBN 1-894255-10-0
1. World War, 1939 – 1945 – Radar.
2. World War, 1939 – 1945 – Arial Operations, Canadian.
3. Canada. Royal Canadian Air Force – History –
World War, 1939 – 1945. I. Title.
D810.R33C85 2000   940.54'4971   C00-911953-4

Book Production:
Bunker To Bunker Publishing.

Printed in Canada

CONTENTS

List of Plates

Acknowledgements

Fair's fair, *Radar Reflections: The Secret Life of Air Force Radar Mechanics in World War Two* would not have seen the light of day but for the singular effort of one Leon Robert McNarry, resident of Calgary, Alberta, Canada, and himself a radar technical officer who served first on various ground stations in the UK and then with a mobile Oboe unit on the Continent. Having read its predecessor, *Beam Bombers: The Secret War of No 109 Squadron* – which focussed on the development and use of a single radar system, Oboe – McNarry reckoned it was high time that someone researched and put on the record the role and the experiences of those whose job was to keep all the many different sorts of ground-based and airborne radar equipment functioning in the various operational theatres of war in which the Allied air forces were engaged around the world. It was his contention that without what he called 'this critical and significant portion', future historians would be lacking when striving to tell the full and complete story of radar in WWII.

'Mac' McNarry (more generally known post-war as Bob McNarry) introduced me to three of his friends in Calgary – Les Card, Tom Lamb and Dick Moule, all of them similarly experienced during wartime service alongside the RAF; since joined by fellow ex-radar vet Harry Carlyle, 'The Calgarians', as I have come to know them, ensured that the net was cast far and wide, the result being my personal contact with groups and individuals in Canada, the UK, the USA and elsewhere, whose war-time recollections are brought together as 'radar reflections' in these pages. Those personal stories have been interwoven with often once-secret material researched among government archives and within the contemporary records of air force commands and operational units. 'The Calgarians' have been the driving force towards the publication of *Radar Reflections*, appropriately with Canada as the place for its first printing; to them, above all, I acknowledge my gratitude and commend their initiative, their encouragement and their support.

A number of groups of wartime radar technicians and radar technical officers have helped considerably throughout my quest for knowledge about the contribution which such people made in helping to build, equip and run ground stations around the world and in helping in the development and the application of airborne equipment carried in aircraft and used around the world. Foremost I would like to place on record the help provided by Bob Linden, whose team involved in the Canadian Radar History Project have been unstinting in their desire to pass on to me a wealth of material to enable *Radar Reflections* to stand as a comprehensive and self-contained work which complements and in no way conflicts with the product of their own painstaking activities over many years. Theirs is the greater task: to assemble and record for posterity as many individual accounts as appears both possible and practicable.

Angus Hamilton has kindly checked through the South East Asia chapter for fair representation; he generously gave me the freedom to draw on his own remarkably detailed accounts. Similarly, Bruce Stewart has been extremely co-operative in making available for an unexpectedly much extended readership the unique and privately gathered 1941/45 recollections of 32 newly-commissioned officers who first met at RCAF Station, Trenton, on completion of their university courses in basic electrical and radio theory. I would like to thank both for taking on the responsibility for ensuring that the extracts quoted in *Radar Reflections* do not vary too far from the originally produced account.

In Canada, Russ Koopman, Secretary-Treasurer, Air Force Telecom Association, through his own endeavors and the AFTA newsletter, opened the way to further useful contacts and I appreciate this contribution. In the UK, Public Record Office staff at Kew have been helpful as ever; it gives me pleasure to acknowledge their willingness to assist in obtaining access to the considerable amount of documentation that it was necessary to research in order to clarify my understanding of individual contributions. In some instances it has been appropriate to include extracts from contemporary records; I am pleased to give due recognition to the fact that the Public Record Office is the custodian of the original documents and in each instance to include the document reference in the Sources. In New Zealand, the Royal New Zealand Air Force Museum has been both fast and thorough in facilitating the inclusion of information to show how radar was introduced and used in that country; such pioneering work and its effective application merits wider recognition at international level. The illustrations have come from various sources, named beside each of them; my thanks are due not only to the providers but also to others unnamed who directed me to them.

I would like to record my appreciation, too, to the many individuals without whose contribution this first-time focus on the role and the experiences of WWII radar technicians and radar technical officers would have been far less complete. Space considerations alone preclude those names – as I am sure each one of them will accept – though each will be aware how much I have valued their assistance. Finally, these acknowledgements would be visibly lacking if I were not to express my grateful thanks to my wife, Rita, and to the family – not only for letting me get on with my work when more pressing needs seemed upon us but for the ideas, the wisdom and the encouragement which I value more than possibly they recognize.

Michael Cumming
Surbiton, England, 2000

Glossary

ACH - Auxiliary Chain Home
AEAF - Allied Expeditionary Air Force
AFC - Air Force Cross
AI - Air Interception, an airborne radar system
AMES - Air Ministry Experimental Station
    (usually radar-related, this title was
    intended to conceal the true function)
Antenna - aerial
AOC - Air Officer Commanding
AOC-in-C - Air Officer Commanding-in-Chief
APU - portable power unit used on airdromes
ASV - Air to Surface Vessel radar
AVO meter - general purpose multimeter
Axis Powers – Germany, Italy and Japan
Big Ben - V2 countermeasures
Boffins - radar experts, usually civilians
Browned off - slang term for dissatisfaction
CH - Chain Home
CHL - Chain Home Low
CO – Chain Overseas, overseas equivalent
    of CH
COL - Chain Overseas Low, overseas
    equivalent of CHL
CRDF – Cathode Ray Direction Finding
CRT - Cathode Ray Tube (as in current TV)
Dad's Army - British TV comedy show based
    on the Home Guard
DFC - Distinguished Flying Cross
DI - Daily Inspection
Dipole - element of transmitting or receiving
    antenna
DSO - Distinguished Service Order
DZ - Drop Zone
E-layer - specific part of the ionosphere
Eureka - Ground homing station of Rebecca-
    Eureka portable guidance system
FM - Frequency Modulation
GCI - Ground Controlled Interception
Gen - slang for information (of any sort)
Genny - see APU
Ham - amateur radio operator
Hz - Hertz (frequency of a waveform)

IFF - Identification Friend or Foe
Lord Haw Haw - derogatory term for a
    German radio broadcaster
MEW - Microwave Early Warning radar
Mark (Mk) - designation for variation and/or
    modification of a particular equipment
Matador - large four-wheel drive flatbed truck
MID - Mention In Despatches
MHz - MegaHertz - frequency in millions
    of cycles
MRU - Mobile Radar Unit
NCO - Non-Commissioned Officer
ORs - Other Ranks
PPI - Plan Position Indicator
Pukka gen - slang for authentic information
RAE - Royal Aircraft Establishment, with
    principal site at Farnborough, Hants
RCM - Radar Countermeasures
RDF - Radio Direction Finding
Rebecca - airborne portion of Rebecca-
    Eureka homing system
RNA – Radar Navigational Aids
Sky waves – radar transmissions reflected by
    the ionosphere
TFU – Telecommunications Flying Unit
TO - Technical Officer
TRE - Telecommunications Research
    Establishment
Tube - electronic vacuum tube in many
    variations
TX - Transmitter
UK - United Kingdom of Great Britain and
    Northern Ireland
VC - Victoria Cross
WAAF - Women's Auxiliary Air Force
WEM - Wireless Electrical Mechanic
Wet Canteen - recreation centre serving beer
WOP/AG - Wireless Operator/Air Gunner
WRNS - Women's Royal Naval Service
Y Service - intelligence gathering service,
    monitoring enemy transmissions
Yagi - Japanese designed directional antenna

Dedication

To Mavis

*One of those who came to understand much of the
requirements but learned none of the secrets
of an air force radar mechanic's life in WWII*

CHAPTER 1: SECRETIVE SERVICE

It was a situation beyond belief – and it confronted an RAF squadron that had barely touched down on its new base after the upheaval of a grueling move from Bone in North Africa to the island of Malta at the height of a wartime summer. In the fierce sun, the planes became almost too hot to handle, requiring work times to be juggled as long as flight test procedures were not prejudiced. Manpower levels had dipped with personnel on leave or off the station for whatever reason; and now, just to add a fresh complication, aircrew and ground teams alike were being pole-axed with sudden bouts of excruciating sickness. Making matters even more desperate, there was an invasion going on too, the Allied landings on Sicily on 10 July 1943; the need to get the planes airborne had seldom been so crucial in this phase of operations in the Mediterranean.

The men and the machines facing those problems belonged to # 600 (City of London) Squadron, flying Beaufighter night fighters; everybody knew and appreciated that there could be no let-up, however extreme the circumstances. The Commanding Officer, Wing Commander C P Green, had already made it clear that maximum effort was required for the next few days, upping the number of aircraft and crews on night-state readiness from eight to twelve. Now, to cap it all, here was one of his top pilots, Squadron Leader A W Horne, raring to go yet there was no-one on hand to accompany him, Flight Lieutenant R T Browne, his usual navigator/radar operator, being in England.

So, unless someone materialized out of thin air – that someone being a person sufficiently competent to use the radar equipment carried in the aircraft and with it to get him close enough to pick out an enemy plane in the darkness – he could dismiss all prospects of flying that night, that night of 12 July 1943. When a full turn-out was imperative in helping maintain the military initiative at a critical stage in the war in the Mediterranean theatre, one of 600 Squadron's Beaufighters – its presence vital and otherwise cleared for operations – would be left idle on the ground at Luqa airfield. Then, to the rescue, came a radar technical officer, Flying Officer Jim Ritchie, Squadron Radar Officer, who knew more about the AI (Air Interception) equipment fitted in those planes than anyone else. He had been up many a time in a Beaufighter – his job was to know inside out the gear that that they carried, of course – but never had he done an operational flight. Most definitely that was not *his* job; there were trained aircrew for that role!

Dawn was breaking when Jim – officially entered on the record sheets as 'substitute navigator/radar operator' and feeling quite at home working familiar equipment –

realized that this début flight was about to turn into a potentially dangerous encounter.   Teamed-up with a Ground Controlled Interception (GCI) unit code-named Blackbear, two hours of the patrol had passed uneventfully; but now, dead ahead of them, a possible 'Bandit' hove into view, flying at 3,000 feet and no more than a dark smudge against the dawn light...

It all happened so fast.   Closing to 250 yards, where all doubts were gone, Horne made a positive identification: it was a Heinkel He 111.   He fired a deflection shot from the nose-mounted guns and the enemy bomber's port wing exploded, the crumpling aircraft diving sharply and crashing some ten miles south-west of Syracuse – the part of Sicily where the British 8th Army had landed with little difficulty, entering the town itself within a matter of hours [*] . Jim Ritchie was 'blooded', a radar technical officer with a ground job, volunteering as an aircrew stand-in simply because he came the closest in competence in an hour of need, sharing in the shooting down of a German aircraft by night.   More remarkable still, he would go on to do more ops and to achieve further successes...

The following summer, when the long-anticipated D-Day arrived, Muir Adair, a radar specialist too, faced the turmoil of Omaha Beach with the task of taking ashore the kind of ground-based equipment which would be used to pick up an enemy aircraft on the screen, the operators continuing to plot its progress and skillfully directing 'Nav/Rads' like Jim Ritchie towards the point of visual contact – hopefully to make a 'kill'.   Muir was with the Americans that D-Day morning, an assignment that saw him under constant fire – and even, as will emerge when he recounts those experiences, finding himself under fire from Allied troops in a blunder of mistaken identity attributable to an instruction to switch from khaki to RAF blue when boarding the landing craft for Normandy.

Before either of those incidents took place – and further away still from Britain, where both Jim and Muir had done the bulk of their specialist training – a third member of the radar fraternity, Neil Turnbull, set up, operated and maintained a different sort of radar set which he had taken into a jungle clearing behind the enemy lines in Burma. By coincidence, each was a member of the Royal Canadian Air Force, though this fact had nothing to do with the job in hand; each had volunteered for war service while in his own country, each becoming a radar specialist because it was a job to utilize his particular capabilities.   Each was there as an active participant; someone else, similarly skilled, might have been there in his place... in that Beaufighter, heading for Omaha Beach or in the Burmese jungle.   First and foremost these were specialists in their chosen trade, which is the reason for their stories being told here, the purpose of the book being to put a first-time focus on the role and the experiences shared by the radar technical officers and the radar technicians of all the Allied air forces, whether serving in the RAF, in one of the Dominions air forces or the USAAF, or indeed in the air force of a country overrun by the enemy and forced to flee to Britain.

---

[*] # 600 Squadron Operations Record Book refers to the move to Malta, the CO's requirement for maximum effort, the personnel situation and the number of men off duty through sickness – it was mostly a mild form of enteritis colloquially known as "Malta Dog". The ORB also describes the encounter with the He 111.

In some respects, it might be thought unusual if there *wasn't* a Canadian running or serving among a squadron radar section or mobile radar units! Canada's record speaks for itself; although there were none too many around to make their presence felt on radar stations during the Battle of Britain, that situation soon changed quite dramatically. Britain put out a special call to Canada... and one wonders what might have happened to the Allies' conduct of the air war had the maple leaf nation not responded so positively. The records show that 'the 5,000 Canadian radar mechanics and 750 RCAF radar officers who answered a manpower SOS from Britain and helped to speed the peace' comprised 'more than half of the total serving the RAF's ground and air installations in the European and Pacific theatres' when almost six years of war ended in August 1945[1]. Giving those figures, the Canadian press quoted the then Director of Radar at the Air Ministry in London, Air Commodore C P Brown, as saying that it would not have been possible to meet 'the vital and increasing demands of radar in the latter part of 1940 and the following years without the knowledge that Canada was undertaking the recruiting and training of men to help us handle this immense weapon'.

Typically, post-war and with the chance to mull over bygone times with his colleagues, a Canadian would probably come to the conclusion that from the mid-point of the war onwards, when the influx had peaked, perhaps one in three radar mechanics in the Allied air forces was a Canadian – leaving aside US air force units. It has been said that 'frequently, Canadians formed as much as half the strength of the radar technicians on mobile units doing their field training in England before embarking for abroad'[2]. Yet in stark contrast, in a draft sailing from Liverpool to Oran, Algeria, around May 1943, there was one person who noted subsequently that 'for the next 19 months I was a lone Canadian on a 35-man British radar crew under an American fighter wing' travelling some 2,500 miles across North Africa[3]. All who served on a radar unit could, if the need was felt, summon their own recollections as to its composition; anyway, it was probably an ever-changing population with ratios rarely constant. There would be no useful purpose in trying to average-out the number per unit inter-nationally when there was a common aim, the aim to do one's best to hasten victory, irrespective of country of birth, serial number, the presence of a certain shoulder 'flash' or, more often than not, simply a give-away accent coupled with a distinct tendency to scorn tea in favor of coffee.

Unlike those with a full or half-wing to denote an aircrew qualification in the RAF and in the air forces of countries in the Dominions, there was nothing on the uniform of radar personnel to proclaim membership of an 'elite', though this isn't too surprising... The public knew that aircraft existed and that these required people to fly them; they knew little or nothing about something the British first called radio direction finding (RDF) until adopting the American term radio detection and ranging (radar), where the men and the women engaged in this work were in a community of their own... in effect a 'secret society' [*] .

---

[*] A variant is that radar was a US Navy-coined word for radio detection and range finding, which appears in Wesley W Stout's book, *The Great Detective*, published in 1946 by the Chrysler Corporation; he expresses the view that 'radar changed the face of war more than any single development since the airplane' and notes that 'more was spent on radar by the US Government than on the atomic bomb'. Elsewhere, American naval officer S M Tucker is given credit for inventing the name 'radar', which was adopted officially by that service in November 1940[4] .

Theirs was a fast-growing coterie where members were introduced to their craft in one or other of a few exclusive schools; there, pupils became inculcated in the mysteries of their 'hush hush' subject, becoming used to being told only what they needed to know – and keeping to themselves all that they did come to know at these primary and successive specialist schools.   Later, when further exposed to the exigencies of this covert world, the closest of friends, following different paths, could well be doing exactly the same job and remain totally unaware of the coincidence because neither would talk about it.

In the course of researching this book, which incorporates many personal stories of intended benefit for future historians wishing to form a definitive judgement on wartime radar, it emerged that neighbors in the same street worked on radar in the Second World War and maintained this secret for 34 years; and for an even longer period, a matter of 40 years, the owner of an electronics company did business with one particular supplier before both realized that the other had also been a radar mechanic during war service!   However, this was not simply an environment where secrecy cloaked their very existence; it was a workplace where people became accustomed to assuming responsibilities beyond their rank, where the prospects for promotion were at times nil and where recognition of a job well done came, in one classic case that ultimately permeated through the 'corridors of power' in Ottawa and Whitehall, an extraordinary 50 years late.   Regrettably, that long overdue gesture of appreciation from one nation to those of another was impossibly late for the many qualifying radar specialists in the RCAF who had passed away in the meantime.

Arguably, 50 years is not an exceptional length of time when set against that of the history of radar itself, which can be said to span a period approaching 150 years.   Though this book concentrates on just one aspect of radar in a mere 6 years – albeit the era of its most dramatic development – it is pertinent to touch on the application and the origination of radar.   In the present context, radar embraces a variety of aviation-related devices based on the use of radio to indicate the presence of a distant object and to determine its position, its size and shape, its speed and the direction of its movement – in the main, detecting and tracking aircraft.   Typically, the radio 'beam' from a transmitter on the ground hits the 'target' in the air and is reflected back to a receiver which is also on the ground, this 'echo' from the target aircraft appearing in visual form on a cathode ray tube, akin to a conventional television screen; the principle, however, applies equally where transmitter and receiver are positioned other than on the ground and, for that matter, the target is something other than an aircraft in flight.   Pioneering work on the behavior of electromagnetic waves in the second half of the 19th century and subsequently on radio-wave reflection and radio range-finding was the foundation on which R A Watson Watt [later Sir Robert Watson-Watt] created RDF.   Suffice here to say that RDF was the cradle of military radar as applied in the defense of Britain from the mid-1930s onwards, those TV-like screens active around the clock to detect the presence of enemy aircraft.   In the hands of skilled operators, these 'tubes' yielded a constant flow of information about the direction, height and numbers of those planes.   This was information of inestimable value and it was put to use with imagination and effect in the critical late summer months of 1940, winning the 'Battle of Britain' and so halting the spread of the aggressor in the Western World [*].

There is an amusing anecdote, which WWII radar technician Craig Knudsen tells, about the period between the continuing use of the pre-war term 'RDF' and its eventual successor, 'radar', a name that has lived-on into the 21st century.   He explains:

> 'At Yatesbury, when I was there in early 1941, we were given a two-week course in electronics and after passing that we were sworn to secrecy and shown the radar equipment.   Of course it was then known as RDF, which stood for Radio Direction Finding, the reason for these initials being chosen was so that the actual use of this highly secret equipment would not be revealed.   We called it RDF for several years, while the Americans wanted to call it 'radar' [a shortened form of the US designation Radio Detection and Ranging].   The story that reached us was that Winston Churchill had said to the Americans, "OK, we'll call it 'radar' if you will call 'gasoline' 'petrol'."   It took us a long time to drop "RDF"... [5].'

It was an experiment in Britain in the mid-1930s, using an RAF Heyford heavy bomber to fly along a beam from a BBC short-wave transmitter at Daventry and a receiver to measure the reflected power, that demonstrated the ability to detect, on the ground and by means of radio signals, the presence of an aircraft high in the sky and several miles away.   In this instance, which took place on 26 February 1935 and made history with the principle of 'radar' being tried out for the first time, the Heyford was at 6,000 ft and measurable signals were being picked up at distances in excess of eight miles, inside a van parked in a muddy field near Weedon [6].   The observers on the ground were among the foremost experts in their scientific fields: R A Watson Watt, generally described as the 'father' of British radar; his colleague Arnold Wilkins, who would join him at Air Ministry when war came; and A P Rowe, later to follow in Watson Watt's footsteps as Superintendent of the Bawdsey Research Station.   Albeit a modest performance, radar foreshadowed the end of constant patrolling of the skies for surveillance purposes.

By the middle of the following year, 1936, with experiments and development in radio location proceeding at Orfordness and then Bawdsey research stations, the range at which aircraft were being detected had risen from those initial 8 miles to a much more comforting 75 miles.   The system had still to prove itself in trials as a useful aid to air defense, but the scientists had good reason to hope that its reliability in detecting and accuracy in locating aircraft could be improved sufficiently to make it so [7].   These were detection methods holding considerable promise because no

---

[*] In his book *The Invention That Changed The World: How a small group of radar pioneers won the Second World War and launched a technological revolution* (Simon & Shuster, New York, 1996), Robert Buderi reports that 'the British admit that they first discovered the practical military application of radio reflection from reports of our [the US] Naval Research Laboratory and of the Carnegie Institution published between 1926 and 1930'.   It was 'possible that the Axis discovered radar's war uses from the same source, though both the Germans and the Japanese long had been experimenting with radio reflection'.   He credits the British, 'under the stimulus of war', as being 'well ahead of us on airborne radar', adding that 'no doubt the Germans were too'.

more would clouds, haze or darkness be able to mask the presence of incoming aircraft, nor would altitude have any affect upon it.   High flying aircraft would be picked up as easily as those at moderate levels.   It was just a matter of continuing heads-down on the development work, which was done, but one particular set of trials over an 11-day period in April 1937 was not especially encouraging.   Even with aircraft sticking to pre-arranged courses over the North Sea, Bawdsey Research Station in Suffolk was experiencing difficulties in locating them – and there was also the somewhat embarrassing situation that the resulting tracks 'mostly bore no recognizable resemblance to the true positions' [8].   The AOC-in-C Fighter Command, looking to the time when he would need the best possible means of obtaining advance warning of the approach of enemy bombers, agreed that 'greater value would probably be extracted from radar in the future, but for the present he regretted that he could not accept the information in the state as it appeared for use in his operations rooms'.

Then, three coastal radar stations only were in operation: Bawdsey was the most northerly, with Canewdon in the adjoining county to the south and next came Dover, which was closest to the Continent.   Greater coverage would be needed if the radar-tracking of incoming aircraft was to be improved, the requirement being to set up more and more of these coastal detector stations so that every part of the area under observation could be under the watchful 'eyes' of at least two stations.

To build up practical detection and tracking experience among the personnel in these stations did not necessarily mean having to go to the trouble of bringing-in military aircraft as mock raiders.   There was already a steady influx and departure of aircraft whose routes and timings could even be obtained quite easily in advance because this information was public knowledge... civilian airliners on services between the UK and countries on the Continent!   Ahead of experiments using radar information for interception purposes, which began on 20 December 1937 and continued with Anson aircraft carrying out mock raids within range of the Dover and Dunkirk stations, airliners were already being tracked by operators at the Bawdsey radar station as part of their normal training [9] .   All in all, though radar fell short of expectations, these experiments did highlight some of the problems which would emerge in an operational application: for example, the frequent unserviceability of the equipment through valve failures and the 'great difficulty' for operators in distinguishing the target among permanent echoes and those caused by other aircraft.   There was also the realization that airliners were not being picked up when the routine action of reducing height when approaching their destination caused them to fly below the coverage of the radar stations in the area where frequent plots were most needed for interception.

Fortunately, in the last year of peace considerable strides were made in Britain's air defense organization which included increasing the number of coastal radar stations to a planned chain of 19, an embryo aircraft reporting and fighter control system in being, a means to help the radar operators tell friendly aircraft from hostiles – this would emerge as IFF * – and filter room plotting and communication procedures

---

* IFF, standing for Identification Friend or Foe, came into the RAF's hands only gradually, 'chiefly because there was a shortage of skilled radar mechanics for the fitting parties which started work at St Athan at the beginning of December 1939'. By the end of February 1940, a total of 258 aircraft had

being honed for maximum and immediate efficiency during round-the-clock operating in readiness for war.

There was an embryonic chain of five stations on the air in time to watch Chamberlain fly to Munich in September 1938 – Bawdsey, Great Bromley, Canewdon, Dunkirk and Dover. With that number trebling over the next six months, on Good Friday, 9 April 1939, an extended 15-station chain went on continuous 24-hour watch without planned interruption for the next six and a half years. That protective 'home chain' now stretched between the Isle of Wight (Ventnor) off the south coast of England and the Firth of Tay (Douglas Wood), well up the east coast of Scotland. Only destruction by direct enemy attack would put any of those stations off the air for an appreciable time [10] .

Six months after the declaration of war, # 60 Group would be formed within the Directorate of Signals, Royal Air Force, becoming 'the technical, administrative and co-ordinative heart of RDF'; it soon assumed 'full control of Britain's "electronic" home defense' and in its time was 'by far the largest organization of its kind'. It is interesting to note that as much as *four years* before the start of WWII, Watson Watt had recommended the eventual establishment of a 'new signals unit responsible for the chain' and that this would control all aspects of air force RDF as well as the RAF personnel who would operate it [11] * .

By May 1940 there were 33 CH and 40 CHL sites under 60 Group's mantle – CH standing for Chain Home and CHL for Chain Home Low, the latter enabling aircraft to be detected closer to the surface of the sea and at longer range. The numbers were increasing daily and there was much movement towards an overseas counterpart, a COL (Chain Overseas Low) chain, to protect the ports of Gibraltar, Malta, throughout the Middle East, India and Singapore, 60 Group being put under the strain of having to source the bulk of the necessary RDF technical expertise and to compete for equipment and spare parts. In the opening stages of the Battle of Britain, six CH stations (Dover, Dunkirk, Rye, Pevensey, Poling and Ventnor) became primary targets of vicious Luftwaffe attacks during the week of 12 to 19 August, the presence of unexploded, delayed-action bombs aggravating the situation at Poling and Ventnor by delaying the desperate efforts to re-activate the stations. It is no exaggeration to point out that in maintaining the vital links in Britain's RDF

---

been fitted with IFF Mark I – 226 of them in Bomber Command, 17 in Coastal Command and 15 in Fighter Command [12] .

* It is possible to pin down, with reasonable precision, the point at which the long-used RAF term 'RDF' would be overtaken in the RAF by 'radar', a word imported from America. An examination of contemporary files held in the Public Record Office shows that on 14 July 1943 the Central Trade Test Board was writing to the Director of RDF in respect of the *remustering of RDF mechanics*; and that on 31 July the Director General of Signals, when referring to that self-same letter, wrote about the *remustering of Radar personnel*. In the second half of July 1943, therefore, so far as the RAF in particular and those in Britain in general who were party to its secrets were concerned, 'RDF' ceased to exist and in its place came 'radar'. The Air Force List, the 'bible' of post-holders in the Royal Air Force and the definitive source for establishing the effective date of promotions of commissioned officers, confirms this timing: there being a Director of RDF in the March 1943 issue and a Director of Radar in the next one, July 1943, the post-holder being one and the same – Air Commodore C P Brown, CBE, DFC.

chain, 60 Group won its own 'Battle of Britain' – and with even fewer personnel than Churchill's famous 'Few' [13]!

Just how few were those of 60 Group?   The paucity can be seen in contemporary documentation, which reveals that Britain's coastal radar chain was in a 'very bad state' with regard to its radio mechanics and that, as part of the remedial action to overcome this dearth, the RAF was in the process of sifting through all its personnel in this and in related trades to determine who could be better employed on the chain. At the end of June 1940, with the Channel and the entire Atlantic coast in enemy hands and its troops just setting foot in Jersey and Guernsey, the disposition of newly-enlisted LAC radio mechanics at that critical time showed 775 earmarked for RDF (compared with 441 for purposes other than RDF) – 376 of them with 60 Group – with more coming along in July and August who were then under instruction at Yatesbury [14] .   Events proved that still this wasn't enough to cope; on 16 August, Group Captain Lang, Deputy Director of Signals (4) at Air Ministry, reported 'a very bad state regarding radio mechanics, personnel on the Chain being heavily overworked by reason of the acute shortage, apart from nervous fatigue etc as a result of enemy action' [15] .   Heed was taken to the extent that 'we are combing out the Service of wireless tradesmen not only for RMs but also for other Signals trades' [16], the purpose being immediately to switch suitable personnel from less effective work to 60 Group to gain experience before training at Yatesbury.

The stories of Churchill's 'Few' are legion, as indeed are those of 60 Group personnel.   There are those who were injured or lost their lives manning the radar stations; and there are those whose bravery in the face of enemy attack earned a medal or else a commendation in some other form; most went about their work as did the majority in wartime, no doubt pushing to the back of the mind the possibility that the worst might happen – and if it did, they'd prefer that it happened quickly and without pain.   Putting aside the drama, the heroics and the personal feelings of those now long gone days – as well as avoiding the temptation to talk in terms of a 'typical person on a typical station' – what was it like on a south-east coast radar site during the Battle of Britain?

A pre-war militiaman whose job was radio servicing and repairs, Eric Folkson entered the RAF, as he had anticipated, in the early weeks of hostilities when reaching the age of 20.   His was a technical background such that he had no difficulty passing a trade test to become a WEM (RDF) – a Wireless & Electrical Mechanic (Radio Direction Finding).   Then, basic training behind him – 'Square-bashing at Uxbridge before Christmas and at Hawkinge after the break' – January 1940 found him lined up, one among upwards of 120 airmen standing 'at ease' in their neat rows on the station's parade ground, anxiously waiting for his name to be called out and his posting announced to the assembly.   He recalls that...

> 'There were all these exotic destinations, like Singapore and Hong Kong, thousands of miles away, so it was a bit of a shock when my name came up and I learned that my posting was to Swingate, close to Dover and within eight or nine miles, as the crow flies, from where we had just completed our "square bashing".   This was one of the first half-dozen or so radar stations forming the coastal chain begun before the war.

'I was on the CHL station manned by three watches to cover round-the-clock working. Each watch comprised about six chaps – a mix of operators, mechanics and wireless operator/air gunners on temporary detachment in view of the shortage of trained personnel. Apart from maintenance, mechanics mucked in and took a turn on all operators' duties, including the "TX" bind – rotating the aerial via the pedals on the modified push-bike arrangement which was the aerial turning gear.

'Although the adjacent CH station had WAAF operators, this was not the case with the CHL which remained all-male throughout the Battle of Britain until late 1940 when I was posted.

'I don't know how my former colleagues fared with their Far East postings, maybe some didn't get back, but there was more than a fair share of the action in the Dover area, which was known as "Hell Fire Corner" because of its proximity to France, by then swallowed up by the enemy whose bombers and long-range guns were intent on giving us little peace night or day.

'The radar equipment was reasonably reliable, although on many occasions we had to improvise repairs to keep on the air. One of the hazards was Channel gales with strong wind-strengths making the aerial uncontrollable – it would behave like a demented windmill. We had to secure it using a large steel pin about six inches long and two inches in diameter – such fun and games on a dark night with lashing wind and rain!

'Generally everything about it was fine, as it was absolutely critical because Jerry was so adept at coming in fast and low, but I do remember there was one peculiar situation where it began behaving in an odd way. We carried out all manner of tests, routine and otherwise... then, by taking a look outside and carrying out a closer inspection, eventually we found the cause. It turned out that a splinter from an exploding shell fired from across the Channel had sliced one of the dipoles in the antenna [17].'

That 'shortage of trained personnel' which caused even WOP/AGs to be detached temporarily from their aircrew duties to help man the severely-pressed coastal radar stations was so acute that Britain would be obliged to take exceptional steps to mobilize sufficient resources. These personnel would be required not for the CH and CHL sites alone – sites overseas as well as those at home – but to provide the technical expertise so crucial to the application of new forms of defensive and offensive weaponry to fight the war in the air. For those who answered that call, this was going to be more than simply helping out in a time of dire need, it would be a chance to get in at the start of a new age – though few would have imagined its benefits and their consequences, its ramifications far exceeding the then confines of aerial warfare. Based on the radio-reflection principle, RDF was a product of pre-war thinking that turned out to be a salvation in the air defense of Britain when this country came under attack by formations of Luftwaffe bombers; what similarly innovative fruits of wartime inventive genius were yet to emerge that would help win the war and, at the same time, be a catalyst for so many developments of a peaceful nature, right on into the 21st century?

CHAPTER 2: RDF RAMPARTS

With the 'Battle of Britain' won in the air and the anticipated German invasion at least deferred, those who were in the know about the radar secret could be excused for taking the view that this was the invention which saved the country. Being the means to track the Luftwaffe's bombers and to direct the RAF's fighters towards them, radar achieved what would otherwise have been impossible: with conventional methods of detection and interception, the pathetically few aircraft that were on hand to protect Britain in this 'darkest hour' would have had no chance against the relentless hordes of incoming bombers... leaving the anti-aircraft gun batteries to wage a lone defensive campaign. A means of salvation or not, the importance of radar cannot be overstated; indeed, there is a school of thought, certainly among those who were closest to its secrets and were instrumental in developing the coastal chain, that had the enemy summoned up more of a knockout punch into its attacks on the radar chain, sufficient damage could have been caused perhaps to alter the entire course of the war.

Nonetheless, 60 Group's RDF chain apparently wasn't functioning as effectively as it might have done; if there was any impediment, achieving a more acceptable performance would have required a strengthening of the chain overall rather than the replacement of any weak links * .

In a tightly-written, strongly-worded paper dated 15 October 1940, issued to a limited circulation list 'for information and necessary action', 60 Group's top man at that time, Air Commodore A L Gregory (its AOC – Air Officer Commanding), reported on what he described as a 'general review' of RDF operational efficiency. He opened with a statement that 'it is generally admitted that the information available on the cathode ray tubes at RDF stations is not passed to Operations Rooms in the volume, accuracy, detail, or with the minimum time-lag, possible.' Although the greater emphasis was clearly to be placed on the handling of information than on the hardware in place to produce it, recipients of the Air Commodore's paper would find that the radio signaling towers – those highly visible signs of Britain's aircraft warning defenses which were the province of the radar mechanics – came in for sharp criticism. The indoor equipment was 'technically good but unreliable', the smaller masts were 'too flimsy for the exposed positions in which they have to be used', the CH aerials were 'very poor' in front-to-back ratio and the CHL array mounting and feeders were of 'poor design', the aerials having to be locked in a high wind, 'thus putting the station virtually off the air' [1] .

Air Ministry reacted with a document comprising Appreciation and Comments, which started by noting that the AOC's survey 'provoked a most interesting and stimulating discussion'. It went on to address each of the points raised, one by one... that it did not agree the indoor equipment could be described as unreliable – 'It will be found that as operators and maintenance men become more familiar with their equipment that the amount of maintenance attention will become less'; that mobile equipment has to be light in construction 'and it is agreed that the particular design in service has erred on the side of mobility at the expense of strength'; and with regard to CHL, that 'an improvement is being sought in designs using higher frequencies and smaller array structure'.

Two other organizations were drawn into the controversy: Stanmore Research Section, whose report ₃ was acknowledged by Air Commodore Gregory on 8 December 1940 to have made 'a valuable and important contribution to the discussions now proceeding as to the measures necessary for increasing the efficiency of the RDF chain', and the Telecommunications Research Establishment (TRE), which wanted detailed information, at the same time countering 60 Group's comments concerning equipment failures ₄. The receiver, calculator and telephone apparatus 'are extremely reliable'; the transmitter 'gives trouble chiefly because of inexperience of the personnel in charge'; 'failures in the recent gale, which have been investigated, were found to be due to insecure picketing'; poor back-to-front ratio of CH aerials 'is frequently due to the station working off spot frequency'; and while it was 'admitted that CHL aerials have to be locked when wind velocity reaches 40 mph', work was being done at that Establishment 'to find how CHL aerials can be screened from the wind without affecting their efficiency'.

Despite all that, radar itself had without doubt proved its value in aerial defense in that epic summer of 1940; furthermore, radar was being seen to offer considerable promise in other fields, the principle of bouncing back a radio signal arousing formidable possibilities both in offensive and defensive applications in the air, on the ground and at sea. The basic facility now existed; it would be up to the military to define the requirements and it would be down to the scientists to create the opportunities for the increasing use of radar to meet those needs.

Faced with the fact that there were nowhere near enough men and women in Britain to install, to service and to operate the increasing numbers and types of radar equipment that were already in use and pending, Britain would have to focus on the problems of where and how to recruit and to train more people of the right caliber. Compounding these problems was the fact that radar was not only a subject which no-one could talk about openly to attract potential recruits, it encompassed requirements so specialist that recruitment would be rendered all the more difficult on account of the educational standards and the technical capabilities that would be needed to warrant selection and training.

The Dominions were an obvious recruiting ground, as evidenced by the steady flow of applicants from these countries who, without pressure to do so, wished to join the RAF in the immediate pre-war years. More specific to the present call was the fact that, just in the last winter before the war began, the Radio College of Canada, noting that the RAF required 3,300 wireless operators, quickly offered its services as an intermediary in placing before Sir Kingsley Wood, Under Secretary of State at the

Air Ministry, the names of graduates meeting the RAF's qualifications. A year or so previous to that occasion, when the shortage of operators had grown acute in England, Marconi in Canada had asked this same establishment to get in touch with all graduates who would be interested in going over to England; and as a result it is on record that 'a large delegation passed the medical examination and joined the Marconi International in England from where they have traveled to almost every part of the globe' [5].

Coincidental with the turning point in the Battle of Britain, when the Luftwaffe's bid for daylight supremacy in the air was ended, much energy was being exerted on measures to resolve the shortfall in radar personnel. All that conceivably could be done was being done; these were epochal measures, on both sides of the Atlantic, including secret discussions between top-ranking diplomats, the eventual agreement of international leaders and, it has to be said, downright subterfuge.

Men of the right sort to ease the 'acute shortage' of RDF mechanics in the Royal Air Force would be 'hard to find' – this comes through loud and clear in a document in the National Archives in Ottawa, dated 4 October 1940, which spelled out Britain's requirements for 'suitably trained manpower'. Three 'main types of personnel' were needed to maintain and operate RDF equipment – these three categories were 'known in England as Radio Officers, Radio Mechanics and Radio Operators'; there was an 'acute shortage' of Radio Officers and Radio Mechanics but not, at that time, of Radio Operators.

The minimum technical requirements for candidates for commissions as Radio Officer were...

> 'a good science degree (or a good law degree and subsequent experience of patent work) and a thorough knowledge of fundamental alternating current theory. They should be absolutely "sound" in this, especially in their knowledge of inductance, capacity, resistance, frequency, phasing and acceptor and rejector circuits. In addition, they must have a knowledge of the basic principles of radio transmission and reception'.

Provided that a candidate's knowledge was thorough, it was possible to 'superimpose the special training' in eight weeks.

Radio Mechanics 'have been recruited mainly from the better-class radio and television shops and from radio factories'; they were employed in 'maintaining the apparatus at the fullest efficiency, in fault-finding and in general technical upkeep'. Ideally, they 'should have about 80 per cent of the theoretical knowledge of candidates for commissions as Radio Officers, and should also have had much more practical experience; but such men are hard to find'.

As a minimum, Radio Mechanics...

> 'require to have a good practical knowledge of modern superheterodyne receivers and of servicing and fault-finding. They should preferably have had some experience of short-wave receivers. It is important that their knowledge should not be purely practical. They should have the curiosity

and intelligence to have mastered at least the elementary basic principles of radio transmission and of modern radio-receivers.'

In a reference to Radio Operators, it was stated that women with no technical knowledge 'have been successfully employed – being enlisted as WAAFs Special Duties, after selection by a board which includes an officer from the Signals Branch'. The 'art of radio operating is still too new for any accurate assessment of the civilian qualifications most suitable for this work. But intelligence, mental alertness, and the ability to think quickly without getting flustered are essential. A certain familiarity and quickness with figures is also desirable'.

RCAF recruiting centres were authorized to recruit immediately up to 100 radio officers and 1,000 radio mechanics [6].

The RAF's urgent need of recruits to maintain and operate RDF equipment had been made known (on 4 October 1940) by the UK High Commissioner to Canada, Sir Gerald Campbell, to the Canadian Department of External Affairs [7]. It became obvious though that, despite strenuous recruitment, even the earliest and most immediate targets would not be met. The net had to be cast further afield and Britain began looking hungrily towards America, even though that country was not yet drawn into the war [*].

Recruiting in America was 'absolutely essential' in the case of radio personnel since men with sufficient basic knowledge to enable them to be trained in any reasonable time 'could not possibly be obtained elsewhere' [8]. The Canadians were all set themselves to launch a recruiting drive for radio personnel and the publicity associated with this was deliberately encouraged to spill across the border into the USA. No time was to be lost, it seemed, because the requirements for radio mechanics were 'very urgent' and, 'by direction of Prime Minister Churchill, had first priority' [9].

A civilian school was envisaged in Canada for the training of radio mechanics generally 'to fill the many civilian radio appointments at present vacant there' – a school for Canadians, yes, but one whose doors would welcome their American neighbors too. Applicants from the USA would be encouraged... but only those who passed muster and professed a genuine intention to enlist in the Royal Canadian Air Force and to serve in Britain as 'Radio-locator Servicemen' would earn themselves a place on one of the courses at this school, plus a railway ticket to get them into Canada. It was admitted that, 'in order to give a more realistic façade to the scheme', it might become necessary to accept 'a few' who did not wish to enlist but who were prepared to accept civilian radio employment in Canada [10]. It was, of course, within the law for an American citizen to proceed to Canada and enlist in that country, provided that he did not take an oath of allegiance to any foreign ruler; what

---

[*] Though unrelated, this appeal to Canada for these first radar recruits from outside Britain came just a fortnight before the British Commonwealth Air Training Plan (BCATP) agreement was signed, with Canada, Australia, New Zealand and the United Kingdom to work together on a combined and co-ordinated training plan, based in Canada, which produced 49,707 pilots, 29,963 navigators, 15,673 air bombers, 18,696 wireless operator/air gunners, 15,700 air gunners and 1,913 flight engineers by the time it came to an end on 31 March 1945.

was illegal was for an American citizen, whilst in the United States, to enlist in the armed forces of a belligerent power.

Air Ministry Signals personnel were already busy trying to work out how best to arouse interest and enthusiasm within the constraints of secrecy; in effect, this was to be an international recruitment campaign designed to invoke the requisite response for minimal disclosure about the nature of the job. It called for a formula in which the world at large would be given a powerful message to attract the right caliber of individual and to make each prospective volunteer feel that here was something well worthwhile.   The thrust of the message turned to talk about 'the new science of radio-location' where wireless electronic watchmen in distant outposts formed the 'radio ramparts' of Britain, 'ever ready to flash up tidings of the enemy's approach with the speed of light itself'.   This new military art required equipment which had to operate perfectly for 24 hours a day for the duration of the war; it would be out of the question for equipment in the field to be returned for servicing, which was why Britain needed 'thousands more men for this work, mostly men with experience of radio' [11].   It was stressed that, while Britain's technical manpower was approaching complete mobilization, beyond these shores there must be many trained men, sympathetic to the cause, who needed only to know of this opportunity for service to be keen to volunteer.

In Canada, on 8 April 1941, 'Chubby' Power, Minister of National Defense for Air, broadcasting to the nation with what he called 'something to catch the imagination of men who can look ahead', focussed on the achievements of British, Canadian and US scientists in the development of a modern weapon against day and night attack by air.   By using a great number of small radio sets of modern design, radio technicians posted at ground points all over the British Isles would be able to detect enemy planes in the air and direct anti-aircraft fire with deadly precision.   It was an invention that, like anything else, called for men to make it work – and although Canada had been combed for several months for amateur and professional radio men to be rushed overseas, 'that source of supply is now dried up'.

The message was clear: 'We are ready to take green men, men of good education who have never seen the inside of a radio.   We will train them in this new work and within a few months they will be holding key posts in the defense of Britain'.

The Minister explained that the age limit was from 18 to 45, but the aim was to fill the requirements with men between 22 and 27; 13 Canadian universities had rallied to the call to fill this urgent need; recruits would spend their first month at an Air Force Manning Depot and then move to one of those universities for a 13-week course, the next step being a posting overseas.   Canada was looking immediately for 2,500 volunteers for a new service which would develop and grow, harnessing to it the initiative and zest of the country's youth [*] .

---

[*] No-one focussed on the exposure to danger that volunteering for active service would introduce to those young men. LAC Doug Paul, an early recruit who arrived in the UK on 17 January 1941, lost his life within a matter of weeks, when on 6 May 1941 a German bomber 'scored a direct hit on the Domestic Site' at Bawdsey, an area of this East Coast radar station that was 'sparsely populated at the time and only three airmen were killed'.   It was reported that two of the three watches were off duty 'and enjoying a dance at the Cavendish Hotel, Felixstowe', the third watch being on duty [12]. There were to be further

With wireless so intriguing in its early days, Canadian recruits especially were often extremely well qualified in its technicalities when offering their services in response to the nation-wide appeals in the autumn of 1940 and the spring of 1941.   Such experience was exactly what was needed; the basic knowledge required for RDF work was there, the hands-on capabilities and the inquisitiveness was there and so was the enthusiasm to continue the learning curve to whatever heights were within their reach.   Roy Taylor was perhaps typical...

'My father had a fascination for the wireless and I remember him building a crystal set so that the family could pick up more distant stations like KDKA in Pittsburg, and WLW in Cincinnati, once our own local broadcasting station, 10AK (which later became CJCS), signed off early in the evening. We – and the neighbors – used to crowd around the kitchen table night after night, when the adults were home from work, listening to these broadcasts.   I still have the plug that accommodated the pin tips of the five headphones that we had to share. Wow! Was there a row when somebody coughed and jerked the set, or slammed a door, and the "cat's whisker" lost the sensitive spot!

'The most impressive model I built myself was a crystal set. The coil was wound on a toilet roll, with a couple of turns for the antenna and ground. The main coil was tapped a couple of places and placed across a tuning condenser. The antenna was the wire from a burned-out radio transformer, in excess of 150 ft in length. I used Fahenstock clips on narrow strips of copper to bring them under the bottom of the window. Across the antenna and ground leads, I soldered a burned-out pilot light. When lightning was around, it was fascinating watching the surges discharge across the broken bulb filament. We could use a loudspeaker when the local station was on the air but we thought it best to have a bit more privacy while listening to police calls from Toronto and Detroit.   Dad lost interest in wireless when he couldn't get rid of the hum on his AC set, so I inherited all his bits and pieces [13] .'

Newspaper advertising for 'amateur radio operators, radio servicemen and radio experimenters' in October 1940 took Roy first to a screening centre in his home town, where he received a letter of introduction to use in the next stage of the enlistment process, and then to the RCAF recruiting office in London, Ontario. There was 'such a queue of applicants – everyone but me wanted to be a pilot! – that I told them I had a letter for the Commanding Officer, which seemed to do the trick'.   Next came an hour-long interview in the Radio Inspector's office across the street, culminating in Roy being given a sealed letter.   The interviewer wished him 'Good luck'... 'Apparently if I wasn't acceptable I would have been told "Goodbye" '. Next day, 16 November 1940, the former Mr Albert Roy Taylor became R78702 Leading Aircraftman A R Taylor, a Wireless & Electrical Mechanic (R) *en route* for Toronto and who-knows-where.

---

fatalities, in the air and at sea as well as on land, some through accidental causes though the majority were the result of enemy action, among them a number who remustered as aircrew.

Before the year was out, Canada's first radar mechanics were in the UK, having arrived on Christmas Day 1940 aboard the SS *Pennland*.   No time was lost in getting them to work in a radar environment.   At Upper Heyford, for instance, Herbert C Bell's job was to remove defective electronic equipment from RAF bombers, which was then sent away for repair at Leighton Buzzard, 60 Group's HQ. Keen to demonstrate that he was no green recruit, Herbert told his Warrant Officer that he was capable of carrying out the necessary repairs himself – there was no need for it to leave the station.   He explains:

> 'He tested my abilities to do this, and I proceeded to do it with success.   I was promoted to Corporal, after which I applied for a Commission. After being interviewed by Senior Officers I was sent to London for tests by a special board, and granted the rank of Pilot Officer – the first Canadian to be commissioned in the UK. I returned to Upper Heyford, went into Oxford to get my uniform, packed my things and was off to Yatesbury for an Officers' Training Course [14]!'

At Cranwell, another of this first group, Francis J de Macedo, ran into his first 'set-to' with the RAF.   He recalls:

> 'An overbearing RAF Warrant Officer addressed us as "You Colonials", which was like waving a red flag in front of a bull. He wanted us for GD [General Duties] work and when he gave us the command "Attention, Right Turn", not a soul moved. Even I was surprised but not more so than our W/O. They never knew exactly what to do with Canadians, and he went red-faced to see the CO. When he returned, one of our braver types said we didn't come over to wash floors or do sweeping. That was for the flyers and we should receive disembarkation leave. I suppose the easiest way out was to give us leave and get rid of these brash, undisciplined "Colonials" and we were all on our way with seven days' leave [15].'

Heading for who-knew-what and no doubt experiencing some sense of pride as pioneers for both Canada and Britain, this handful of kindred spirits was quickly followed by another group, this time on the *Nerissa*, which was at sea over the New Year.   Together, that vanguard numbered but a fraction of the first major contingent – the 161 members of what would become known as the 'Leopoldville Group', taking this name from that of the ship which carried them to Britain.

For Roy Taylor, a member of that 'Leopoldville Group', Christmas 1940/New Year 1941 was spent on embarkation leave.   On 2 January, having 'fallen-in' adjacent to the railway sidings at the Toronto Exhibition Grounds, 1914/18 war hero Billy Bishop VC shook each of them by the hand and wished them luck * .

A three-day train journey took them via the Gaspe Peninsula in Quebec to Port of Saint John, New Brunswick (a detour because the United States was a neutral country), where stood the SS *Leopoldville*, a passenger vessel used between Belgium and the Congo, whose colorful livery of pre-war days was now replaced by

---

* As Air Marshal in charge of recruiting for the Air Force, Billy Bishop's personality, drive and fame as a WWI air ace attracted so many recruits that applicants had to be turned away.

drab gray overall. 'One look at her,' said Roy later, 'and you could understand what the incoming RAF draft meant by reference to it being "a tub" [16]. These lads made it plain that they didn't envy anyone who was returning to Britain on the *Leopoldville'* .

The RCAF WEMs on this Britain-bound draft soon discovered that the vessel was not best suited for crossing the Atlantic in winter.   Being more used to providing a tropical service, 'she had fans but no apparent means of heating.   When the wind blew down from the north, on to the port side, we had to move to the starboard side'. For all but the first and last days of the 12-day crossing to Liverpool, Roy was in the sick bay with what he suspected was either sea sickness or flu; in fact it was related to his appendix, which caused him problems on and off until its removal in October 1942. Other than the ship's officers, most of the crew were nationals from the Belgian Congo, which created communication difficulties; Roy's doctor spoke English but sign language had to be employed when in contact with the orderlies.

There was much common ground among the 'Leopoldville Group'; at minimum, all were Canadians answering the mother country's call and all were excited about putting their interest and their skills in radio to best use in the war effort.   Individual backgrounds varied, no doubt largely dependent upon which part of that vast country was their home.

A radio enthusiast from the moment the family bought a battery set in the mid-1930s when he was around 16 years of age, Craig Knudsen was an Ontario farmer's boy, as were a fair proportion of his countrymen who answered the early calls for recruits to go into RDF in the UK.   He didn't have a high school education – it seemed totally irrelevant in a farming community – but what he did possess was the necessary competence in understanding and handling radio equipment.   For this he could thank the fact that he had seen and answered a magazine advertisement for an electrical and radio correspondence course costing 35 dollars; this was a sum beyond his means until he had saved up the proceeds of shoveling snow at 25 cents an hour.   Having gone to London, Ontario, on 6 November 1940, to see if he would make a suitable candidate, Craig wasn't a bit surprised to find that he had the right technical qualifications to become a Wireless & Electrical Mechanic (WEM) – 'It was obvious that the people questioning me knew less about radio than I did... I had no trouble at all, passing that test [17] .'   What did surprise him, though, was the apparent haste to get him into uniform – he was asked to go to Toronto that very day to complete the process!   No, he said, he couldn't do that: his car had broken down on the journey to the recruitment centre and he had to get it towed off the roadway. Three days later he was in Toronto and a member of the 'Leopoldville Group', reaching Liverpool on 17 January 1941 after 'a rough crossing with equally unpleasant food'.

Pals and neighbors Ev Brown and Art Blachford, successful in their amateur radio examinations given by venerable Radio Inspector Sam Ellis in Toronto back in 1935, when only 14 years of age, each received a letter from Sam in 1940 which invited them to join the RCAF for service in the UK where, as Ev puts it, 'radio technicians were in short supply'.   The pair became LAC WEM (R) recruits and members of the

---

* SS *Leopoldville* was torpedoed on Christmas Eve 1944, within sight of the French port of Cherbourg, with the loss of more than a third of the 2,200 American troops who were on board.

first group to be sent to the UK, sailing on the *Pennland*, arriving on Christmas Day 1940 and going first to RAF Station, Uxbridge. Ev takes up their story:

'We were given our choice of some 15 RAF stations and decided on Church Fenton because it wasn't far from Manchester where friends lived. When we arrived, in mid-January 1941, # 54 OTU had just formed; there was a shortage of Signals personnel so we found ourselves very busy servicing some 100 aircraft. There were 60 Blenheims (both the short-nose Mk II and the long-nose Mk IV), some 28 Defiants and a miscellaneous collection of Ansons, Masters, Magisters and Tiger Moths. In those days Signals was responsible for all electrical equipment as well as radio on the aircraft so we soon became skilled at turning down commutators on motors and generators, changing bearings, adjusting carbon pile voltage regulators and knowing all about the care and feeding of accumulators, both lead acid and alkaline. The more modern radio equipment was "user friendly" to us, containing American tubes with which we were familiar. For example, both the AI RDF and the VHF ground transmitter T1131 contained Eimac 35Ts and the airborne VHF transceiver, the TR1133A, used Type 807s in their output.

'Art and I were promoted to Corporal in March 1941 and to Sergeant in June. He looked after the dispersed aircraft and I supervised the hangar maintenance [18].'

It was while the Canadian pair were at Church Fenton that there occurred what Ev describes as 'most curious' air raids – odd because there was one virtually every Wednesday night, odd because 'Lord Haw-Haw' referred to a certain pilot having paid 'his usual visit to Church Fenton last night' and odd because all were carried out by a single Junkers 88. One brilliant moonlit night, while walking in the direction of one of the hangars on the airfield, it passed over Ev's head with its flaps and wheels down 'as if coming in for a landing'. He continues:

'The Ju 88 carefully dropped a stick of bombs between two hangars with the result that little or no damage was done. The avoidance of damage was obviously deliberate in view of the splendid visibility. On another occasion I was attending an ENSA show in a hangar fitted out as a permanent theatre. During the show we had an air raid and I remember it sounded as though every ack-ack gun on the station opened up. The entire audience went flat on the floor and then, when things had quieted down, the show resumed. I was seated near the door and was one of the first to leave. Someone ahead of me stumbled against something in the darkness and cursed. A man behind him had a torch and what this disclosed was a set of fins sticking out of the ground. It was a bomb – and judging by its size, a 250 kg. We found five others in a straight line so the crew had either forgotten or purposely had neglected to fuse the bombs.

'Prior to every one of these air raids a number of aircraft radios would be turned on, usually in the vicinity of # 1 hangar, and the Ops Room would call me to ask that I turn them off. It has long remained my contention that those radios were turned on to allow the Ju 88 to home-in on Church

Fenton.   On the assumption that we had a German agent in our midst, one Wednesday night I stationed three of my men inside # 1 hangar, each armed with one of the Thompson sub machine guns, part of some 40 weapons supplied by American Lend-Lease for my little band of 30 men. Sure enough, there were aircraft transmitters turned on in and around the hangar but my men had seen nothing.   Then we had an air raid with incendiaries coming through the roof, which kept me busy dumping buckets of sand on them, but none landed close to the few aircraft in the hangar. Several of the incendiaries hung up in the roof, burning fiercely, and our Fire Detail Corporal went up the steel ladder on the side of this 80 foot high hangar with a large fire extinguisher under each arm and put out the fires. He received the BEM for his trouble.

'There is something very mysterious about these raids.   I got the feeling that they were somehow sanctioned and assisted by high authority. Permission was never given to the anti-aircraft gunners to shoot until the Ju 88 was disappearing in the distance – then the gunners would fire a few rounds in frustration.   I wondered then – and I've been wondering ever since – if the aircraft was dropping information by some means or another... that it was a conduit for communication from inside Germany.   I guess we'll never know! [19] '

Commissioned in the autumn of 1941, Ev Brown went on to serve as a Station Signals Officer in Fighter Command, Coastal Command, the Tactical Air Force and finally in Bomber Command, returning to Canada in 1945.

The day that 'Chubby' Power was making his major radio appeal in Canada on 8 April 1941 and Ev Brown had his hands full in Britain, serving the needs of the RAF at Church Fenton, Wylie Barrett was already in uniform, by trade a Wireless & Electrical Mechanic (Radio) – a WEM (R).   Despite being older than most of his contemporaries and a family man with four young ones, he was on the way to Debert, Nova Scotia, a period of embarkation leave behind him and, ahead, service in some unspecified overseas country or countries for an also unspecified length of time.   One of the first of his country's radar technicians, Wylie had answered a previous though much less publicized appeal for men with experience in radio and communications for service overseas – 'I felt that my conscience would bother me all my days if I did not volunteer,' he has confessed subsequently [20] .   So, having answered the call, during the first week in February 1941 he was sworn-in as R72820 Barrett, A C W, a member of the Royal Canadian Air Force and two steps up the promotion ladder to hold the exalted classification of Leading Aircraftman, by virtue of his background in the wireless trade.   A radio amateur for four years and a licensed electrician of journeyman level, Wylie had been working for a Summerside, Prince Edward Island, firm which owned and operated a broadcasting station, CHGS; so, not only was he familiar with transmitter maintenance, he was part-time announcer/disc jockey too.   With such technical qualifications and experience, he found no difficulty passing the RCAF trade test and leapfrogged AC2 and AC1 to become an LAC Group (B), with a posting first to the Manning Pool in Toronto and then to Debert, Nova Scotia, which was functioning as a holding depot for personnel waiting to go overseas.

He sailed out of Halifax on an armed merchant cruiser, *California*, with some 300 RCAF personnel, most of them aircrew Sergeants, which was rather unfortunate as the three-stripers were not called upon to volunteer for any duties aboard ship, unlike lesser mortals. Wylie reckoned that the first to volunteer would get the best jobs so, with one of his buddies, Ray Dempsey, he put his hand up and found himself operating the elevator between the galley and the officers' mess several decks above. It was a job which brought certain fringe benefits which are not difficult to imagine. WEM (R)s who were reluctant to volunteer were less fortunate: these became expert at peeling potatoes and washing dishes.

'Our route across the Atlantic took us far north and for most of the time we saw nothing exciting until a couple of days short of Iceland we were met by several lease/lend destroyers which Britain had acquired from the USA. Then, there was some action. The destroyers dropped quite a number of depth charges and smoke markers, though whether this was a practice or for real we would never learn. As we came into the fjord near Reykjavik, we were greeted by the sight of the battle cruiser *Hood* and there to salute us was a band playing on the foredeck – a most impressive sight. Little did we expect this mighty warship to be on the bottom of the Atlantic within a matter of weeks.

'Iceland would be, I thought, a land of nothing but snow and ice. To my surprise the grass was green near the sea although snow could be seen on the higher elevation inland. We didn't have an opportunity to see anything of that country, however, because we were quickly transferred to a smaller vessel, *City of Belfast*, a troop transporter which was said to be too fast for submarines that it traveled without an escort. That was the story, anyway, but I did hear later that she had been sunk by a submarine – maybe she slowed down... My experience was more that of transportation aboard a stinking ship, rather more than a sinking ship. I couldn't stand the stench below decks so, with my one blanket and greatcoat, I spent the nights under one of the lifeboats. The food was no better, certainly not up to the standard we had enjoyed on the *California*, and there seemed to be the same old menu: a can of fat USA bacon with dry bread for breakfast, a tin of McConniky's Irish stew or a tin of bully beef for lunch and supper.'

The voyage from Iceland to Greenock in Scotland was uneventful and this was followed by the long train journey south to London and across to Uxbridge, from whence the next destination was RAF Station, Wilmslow, where he heard the sound of enemy aircraft for the first time, droning overhead in all probability to bomb the Liverpool docks. At Wilmslow, an unexpected further trade test sorted out some 150 WEM (R)s into 20 who were selected for training at Yatesbury and 100 to go for *ab initio* training in London, the remainder being shipped back to Canada. Wylie Barrett was one of those who 'guessed right' during the exams and secured a place on a radar training course at Yatesbury, a member of Class RM13, which was all so secret that no notes were allowed outside the secured compound and there was a total ban on discussing with anyone what was being learned on the course.

By chance during the brief stay at Uxbridge, with a free weekend in which to settle down in surroundings so different from those on the long journey across the Atlantic, the new arrivals had been given a rare chance to do something far removed from the thoughts and the deeds of war, at the same time meriting the privilege of a rare 'audience' with royalty.   It came about when offered the opportunity to make a Sunday afternoon visit to Windsor Castle, a country location which members of the Royal Family used on occasions instead of Buckingham Palace which was in the heart of London.   In this group was Fred Grahame, who had been so keen to 'do his bit' that he volunteered for the RCAF the month the war began, only to be told that despite his educational qualifications and practical experience, there were regrettably 'no vacancies for you', the medical requirements being 'very strict'.   A full year would pass before he was called to take a trade test in which he was successful, enlistment within 24 hours as an Aircraftman 2nd Class being followed by time at Moose Jaw, where one of the perks of the job was being able to accompany student pilots and navigators on training flights; he remustered to WEM (R), which gave him reclassification to Leading Aircraftman, and following passage to Britain on the *Laconia* he reached Uxbridge on 2 May 1941 [21].

Looking back on that treat when able to visit Windsor Castle, Fred goes on to recall that although some members of the group carried cameras there was a strict ban on taking photographs while inside the grounds of the royal residence.

> 'We were escorted past St George's Chapel and up on the wall where we could look down on the gardens. There were a few anti-aircraft guns hidden in the bushes but we saw no other military equipment. Our group, numbering about two dozen, continued along the walled embankment until we were stopped at a rope barrier because the Queen and the two Princesses, Elizabeth and Margaret, then aged about 15 and 11 respectively, were on their way up from the garden to speak with us.   Her Majesty noticed that some airmen had cameras and she told us that we could take a few pictures. She spoke briefly and quite casually with about five or six of the airmen in the front row.   When she asked the first man where he was from, he happened to be an American who had come to Canada to enlist.   As we left, those who had cameras had to remove the films; these were developed by the security staff and returned a few days later to the owners'.

By the spring of 1941, by drawing upon the availability of suitable recruits in North America, Britain was effectively saying that the input obtained in this manner would be sufficient to meet the RAF's requirements for radar technical personnel to work on the ground and in the air for the next 12 months.   Indeed, 'the facilities have been utilized for the training of USA and Canadian personnel on the assumption that no further "skilled" personnel will be recruited in this country' [22].

A steady flow was envisaged, linked to the training facilities available, but there would be at least one occasion when a glitch would upset its smooth running.   In the last week of February 1941, with some 250 Canadians in the UK or on the way, an outbreak of scarlet fever put the next batch, 150-strong, into quarantine at the embarkation port * with a further 100 quarantined at the Manning Pool [23].

---

* The incident is recalled in a commemorative brochure produced for the WWII Radar Reunion in London, Ontario, 21/23 September 1999, based on details supplied by Bill Barrie and Len McMillan,

Furthermore, it should not be assumed that, despite the care taken in their own countries, that all UK-bound recruits were able to fit happily into the training and posting processes once those individuals had reached the UK.   It is shown, for instance, that '71 Canadians and 21 New Zealand radio mechanics have arrived during the past 10 days and have been trade tested at West Kirby.   46 were found suitable for advanced training and will proceed either to Yatesbury or Cranwell; 37 will be absorbed into *ab initio* training; and 9 are considered unsuitable', these last 9 being destined either for training in other trades or a return passage back home (which happened to be Canada in all 9 instances [24]).

An indication of the severity of the shortage of radar mechanics can be judged from this estimate of the new ground stations alone that would be required during 1941 and in the first half of 1942: British Isles, 92 (at 31 December 1940) rising to 310; Middle East, 22 rising to 110; and in the Far East, including India and Ceylon, 2 rising to 55 [25] .   Fortunately, with the first 1,000 of the tentatively planned 8,000-plus embryo radar mechanics having enlisted in Canada by mid-July 1941 (three quarters of them by now in the UK or on their way), by end-October in that same year the RCAF was 'experiencing no difficulty at present in enlisting 300 suitable men per month for pre-training in units' and it was considered 'that this figure can safely be increased to 400 per month without lowering the present physical or educational qualifications [26] '.   By the time the year was out, some two and a half thousand were in RCAF uniform and in training, though not all would be sent to the UK.   Canada had requirements of its own: she needed instructors and, of course, she needed technicians in her own radar installations.

Throughout Canada, the recruitment message traveled far and wide, Julien Olson, for example, hearing about the need for 'radio specialists' as a result of RCAF recruiting officers talking to a high school graduation class.   They outlined the requirement, indicated that the successful recruits would go to a dedicated training facility that the RAF had established in Clinton, Ontario, and right away he was 'hooked'.   He enlisted in September 1941, trained in Canada and in the UK, then joined the RAF's # 23 Operational Training Unit which had GEE- and IFF-equipped Wellington bombers.   Julien stayed there until February 1944 when he specialized in Oboe airborne equipment for the remainder of the war, serving with # 109 Squadron in the RAF's Pathfinder Force... but those were operational experiences that were far beyond high school, enlistment and an introduction to something that eventually the world would know as 'radar'.

That dedicated training facility that the RAF had established in Clinton was # 31 Radio Direction Finding (RDF) School.   Its first CO, Group Captain Adrian Cocks, gave the reason for its creation when writing in a special edition of the *Clinton News-*

---

explaining that a draft of 130 WEM (R)s, having boarded the Dutch ship *Johan van Oldenbarneveld*, disembarked next day when it was discovered there was scarlet fever on board. First they were sent to a camp at North Sydney, Nova Scotia, and then to Debert, where conditions were 'primitive and unpleasant'.   Needed in England, this group was 'stalled around a hangar' or 'loafed in a bunk'. After a two-month wait, they joined the troopship *Georgic*, sailing at last for the UK. A poem about the well-understandable frustrations of this self-named 'Gypsy Squadron', published alongside that article, concludes with the telling comment: 'Sure we're just a Gypsy Squadron, that came from far and near; we started out for England, but we only reached the pier.'

Record on 24 August 1994 which commemorated the 60th Anniversary of the Air Force Telecom Association of Canada (AFTA).   The decision to have an RDF training school outside Britain was, he said, to expand the output of RDF mechanics and as an insurance against either of the two UK schools, Yatesbury or Cranwell, being bombed out.   A former Chief Instructor at Yatesbury before taking up a post in the Directorate of Signals at Air Ministry, Cocks noted that 14 weeks after he arrived in Canada ('and remember that a site for the School hadn't been selected at the time of my arrival'), Clinton was able to accept its first trainees, who were from the USA. He wrote:

> 'When the Americans first arrived at Clinton, I asked whether their Stars and Stripes could be flown at my mast at the same level as the RAF Ensign, but this was not allowed.   There was no official 'opening ceremony'.   If there had been one, more likely than not it would have taken place in a cloud of contractors' dust.   Once they had started to roll out of the Canadian Universities and had survived their recruit training at the RCAF Depot in Toronto, there was no holding the flow of Canadian trainees into Clinton and the population built up weekly.'

Clinton was opened on 20 July 1941 and Cocks was in command for two years; they were, he wrote, 'my best two years out of a total of 34 years in the RAF'.   He was succeeded by John Martin, who had gone to Clinton from Yatesbury at the outset and become its Chief Instructor.

Roger Richards, having enlisted for the Royal Air Force in June 1940 when he was aged just 18, hoped to train for aircrew but found that he had a problem when tested for color vision.   So he opted for a trade, that of wireless/radio mechanic – and not unnaturally, given his background.   Roger had been a radio hobbyist, building short wave receivers and so on, since the age of about 13, and while at school he had been aiming at a university scholarship in physical science.   The Air Ministry was calling for people who knew enough of the fundamentals to be able to be trained very quickly as technicians, so it 'seemed to be a natural move' [27].

An instructor in 'RDF' (as radar was then called) at Clinton from its creation, when the first students were all American citizens and serving members of the US armed forces, Roger Richards gives some of the background to their presence.   He explains:

> 'The Americans were not then in the war, of course, but we were trying to get them to manufacture British types of radar sets rather than take the time to develop their rather primitive ones into useful equipment which we could use at once.   There was an Act of Congress in effect which forbade US companies from manufacturing military equipment for foreign governments if that equipment was not in use by the US Forces.   So, if we were to get access to American production capabilities it would be necessary to have their armed forces actually agree to use some British radar equipment. Then, they could produce it for themselves and also, legally, for us.   We were desperately short of equipment so the exposure of American service personnel to British radar at Clinton was an important though small link in the chain of a complicated lobbying process [28].'

In many respects Clinton was an ideal site for a training establishment in this innovative and highly secret technology. It was located near Lake Huron where there were high bluffs along the shore that simulated parts of the English coastline – a benefit in demonstrating the principles and applications of radar; it was fairly well isolated, which offered security given the nature of the school, but it was also close to large centres for leave. Roger remembers the two 240 ft antenna towers built there in 1941 as being the 'UK West Coast Type' as used for receiver aerials at western CH stations such as Sennen Cove – 'handsome wooden structures, quite open and in a way graceful, as opposed to the eastern variety, which were "clumpy" with a large number of cross members, making them look almost solid when seen from some angles [29]'. On his arrival, with the radar equipment [*], Clinton was still under construction – 'we were using pit latrines for a little while, there were some tents and the canteen was a big marquee'.

A booklet produced post-war to welcome people to Clinton recalls that the first course conducted on the station was composed of members of the United States Navy and United States Marine Corps. In the ensuing years, Clinton graduates took their places in theatres of war all over the world. The majority of the radar mechanics serving in the British forces were Canadians – this booklet states – and most of them, it adds, trained at Clinton. The school's record is impressive, with over 5,000 Canadian technicians and over 750 technical officers having gone through during the war years, additional to these figures being 2,325 American graduates.

By the time Clinton was training its first embryo radar mechanics (although the terms 'RDF' and 'Radar' remained secret), some of the mystique surrounding radar's role in the Battle of Britain was set aside when, to quote the 18 June 1941 Metropolitan edition of the Toronto-based newspaper, *Globe and Mail*, 'Britain today divulged her best-kept secret of the war with the announcement that radio location – a scientific device which warns of approaching planes miles away – is her great mystery defense against German raiders'. Radio location had had 'a tremendous influence on air, military and naval strategy', the device itself being 'a complicated apparatus for which it took longer to train a man to service one than it did to make one' [30]. Radio location had been kept so secret that in the military services it had been 'referred to by three letters only, and even these could not be whispered outside', according to a further quote, this time attributed to the Air Ministry.

The prime source for the information in that article, Air Chief Marshal Sir Philip Joubert, describing how 'the device' performed, said that for security reasons its operational methods were 'a close secret'. Radio location had started an entirely new military art; it worked by sending out electric waves unaffected by darkness and fog. The article continued:

> 'These become distant outposts constantly "manned" by wireless electronic watchmen which send back a signal of any object coming into its path. It

---

[*] Roger Richards notes the equipment brought from the UK for setting up the school as being CH Transmitters (2 - MB2A); CH Receivers (2 - RF 6/7); CH Mobile (1 - RM 3A Receiver, complete with 105 ft mobile aerial tower); CHL (1 Transmitter and 1 Mark 5 Receiver, with PPI display); a number of ASV Mark II and AI Mark IV sets; and power devices (400 Hz motor generator units for the airborne sets and some 230 volt 50 Hz converters for the heavier ground-based equipment).

keeps a 24-hour watch.   The device was given much credit for winning the Battle of Britain last Fall.   Sorely overworked Royal Air Force fighters, through radio location, were relieved of keeping up standing patrols and relied on the weapon to tell them in plenty of time when the raiders were coming and from what direction.'

The summer that Clinton opened, as # 31 Radio Direction Finding (RDF) School – 'RDF' of course being the three-letter code for radio location that no-one even whispered outside the military services – one of its soon-to-be students was on a training course of a different sort.   Bob Warner had been accepted for training as a radio technician in Hamilton, Ontario, under his country's War Emergency Training Plan (WETP), and a visit from an RCAF recruiting officer led to his enlistment as a Leading Aircraftman with arrival at Toronto Manning Depot on 15 October 1941.

For the new recruits, the time spent there was largely a combination of foot drill on the grounds of the Canadian National Exhibition, route marches through the city streets accompanied by a band and, if you were there at the right time, seeing ice hockey games, an ice show or, as was the case with Bob and the others, 'we were entertained by many well-known people like Paul Robeson and Gracie Fields. There were also boxing and wrestling events once a week – boxing conducted under military rules, meaning the action was stopped whenever the crowd started to cheer or applaud, and wrestling under professional rules [31]'.

Not every radar technician with the RAF was in air force blue from Day 1 of his service; Canadian Allan Paull, for example, decided that being ordered by Ottawa to report to the Royal Winnipeg Rifles in Brandon for 30 days' training as a foot soldier in a temperature of minus 30 degrees Fahrenheit was probably OK as an interim character-building exercise but it didn't hold much of a future.   He said:

> 'It made many of us start thinking seriously about what part we might play in this war before we would once again be told what to do by orders from Ottawa.   David Baker and I started shopping the different branches to see if a university degree counted for anything towards getting a commission, but we soon discovered that it did not.   About that time, though, there was a program where the RCAF was selecting and training people for what eventually became known as 'radar technicians'; although we didn't know much about what that would entail, we had previously heard that in the air force even the 'other ranks' slept between sheets in their bunks, so we decided to apply to the RCAF.   We volunteered, joined as AC2s (Aircraftman 2nd Class) in December 1941 and we were on our way, first to Brandon Manning Depot and then to UBC for basic radio training [32].'

Universities and dedicated radar-training establishments, Clinton in Canada and Yatesbury in England predominating, all had their part to play in turning raw recruits into confident specialists.   The spit-and-polish of 'Boot Camp' behind them, the emerging jargon of cathode bias, capacitor-resistance combinations and their associated time-constants, instantaneous peak power, blocking oscillators, antenna impedance and other such mind-bending terms was now but a classroom away...

CHAPTER 3: LEARNING CURVE

A variety of vessels were pressed into service as troopships on the Atlantic run; their availability at a given time meant that while some of Canada's subsequent radar recruits would travel in comparative luxury, others like Les Card and fellow direct-entry LAC WEM (R)s Bill Barrie, Art Scott and Bob Broughton in one of the vanguard groups, headed out of Halifax on nothing more salubrious than the mail packet ship SS *Nerissa*. New Year 1941 saw them quartered above the drive shaft ('noisy and smelly'), there being no-one less superior in their status or less deserving in their treatment among the 130/140 passengers who were to make this trip. Les recalls:

> 'We expected that we would be joining a convoy; instead we made a lone dash to the UK, diverting southwards on occasions presumably to escape submarine attacks. Lord Haw-Haw [who made propaganda broadcasts in English on the German radio] mentioned our ship; he said who was on board and he stated that we would never make it. We did make it, though most of the passengers were suffering from sea sickness [1].'

On his first night in the UK, while at Uxbridge awaiting a posting, Les Card had a very quick and salutary lesson in the English currency as a result of being short-changed by 10 shillings out of his first one pound. Successive postings were to a station in Norfolk, Hendon, Yatesbury (where, as member of # 2 Canadian Course in April/May 1941, he played double b flat bass horn in the band) and to Prestwick for an ASV air course before joining Coastal Command at Limavady in Northern Ireland with # 221 Squadron on 27 June 1941 [*].

Roy Taylor, one of the 161-strong contingent which came to Britain on the *Leopoldville*, constituting the first major group of Canadian radar technician recruits to reach the UK, recalls the Yatesbury site as having # 1 Radio School, where he and those in his group received their instruction, and # 2 Wireless School where group members were billeted.

'We were marched there and back each day by our Canadian Flight Sergeant, whose name I seem to remember was McGee. The 'Radio School' was in fact a 'Radar School', though this was unknown to anyone but our teachers and ourselves. We could not discuss anything about our school and we could not keep any notes;

---

[*] Bill Barrie, who crossed to the UK with Les Card, became an instructor at Prestwick and during a visit to New Zealand in the late 1990s met one of his fellow instructors, Angus Tait – 'to our knowledge the only survivor of a group of about 25 RNZAF radar people who answered the call from the UK under similar circumstances to the Canadian case'. From the Commonwealth, Bill recalls Australians, a few Rhodesians and South Africans coming through for instruction on AI and ASV airborne radar during his time there in 1941/42 [2].

we "came under the Secrecy Act", so we were always being told'. It is odd, the memories that Yatesbury students like Roy have retained...

> 'When I first went to this station the Women's Auxiliary Air Force personnel (WAAF) were assigned to each Wing, but after the influx of Canadians increased substantially, the WAAFs were all put in HQ Wing accommodation. I suppose they thought it was for the girls' safety and perhaps it was. Anyway, this led to one of the RAF airmen getting into trouble. It seems that he was on a fortnight's leave when the WAAFs were moved and, naturally enough, when he came back to Yatesbury, after "Lights Out", he had to find his bed in the dark.   Well, it was in HQ Wing accommodation.   All was dark, all was quiet, so he tiptoes across to his old bed and it is empty, as he expects.   He gets in, goes to sleep, then it's morning and there's a WAAF Sergeant calling "Wakey-wakey", at which point he finds himself surrounded by women. He dashed out, wrapped in a blanket, only to be arrested by the SPs (Service Police). The CO had a laugh and dismissed the incident. I think a lot of other guys would have liked to have had that experience and been less inclined to leave in such haste. Oh, what a war! 3 .'

On course # 14, Roy and his group were required to learn about British valves so, being keen to supplement the classroom documentation with material of a less confidential nature, he visited the Foyle's bookstore in London and bought a book on British valves. Then, he says, 'I spotted a book on "Wireless Direction Finding". There was a picture of the German liner *Bremen*, in New York harbour, and I was amazed to find that it was equipped with a pulse-operated radio direction finder, using a cathode ray tube. Wow, we thought our stuff was *so* secret'.

He remembers the first several weeks of the course being concerned with general radio, the way that cathode ray tube sweep circuits functioned and the principles of radar. It was explained that the transmitter sent out a high-powered pulse and the receiver picked up any signal which bounced back from an intervening object. The cathode ray tube's trace started the same time as the pulse transmission. Since the calibration was in miles, one could read on the trace (a thin green line running horizontally from left to right) the time that it took for the signal to go out and return. The returning signal, bouncing back from the aircraft or other object, deflected the trace to create a 'blip' on the tube.

In post-war years, Yatesbury students who were on courses later than Roy Taylor might have wondered to what extent the eminent writer Arthur C Clarke had recalled his own days as an embryo radar specialist when writing *Glide Path* * .

---

* *Glide Path*, Arthur C Clarke, Dell Publishing Company, 1965.   In his foreword, the author states that many incidents in the book are based upon real events, adding that as 'some may be tempted to identify the leading characters with real people, I would therefore like to stress that all characters are entirely imaginary'.   Readers of *Glide Path* may remember references to '# 7 Radio School' and to '61 Group'; no doubt many who were at Yatesbury will ponder over what Roy Taylor describes as the 'one or two interesting highlights about the extra-curricular activities at "Gatesbury" which even I did not know about!'.

Everyone has their own memories of Yatesbury, Craig Knudsen recalling that 'it was so cold, there was no heating in the classrooms and we were taken outside to run up and down the paths to generate our own internal heat'. In those early months of 1941 he learned quickly about the impact of war when, midway through the three-month course and allowed weekend leave in London, he not only saw the devastation caused by the air raids but he experienced their effect on human life. Two members of his course were killed when a landmine fell and demolished the building where they had been staying overnight, the first survivors of the group walking into the room where Craig was having his breakfast – 'they were covered in plaster dust and some had lost parts of their uniform'. Craig might have been there too, had there not been a mix-up with his pass that caused him to miss the train and hitchhike to London. He couldn't find the intended overnight accommodation and had to make his own arrangements, staying in a one-shilling-a-night servicemen's hostel on a straw-filled mattress with his gas mask for a pillow.

Arriving at Yatesbury in April 1941, Bill Barrie found it to be...

'a wonderland of radio towers, antennas and gen men. The technology was advanced, the instructors good and the pressure to get going was great. The principles of detection of airplanes by radar were easy to learn. The fact that Britain had a successful working television system gave radar the availability of receiver elements and suitable circuit components. We saw flexible RF cables, both 52 ohm coaxial, and shielded balanced 72 ohm line. Also of importance were high-gain, low noise VHF vacuum tubes. Cathode ray tubes of an advanced nature were in use, also stemming from the receivers in British television [4].'

A radio 'ham' himself, it was not too much to expect a number of the Yatesbury students to tune an RF7 ground radar receiver to the subsequently banned 10 meter waveband. Bill notes that 'with the big antenna tower and spring propagation, there they were, the US "hams", lucky devils, still having fun and working all over the world'. Canadian colleagues on that particular course included Johnny Bolton, Les Card, Charlie Grove, Marshall Killen, Len Kobel and Art Scott.

Doug Gooderham takes the view that the eight-week course at Yatesbury 'clearly presupposed that all of us had a good grasp of basic electronic theory'. Going into more detail about the particular time that he was at Yatesbury, which was the spring of 1941, he says:

'It started off with a detailed analysis of an assemblage of radar circuitry called a "spongy lock oscillator". We were encouraged to take full note with circuit diagrams, primarily to enable us to swot on the subject in the evenings, and also to cover the possibility that we might find ourselves on stations that had not received technical manuals; as a result our notebooks were highly classified documents and a damned nuisance. By the end of the eight weeks the Course had covered the circuitry of the three types of ground air-defense radar then in general use in the RAF: CH (Chain Home), ACH (Auxiliary Chain Home) and CHL (Chain Home Low), as well as GCI (Ground Controlled Intercept). Little or no mention was made of microwave radars being developed. Airborne radar gear was taught at another school [Prestwick, in Scotland]. Yatesbury had a few pieces of ground radar equipment on which we were given a few hours of hands-on fault-finding instruction [5].'

Training programs at Yatesbury varied in structure and length, depending when a student was there and the reason for being sent there. On a pre-commissioning course that was supposed to run for 16 weeks, Wylie Barrett was one among the small number who were singled out in the first week and given the syllabus before being told that those 16 weeks of instruction were to be halved. This presented the daunting prospect of their career-critical end-of-course examinations now taking place in a matter of just 7 more weeks.

In this 'grin and bear it' situation, these high-flyers of their day began looking around for comfort, encouragement and assistance among their fellow students. It is worthy of note that one of them on this accelerated course in that spring of 1943 was Arthur C Clarke [*], then in his mid-20s and some years younger than Wylie, who has since said of him:

> 'Being in the same class as Arthur C Clarke was really a stimulating experience. Even at that time he was promoting the idea of space travel. I was particularly fortunate as I was paired with him for guard duty, which we all had to do in rotation. I still remember some of what he used to talk about in those far distant days. It was fascinating, just listening to his theories of movement in space, but I'm afraid that not all of the class took him seriously. He had been a member of the British Interplanetary Society since the mid-1930s – and its chairman, of course, during later years – and I well recall his contention that it would not be possible to go to another planet without first building a space station. The reason, as I understood it, was that it was impossible to carry enough fuel; he was considering solid fuel propellant although more efficient fuels have since become available for the purpose [6].'

At Yatesbury, 'thanks largely to the instructional skills of classmate Arthur C Clarke', the entire class passed the exams and soon were on their way to the RAF Officers' School at Cosford, where rank designations were removed and all cadets wore white flashes in their field service caps. Course # 39 was 'a busy one…

> '… where the study of King's Rules and Regulations (AIR), Manual of Air Force Law, Air Ministry Confidential Orders etc occupied a large part of the day. We had periods of drill and each cadet had a turn playing the part of

---

[*] Probably best known around the world as the creator of *2001: A Space Odyssey*, which had its film premiere in 1968, Arthur C Clarke had already drawn on familiar material, that of his wartime radar experience this time, when writing *Glide Path*. International honours bestowed in his remarkable career include the NASA Distinguished Public Service Medal. In Britain, his achievements were celebrated in 1995 with a special exhibition at the Science Museum in London; already a CBE, awarded in 1989, he received a knighthood in the New Year Honours List, 1998. Post-war, Wylie Barrett met his former classmate just once when, back in Britain with the RCAF and serving on a two-year attachment to RAF Coastal Command, he took Arthur C Clarke to a meeting of the Radar Association in London in 1953, shortly before the latter made his first visit to the country which became his permanent home, Sri Lanka.

parade commander. We had periods in the swimming pool and in the gym – and everywhere we went on the base was at double-time. We were not totally deprived of the opportunity for socializing; in fact I remember that we had numerous Mess dinners, though there was a downside even to this... it was on occasions like these that our dexterity at handling the cutlery was noted, as was our general attitude and our personal qualities to confirm that we were officer material.'

Graduating on 27 May 1943, Wylie Barrett and others on the course (for the record, Arthur C Clarke was among them) became Probationary Pilot Officers and received one week's leave during which to acquire their new uniforms. Wylie chose to get kitted-out at Isaac Walton in Newcastle, although probably for no better reason than that he enjoyed fishing! For those few days, 'with nowhere else to go while waiting for the uniform to be made', he boarded at a rooming house in South Shields until it was time to move from Newcastle to Newquay, where the radar station at Trerew – 'a typical West Coast type CH with dual transmitter, receiver and antenna facilities, together with a GEE navigational transmitter' – became his first posting as a radar technical officer. This remained his function until returning to Canada in September 1944.

A feature of the recruitment program in Canada was the introduction of initial technical training in one of a number of universities. As many as 500 places were made available in the bigger ones, 50 and less in others, with as much knowledge to be absorbed in some 13 weeks as was possible. Doubtless the success rate varied, in line with the respective aptitudes of students to learn and tutors to instruct, some of the new recruits faring better than others.

The harvest over and 'time to go to war', as he put it, Allan Beattie enlisted in November 1941 and found himself at McGill University where he couldn't have been in better company... seeing that 'father' of British radar Sir Robert Watson-Watt was one of his tutors. Allan recalls:

> 'He came and spent a number of one-hour lectures with us, a fine teacher and a man I came to admire. We didn't appreciate how important he was; he didn't tell us. He simply told us what we had to understand and he really did teach us. My belief is that he was doing some research at McGill and seemed to come to the classroom whenever he could; sometimes he wouldn't show and then, next time he saw us, he would apologize. My guess is that we saw him as many as nine or ten times during our three months at McGill. Understandably, he was especially interested in teaching us what this new science of his was all about. He already had a vision of what H_2S (operational in 1943) was going to be... and I recall that he was always emphasizing the need never to let our minds stop keeping active [7].'

It is of interest to ruminate on the lessons that were there to be learned in those formative times: one's first experience of Service life, mixing with such different personalities, maybe obtaining a taste of university life in parallel, and testing oneself against the strengths and the weaknesses of others in a desire to make the best of available opportunities. For some, the transition from civvies into uniform was seemingly particularly brief, the requirements of the Services being the determining factor.

No more than a fortnight passed between Sydney Goldstein, aged 20 at the time, applying to join the RCAF as a radar technician (or be conscripted a year later, probably without the chance to do what most interested him) and receiving a notice to report to the Manning Depot in Lachine for basic training. Radio was a hobby, he had heard a bit about radio direction finding and he was keen to pick a branch of the Service that would leave him with a vocation when discharged.   In those first few days, when finding that someone had made off with his pillow and his Corporal's only advice was to steal another one, he learned the cardinal rule in the armed forces that 'God helps those who help themselves'.

Basic radio principles were digested at the University of Toronto; while his classmates 'did not know much or anything about radio but did have some knowledge of High School physics', Sydney had the advantage of being a graduate of Montreal Technical School in electricity and he had been 'playing around with radio sets for a few years'.   It was a 'very elementary and not too interesting' course which left him longing to get to Clinton, which he joined in the autumn of 1942, to learn about radar.   He remembers that...

> 'We marched to classes to band music played from a watchtower located at the corner of the compound.   When there was no wind we could hear the music and could keep in step.   But since Clinton is close to the shores of Lake Huron, there was usually a strong wind blowing, especially as winter came along, and most of the time the music was so terribly distorted that it was tough trying to keep in step.
>
> 'To get to our classes we had to march through the compound gate, which was manned by Service Police from England, one of whom was a big brute some 6 ft 6 ins tall and weighed about 250 lbs.   He went out of his way to be miserable to us poor LACs.   I came across him again when I was posted to 60 Group HQ in England and, being a Pilot Officer by then, I took a fiendish delight in going out of my way to make him throw up a salute to get even for his behavior at Clinton [8] .'

Clinton's function was to prepare its students for their future role in radar, with several examinations to help determine who would work on airborne systems and who would work on ground radar.   At the end of Sydney's course, about ten per cent were commissioned and posted to England; those who were to be on airborne equipment were posted to Corpus Christi, Texas, for further training.

Awaiting a ship at Halifax, Sydney Goldstein, newly-commissioned and straight out of Clinton, remembers 'the usual hurry up and wait' syndrome with nothing much to do apart from a parade every morning 'so that they could count heads and make sure that nobody had become bored and left for home', plus 'the famous short arm inspection to be sure we were all still healthy'.   He had been in the RCAF now for nearly a year; he had never been near an aircraft and he had never handled a gun.   In Halifax there were no aircraft nearby but there was a rifle range on the station to which he wangled access.   Sydney felt that 'if you were going to war, even if you didn't expect ever to need the knowledge, it wouldn't hurt to know the appearance and feel of a rifle... and besides, it killed a whole afternoon'.

The liner *Queen Elizabeth* was his transportation across the Atlantic, sharing a cabin for two with 12 of his fellow officers, prompting these memories:

'Sharing the one bathroom took some getting used to... and our bunks were so close that it was worth your health to yell when you were coming out of your bunk so that no-one stepped on you. This was one of the ship's early troop-carrying missions and there were still a lot of decorative artifacts to recall her bygone luxury. We were served two meals a day and each was an adventure with a choice for every course. Compared with the men, we were well off; there were more than 10,000 troops aboard, sleeping in hammocks wherever there was space – the ballroom, the swimming pool even – and there was a continuous line of them along the stairwells while queuing for their turn to be fed, in shifts, twice a day. Being early March, we were concerned whether ours might be a rough crossing so when we boarded we asked the steward assigned to our cabin for a sea sickness remedy. He advised us to have some bread to eat as it was best to have something in your stomach, like bread, if you felt sick. So, at the next meal, everyone brought back a bun and put it under his pillow, just in case. In fact very few did succumb so, when the time came to do our packing, it was punctuated by the thud of those four-day-old, stale and by now concrete-hard buns landing in the wastepaper baskets when we realized, one after the other of us, that we hadn't needed them [9] .'

As noted, Canada retained some trained or part-trained personnel for its own radar establishments; also, as noted, some who had gone through Clinton were earmarked for additional training of a selective nature in the United States, at Corpus Christi. For Dave Roumieu, it was quite unexpected that he would find himself at Corpus Christi, attached to this US Naval Air Technical Training School in Texas. After all, there he was at the railway station in Burns Lake, British Columbia, saying his good-byes to parents, family members and friends, when along comes the Station Master running towards this group with a telegram in his hand. Dave was due to go to Halifax, presumably to catch a boat for Britain, when that surprise message unfolded a change in plans: he must return to Clinton, one of a dozen airmen who had been selected for specialist instruction at this important training establishment before going overseas [10] .

He goes on to say that

'At Corpus Christi, under capable instruction we were concerned with studying ASV 10cm PPI airborne search radar as well as being introduced to the most secret magnetron. This equipment I found to my liking and felt I did well on the final exams, both practical and theory. I think it is safe to say that we RCAF or attached RAF members consistently led the classes. Our university training and subsequent Clinton radar training was very intense with a high percentage of failures and remusterings.

'Texas hospitality was fabulous and in small groups we visited Houston, San Antonio and even Mexico.   I flew in a Catalina flying boat for about three hours over the Gulf of Mexico and on another occasion went up with an instructor in their equivalent of the Harvard single-engined trainer... when he had three students in the air at the same time, each in his own plane.   It was quite an experience!   When the course came to an end, the US Marines and Navy personnel were promoted to Master Sergeant, Ensign etc, while we stayed as LACs... posted to Lachine to fly overseas.'

In Orv Marshall's time at Clinton, which began around Easter 1943, the introductory training course lasted six weeks; on completion, those who were successful were posted either overseas or within Canada or stayed for further training in other types of equipment, the remainder having to re-take the course.   Unusually, Orv remained at Clinton for close on a year... though, it must be stressed, not through any learning difficulties!   He had been recommended for a commission and this process delayed his intended posting to the US Navy radar school at Corpus Christi for training on newer microwave radar and on a new navigation system, Loran.   However, during this period it was announced that there would be no further postings to Corpus Christi, those courses now being transferred, which meant that Orv would be on the first one at Clinton 11 .   In the event, he still achieved a posting into the USA, additional training being required in Washington, DC, before starting his operational service, which would be with Liberators in the Mediterranean theatre.

By far the majority of the radar technicians whose initial training was in Canada alone or in Canada and America made the journey to the UK by sea, one of the exceptions being someone who became involved with radar almost by accident: Tom Lamb, in 'Civvy Street' a civil engineer rather more accustomed to finding his way around the blueprints on a major construction project than tracing a path through the intricacies of circuit diagrams for a comparatively hi-tech electronic system. He explains how this came about...

'In 1940 I was working as a junior resident engineer building airfields for the British Commonwealth Air Training Plan.   In my time, we went to classes only from the beginning of October to the end of April, which allowed us five months to gain work experience and earn a little money. When the Canadian Department of National Defense began construction of the many facilities that were required to implement the BCATP, they needed engineering students as well as experienced engineers to design and supervise the work and we were available for that five-month period.

'So the following year, when I had graduated as a civil engineer and went to join the RCAF, I expected that I would be involved in airfield construction and maintenance.   However I was told that they were not looking for that type of recruit so I continued what I was doing until January 1942 when I went back again.   This time I was asked if I would be interested in RDF, which suited me fine because I had been interested in amateur radio for a number of years.

'I went through the usual basic radar training including Clinton, starting in the summer of 1942, followed by several months at the US Navy Air

Training Centre at Corpus Christi, Texas, in 1943.   There, the equipment on which we trained included both ASG and ASC – these were 10 cm anti-submarine systems; ASD, a 3 cm torpedo-bombing system; the AYD radio altimeter; and ABK, a radar transponder.   On completion I was posted overseas, in common with most radar technicians who began their training at Clinton.   The difference was that I crossed to the UK in a Liberator bomber destined for use by the RAF.   I assumed that, because the Americans were supplying both aircraft and radar to Britain, I was wanted in the UK right away to start training the RAF on the installation, operation and maintenance of US radar equipment.

'Much to my surprise, when I reported to RCAF Headquarters in London, I found that I had been posted to # 60 Group HQ at Leighton Buzzard, the reason being that I was a structural engineer in civilian life and someone was needed to design supports for a new type of ground radar antennae. It was five weeks before the RCAF realized that the reason I was flown to Britain was on account of my training on US radar!   Immediately, I was posted to St Eval, a Coastal Command station, where # 224 Squadron was being outfitted with Liberators and ASG. This was to be my home for the next four months [12].'

By the time the Japanese attack on Pearl Harbour brought the United States into the war in December 1941, American civilian radio operator James S Farrior had not only enrolled to work with 'the air-defense weapon known as radiolocators, now in active use against enemy air fleets all over the British Isles' (to use the contemporary wording in the recruitment literature), he was two-thirds through his RDF training course at Cranwell and he had twice been in close proximity to His Majesty King George VI.

Telling his story later [13], James Farrior explained that it all began in August 1941 when he read where the British and American governments had agreed to allow Americans having radio experience to serve with the RAF in England as radio mechanics – 'This seemed like a good chance to get into something exciting, interesting and very technical.'   His application was quickly acted upon and on 17 September 1941 he boarded a train for Montreal, leaving behind him 'a well paid, very demanding, high traffic job which I liked very much', in the Net Control Station for the US Army's 4th Corps Area located at Ft McPherson in Atlanta, Georgia.

Arriving next day at the Civilian Technical Corps (CTC) headquarters in Montreal, he joined a small group of men who were being outfitted with RAF uniforms and awaiting orders to travel to Halifax, Nova Scotia, his enrollment certificate bearing the serial number 149.   At Halifax...

'# 1 "Y" Depot was filled to overflowing with men waiting to sail to the UK. For much of the day we were drilled on the parade ground and marched through the hills above Bedford Basin, thoroughly tiring us out and keeping us out of trouble.   One day each of us fired 25 rounds from an ancient rifle; on another we were briefly put in a tent as part of the gas-mask training. On Sunday we were divided according to religion and marched to the appropriate church.   By the time of our departure we had become accustomed to more military life than any of us had anticipated.   Then came the moment to board ship and thousands of us marched through the streets of Halifax with people waving from the sidewalks, as they must have done many times before.   Our group sailed on the *Andes*, a converted luxury liner; with five times the normal number of passengers there was no sign of luxury.'

Leaving the ship at Liverpool on 19 October, James Farrior's group traveled to Bournemouth, where the CTC was then headquartered, to be lectured on 'how to act and what to expect'.   What he probably didn't expect was to be marched to a large paved area in front of the Bournemouth Pavilion for an inspection by King George VI and Queen Elizabeth, while waiting to go to Cranwell.   There, 'the RDF training we received was first-rate with highly competent instructors, well divided between classroom lectures and hands-on experience with the same equipment used in the field.   We also had comprehensive written and oral testing.   It was serious business and those showing inadequate capability of becoming good radio mechanics were quickly culled out.   At night we studied hard in our very dimly lit, very cold and very crowded hut'.

On the morning of 13 November, the principal instructor advised that...

'We should come to class in the afternoon looking our best, as our classroom had been chosen for a visit by King George VI,, who was on one of his regular inspection trips to Cranwell.   He also made it clear that if we had any gripes, we should express them to him and not to the King.   His Majesty wore RAF uniform with his pilot's wings and service ribbons, as he had done at Bournemouth.   He appeared very relaxed and pleasant and in no hurry to leave.   He was aware that he had met us before, asked where we were from, how we liked England and what we thought of the training we were receiving.   Needless to say, our instructor's admonitions were well heeded.   Upon leaving, he wished us well and thanked us for our help in the war effort.   Most British subjects would go through their entire life without seeing their monarch; we had seen him twice in the short time we had been in Britain.'

On 19 January 1942, final grades for the entire course were issued and postings notified which were scattered over the UK.   James Farrior received what he believed to be the best of them, which was to RAF Scarlet at Castletown on the Isle of Man, a CH station.

Radio enthusiasts, college students, even farm boys, those who had answered Britain's call were in the process of being schooled in understanding and maintaining some of the most sophisticated electronic equipment that the best brains in the free world could devise.   The rapidly evolving nature of this new technology meant that the emphasis was more on the blessing of high intelligence than on the capability to display high skills in a trade; by comparison, aero engines and airframes were 'old hat' when what was demanded was a quick and thorough understanding of circuits and components designed for specific functions.   Those who came forward to take their place on this helter-skelter of burgeoning technology which promised so much were participants in a scheme on a par with the British Commonwealth Air Training

Plan, which provided a continuous stream of aircrew to man the planes. Like that resource, this one too was beginning to do what was expected of it – to produce a flow of sufficiently competent volunteers to occupy radar technician positions that couldn't be filled without them.

Where James Farrior was destined for a CH station on the Isle of Man, some would be going to far more remote parts of the British Isles and further afield still; and others would serve in an altogether different environment, perhaps on a front line squadron in one of the operational Commands, maybe even being posted to a research centre to work alongside the scientists designing new forms of radar. No matter the posting, the learning wouldn't stop. When there was fresh knowledge to be imparted, it was 'gen' that just had to be digested – going back to school if needs be, time and time again. Life would be punctuated by a succession of new kinds of radar, variants and new 'Marks' of an existing device and the 'mods' that someone, somewhere, decided was a mandatory modification. All had to be understood and applied because the benefit of radar was a dominant possession in the Allies' armory; it was ever-evolving, a product of promise, a catalyst for change in a war that was yet to be won.

CHAPTER 4: CHAIN REACTION

S traight out of radar training school at Yatesbury, where he graduated on 31 March 1941 among the first group of Canadians whose instruction was biased towards its use on Britain's coastal ground stations, Roy Taylor found himself in a privileged position: he had a geographical choice of posting. A direct entry Wireless & Electrical Mechanic (R), he wore the propeller badge on the sleeve of his uniform to denote classification as a Leading Aircraftman; he had gone into the RCAF as an LAC, leapfrogging Aircraftman 2nd Class and Aircraftman 1st Class on the strength of his knowledge and experience of radio, and here he was with the opportunity to pick whereabouts he wanted to go after Yatesbury. He had better make the most of it; there would never be another chance to choose his own posting!

He opted for the radar station at Formby – 'I had cousins in Lancashire and my father was born in Rochdale' – which turned out to be…

'A two-storey red brick building on the beach which had been a Catholic orphanage before the RAF took it over. A newly-operational CHL station with a rotating antenna, it had an accessible flat roof and inside was the operations room with other areas which were eventually converted to sleeping and eating accommodation. To my surprise I found three other Canadians there (Clarence Brown, Russell Heagle and Irving Musselman), all from my course, so each was assigned a different shift [*] .

'A few of the British radar operators said: "What are you colonials doing here, this is our war!" Well, I guess they managed Dunkirk and the Battle of Britain without seeming to need us. It was encouraging, however, to find that when Hitler threatened invasion, we didn't hear any more unfriendly comments [1] .'

During this period, a German bomber dropped his bombs north of Formby one night, possibly jettisoning them because a fighter was after him. This started a blaze which the fire service began tackling. Then it became obvious that other enemy planes were now moving in that direction, believing the flames to result from the 'trail-blazing' efforts of their pathfinder aircraft beginning a fresh attack on Liverpool. This prompted the firemen to be told to let it burn – it was, after all, only coastal scrubland. The result was a lot of bombs falling in an area where little harm could be caused, so that the fire brigade, with more then enough serious demands upon its services, could return later to complete the task. It is worth noting that the deliberate use of this same technique (an operation known as Starfish, where decoy

---

[*] These were 4 of the 161 members of the 'Leopoldville Group', the third and by far the biggest contingent of Canadians to reach the UK in the period December 1940/January 1941, the first of 5,000 promised by the Canadian Government to meet Britain's acute shortage of radar technicians.

fires were lit to attract enemy raiders) caused as much as 60 per cent of the effort directed against Hull on the night of 31 August/1 September 1941 to be aimed mistakenly at a Starfish site, those bombs falling in fields and villages within a two-mile radius 2 .

While at Formby, Roy was able to discover first-hand how stretched were Britain's defenses which, without the benefit of the radio direction-finding and similar techniques where he was increasing his familiarity with every passing day, would have been swamped.   He suggested an exchange of personnel between the area where radar equipment picked up the presence of enemy raiders and the filter room where the location of those aircraft was plotted and displayed as counters moving across a huge map, so that defensive action could be directed with maximum advantage.   He says that some of those working in the filter room thought that the radar screens showed real aircraft, instead of just a 'blip'; and the radar operators had no real understanding of how their role linked-in with those in the filter room. One day, while Roy was there...

> 'The filter room was plotting two "Photo Freddies", which was Formby's name for German reconnaissance aircraft coming in ahead of a night raid on Liverpool.   I queried why no move was being made to send up fighters to attack them.   The person in charge said that he didn't want what he was going to tell me to go outside those four walls.   It seemed that if we were to send up a squadron of fighters, they would not catch them; and there would not be enough aircraft left to intercept the bombers that it was expected would be coming in that night.   He told me that there was only one front-line squadron available to be scrambled in the event of an attack... and one other squadron whose equipment was being overhauled.   As it turned out, while we watched the plotting table, one of the counters representing an enemy aircraft was removed.   It was reported that the anti-aircraft defenses, perhaps with a lucky shot, scored a direct hit and brought down one "Photo Freddie" while the other scooted home 3 .'

That summer, Roy was posted to Singapore; however, as he was close to West Kirby, which was the embarkation centre where he would be prepared for this draft, he had to remain in his billet at Formby.   Subsequently he learned that several of the 'Leopoldville Group', who traveled with him from Canada to the UK, remained on that posting while his was cancelled.   Of five Canadian radar technicians he knew made the journey to the Far East, all were captured and four of them died – one of them as a result of a beating by the Japanese * .   Withdrawn from standby for overseas service, Roy became an instructor on IFF (Identification Friend or Foe) equipment until the time came for a move to North Africa with a mobile radar unit and

---

* An article in a Canadian newspaper, *The Hamilton Spectator*, on 19 July 1994, tells how Ed Goodchild was 'ordered to beat a fellow prisoner who had pilfered a few sticks of firewood' and, when refusing to do so, 'his Japanese captors beat him as an incentive'.   Four times he defied them, each time with the same result.   Although this caused the Japanese to stop forcing prisoners to mistreat each other, Ed Goodchild paid with his life; he 'died of his injuries two weeks later'.   It was, wrote Shaun N Herron, 'the death of a decent man, a man who refused to mistreat his comrades for the entertainment of his captors'.

often non-stop action in Sicily and Italy as the Allies battled to maintain the upper hand in the Mediterranean theatre of operations.

The period that anyone spent at a radar station would vary: Roy Taylor was at Formby CHL station for a little over a year whereas RAF radar technician John Glen, who was at Anstruther in Fife, Scotland (the first operational CHL station in Britain), remained for more than a year and a half on this, his first posting. When he joined that station in February 1940 he was among the earliest RAF arrivals. The work was hard... but it was rewarding... With just 4 months' service behind him, he had been posted in as an AC1 (after basic training at Padgate and further instruction at Leuchars) and he was posted out as a Sergeant; as it happened, another promotion followed immediately when, on joining his new radar station at Point of Stoer, it was to fill a position as Flight Sergeant.

Looking back on those days at Point of Stoer, when it was hit and miss whether a fresh posting turned out to be to one's benefit or liking (a missed boat to the Shetlands to take up duty at Sullom Voe was apparently the reason that John was posted instead to Point of Stoer) he says that

> 'Our main task was the protection of shipping lanes through the Minch where U-boat activities were intense around the Butt of Lewis, Cape Wrath and Pentland Firth. We had our frantically busy days, we had our relaxing occasions and we had our times of sadness. I remember, for example, that we were using our radar equipment to search for a plane with the Duke of Kent on board. It went down, unfortunately, and I recall that the Duke's body was recovered from the hills and taken to Dunrobin Castle. And there was the time when the unidentifiable body of a seaman was picked up on the shore, the funeral taking place on a bitterly cold, sleety sort of day. The burial was carried out according to local custom in the village cemetery, which meant successive pallbearers, supplied by the RAF, having to carry the coffin for some two miles along a hilly road with a pacemaker at the head of the procession to mark-out the time for each new change of pallbearers 4.'

There was a brighter side to a radar technician's life at Point of Stoer... for example there were impromptu dances which would start in the village hall around 10 pm when a pianist would turn up, followed by someone else with an accordion and then maybe a violinist. Square dancing was the order of the day and the dance would finish only when everyone was exhausted, generally about 4 am. Additionally, as John Glen notes, 'the local policeman was most accommodating when it came to closing time at the Cuileag Hotel'. Occasional moments of drama intervened, such as 'one hairy experience when a small group of us found ourselves cut off by the tide while walking along the shore. Dick Kupkee, a Canadian and a former 'Mountie' who never seemed to say much, reckoned that we could climb the cliffs to reach the site. We did just that, arriving at the top absolutely whacked out, only to hear Dick's admission that he had never before done any climbing of any sort in his whole life'.

Although the more cynical radar bods reckoned that civilization had yet to reach some of these more remote island bases, John Glen was sometimes more inclined to the view that it was the uniformed visitors, unaccustomed to the ways of the long-established inhabitants, who were in need of basic instruction in coping with particular situations.   He casts his mind back to Christmas at Rodel Park in the Outer Hebrides where

> 'The postmistress at Leverburgh promised us a turkey.   We duly arrived, only to find that our Christmas Day dinner was still alive; and not only alive but running around in what I can only describe as a particularly angry mood! We were greenhorns, of course; nobody knew how to kill it.   So we bundled the bird into the truck, drove back to camp and locked our precious gift in the boiler house, while the camp cook held a meeting to decide how to end its life in as reasonably humane a manner as was within our capabilities.   It was a big bird, which didn't help matters, so the cook was of a mind to chop off its head.   Eventually one of the "locals" came to the rescue and performed the required task with consummate ease – he caught the turkey by the back of the neck and killed it there and then.   It was so simple to these islanders, so impossible for us [5].'

Being on the Isle of Harris, Rodel Park was regarded as a worthwhile posting and an even more worthwhile site for a visit, on the grounds that lengths of tweed bearing the name of the island were ever-popular.   However, while posting parcels of Harris tweed to relations and friends wasn't a problem, transporting people to and from the island was something else.   The mail boat came into Loch Rodel twice a week, during John Glen's time at this radar station, and a rowing boat between the mail boat and the shore was the sole means to ferry passengers and the mail to and from the island.

At the School Hill CH station near Aberdeen where, incidentally, its location and the height of its aerial towers (250 ft for the receiver, 360 ft for the transmitter) no doubt contributed to a reported success in continuing to follow one departing aircraft for as much as 215 miles, Craig Knudsen 'was amazed to find that I was the only male in the operations room on the night shift, some of the girls looking no more than 17 years of age while those in charge were only in their early 20s [6]'.   While there one night he shared the anguish of a WAAF who was going out with a pilot from a nearby fighter station, Dyce.   He recalls:

> 'In the early hours there was a "hostile" plotted 60 miles out and the WAAF sergeant who was in charge contacted Dyce, a fighter then taking off to intercept.   As he didn't have his IFF working, we couldn't identify which was "Friend" and which was "Foe" when the two echoes on our cathode ray tube began to get closer and closer together.   The situation was especially tense because the plane from Dyce was being flown by the pilot who was going out with one of our girls.   Talking to the pilot, the WAAF sergeant who was directing him towards the enemy aircraft said that he should be able to see its exhaust "about now".   Then, one of the echoes disappeared from the tube.   The tension heightened because without the IFF to tell one from the other, there was no way to tell which aircraft had gone down. Relief came only when we heard the fighter pilot say: "Made my kill, I'm coming back."   For a moment the girls cheered; then they fell silent, thinking about those in the other plane who, in all probability, they themselves had helped towards a cold grave in the North Sea. I remember

just two of the girls who were with me at School Hill – one of them told me that while on leave she had been asked to identify her boy friend's body, which had drifted back to the shore when he was shot down at sea. Later, she and the other girl were posted away... and both were killed in a bombing raid on their new station.'

There were, of course, less harrowing experiences among radar technicians, as Craig would be quick to testify. During a time of increased tight security, due to the possibility of a retaliatory raid on one of the coastal radar sites in Britain, he was temporarily alone in the transmitter room at School Hill when he sensed someone watching him. Immediately, his mind flew back to the raid warning and he wondered not only what had happened to his colleague Des O'Callaghan but how someone could have entered a room they had locked behind them. Momentarily he was too scared to turn around... but when he did so it was with considerable relief. Instead of facing a member of an enemy raiding party, as he feared might have been the case, Craig found himself in the presence of a massive rat. It was standing on its hind legs, looking straight at him, its mouth exposing two big front teeth and its face taking on what seemed almost to be an evil grin. He explains:

'I knew then that I was looking at the cause of our equipment going off the air intermittently recently – this was a problem that had been baffling all three crews. We couldn't work out what was happening. Now I knew... the rat had been walking over the shut-down relays of the transmitter! By this time Des was back from the power-switching room and there were two things we knew we must do: first we had to stop the rat from getting back into the cable trenches, which I did by shutting the door from which it had emerged, and then we had to stop it going anywhere else or we might never find it again. So, we fixed our bayonets on our rifles and charged – the rat, being pretty agile, meant that we were stabbing around for all we were worth and I was more concerned about being on the wrong end of my colleague's bayonet than I was about getting the rat! Anyway, Des managed to spear the rat, which began shrieking... as did Olive Kenyon, the WAAF telephone operator who made us tea and toast midway through the shift and had just come in to see us. She had seen the rat of course, jumped on the chair that I had previously vacated and begun screaming at the top of her voice. With Des having put an end to the rat, this was also the end of that particular fault with the transmitter... but we had to put in for new cutlery and never again did Olive use our bayonets to margarine the toast!'

A subsequent posting towards the end of the first half of 1942 saw Craig helping to assemble, maintain and operate radar sites in the Faroes, roughly 250 miles from Scotland's most northerly island and some 250 miles south of the Arctic Circle – a group of islands where the winters were generally cold, wet, foggy, with storms from time to time, and at the height of summer there was practically no darkness. The civilian population was around 15,000 during the war and with Denmark and Norway in enemy hands, the British were in the Faroes to prevent their possible use by the Germans as a submarine base. Craig hadn't anticipated going there; he had been intended for Burma but by this time the Japanese were in occupation and a switch in postings saw his draft heading for Scotland, the presumption being that this would be a prelude to an invasion of Norway.

Craig admits that, geographical locations aside, it was preferable going to the Faroes. He puts it this way: 'For Burma, we had been trained on ASV and that would have been a great disappointment after working for so long and so hard on the big CH transmitter. With ASV, which fitted inside a tent, I could carry the transmitter under one arm and the receiver under the other. Apart from the relative sizes, the transmitter output was about 80 kilowatts, a far cry from the 750 kilowatts of the CH transmitter.'

It's often enlightening when hearing about the less routine experiences of radar technicians like Craig Knudsen. Who, for example, would have expected to find him down in a ship's hold, bagging coal, the lifting winch having broken down? This state of affairs occurred because the coal was needed for a radar station under construction and the only way for it to be delivered on time was if he and his colleague 'mucked in' to help the ship's crew, some five truckloads of coal having to be heaved out of the hold. The job done and the radar pair looking as if they had just emerged from a grueling shift at the coal face, it was by now too late to get any food. The Faroese came to their rescue by tackling a pile of fish-heads discarded by the local fishermen, cutting out the cheeks and cooking them in a tin bucket. It was, he recalls, 'very delicious and one of the tastiest fish meals I've ever had, despite all the coal dust that was mixed in with it'.

While on one station in the Faroes, agreement was reached for Craig to help maintain a Type 273S, a centimetric radar system which in this instance was set up on land although customarily it would have been mounted on the deck of a naval vessel. He recalls:

> 'We had just got this radar operating when two British vessels were picked up going north; they passed the 30 nautical miles range limitation so this was increased to 90 miles, at which point they disappeared off the tube. Later, when their captains returned to Royal Navy Headquarters at Torshavn, they expressed amazement that they had been tracked for such a distance. The ships' navigation charts and our radar plots compared favorably and the Admiralty in Whitehall sent its congratulations to our site for recording the longest track of a naval vessel by radar. There is no doubt that this was helped by the site's location being at a height of 1,200 ft. It is interesting that although we hadn't told the Faroese that what we were operating on this mountain top was a radar station, they themselves knew this – apparently its location and its purpose had been announced, by the Germans, over the Danish radio service [*].'

Another Canadian, Wylie Barrett, who was one of the 13 successful graduates in Class RM13 at Yatesbury from 18 May to 26 July 1941 (the remaining 7 were held

---

[*] Craig Knudsen returned to the Faroes in 1948 and married his Faroese girl friend. The couple marked their golden wedding in 1998 with a holiday in the Faroes, accompanied by their son, daughter-in-law and three granddaughters, visiting the former radar site at Eide with its then still-standing though derelict buildings.

back for further training), found himself assigned to RAF Station, Saligo Bay, on the Isle of Islay in the Western Hebrides.   First, though, a night in London gave an early indication of what the civilian population was continuing to endure from German bombing raids.   During the night it was the sounds which were predominant, as if there was an anti-aircraft gun on a roof of the building where he was staying – there probably was, or else it was in an open space nearby; in the morning it was the sights which were uppermost with the revelation of damage so indescribable that it was, to him, unreal.   How different it would be, surely, a new life ahead in a remote part of Britain compared with what he had just experienced on leave in its capital city.

On the way, Wylie was required to report to # 72 Wing HQ at Dollar, Clackmananshire, Scotland, where the combination of the initial letters of his rank, L A C, and the initial letters of his three first names, A C W, caused immediate consternation to the Wing Operations Officer.   Informed by his clerk that LAC ACW Barrett was in the outer office, awaiting his pleasure, he must have been wondering how anyone could be both an LAC – Leading Aircraftman – and an ACW – Aircraftwoman.   So, which was it going to be, an LAC or an ACW?   In those less enlightened days, it has to be said, no-one would ever have queried the possibility that the person awaiting the Wing Ops Officer's 'pleasure' might have been a sex-changed airman/airwoman!   He had his answer when in marched Wylie, whose demeanor made it perfectly clear, beyond the slightest doubt, that he was, in fact, every inch a gentleman.

The route to the ultimate destination on Islay was tortuous: a train from Dollar, via Glasgow, to Wemyss Bay; a ferry across to the Mull of Kintyre and a scenic voyage through the Kyles of Bute to the fishing village of Tarbert, where a group of lady volunteers provided a real treat of seldom seen bacon and eggs, before it was time for a bus ride, a further ferry to Port Ellen and finally RAF transport to a former distillery warehouse at Port Charlotte, which was to be this group's home for the next nine months.   Possibly this was typical of life for a radar technician in one of the more remote locations – a life allied to the use of chemical toilets, washing one's clothes in brown peat water heated on the stove or in a stream flowing near the radar site, with a once-a-week bath that meant, in this instance, a bike trip to the distillery at Bruichladdich about two miles distant.   Home comforts were indeed few – no sheets, no pillows, yet no-one complained [7].

Wylie recalls that radar site as being, in that summer of 1941 onwards, an ACH type with the transmitter and receiver buildings wood-framed and surrounded by sandbags to a height of about 4 ft.   The aircraft detection equipment comprised a T3018 transmitter and an R3020 receiver, both having transportable towers 105 ft high; additionally there was a T1087 transmitter and SX-25 Hallicrafter receivers for passing plot information by CW (Morse) to Dundonald in Northern Ireland.   It was an all-male station though under construction for some of the time that Wylie was there was a West Coast type CH station with living accommodation at Coille, some three miles away, where the planned refinements were said to include even WAAF operators.

He remembers that

'During a bad storm a cargo ship was wrecked on the rocky coast nearby and her cargo was unusually mixed – railway locomotives, bolts of cloth, whiskey, cigarettes and boxes of pocket combs. The crew were able to reach land and we put them up for the night, during which time the vessel broke in two and anything that would float came ashore, liberally coated with oil and tar. The authorities put a watch detail on the land approaches but overlooked an alternative access by way of the beach, which a number of us took on a personal salvage operation. The night was particularly dark and light rain was falling as we made our way in silence, with blackened faces, to the scene of the wreck. Each of us carried an empty sandbag and in no time we had filled them with tins that we realized contained 50 cigarettes. Back at camp we stashed our haul until morning, when we cleaned the tins with turpentine from a salvaged 45-gallon drum. Imagine our delight to have this enormous haul of State Express 555, Philip Morris etc – and imagine the chagrin of just one of us (not me, I was too careful!) who misjudged the weight of a can of cigarettes and found, having cleaned-up his booty, that instead he had gathered nearly 50 cans of Andrews Liver Salts.'

Perhaps it is only fair to note, in mitigation, that there was a subsequent occasion where a foraging expedition was used to the nation's benefit instead of personal advantage. A destroyer had gone aground a mile from the radar station where Wylie was working and he was able to salvage a considerable quantity of copper pipes, valves and shut-offs. These he installed in the diesel house so that refueling could be achieved 'by merely opening the right valves and wobbling the rotary pump. I remember when "Ned" Fennessy came up from # 60 Group HQ, the polished copper plumbing caught his eye and prompted a question on where it came from'.

There was more island-hopping when Wylie, promoted first to Corporal and then to Sergeant, received a posting from Saligo to Port Mor, on an island without trees and flat except for a single hill, Ben Hough, which became the site for a CHL station. With an ACH station at Port Mor and a GCI station at Barrapol, this tiny island was the home of three radar stations. In his six months on Tiree, the ACH station was closed and the equipment moved into new concrete transmitter and receiver blocks and connected to the typical aerial arrays: two receiver towers of wooden construction, 240 ft high, and the transmitter aerials supported as curtain arrays between pairs of steel towers 365 ft high. It was at Tiree, where by now he had been further promoted to Flight Sergeant (an acting though paid rank), that he flew for the first time and, aboard a Blenheim aircraft, maintained communications with a radar station to calibrate the newly installed equipment. Earlier calibration flights produced 'some unlikely results – the aircraft disappearing when, according to theoretical polar diagrams, it should not'.

There being no radio link between station and aircraft, re-runs became necessary and it proved difficult scheduling aircraft for calibration flights. This introduced unacceptable delays in carrying out the critical function of calibrating the radar equipment so it was decided to speed up the process by having a radar specialist join the crew, operating a T1083 transmitter and R1082 receiver and in touch with a similarly qualified person at the ground station. It was 'a good move', according to Wylie, who was nominated to fly, and soon solved the mystery of the disappearing aircraft. He explains that, previously, aircrews engaged on these calibration flights had not appreciated the importance of maintaining azimuth and altitude on the pre-arranged radials 'and sometimes dropped down to little more than wave-top height to get a look at a fishing boat or to test their machine guns on gulls'.

Further north still, up in the Shetlands, where RCAF radar technician Pacifico 'Puss' Valeriote spent several months of his time in the UK, which lasted from 15 January 1941 to 14 November 1942, he was on a Royal Navy base in the village of Haroldswick on the island of Unst, the civilian distinction being that Haroldswick claimed to have the northernmost post office in the British Isles. A series of moves on and off the Scottish mainland are recalled by diverse memories, for example... retrieving souvenirs from an enemy bomber brought down while attacking Aberdeen... plotting marine activity going to the Arctic ports of Murmansk and Archangel in Russia and keeping track of the daily incursions of German photo-reconnaissance planes coming over from Norway; and sitting on top of the receiver building in the early hours, watching for escaping Norwegian sailors he never once saw and flashing 'V' signals on an Aldis lamp to direct them on shore where, if any made it after their perilous journey, 'Puss' didn't spot them [8].

Arriving in the Faroes in November 1942 in a 14-man radar crew posted to a site on Nolsoe Island where the primary job was similarly detecting the presence of enemy aircraft and plotting the movement of shipping, Earl Moore was more fortunate than 'Puss' when carrying out the form of 'spotting' in which he was engaged one night in January. 1943. One radar response 'simply appeared and grew larger before my eyes', a visual sighting in the light that was still available confirming his suspicion that this was a surfacing submarine. A series of unidentified shipping plots earlier in the month had already pointed to the possibility of U-boats being in the area. Alert for any opportunity to have a crack at one of them, in response to this particular plot the Royal Navy dispatched a gun boat and a corvette 'which came charging around the point of our island and the U-boat did a crash dive'. It had made a fatal mistake in surfacing and it was now too late – a pattern of depth charges from each vessel 'practically blew the U-boat out of the water' [9].   The destruction of what was apparently the U-553, just a week out of its base in France and destined to do battle with the Atlantic convoys, likely saved Allied troop and supply ships and the lives of those on board them [*].

Earl returned to the UK towards the end of 1943 with the comment that 'it had been a long and often rough year... an interesting and on occasions exciting experience where the many challenges included mastering strange types of radar we had never seen before – in the main, ASV converted to ground use and dealing with the violence of the weather'. Gales were the big weapon in the weather arsenal, with storms with hurricane-force winds closing down the Faroes' radar stations for hours and even days on end, the crews becoming increasingly aware that there was little that could be done but to 'lash and wait it out' [10]. Earl recalls:

---

[*] U-boat Net, an invaluable source on the world wide web (http://www.uboat.net/boats/u553.htm), credits U-553 with 13 ships sunk (a total of 64,612 tons) and 2 ships damaged (a total of 15,273 tons) before embarking on her final patrol; this source lists her as missing, presumed sunk, with the loss of all hands, 47 persons, and quotes her last radio message as one sent on 20 January 1943: 'Seerohr unklar', which translates as 'Periscope not clear'.

'We saw RT aerials, guyed to withstand winds of 130 mph, twisted like so much matchwood.   We saw well-lashed aerials have the shaft broken at the roof by motion we could not stop.   Wind was indeed the enemy.

'Even in summer the wind could be a problem and we began to think about ways we might deal with it.   The idea of creating some type of shield against wind came up for discussion and someone suggested using Plexiglas, a transparent plastic material.   We didn't know whether or not it would have any affect on the efficiency of the radar set but it seemed worth a try!   So at Vaagar we set about building a scaffolding support around the tent containing the radar and then, on a platform at a level where the aerial mast came out of the tent, erecting a protective dome made from Plexiglas panels held in a wooden frame.

'There were large sheets of this material in store, presumably for aircraft repairs, and we were able to requisition and obtain them.   The result: with much effort we soon had a completely encircled, stacked Yagi aerial.

'It is interesting to note that while the aerials were now screened from the wind, the crew were living in tents, cooking in the open and even sleeping in the boxes in which the gear was packed.   We had been operational long enough on this site to have a good pattern of our area of coverage and could use this for comparison once we were ready.   For a start, a record-distance plot of 86 miles proved that you could send a radar beam through Plexiglas!   Next day we had a pick-up at 89 miles and before the end of the first 48-hour shift we hit 100 miles.   In the two months before the station closed, we never shut down because of wind – even though on one occasion we lost a tent blown over the cliff.   It was top marks for what was perhaps the very first, primitive radar dome.'

Of course within the fraternity of radar mechs there were less remote locations and there were less pressing tasks… for instance on the southern coast of Cornwall, at Polruan, there was one which RAF volunteer Len Betts considered to be 'one that time forgot'.   An early posting after finishing his training at # 8 Radio School, Cranwell, this was a coastal defense CHL station which he describes in these words:

'It was operated by the Royal Artillery with a crew that might have come from "Dad's Army"; it was maintained by the RAF with a staff of three and it plotted only on shipping, the plots being passed to the Royal Navy.   This was a real Combined Operations job, although to my mind the station had outlived its usefulness.   The equipment was archaic, with an aerial capable only of scanning a limited sector because it had been built before rotating aerial couplings were introduced.   The bearings were taken from a large circular scale mounted on the ceiling and driven by a bicycle chain from the aerial.   Keeping such ancient equipment serviceable was quite a challenge but we plotted only every 15 minutes so life was not particularly stressful – in fact it was pretty comfortable.   Sadly, this didn't last long…   A welfare officer passed by, was horrified at the conditions and before we knew what was happening the station was closed down and I moved on to Beer Head in Devon… a "real" CHL station [11].'

Although Len Betts didn't have a say when it came to the sort of posting that was coming up next, sometimes there was a choice on offer.

Sydney Goldstein, Clinton-trained, commissioned as a Pilot Officer at the end of the course and posted to the UK, found himself at 60 Group HQ to be made aware of the different types of radar stations located around Britain.   Given the option, Sydney chose a GCI station and his posting was to one of the latest types near Penzance where, he recalls, it was 'camouflaged to look like a field in the middle of a farm'.   A row of trees 'were posts with the branches nailed on, the idea being to change the branches with the seasons but I doubt if this ever happened 12 '.

The first enemy action came when a posting took him to Wartling, a GCI station in the marshes some 20 miles from Eastbourne, where a Type 7 was being built on the same site as an existing transportable GCI.   Sydney divided his time between maintenance of the present station and construction of the new one; with a fellow Canadian, a Sergeant radar technician totally able to take care of most of the routine matters associated with running the technical side of the operating station, Sydney was able to spend 'many an evening, into the early hours, witnessing our activity in having patrolling aircraft, under our control, intercepting bombers attacking London'.

Besides air raids there still remained the threat of an enemy invasion.   One night he was awakened by the sound of stones being thrown at his window in the house he occupied in the village of Pevensey.   He had to get dressed and return to the station – 'There was an alert on, there being a possibility that a German parachute regiment had landed on Beachy Head and might be on the way to attack our station.

> 'The RAF Regiment lads were out in full battle gear, patrolling the perimeter, and my first job was to gather up all the secret radar documentation and be ready to destroy it – though only when we were certain that we were under attack.   All the radar stations had a large lead-lined box for this purpose, with acid inside to make immediate inroads into whatever we put in the box.

> 'Of course nobody had checked our box, I guess since the station was first set up; no-one had even thought it was sufficiently important for me to learn of its existence.   I decided that, to be ready to do as required if an attack materialized, I should test its efficiency.   So, throwing in a piece of printed matter of no particular relevance, I watched with fascination to see the sheer speed of its disappearance.   The paper just lay there... nothing happened... nothing at all.   I had visions of the same occurring on other stations.   Anyway, the alert being still on, I set about finding an alternative method to set fire to my documents.   I needn't have bothered because the alert was called off; the so-called landing had been an unfounded rumor.'

Britain's coastal radar sites in 1942 were on heightened alert for enemy commando-style attacks.   Although none occurred, their likelihood stemmed from raids made on German RDF installations on the French coast.   The first (Operation *Biting*, 27/28 February 1942) went in north of Le Havre at Bruneval.   One RAF radar technician with 120 paratroops were used in a foray dedicated exclusively to obtaining information concerning a Wurzburg radar recently photographed there.   The already-familiar Freya equipment, a 240 cm long-range early-warning set used for coastal and air defense, which was located nearby was not scheduled for attack. A top-level civilian scientist, although not risked ashore, went with the ships evacuating the raiders and their booty [13] . At least three unsuccessful radar-related raids were attempted by small seaborne landing parties at various French locations in April, June and August. Their intent was strictly demolition and no reports of radar technician involvement have been found [*] .

The large-scale operation at Dieppe (Operation *Jubilee*, 19 August 1942) presented the next opportunity to land a radar technician in France, this time under the cover of thousands of infantrymen and with reasonable expectation of capture of the local Freya station. This stood on the cliff-top above Pourville, immediately to the west of Dieppe, and the Army needed that heavily-defended high ground to protect its right flank during their day-long operation. The Freya itself was of no interest to them but, in certain quarters at the Air Ministry, its likely capture seemed an ideal 'target of opportunity', even though its own Director of Scientific Intelligence, Dr R V Jones, who had instigated the Bruneval attack, did not hold that view. The risk of any technical personnel of high-grade security category was declined and only one RAF NCO radar technician was assigned to the job. This was no more than an adjunct to the overall Dieppe raid although subsequent publicity has created what some regard as being a distorted impression of its importance.

The two raids stand in sharp contrast in intention, scale, achievement and cost. At Bruneval a little-known type of radar was captured, inspected and photographed by the technician, then essential components and two prisoners were returned to England for detailed examination. The operation was an unqualified success. Total British casualties, all categories, amounted to nine [14] . Thus were unfolded the secrets of Wurzburg, the 53 cm anti-aircraft, gun-laying, searchlight and fighter-control radar system 'which now were as well-known as were those of the Freya' [15] . At Pourville, however, no similar prize existed, entry to the site and its equipment was thwarted and, unhappily for this operation, the success at Bruneval had 'motivated the enemy to stiffen the defenses at all of his RDF stations and the Canadian attackers were to pay heavily on that account' [16] . The cost in Canadian lives must be shared between the Army's need to secure the heights and the Air Ministry's request to inspect the Freya. In all categories, the total casualties of the regiment assigned the task amounted to 340 all ranks – 65 per cent of the force landed [17] . The well-protected RAF technician, although he did his best and suffered a very rough day, returned to England unharmed but empty-handed.

Breaking new ground, Canadian radar specialist J R ('Rus') Robinson studied the Dieppe attack in detail from the aspect of its effectiveness in obtaining new radar information. Casting doubt on the necessity of incorporating such an operation within Operation *Jubilee*, he refers above all to the opinion of Dr Jones who described it as not only unnecessary but also as unproductive. The sole operating radar at the site was the Freya and Dr Jones states that 'the Dieppe raid did not provide sufficient new information regarding the German Freya radar system to justify the preparation, subsequently, of any Scientific Intelligence Report about it' [18] .

---

[*] These were Operations *Abercrombie*, at Hardelot, 21/22 April; *Bristle*, at Plage St Cecily, 3/4 June; and *Barricade*, Barfleur/St Vaast, 14/15 August.

More recent research has strongly reinforced this view. With regard to radar, there was at least one achievement on the positive side. Dieppe saw 'the first successful ship-board use of the radio-navigational aid GEE in action against the enemy' [19] and it 'played a big part [at Dieppe] in the first rehearsal for an attack on Europe' [20] . Although requiring development, the great potential of GEE for providing accurate landfalls from the sea was proven by the Navy at Dieppe and on D-Day, 6 June 1944, at least 860 ships were fitted with GEE for the Normandy landings. In the context of radar personnel serving in the Allied air forces, it is of greater relevance to focus on the development and application of GEE as a navigational aid to benefit air crews, especially those of Bomber Command.

It is possible that there were intended to be more operations of a covert nature where German radar equipment would have been the target. RCAF member Lenny Palmer, who trained at the University of Alberta and at Clinton, subsequently working on AI-equipped squadrons during the first half of 1942, responded that summer to 'a request for volunteers from radar technicians to take training and then jump with the Commandos into Northern France and blow up the enemy's coastal radar stations'. Later he was told he had been accepted, having had an edge over other applicants in that he had gone through infantry training for six months with the Calgary Highlanders. As must have happened many times in many circumstances, 'apparently the War Department had a change of mind as I heard no more of it [21]'.

Posted into 60 Group as a technical officer and electing to serve on a GCI station, Sydney Goldstein provides an intriguing insight into one particular form of enemy radar and the insistence of Prime Minister Churchill in allowing nothing to stand in the way of measures to save lives in a dire emergency. He explains that, while at Wartling, RAF night fighters controlled from the ground would attempt to intercept German bombers, which were equipped with 'backward-looking radar', exiting England over the South coast. He goes on [22] :

> 'When one of them picked up a fighter on its tail, Jerry would release its bombs and "hit the deck", fleeing at no more than a few hundred feet. Of course if he wasn't intercepted, he would be expected to bomb his proper target. It seems that the presence of this "backward-looking radar" was raised at an air defense meeting where Churchill was present; he was assured that there was a plan to have our ground stations able to jam it within six months. "Six months be damned – you will have it working by six o'clock tonight", he retorted. By six o'clock a number of jammers were indeed working, some portable early warning radar sets having been modified to operate at the enemy's frequency and raw AC applied to the plates of our transmitters. The sets burned out after one or two nights' use but the technique was successful. After a few weeks, enemy aircraft that were shot down no longer carried this form of radar. I was told the gist of all this by someone who attended that meeting with Winston Churchill – and I was present about five months after that meeting when contractors turned up to start installing the jamming equipment. My technicians were trained to use and to service it, but not once was it needed.'

Newly-arrived in the UK as a newly-commissioned officer, Allan Paull was in May 1943 posted to serve as technical officer in charge of a ground radar installation at

Great Ormes Head, near Llandudno, a station set up high on a bluff to provide surveillance over the Irish Sea. Previously, he says, 'the installation was being run quite efficiently by a seasoned RAF Flight Sergeant and I, an inexperienced Pilot Officer, was sent there to take charge. I had to become a fast learner'. He goes on:

> 'I remember that the station was armed with a Browning machine gun (left over from World War I), mounted at the top of the cliff and pointing out toward the Irish Sea. We fired it once a week to make sure that it remained operational – it kept jamming – but we never had to fire it in anger. My only other recollection of that station is when the radar antenna, a large bed-spring-sized device, became unserviceable and we had to go up on the roof in a blinding rain storm to work on the antenna and find the fault. It was after this incident that I first heard the frightening rumor that exposure to radar waves could make a man sterile. It ain't so – and that's "pukka gen", as we used to say! I don't recall that we picked up any enemy aircraft on the tube but we monitored most of the friendly flights from across the Atlantic on their approach to destinations in the United Kingdom [23].'

Fellow Canadian Al Revill, appointed Commanding ('and only') Officer of a CHL station perched above the village of Castlerock in Northern Ireland, tells how he was able to circumvent the paperwork covering the petrol usage returns and enable the airmen to have a weekly liberty run into Coleraine to go to the movies. These returns, which were sent to Wing HQ, itemized authorized travel, mileage and odometer readings; by lengthening each authorized run 'by just a bit', Al was able to accumulate enough spare miles in the week to make the required liberty run. There is a sequel though, which soon dissipated whatever concerns he may have had for encouraging this trivial waste of resources. Visiting his brother for a drink at a nearby Coastal Command squadron, Al commented that the sherry was excellent and apparently available in quantity, to which came the answer: 'Oh yes, if we run short we send a Lib for some more!' – a 'Lib' meaning Liberator, the four-engined long-distance aircraft widely used in Coastal Command though not necessarily for obtaining supplies for the Officers' Mess [24].

When, after service on a number of radar stations in Canada, Bob Warner was able to join an overseas draft, it was at RAF Kingswear, Devon, just across the harbour from the Royal Naval College at Dartmouth, that he saw for the first time the contribution that the female branch of the RAF was making in radar. There was, he recalls, 'a very high percentage of WAAF personnel, including four radar technicians, although most were radar operators' [25]. In the main, Kingswear personnel were billeted in private homes in nearby Brixham, to keep off-duty personnel away from a potential target. He understood that the radar station had been attacked on two or three occasions, without casualties, though by the time Bob arrived there towards the end of the European war, the possibility of an air attack was considered to be very low. Although the WAAFs were still in accommodation off-site, their male colleagues were by now in quarters on the station, which had two different types of radar at that time, one a CHL/GCI type and the other a 10 cm Type 52.

Canadian radar technician Harry Carlyle saw service in the UK first as an airman on Home Chain stations and then as a technical officer on Oboe ground stations; he was among what might be described as 'second wave' officers, graduating in November 1943 when already a comparative 'old stager' on active duty overseas.

Harry had gone from the CHL station at Prestatyn, North Wales, to TRE in Malvern in March 1943 for his Oboe training course; and this was followed by time spent on the Oboe station at Hawkshill Down, more Oboe training at Yatesbury and on officer training at Cosford. At Swingate as an Oboe technical officer, during a seven-week spell there and at Winterton, Harry found himself on the receiving end of a number of cross-Channel artillery exchanges. It was already 'a very active period for us without those barrages.

'It seemed that whenever our own guns fired on shipping along the French coast, the enemy's return fire was liable to land in our vicinity. The station was heavily sand-bagged, so as to try to provide protection, but this didn't always save us from damage and casualties. The hits created a lot of dust and from time to time their reverberation would cause a clock to fall off the wall. We had some close calls: more seriously I recall one hit on the NAAFI that killed two of our airwomen; and another that blew up the adjacent CHL Nissen hut, some 50 feet away from our Oboe room. The hut was devastated though no-one was hurt, everyone having taken cover beneath the plotting desk. Funny thing was that even though not much remained of the building, the radar equipment in it was happily percolating away in the open air [26].'

Radar technical officer Rus Robinson, 'browned off' with a year spent mainly on administrative duties in charge of RDF units in the UK and in the Faroe Islands, spent nine months at TRE. Being posted there in July 1943 worked to his advantage as well as to that of 60 Group, to which he belonged: they needed more 'trained hands' in their radio technicians detachment at TRE and he wanted to make better use of the training he had received in electronics since joining the RCAF.

He was assigned to the Oboe group, which was then busy on ground-station equipment capable of mobility, ready for eventual use on the Continent of Europe to extend the Oboe-led bombing capability in step with the advancing armies. Immediately he sensed 'an atmosphere of dedication, urgency and the supreme importance of their work', which he says was leavened by a friendly and co-operative acceptance to 'the family'. Each of the various groups in TRE was engaged in research into dedicated aspects of its own type of radar, the personnel at TRE tending not to mix much. Rus explains that 'all of us were strictly governed by the "need-to-know" security principle and even within the Oboe team there were development groups, the details of which I knew nothing at the time' [27].

He notes that 'as a measure of our acceptance by the Oboe civilian scientists, we 60 Group "loaners" had their complete trust and we were given proportionate responsibilities'. To make this point he continues:

'We took full part, if not in primary conception, at least in the modification, improvement and installation of the new centimeter system's development – draughting blueprints, experimenting with minor circuitry changes, installing modifications ordered by the circuit designers... all of the activities of prototype production. In my case this often resulted in travel and personal contact with industrial engineers or with RAF squadron-users, much more than being merely "a pair of hands". In addition to technical skills, good health and ability to put in long hours, to drive a balky van by day or in the blackout, to communicate technical information clearly over the scrambler phone, and a measure of negotiating tact were also requisites of the job.'

There were some seven civilians and six air force personnel in his immediate group, the 'on-site' manager of the Oboe development team being J E N (John) Hooper, one of the original group of six convened by 'F E' Jones in May 1941 – 'greatly experienced in Oboe development, enthusiastic, efficient, capable and a great inspiration to those who worked for him; like "F E", John inspired others by example'. The job supervisor on Oboe Mk IIM was Keith ('Jock') Russell, 'a patient and fatherly Scot who taught, and insisted, that all of our soldered joints and layout must be "sanitary", a term which he apparently borrowed from that magician of electronic design, Dr F C Williams, a legendary figure who occasionally sent us scurrying to modify the circuits and schematics'. Williams had applied his talents to RDF circuit-design in the early days at Bawdsey and later made significant advances in IFF, GCI, Rebecca-Eureka, Shoran, G-H and especially to 'lock-follow' AI.

When working away from Malvern, Rus would 'serve as a bridge' between the civilian scientists, the manufacturers and the users of both airborne and ground equipment. In this latter function he came into close contact with Oboe pilots 'Hal' Bufton and 'Slim' Somerville, each of whom commanded one of the only two RAF squadrons to operate with Oboe Mosquitoes, and with Frank Metcalfe, one of the first of the Oboe ground station controllers.

In March 1944, Rus left Oboe development work to go operational with the mobile equipment that he had seen progress to fruition, being located first at Beachy Head in the build-up to the Normandy invasion and then, on D-Day itself, marking enemy coastal batteries that were thought to threaten the success of the landings. Soon he was in France himself, a member of AMES 9432 – the first mobile Oboe ground station to set up in continental Europe, with one of his contacts from his TRE days, Frank Metcalfe, its senior controller [*] .

TRE had its own dedicated flying facilities, under the name Telecommunications Flying Unit (TFU); these were at Defford, some eight miles to the east of Malvern, where TRE was itself located. It had moved to Defford from Hurn in parallel with TRE's move from Worth Matravers to Malvern. A Canadian radar technician, H ('Red') Macaulay attached to the RAF, who was stationed there for a while, recalls:

---

[*] Rus Robinson remained with AMES 9432 until severely injured in Belgium in November 1944. Following medical retirement from the RCAF he returned to university, graduating as a specialist in organic chemistry and making a career as a research scientist in public service with Agriculture Canada. In retirement, Dr Robinson has conducted research and published several critical studies concerning the history of radar. He has provided on-going funding for a collection of books at the Weldon Library, University of Western Ontario, all relative to radar history and technology and available for loan to historians.

'Malvern was secure, Defford was even more so – if that was possible!   I remember there was a large contingent of the RAF Regiment at Defford to maintain security, possibly 200 personnel. We also received weapons training, including the Sten machine gun, and some of our personnel assisted in digging slit trenches surrounding the airdrome.   On the airfield, security was so tight that no-one whose job required him to work in one of its hangars was able to enter another without authority. However with radar personnel, sometimes it would be necessary to move about between hangars and dispersal areas to work on different aircraft, so certainly I had a pass which enabled me to do so. We were continually briefed on the importance of security and aware of the fact that we confined discussion on any radar activity between those who had a need to know [28] .'

Red Macaulay came to Britain in the troopship *Stratheden*, one of some 250 radar mechs stowed in an area on 'G' Deck at the bottom of the vessel, accessible only by steel vertical ladders to the last two decks, arriving at Greenock after a 'two-week miserable crossing'.   Those '*Stratheden* survivors must have been', he said later, 'a sick-looking bunch to the locals viewing the new arrivals sent to help win the war [29] '. Though all of his buddies 'seemed to have been selected for more romantic spots, such as the Hebrides or Shetland Islands', Red was sent to TFU Hurn, by comparison a 'privileged posting' near Swanage in Dorset.

When the move to Defford occurred in the early part of 1942, this base was under construction and the spring rains resulted in mud everywhere – 'We lived in our Wellington boots, only to take them off when we entered our sleeping quarters – a row of bell tents'.   The majority of the work carried out by the radar section involved DIs and servicing of Mk IV and Mk V AI and IFF equipment fitted in Blenheim, Halifax, Anson and Beaufighter aircraft, though occasionally their duties encompassed other aircraft used for transport and experimental fitments, including the Hurricane, Wellington, Lysander and Oxford.   There was a time when Mk VI AI radar was tried out in a Hurricane, a single-seater fighter, but it meant the pilot having to watch the tube, search in the darkness for the enemy aircraft and fly his own plane, all at the same time, thus creating what must have been insurmountable difficulties.   Noting another and much more significant radar application undergoing tests at TFU, Red states:

'Aircraft with unique aerial configurations were often seen at TFU, but if we were not involved we knew enough not to discuss the different types of installations.   It was many years later that I read the story of a bulbous-nosed B24 Liberator aircraft that arrived at Hurn in March 1942, fitted with the first centimetric air-to-surface vessel (ASV) radar, a variant of AI used by Coastal Command for surface vessel detection and control.   British equipment was used to develop this radar system at the Massachusetts Institute of Technology (MIT) and flown to England for extensive testing and evaluation by TRE.   Two Royal Canadian Air Force Sergeants, Gilbert Edgerton and James A Leach, were with this Liberator, having been on the project since Day One, and they continued to fly with it – it was known as "Dumbo" – on the Atlantic coast off the USA until October 1942.   World War II was only a month old when these two wireless telegraphy operator mechanics were selected for special training by the National Research

Council of Canada.   In October 1940 they were attached incognito as "civilians" to MIT in Boston, USA.   They were indeed RCAF pioneers in radar maintenance.   Later, I came across Gil Edgerton again when we were on the same commissioning course at Clinton in 1955 and we met for the first time [30].'

While Red Macaulay remained within the strict security environment of TRE, first at Hurn and then at Defford, centimetric ASV and other radar applications were being further developed for operational service with RAF squadrons.

Squadron life was probably better for radar mechanics than for those in other trades; and security had much to do with this, according to Dick Moule.   He explains that the secrecy of the radar gear 'had to be protected in every way possible' and for reasons of its highly-classified category, regulations called for the radar shop to be set apart from the rest of the station and only authorized personnel could enter.   As a consequence, 'this made the radar people a group unto themselves.

'A radar section would have its own officer, usually with the rank of Flying Officer or Flight Lieutenant; a senior non-commissioned officer with the rank of Flight Sergeant; plus a Sergeant and two or three Corporals.   The ordinary ranks all received trades pay and most were Leading Aircraftmen.

'The other trades, such as the aero-engine mechanics, wireless mechanics, fitters and electricians, worked more closely to one another, often sharing workshops and coming under the general administration of Station Headquarters.

'But the radar section ran its own show.   They arranged their own work schedules, days off and leave.   They weren't called for guard duty or kitchen fatigue.   This special treatment gave radar mechanics a distinction that was sometimes resented by the other trades.   The fact that most of the radar men were Canadians added to this "prominence" [31].'

Dick spent three and half years in England, serving on various RAF squadrons though never on a Canadian squadron; during the first six months he was the only Canadian on his station.   This period was 'a lonely time' for him; he was 'well treated by my English friends, but I found their habits a bit different and their jokes not very funny – not then anyway.   I was like an alien in a foreign land, but I learned to chug-a-lug a pint of beer!   Generally I had a "good war".   I enjoyed my work – we were the "gen men" on the squadron'.

An insight into the relationship between the lower ranks in a radar section on a UK-based squadron comes from Gregory Biefer, noting that where the corporals were friends and sometimes counselors to the 'erks' (Gregory was a Leading Aircraftman on five squadrons in Bomber and Coastal Commands between 1943 and 1945), the senior NCOs (Sergeants and Flight Sergeants in the main) 'represented authority'. He recalls that:

'Some of the senior NCOs I served under were excellent, but others – while probably well intentioned – were simply not up to the job of supervising the

Metropolitan
Edition

The Globe and Mail.

Forecast:
Fair; Warm

VOL. XCVIII. NUMBER 28,550.   TORONTO, WEDNESDAY, JUNE 18, 1941.   3 Cents Per Copy   10 PAGES

Radio Secret Dooms German Raiders;
Score 13-10 for R.A.F. in Channel Fight:

The date 18 June 1941... and Britain divulges that 'radio location' was her 'great mystery defense against German raiders'-a 'scientific device' and her 'best-kept secret of the war'.

Wooden CH tower at RAF Station, Sennen Cove, in Cornwall, England; this view was taken looking towards Land's End, with a TX (transmitter) curtain array at right. [Via Art Craig]

Radio Men Credited With 1940 Repulse of Germans

Canadian Press

OTTAWA, June 8.—Air Minister Power Monday transmitted to the House of Commons the word of Prime Minister Churchill that radio mechanics were largely responsible for the United Kingdom victory over the massed German air fleets in 1940.

Major Power gave the information when answering an inquiry about dissatisfaction a m o n g highly-educated men handling secret radio equipment. These men, who had been sent all over the world, felt their chances of promotion were not as good as those in other branches of the service. He reported the condition improved, with more commissions granted and trade pay

versity degrees graduates when About 54,000 had lation or better. T program would per a B.A. degree to studies, if he Government wou "I happen to h. matter of radio n higher authority, . England, and he w tory in the Battle c to radio mechan in the R.C.A.F.

Major Power and his parliamentary assistant, Hon. Cyrus MacMillan (Lib, Queens), answered a long series of questions about R.C.A.F. activities.

They revealed:

The R.C.A.F. bought some gliders but they were not quite satisfactory. Six helicopters have been purchased from a United States firm but the date of delivery was uncertain. The R.C.A.F. has "quite a few" good transport planes which could be used for training airborne troops but they are not now being used for that purpose.

Negotiations are proceeding between the army and the air force to increase the flow of men desiring air crew training from the army and also to arrange for enlistment

Government allott Kingdom had aske locators, and the t priority to them," s in his answer to (N.D., Camrose) F motion and pay of In January, 194 Kingdom had aske this was increased Canada felt that high qualification versity students a "Somehow or ot! have demanded to.

Ether Waves Warn Defense of Approach of Hostile Aircraft

USED LAST FALL

London, June 18 (Wednesday) (CP)—Britain today divulged her best-kept secret of the war with the announcement that radio location—a scientific device which warns of approaching planes miles away—is her great mystery defense against German raiders.

Air Chief Marshal Sir Philip Joubert, who described how the de-

Above, left: Two years after disclosure... and 'radio men' (actually radar personnel) receive due credit from Prime Minister Churchill, being 'largely responsible' for the United Kingdom victory over the massed German air fleets in 1940. Above, right: Radio location is said to use 'ether waves' to warn Britain's defenses that hostile aircraft are approaching.

Portion of a photograph of RCAF WEMs at Toronto Manning Pool, Craig Knudsen being circled; the 161-strong 'Leopoldville Group', as they came to be known, constituted the first major group of Canadian radar technician recruits to reach the UK. [Via Craig Knudsen].

WITH THE RADIO MECHS.

RADIO ROUND UP

Five gents with a sizeable chunk of RAF jankers and night watches under their belt, skipped through Smoke recently on privilege leave. They formed part of a healthy hunk of radio gen men who have clustered around mobile equipment, and will be wearing that pretty red combops badge shortly.

What a Team!

The quintet included LAC Pete Marshall, Toronto; LAC Frank Bricault, Sault Ste. Marie; LAC "Mac" Chown, Hamilton; LAC Hilton Hunter, Amherst, N.S.; and LAC "Baz" Mulligan, Toronto.

On arrival, they had just completed a taste of things to come after a three-hour ride in soaking clothes, preceded by a three-mile walk in the elements (censorship permits mentioning it was raining at the time).

work, and we've never seen him work so hard.

This week we say Hello to P/O D. E. Jones, newcomer to our unit. He brings the number of Hamiltonians here to five. He has been over a few years, and has had his spell at Jeep pushing with the rest of us.

—LAC J. B. Scarcliff.

Tiger Hours

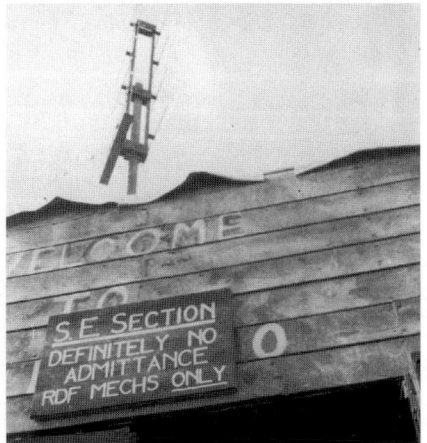

Above, left: *Activities of radar technical officers and radar technicians were the focus of a dedicated column, 'With the radio mechs', in the RCAF newspaper* Wings Abroad. *Above, right: The "Special Equipment" (SE) under the care of the radar mechs was most definitely out of bounds; this sign appeared at a workshop at Korangi Creek, India.* [Via Bill Barrie].

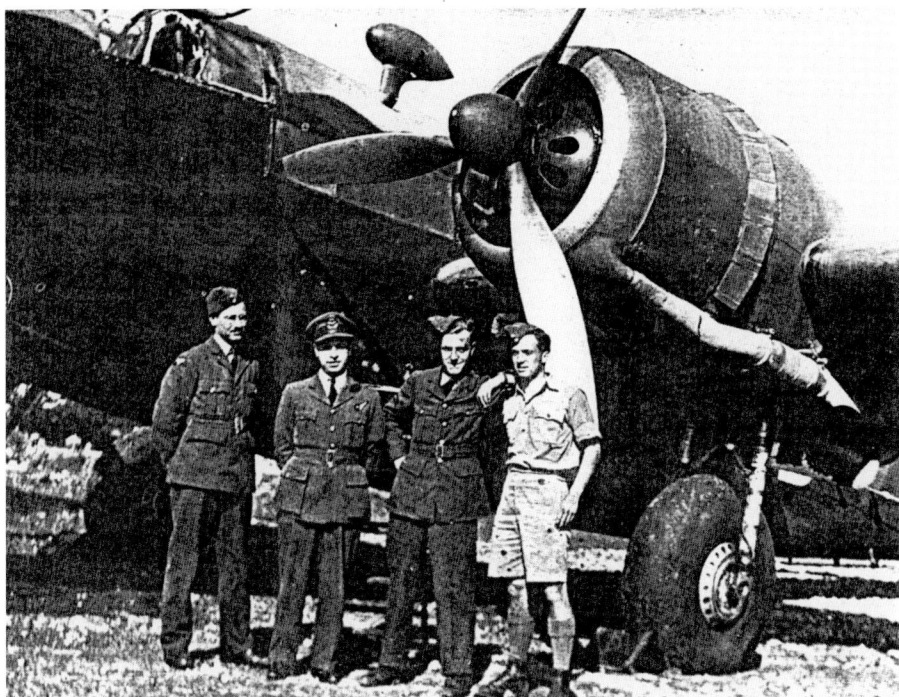

Carefully positioning themselves to avoid showing the antennae on this ASV-equipped Welling-ton of #69 Squadron on the island of Malta in the autumn of 1941 are, left to right, Canadian radar mechs Les Card, who was then a Leading Aircraftman, and Flying Officer Al Glazer, with RAF radar mechs Corporal Fred Few and ACI Tom Rogers, all of them contributing to the war effort with operational flights as aircrew members as well as carrying out their more customary maintenance and installation duties on the ground. [Via Les Card].

Chicken for the radar section on #106 Squadron at Metheringham, with (from left) recipients Al Beattie, Jim Chisholm and Norman Yates. [Calgary Radar Reunion '96 brochure].

Going up... a CH tower at Clinton, the radar training centre in Ontario where more than 5,000 Canadian technicians and more than 750 technical officers, as well as 2,325 Americans, were taught during the war. [1999 London (Ontario) Radar Reunion booklet].

CHL tower straddling a Clinton classroom. [1999 London (Ontario) Radar Reunion booklet].

Canadians abroad: Serving on #614 Squadron in Italy, which flew Halifaxes before converting to Liberators, were these radar mechs – left to right – Corporal L. A. Phillips, Flight Lieutenant O. H. Marshall and Leading Aircraftmen E. C. Helson, E. L. Fulton, W. Pankratz and J. H. Leveille. It will be observed that the working environment on an operational unit did not always allow its personnel to maintain quite the sartorial elegance invariably instilled into recruits in successive training establishments! [Via Orv Marshall]

Canadians at home: Pictured at the Ucluelet camp site of #13 Radio Detachment, Amphitrite Point, British Columbia, in the fall of 1942 – this was their country's first operational radar station – were (top left to lower right) radar personnel Jim Skuce, George Rutledge, Stan Williams, Ernie Foychuk, Jack Webb, Bob Millar, Bill Moir, Ed Hall, Doug Finlayson, Marty Moore, Jeff Ingraham, Bob Warner, Joe Sherk and Ed Saunders. [Via Bob Warner].

ENEMY RAIL MOVEMENT
CAUGHT AT NIGHT BY
69.

Night-time photo-reconnaissance, which could obtain unexpected intelligence such as the enemy rail movement caught in this picture taken by #69 Squadron, combined the use of specialist squadrons in #34 Wing and eight Eureka-H beacon units which were used in Normandy from soon after D-Day through to VE-Day. The crews in these squadrons used the ground beacons for pinpoint accuracy in navigation.[34 Wing, An Unofficial Account].

At Manston in Kent, #584 Spitfire Squadron radar officer Roy Cuthbert greets a visitor from a Canadian infantry unit, this squadron's role being close support for the Allied armies in North West Europe, the pilots being directed to their targets by radar. The squadron took its numerical identification from the type of radar it used – the SCR 584. However theirs was a mobile system modified from its more customary gun-laying role. [Via Roy Cuthbert].

D-Day, 6 June 1944, and a Type 14 in AMES 15082 is on this landing craft on its way to Omaha Beach, the whole unit being carried in this and other vessels to land and then to form a ground-controlled interception facility for the Allied air forces. The sea crossing was uneventful but near and on land there was heavy gunfire. Fierce opposition meant that it was not until evening on the fourth day that AMES 15082 was 'in Business' - and that very night notching-up the first 'kill' by the night fighters under its control. [Via Muir Adair].

A US Navy photograph showing a section of Omaha Beach on the morning of D-Day+1, 7 June 1944, including beach obstacles and burned-out vehicles belonging to AMES 15082, whose losses in this 'disastrous' landing included equipment carried in the LST in the previous photograph, which was drowned off the shore. The landing craft carrying AMES 15082's vehicles, equipment and men stopped in the water that was deeper than anticipated while another came to an abrupt halt on a sandbank. [National Archives, 80-G-45714].

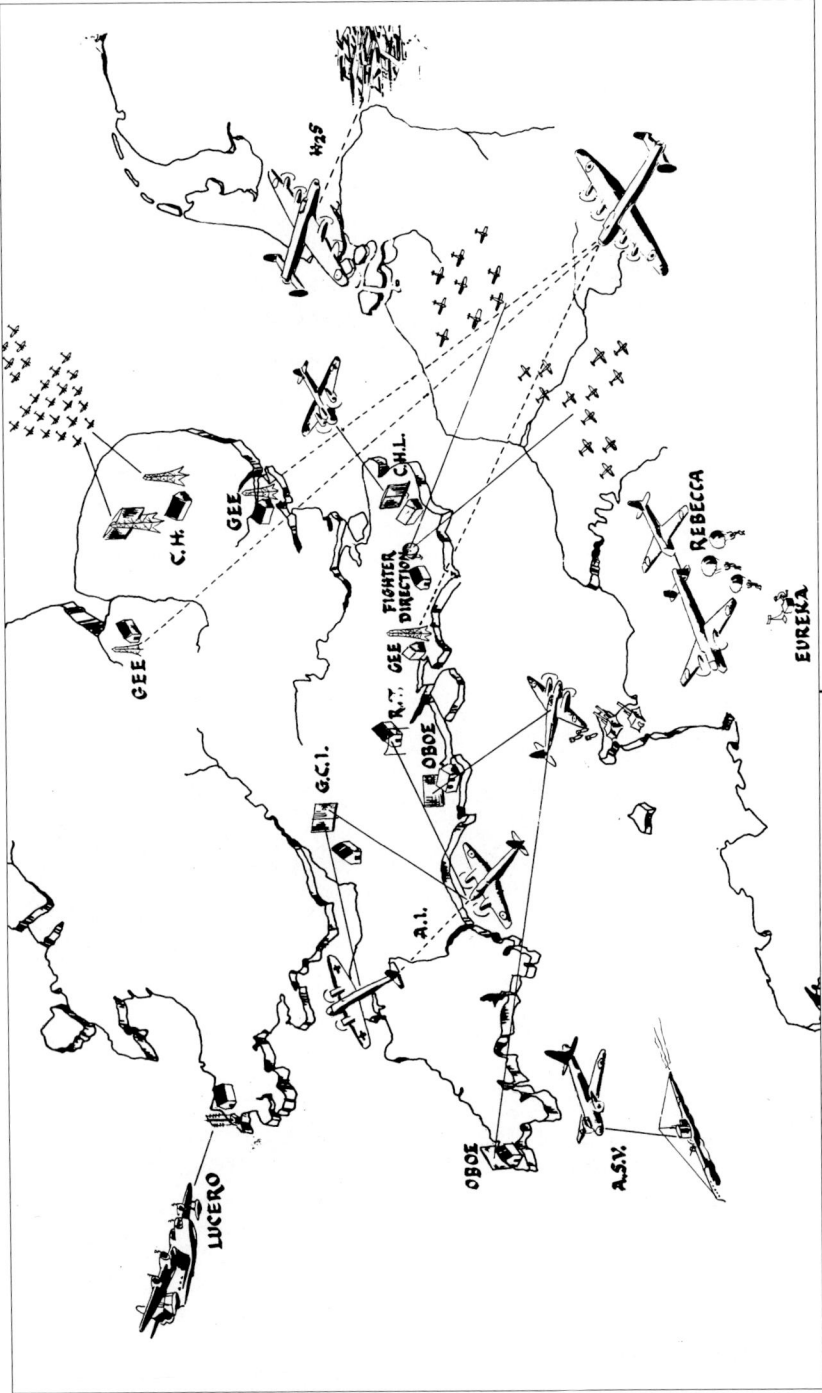

Composite picture of drawings by TRE artists to illustrate the nature of various radar devises originating there ande used by the RAF in Europe. It was created for a visit by King George VI and Queen Elizabeth in July '44. [Imperial War Museum: E1428].

activities of a dozen or so radar mechanics. Unfair treatment was sometimes coupled with a refusal to listen to any complaints. In this frustrating situation one airman resorted to carving a wooden doll to represent the offending NCO, then sticking pins into it while uttering suitable curses. It is not known whether this had its intended effect [32].'

The commissioned officers in command of a radar section were, he remarked, reasonable men having little direct contact with the other ranks, their activities 'hidden behind the same curtain of secrecy as those of all other officers'.

A function that was easy to forget was that of 'fine tuning' the radar sets on ground stations; yet to Harold Mason, one of those doing this work with # 75 Wing Calibration Flight at Biggin Hill, it was 'probably the most interesting posting of my career'. It was in April 1942 that he was posted to Biggin Hill, an airfield which had become perhaps the best-known fighter base of all during the Battle of Britain, so far as the general public was concerned. For calibrating, Blenheim aircraft were used; normally these planes had a crew of three but for this work there was a fourth person on board – a radar technician with specialist equipment of his own and the facility to keep in touch with the ground station by wireless. The Blenheim would make successive 'runs' over the Channel, flying at previously agreed altitudes, while the ground station calibrated its equipment to ensure the production of accurate aircraft-positioning data when on watch for enemy raiders. One of Harold Mason's more routine flights, lasting two hours and in conjunction with Dunkirk, involved two runs at 7,000 feet and one at 15,000 feet; less typical were ones when the Blenheim's air speed indicator became unserviceable, the flight aborting after 20 minutes, and when the pilot's cockpit hood malfunctioned and the flight had to terminate after 40 minutes. Such flights were not without the potential dangers. Once, airborne and working as scheduled with a ground station at Pevensey, the area chosen for the calibration runs was designated 'not clear'; this was the parlance of the day to indicate the presence of enemy aircraft in the vicinity. In double-quick time, the Blenheim cut short the job in hand and headed hastily for home, causing a rather relieved radar technician to remark to his colleagues that 'it wasn't our job to take on the Luftwaffe! [33]'

On leave in London between leaving Cranwell and taking up his first posting, James Farrior was inducted as an 'Original Eagle' at the American Eagle Club. Posted to the CH station at Scarlet on the Isle of Man, where his 'USA' shoulder patch was the first that anyone there had seen, he arrived towards the end of January 1942 to find a warm welcome awaiting him, especially from the RDF mechanics who were 'very much under-staffed'. Subsequently he noted that the only radio operator, who sent plots to the Filter Room at Preston by Morse code during underwater cable outages and drills, 'was happy to learn that I could relieve him up when needed' – James having been a civilian radio operator working with the US Army before joining the Civilian Technical Corps (CTC). He explained that, although technically civilians, CTC members were treated the same as members of the RAF or one of the Dominion Air Forces; they wore RAF uniform, 'slept in the huts, ate in the mess, did camp duties and worked the same shifts'. By mid-1943, when he took his release from RAF service to join the US Merchant Marine and become a Chief Radio Officer, it was his understanding that there were at least 1,000 men in the CTC and that the majority were RDF mechanics [34]. Several were with him on the Isle of Man, among them George Fulton and John Boor at Scarlet, Floyd Harkom and Harold Wright at another CH station, Bride.

But what about the Canadians, who were the more numerous among arrivals from the North American continent? It would surely be revealing, as a unique historical record, if it were possible to put a retrospective focus on an entire group of embryo radar technicians who, having answered 'Chubby' Power's appeal and begun their training course between 26 May and 19 June 1941 in one of the 13 Canadian universities taking part in this program to prepare up to 2,135 of these recruits for service overseas, formed what could perhaps be called the 'Class of September '41 at Trenton'. What happened to them during and after their transportation to foreign parts; what were these 'foreign parts' and what were the duties performed by each of those men; and how many would still be around, half-a-century hence? In fact, such a chronicle *has* been compiled: it stems from early note-gathering by Craig Cooper and blossomed with assistance from several others who were united by a single yet sturdy thread. All shared the same career starting point, being members of a group of 32 newly-commissioned officers in the Royal Canadian Air Force who, with their 12 weeks' instruction in basic electrical and radio theory now behind them, assembled for the first time on the parade square at Trenton on 17 September 1941. Suffice, for the moment, to be able to take comfort from the fact that, 58 years on, at least 18 of those 32 fledgling Pilot Officers were known to be still 'in the land of the living' and well able to recall so much of that memorable chapter of their lives [35].

It might be tempting to regard the experiences of this 'Class of '41' as a microcosm of radar technicians recruited in that period within the British Empire at large; as a group, however, these were already far from being considered any sort of 'norm'. Each was already 'an officer and a gentleman' when by far the majority were plain airmen (some, as will emerge, progressing no further up 'the totem pole' than the classification of Leading Aircraftman); and more significant still, each of those 32 members of Administrative Course # 21 at Trenton from 15 September to 18 October 1941 for conversion to officers was there by virtue of being top student in whichever university he had done his groundwork. From Trenton, all were sent on to Clinton for radar training and entry into 'a new world' to be faced with 'knowledge far beyond our imagination'; on completion of eight weeks' intensive training, all but two (who were retained to teach subsequent courses) were UK-bound in the first week of January 1942.

If those 32 *were* to be viewed as typical radar technicians, a picture would unfold to show that at least three in four were destined to see service in the Middle East within a year or so; while among the remaining one-in-four, the campaigns in Northern Europe were a shade more man-hungry than those in India and Burma. All 32 survived their period of active service and the majority were home in early 1945, though some were re-trained in the expectation of serving in the Pacific. Most returned to civilian life before the end of 1945; however 2 of the 32 were still in uniform and still overseas for a further period while with the RCAF occupation forces in Germany until the summer of 1946. Reunion dinners were held in Hamilton and Toronto shortly after the war but, inevitably, these 32 former radar technical officers then went their separate ways... until Craig Cooper (Egypt, Cyprus and Palestine in 1942/44) and Jack Brown (Palestine, Cyprus, Tunisia and Italy during the same period) reunited the group in 1981 after a 30-year gap.

It was a time to recollect days gone by... a time to remember one's comrades, some of them having by then passed on, when radar in the early 1940s seemed to embrace no more than the CH and CHL stations which helped save Britain's life in a critical period, the MRU mobiles that were the backbone in more distant theatres of operation and the GCI system to point fighters toward their quarry.

Some radar technicians spent many hours in the air while others were hardly ever given an opportunity to fly, even if wishing to do so; and there were times when some 'radar tecks', because of the nature of their work, logged more hours than did aircrew on the same squadron over a similar period of time [*].

Ground radar specialist Sydney Goldstein's entire flying experience was confined to a single trip in an Anson that had probably seen better days – a flight between two airfields to check on a new type of radar equipment: 30 minutes in the air, 3 hours by train to make the return journey because worsening weather conditions grounded the plane.   Back at his base, Sydney's first and only flight became an occasion for celebration.   He was given a 'gong' comprising a ribbon, safety pin and beer bottle cap which was presented with full honours and inevitable ribbing in the Mess.

It needed fun times like that to make one forget that there were many occasions when planes didn't return, when crew members came back wounded or dead or didn't get back at all.   If you were a radar technician posted into RAF Bomber Command, you had to be resilient... to be able to face the tragedies with the triumphs...

---

[*] LAC John Livick, whose experiences as an early veteran came to the attention of a contributor to the RCAF newspaper *Wings Abroad*, saw service 'in the days when radio men got in as many flying hours as aircrew'. He seems also to have seen more action than most – he was 'bombed, mined and torpedoed... spent time floating around the Channel before being picked up... participated in the D-Day operations and spent three weeks across the Channel'.

CHAPTER 5: BOMBERS' BOON

With three radar-based navigational aids introduced successively for operational service with RAF Bomber Command, GEE in 1941, H₂S in 1942 and Oboe in 1943, its crews were able to find their targets more easily and to hit them more effectively than was previously the case. GEE enabled them to cross-check their position on both the outward and return journey, H₂S provided the means to determine important landmarks invisible to the naked eye, thus helping to confirm target areas, while Oboe guided crews to the aiming point and signaled when to release the bombs for maximum accuracy.

Arriving on a bomber base at Leeming in Yorkshire on his first posting as a radar technician – it was to # 10 Squadron – Bill Lee wondered what was going on... He recounted later that 'nobody knew what I was there for, there was no radar equipment and I was the only Canadian ground crew on the station. I just hung around with the wireless people for a while'.

It was a time of transformation and this was the reason for the enforced inactivity. There quickly followed a three-week course on GEE, after which he returned to Leeming to install this and IFF in the four-engined Halifax bombers newly-arrived on the squadron – IFF being a device carried inside an aircraft to identify it as 'friend' not 'foe' when interrogated by the radar defenses * .

The sense of achievement that he experienced at Leeming was to some extent tempered by what he calls his 'first introduction into the shock of sudden death'. One of the bombers, returning from a training flight, 'dropped short of the runway, hit a horse in a field and bounced over a farmhouse. Then it ploughed into a grove of trees, hitting a bunch of ground crew who had run with the aircraft instead of to one side. We were ordered to remove the radar gear immediately through all that carnage ₁ '.

Serving elsewhere in Bomber Command, as a member of # 106 Squadron, Allan Beattie remembers that 'we radar mechs were very busy fellows and didn't get to know many people on the station.

'As an indication of what life was like in those days, I recall that in October of '42 there were supposed to be ops 30 times and that 28 times they were scrubbed because of bad weather. We had the same routines to follow, though, whether an op was on or off, the difference being that we wouldn't

---

* An item about IFF in the Calgary Radar Reunion '96 Souvenir Publication notes that when crews were advised of a change in the frequency of this 'comfort signal', they were expected to take appropriate action at once. If the early frequency was on # 2 and the new one was # 5, 'better be squegging on five in very short order'. The IFF sets were 'very dependable' and radar mechanics 'rarely' had to fix them.

have to wait up for the aircraft to come back. Sometimes it was unlimited hours seven days a week if we were needed. We didn't mind, we knew we were doing something that was important. We reckoned that we were the "gen" men on the squadron; you see other trades didn't savvy radar and were careful about asking too much about this "secret gear".

'When H_2S came along there were special courses for two weeks at TRE in Malvern for some of us who were a little more senior in the section. A special crew arrived to install H_2S in the aircraft; they did that in two nights. H_2S was a great system and now it would be up to us to see that the equipment worked – quite a responsibility considering that we had been given only that two weeks' training!

'The next big installation for us was Loran, the long-distance beacon-guide system which the Americans had developed. Loran put us in a preferred category as far as communication and exact placement of target were concerned – and with H_2S it worked very, very well.

'One thing about radar that needs to be stressed: you were forever doing a modification that was required by the next op... or sooner! Mods, as we called them, were always important but for us they were the bane of our existence [2].'

Commensurate with the increasing use of radar within RAF Bomber Command was the call for more and more technicians to install, to test and to service this equipment. On Allan's squadron for example (106 Squadron), the size of its Radar Section would virtually double in three years, the complement growing from a single NCO and eight airmen in the late summer of 1942 to one officer, five NCOs and eleven airmen in mid-summer 1945 [3].   Based at Coningsby, Syerston and Metheringham successively over that period, the squadron's Lancaster bombers operated initially with only the early versions of GEE and IFF.   Then came a new generation of devices to add to the RAF's radar repertoire, all of them utilized by 106 Squadron during 1942/45, including Monica, to provide early warning of   an approaching enemy fighter [*] ; Window to confuse – and Mandrel to jam – enemy ground-based radar; H_2S incorporating Fishpond, a fighter early warning indicator; and Loran, capable of operating in two modes – 'line of sight' transmission, where the range was similar to that of GEE, which was about 300 miles from the trio of ground transmitters, and 'sky waves' transmission, where target distances were greater.

This particular bomber squadron, 106 Squadron, on one occasion attracted the attention of TRE personnel, whose scientists visited Syerston when a problem with

[*] Monica could be a life-saver as RCAF radar technician Lenny Palmer can testify. At one stage he was the only person on # 432 Squadron who had been trained on Monica, having been sent to Bomber Command HQ for a course on it. He reports: ' After a couple of months I was wondering if it was any use until a crew came into our workshop looking for the Monica tech. They came over and thanked me for saving their lives: the rear gunner had been dozing when he was awakened by the Monica peeps on his intercom, an enemy aircraft closing in fast. He gave them a burst of fire and the plane dropped out of sight. They were not sure if it was a kill but they continued safely back to England [4].'

Monica appeared to threaten its further use; and on another, that of the US 8th Air Force hierarchy, when GEE was introduced in favor of Loran. These two occasions have been recalled by two members of the squadron's Radar Section, Jim Chisholm and Mike Burke, who explained that...

'Despite Monica's success in enabling bomber crews to drive off enemy fighters, the continual sound of the pips on the intercom in flight was distracting; these occurred at a rate of one a second at maximum range, which was about 1,000 yards, and increased to almost a continuous note at minimum range. Learning about the distraction that the pips were causing, TRE formed a team of "boffins" who came to Syerston to effect a solution to this problem, short of withdrawing the equipment from service. It was decided to eliminate the audible warning and change it to a visual indication. Accordingly, it was proposed to utilize some redundant ASV equipment from Coastal Command and convert it on the station, utilizing the Monica transmitter together with an ASV receiver and indicator and azimuth aerials. This concept provided the wireless operator with a visual indication of the range and quarter of approach of any hostiles.

'With regard to the navigational aids which used radar, it had been intended that the Americans would use the Loran system when bombing in daylight, the 'sky waves' mode being achieved by directing the transmission upward some 70 miles to the ionosphere and having pulses reflected off the 'E' layer to the aircraft, thus overcoming the problem of the curvature of the earth. However, due to unstable conditions of the ionosphere during daylight, the intention to use Loran was abandoned and the 8th Air Force initially installed GEE in their B-17 and B-24 bombers. Because of this, during the summer of 1943 several newly-arrived American radar personnel came to Syerston and were trained by 106 Squadron Radar Section to service and maintain GEE prior to their assignment to the 8th Air Force Bomber Groups [5].'

That same squadron played a significant part in the development of Fishpond. With the wireless operator at the controls in concert with the air gunners, Fishpond initially 'had a range of five miles and in the bomber stream many echoes were displayed on its screen. This made it difficult to quickly detect enemy fighters amid all of the echoes from the bomber stream. 106 Radar Section designed a modification to the range and reduced it to two miles. This modification was submitted to Bomber Command HQ and a subsequent Air Ministry modification was issued [6]'.

David Acaster, serving with one of the RCAF squadrons in Bomber Command, # 428 Squadron, recalls radar 'coming into its own' in the summer of 1943, with the installation of Monica and Fishpond and the GEE range extending. Mounting optimism came with a succession of significant bombing operations against important targets in Germany, the invasion of Sicily and the surrender of Italy; understandably, 'we felt the back of the war had been broken' [7].

Jim Chisholm and Mike Burke, whose time with 106 Squadron Radar Section spanned the period between late summer 1942 and June 1945, make the point that 'while awards to ground personnel are normally few and far between, there were 4 Mentions in Despatches awarded to the 106 Squadron Radar Section' [8] .

A Mention in Despatches was a means of recognizing ability and effort and radar specialists fulfilling a gamut of duties were similarly honoured, for example a Senior NCO at Linton on Ouse for showing 'exemplary leadership in all phases of his work during periods when the very maximum was exacted from each individual'; the Radar Officer in charge of servicing and repairs at Middleton St George, whose 'keenness and technical ability have been instrumental in achieving the highest state of serviceability of any station in 6 Group'; the NCO i/c Base Servicing at Skipton on Swale for displaying 'a quality of leadership which has been an inspiration to those serving with him, encouraging them, through personal example, in many circumstances requiring special effort to get maximum radar operation serviceability'; and a Senior NCO at Tholthorpe who, when that station was chosen to convert AI Mark IV night fighter radar equipment into an efficient early warning device for bomber aircraft, 'personally conducted the experimental work and later supervised the installation of this equipment in all aircraft of this station' [9] .

With regard to the principal radar-based bombing aids, whereas H_2S operated with equipment inside the aircraft alone, Oboe required equipment on the ground as well as inside the aircraft, the function of one of a pair of ground stations being to provide tracking information for the run-in to the target while that of the paired station was to signal the optimum moment for bomb-release.   Thus with Oboe there were radar technical officers and radar technicians both on the ground stations whose equipment was dedicated to this system and on the squadrons whose aircraft were equipped with it.   Although Oboe was used during December 1942, it did not come into significant operational use until the night of 5/6 March 1943.   On that night, when eight Mosquitoes of # 109 Squadron were dispatched to drop target-indicator flares over Essen, ahead of Main Force bombers and relying entirely on the Oboe ground-controlled, blind-bombing system, some of their primary markers were reckoned to have fallen as close as 75 yards from the aiming point – it was within the Krupps works itself – and most landed inside 200 yards [10] .   To 'Bomber' Harris, who had taken over Bomber Command at the beginning of 1942, this was the 'precise moment' when the RAF's main bombing offensive began [11] .   Initially a single squadron was given Oboe: 109 Squadron, based at Marham.   Then, in the summer of 1943, # 105 Squadron was re-formed with Oboe-equipped Mosquitoes and both squadrons left Marham, 109 going to Little Staughton and 105 to Bourne.

While at Winterton, one of the Oboe ground stations on the East Coast and then under the command of a fellow Canadian, Carl Conway, Art Craig had an opportunity to meet – at one and the same time – three of the people most intimately concerned with the creation and use of this remarkable system.   He recalls that, although he had met one of them previously – 'Hal' Bufton – this was the first time he had met either Alec Reeves or 'F E' Jones, who accompanied him on that occasion.   Alec Reeves was running the Oboe project at TRE, where he invented and improved on the system, and 'F E' Jones was his '# 2'; Bufton was an RAF operational pilot and squadron commander who had long flown aircraft equipped with Oboe and its predecessor bombing aids, right back to the time when enemy beams laid across England to guide bombers to their targets were followed back to their source and attempts made to knock out the transmitters.

It was at TRE that Art was initiated into 'the mysteries of Oboe' by Reeves, Jones and others, one of his first tasks on the completion of this course being to put together the Treen ground station, which was intended to facilitate attacks on the enemy's submarine pens on the Atlantic coast of France using Oboe to mark the targets.   Several subsequent visits to TRE improved his overall knowledge of what he calls 'this fascinating thing, Oboe'.   From Treen he moved to Winterton, his new station turning out to be 'hot and heavy'.   For the visiting trio of Bufton, Reeves and Jones arriving at Winterton, there was probably no better timing; they were 'pleased to see a fully operational ground station', Bufton expressing his thanks with an invitation for Art to visit his squadron – # 109 Squadron, the one whose aircraft performed the target-marking over Essen on that night of 5/6 March 1943.   He had 'a great couple of days there', with the chance to have Bufton introduce him to many of the two-man Oboe crews; this was 'a good move because when I returned to my ground station, the blip on the CRT was not just an aircraft but two wonderful men doing what they knew best – and we were helping them.   We always knew when Bufton was flying [with 'Ding' Ifould his navigator most times when on ops] because they always showed up Johnny-on-the-spot and Bufton's approach to the target was consistently immaculate $_{12}$ '.   Besides meeting squadron members, Art found that arrangements had been made for him to enjoy 'some Mosquito air time' – non-operationally of course – 'but that's another story!'

An idea of the tension gripping Oboe ground station personnel in the winter of 1943/44 can be gained by sharing the sentiments contained in a letter that RCAF radar technical officer 'Mac' McNarry wrote home to his wife, Mavis, in Canada.   To combine a sense of the extent of the burden which he was experiencing and the concern that he was feeling about his consequent inability to spend as much time as he would have wished on their correspondence, he wrote in one letter during that period: '*Worked all day, all night, all next day until 5.30 pm – it's things like that that don't let me write you as often as I want to.*'

He explains:

> 'I joined Trimingham during the second week of October 1943 and by the end of November I was on sick leave due to exhaustion.   In the interim, throughout my letters home, I see that I mentioned being very tired most of the time.   This was probably caused by a combination of responsibilities, those of a technical nature relating to the equipment, which I had to keep operating at peak efficiency, exacerbated by the many other duties which, as I was the Technical Officer for the station, I considered were "down to me".   Perhaps I was too conscientious – I would not rest until I was certain that all was well with the equipment.   It was right to have concerns about maintaining good attitudes toward the necessary maintenance schedules – and ensuring that adequate spares were always on hand – but maybe other TOs were less rigid than I was in other aspects.   For instance, it was my contention that ours should always be a neat and clean-looking environment; to this end, on all the watches, I established a floor cleaning and polishing schedule, as well as a procedure to ensure that our test gear and our spares were always in top condition.   I cannot recall any adverse reaction – though I'm sure there was! – but I felt vindicated when, on being

posted to Hawkshill Down, I received a warm and appreciative message of best wishes from all the staff at "dear old Trim" [13] [*] .

In that reference to a period when he was working 'all day, all night and all next day until 5.30 pm', it should be noted that although Oboe operations were still confined to the hours of darkness, major Oboe-led bombing attacks were often supplemented by 'nuisance raids' performed by individual Oboe-equipped Mosquitoes, so that the ground stations were handling more than one raid in the course of one night. In addition, the fact that there were now two Mosquito squadrons using Oboe called for an increase in the number of aircrew training flights during daylight hours, with a consequential requirement for the ground stations to maintain an operational or pseudo-operational status right around the clock.

Having worked on a CHL station before going to Trimingham, 'Mac' recognized in the Oboe ground equipment many CHL components and racking, as well as the same antenna. This 'was mounted on a short wooden tower above the receiver hut and was rotated by mechanical gearing attached to a hand-crank beside the operator's position to the right of the CRT chassis. When not carrying out an active raid operation the antenna was pointed to various bearings that could be target areas and we performed mock operations. The intent was to keep the German monitoring stations on edge so that they could not anticipate a real raid. We had very little "down time" for extended maintenance – and I don't recall one failure of ground equipment during my entire Oboe experience [14] .'

With the Oboe system, a pair of ground stations handled a single Oboe-equipped aircraft, one acting as if holding the plane on an invisible dog-lead while tracking along an arc towards its target, the other station giving the signal to the plane to release its load of target-marking flares or high explosive bombs. A typical operation would begin with the Senior Oboe Controller receiving the target and timing information in a scrambled message from # 8 (PFF) Group Headquarters, he then notifying the Technical Officers (TOs) on the respective Oboe ground stations who had to make sure that the equipment was fully functional. When the Oboe Controllers arrived to take control of the station, they would initiate the setting-up procedures and check the work of the WAAF operators whose function was to plot the target and flight path of the aircraft under their control, using long rulers pivoted on the precise location of the paired ground stations. With his team, the TO 'hovered in the background, like a nervous mother hen, hoping all was well'. 'Mac' goes on:

> ' The Controllers were all ex-aircrew and knew the situation in the aircraft, but they did not necessarily know much of the complexity of the ground equipment, though some were tip-top. Given the pressures under which we were required to perform, in close proximity to each other, it will be appreciated that liaison between the TO and the Controllers was sometimes in a delicate balance. There was an occasion when, having begun their

---

[*] From the then Corporal Margaret Easting to 'Mac' McNarry, the unit's former Technical Officer, the letter opened by teasing him that it was written 'as we have a few minutes to spare between bouts of floor burnishing', to let him know that 'we are still coping!'. It was signed with 'Love from "A" Crew and its mechs'.

initial calibrations, the Controllers found that it was not possible to set the target range marker, which was crucial because it determined the controlling signals to guide the aircraft onto a constant range track to the target. We knew that there was a substantial bombing force already airborne and that there was a Pathfinder Mosquito soon to come under our control to put markers on to their target. Some ten minutes remained for us to find a way round the problem – and this would be down to me – or "our" Mosquito would have to abort the operation.

'In fact the problem was one which the Controllers on my station had recognized immediately as stemming not within our Oboe station but from the planners at Group HQ, where the bombing strategy was initiated. It was all to do with "ground clutter" when a very short range target is selected, as it was on that occasion. With the minutes ticking by, the Controllers were in a desperate state, trying to set the target range marker. I decided that it just might be possible to make an adjustment to a particular component that wasn't easily accessible; it would mean opening a panel, removing a chassis from within the cabinet, taking it into another room to make the adjustment, then reinstalling it. With some trepidation, which I hoped I would be able to mask with a breezy "Don't panic" addressed to the Controllers specifically and to all in earshot, I took off the panel and proceeded as intended. Not only was the modification successful, it was done in time to call-in the lead PFF Mosquito as if nothing untoward had happened. The target was marked correctly for Main Force and the record shows that the bombing was successful too [15].'

Although extremely rare, Oboe ground station personnel sometimes saw those target-marking flares during their descent. While at Hawkshill Down, with the bombers' objective Dunkirk, just across the Channel, 'Mac' had one such opportunity. His was the station giving the Pathfinder Mosquitoes their release signal so, the weather conditions being favorable, he started his stopwatch as the signal was being given, dashed outside and at the exact second expected, saw the flares bursting over Dunkirk. It was, he said later, 'my first unequivocal proof that the system worked!' What he hadn't expected, however, was to both feel and hear the concussion of the high explosives as the bombs burst on their target.

At TRE Malvern, where Julien Olson began to train on Oboe equipment on 28 February 1944, following more than a year spent with a Bomber Command OTU at Pershore, the course was intensive and there were lectures from 7.30 am until 6.45 pm. Everything was done under conditions of high security and no notes were to be taken out of the classroom – an echo of his introduction to radar while at Clinton. Malvern was, he says, 'a very pleasant place as normal RAF discipline was greatly reduced' and the rapport that he built up with the civilian staff would prove especially beneficial when, while he was working in a squadron radar section, some of them would visit to initiate the frequent equipment modifications [16].

The emphasis on the exceptionally tight security that embraced Oboe was mirrored at Little Staughton, the RAF Pathfinder Force airfield where he was a member of # 109 Squadron. The radar section building 'was isolated and out of bounds to everyone not "Radar", being staffed right around the clock by the radar mechs'.

Another indication of maintaining the secrecy of Oboe was the order that in the event of one of their aircraft making an emergency landing, an armed guard was to be placed with it until a mechanic was flown in to retrieve the Oboe gear before the aircraft could be serviced.

As a radar technician with 109, Julien was involved in testing the equipment before each operation and changing any defective units; besides the workshops, there were test vans which the mechanics used to simulate ground station transmissions and to carry replacement units.   Once, while driving one of these test vans along the perimeter track after completing checks on the squadron's Mosquitoes, just back from operations where a total of 22 aircraft were detailed to mark two targets and bomb three others, he had a close call when there was 'a tremendous explosion and balls of fire rolled by me', those blazing bits and pieces later being identified as the engines of an American B-17 Fortress bomber that pancaked on the airfield.   Debris was scattered for half a mile and 'as soon as we were able we ran to where we thought there might be survivors'.   There were flying jackets strewn around but no evidence of any crew members, alive or dead; apparently the plane had been abandoned with engine failure and simply glided down upon Little Staughton airfield, fortunately without damaging any of the Mosquitoes or Lancasters at their dispersal points and, more fortunately still, coming to rest well short of a bomb store which was directly in its path.

Talking of bombs...   Drama of another sort came Julien's way when, sitting in the navigator's seat of one of 109 Squadron's Mosquitoes and running a test on the Oboe equipment, 'a great thud shook the aircraft'.   The armorers had been hoisting a 4000 lb bomb into position within the fuselage when a cable broke and the bomb dropped to the ground.   For 'a horrible few minutes', no-one moved, hearts all but stopped; since nothing untoward happened, relief came with the realization that the bomb was not 'armed', allowing the armorers to continue the bombing-up procedure by replacing the cable [17].

On a bomber squadron, it was radar technician Gregory Biefer's experience that there was what he describes as 'a gigantic gulf' between the duties of air and ground crews, he and his colleagues being usually disregarded and treated more as hired hands than as members of the family, the triumphs and tragedies of aircrew rarely filtering through except perhaps as something heard on the grapevine [18].   During his first winter with the RAF, when Bomber Command's losses were at their highest in his time in the UK (1943 to 1945), the pale, suffering faces of the overstressed aircrews moved him deeply.   Lack of close contact had its blessings; comfort was possible and the sense of loss, when a crew didn't make it back to base, impersonal.

By the beginning of 1944 the magic figure of 5,000 Canadian radar technicians to work on behalf of the RAF had been all but achieved.   A survey showed that, once the number of radar mechanics either posted to the UK or under training specially for overseas service was taken into account, an additional 291 mechanics were required to complete Canada's commitment of 5,000 personnel for the UK [19].   On the surface this seemed to be a matter of bookkeeping: 5,000 promised, 4,709 supplied, leaving a 291 deficit.   It was the view within the Air Ministry that these could be 'very usefully employed in the UK and their dispatch to this country should be requested forthwith'; the RCAF offer would be 'of considerable assistance to the combined war effort'. The wheels indeed turned quickly, RCAF Headquarters in Ottawa advising Air Ministry that 'approximately 262 repeat 262 radar mechanics will be posted to depot March 15 for onward transmission to the UK'. In an additional and separate move to alleviate the continuing acute shortage of radar technicians in these few months remaining before the scheduled Allied invasion of Northern France, steps were begun to obtain 'at an early date' some or all of 970 radar mechanics who were likely to become surplus to Canadian Government requirements. For 60 Group alone, their arrival couldn't come soon enough; 60 Group had a 'serious deficiency' due, mainly, 'to the heavy calls that have been made upon us to fulfil the overseas crew requirements of AEAF and to the rapid growth of the RNA chain [20] '. Although a number of Coastal Command mechanics had been transferred to AEAF, AEAF were 'still very perturbed about the shortage of mechanics' and there were moves afoot to see about 'bringing mechanics from overseas to meet AEAF and other commitments' [21] .

In the early part of the war until the end of 1943, most RCAF radar officers were assigned to ground installation stations around the British coastline which provided early warning of approaching enemy aircraft. As the tide turned in the winter of 1943-44, after Italy's secret armistice with the Allies and the Russians had broken the siege of Leningrad, Britain began moving from a defensive mode to an offensive one in preparation for the invasion of Europe. Allan Paull recalls many radar technicians being put to work on aircraft installation duty at RAF Maintenance Units, where…

> 'An aircraft would arrive for modifications to its engine, to its airframe and to its complement of electronic gear. Once the modifications were completed a test pilot would take the aircraft for a test flight, checking out all the work that had been done. I recall that, as Signals Officer, I would frequently go up on those test flights, sitting in the co-pilot's seat, to check out the radio and radar equipment and, if memory serves me correctly, whenever I did I collected $2.00 per day flying pay. Another day, another two dollars [22] .'

Something that many remember is the effect of the prevailing and forecast weather conditions in the immediate run-up to the Allied invasion of Normandy on 6 June 1944. In fact, where Bill Milligan was concerned, climatic conditions seem to have influenced his radar service on several occasions including, it will be seen, the role he was to play in Normandy. For example, when in the Shetlands to open-up and run a CHL Type 2 station at Watness, Bill was posted to India; then, making the first leg of the journey, his plane was forced down in the Orkneys due to violent storms. Later he would explain:

> ' I was unable to get out by air for a week so I took a boat to the Scottish mainland and proceeded by rail. Upon arrival I discovered that my draft to India had gone and I was posted to 2nd Tactical Air Force to prepare for the invasion of Europe. At Swanage, where a GCI unit was being formed, AMES 8024, with new equipment, 29 airmen, an adjutant and myself as CO, we moved all over the South East reporting to various CH stations who relayed our plots. Also, we took part in exercises in preparation for the invasion. Shortly before the landings we became 483 GCC and four controllers joined us; one of them was higher in rank than I was so he

became the CO.   We were scheduled to land in France on D+9 but the weather was unsuitable for our landing and we were held up for a further week.   In Normandy and onwards, as the line of battle moved forward, so we moved too to give close support.   Then I received a signal asking if I wished to stay in Europe for another year or be repatriated.   I chose repatriation and my draft to Canada sailed in March 1945, unhindered (!) by the weather [23] .'

By the time D-Day arrived, Canada's 5,000 radar technicians were dispersed around the globe: though some remained in their homeland, by far the most were in one of the principal theatres of operation – the UK mainland and islands small and large that lay to the north, the Mediterranean and the Middle East, the Far East and the Pacific.   Some were still doing the same work as in their early days while others had moved on, as radar-based equipment had done; depending on the posting, a radar mech could be in the forefront of this new science... or immersed as ever in tried and trusted equipment.   He might spend the majority of his duty hours in a workshop or somewhere with this so-sophisticated, so-secret gear that he alone can handle – one of those indispensable 'unsung heroes'.   Conceivably, if he were to be sent to the battered and besieged island of Malta, he just might be in line for a medal that usually goes only to aircrew members serving on operational squadrons... the Distinguished Flying Cross.

CHAPTER 6: WAR IN THE DESERT

I t has already been noted that some radar technicians spent many hours in the air while others were hardly ever given an opportunity to fly, even if wishing to do so. In the Mediterranean theatre of operations, as will now be seen, 'air time' for a radar mech was less a joy ride, more a flight into uncertainty...

Posted to Malta in the autumn of 1941 and soon on attachment to # 69 Squadron, Les Card, though still only a Leading Aircraftman, and three of his colleagues (Flying Officer Al Glazer, a fellow Canadian, and Corporal Fred Few and AC1 Tom Rogers who were both in the RAF) started flying as members of an aircrew, Les going on to complete a tour of operations before leaving the island on transfer to Egypt in October 1942.   Cynics might well have taken the view that this was a stage of the war when it was probably safer to be in the air than on the ground – because in those 12 months on Malta, Les experienced well over 2,000 air raids.   It was a memorable period: all maintenance of the ASV equipment, the aircraft and the engines was done outdoors; there were no hangars, all of them long gone and reduced to piles of rubble as a result of the bombing.   Recalling those days on the George Cross island, Les said:

> 'The tools of our trade consisted of our own little tool box with pliers, screwdriver and adjustable wrench, with one AVO meter for the use of our section.   Our soldering irons consisted of one 220-volt for inside work and a Mock for outside work, the latter working with a magnesium and iron capsule which was placed on the iron and then lit with a special match. This we used to repair co-axial cables and to solder the breaks and cuts from bombing, strafing and enemy fire when on operations, strafing being a regular occurrence at times and all you could do was to shelter behind the many stone fences and walls.

> 'Our first barracks were destroyed in the bombing, as was our maintenance section, so we had a wooden shack hauled on to the airfield and that combined as our home and our place of work until it became so badly bent and suffered so many holes that we had no option but to evacuate the airfield and move to a radio monitoring station.   I put up a machine gun post behind our shop and managed to get one Me109 down and another on fire, as well as scoring direct hits on a Ju 88.   Also, I filled the air with lots of lead.   I recall that my ammunition line-up was rather impressive: incendiaries, tracer and armor-piercing.

> 'Despite there being so many air raids, which were regular occurrences morning, noon and night with anything from a single aircraft to 50 to 100 at a time, life on the island carried on as best it could, even to cinema shows in the main town, Valetta.   One incident stands out, the time when Tom

Rogers and I had sneaked out of camp to see the film *North West Mounted Police*. We were just going into the auditorium when the building received a direct hit, unfortunately killing about 200 people. Tom got a piece of shrapnel in his hand; both of us got part of the theatre on top of us, a Paulette Goddard billboard being the first to collapse upon the pair of us before the entire structure began falling to pieces. This happened on a Sunday, yet people were still being dug out on the Tuesday, among them a couple of sailors in the bar area who were hauled out in a perfectly OK state except that they had to be sent to a rest camp to sober up.

'Certainly we lost a lot of our own planes due to bombing and strafing, though we were very fortunate in our operations by losing only two planes with their crews while I was there. On one of them, Corporal Fred Few was the radar operator; I guess that's why, suddenly, I became first a Corporal and then a Sergeant ₁.'

Many radar personnel who were ground-based as distinct from being an aircrew member, necessarily flew as a normal function within the routine of their job. This was the situation, initially, with Fred Few, Al Glazer, Tom Rogers and Les Card. Les and Tom were the first to arrive, on 1 October 1941, flying out from the UK to Malta in ASV-equipped Wellingtons and entering the operational flying mode right away, alternating the nights and the aircraft between them as members of a Special Duties Flight. It was their role to operate the ASV equipment, additionally to maintain and service it in flight to ensure the success of whatever was the crew's mission. Les recalls that this was the practice for a fortnight; then, with Al and Fred having turned up in a Sunderland flying boat with spare radar and test equipment to set up maintenance facilities, all four were rostered in aircrews on all operations of major importance where the application and serviceability of the ASV equipment was especially critical.

Les continues:

'Al Glazer, who was on good terms with the Fleet Air Arm crews, flew with them on operations as well as with our own squadron so his flying log was positively bulging * . He was on some very successful sorties, sinking and damaging shipping vital to Rommel. All four of us knew the risks that we were taking by continuing with these "extra curricular" activities, nonetheless we regarded them as a part of our job. We were individuals, specialists in ASV radar, who each belonged to a team whose task was to search for enemy shipping, especially tankers, which we would hope to find and to attack with bombs or torpedoes.

'Fred Few was especially keen and the night that he didn't get back, I was the one who had been scheduled to fly. He wanted to go so we exchanged places, Fred to go that particular night, me the following night. The swap

---

* For taking part in 'a large number of sorties' when he had non-flying status, Al Glazer received the DFC (Distinguished Flying Cross), the citation referring to his 'courage and devotion to duty' being 'worthy of the highest praise'. A Flight Lieutenant by this time, he left Malta on transfer to RCAF Headquarters in the UK shortly after receiving the award.

was fortunate for me, fatal for him, and the next night's operation proved to be most successful.

'By then, like Al, Tom and myself, Fred had been granted the "RO" half-wing brevet which the four of us were proud to wear [*] . This award came on completion of 100 hours as an aircrew member; it was granted by the AOC and it was "Gazetted", so it was very official if (as I'm sure it must have been) it was somewhat exceptional.   Traditionally, aircrew members go through a training course to qualify for their brevet and then fly on ops, whereas we did our own training "on the job" and received ours "on the field of battle" when already seasoned aircrew members [2] .'

While on a Wellington bomber squadron operating from LG (Landing Ground) 109 in Egypt, where he continued to fly as radar operator as well as performing his normal non-aircrew function to maintain the ASV equipment carried in those aircraft, Les Card, as did countless thousands who served in the desert, gained personal experience of the effect of all that sand – effects ranging from mere irritation to potential death.   He recalls:

'Ours was a tent camp with roadways between the living quarters, the mess hall and the aircraft dispersal points.   All these roadways were lined with a railing of rope, which was something I couldn't understand, until there was a sandstorm.   To get our food, we had to hang on to that rope both to stay on our feet and to find our way.   Then, with some bully beef, biscuits and bread, or perhaps a tin of beans, we would struggle to negotiate the return journey in the same manner, gripping our food for all we were worth and crawling into our bed, pulling the blankets over our heads before opening-up the food and eating it.   This way, we kept out most of the sand. Personally, I found it very unappetizing to try and eat gritty food...

'Sandstorms were, to say the least, inconvenient.   Aside from sandstorms, to a lesser degree there was sand everywhere, all the time, the wind depositing the sand in the most unlikely places besides the most obvious. In the worst conditions, aircraft engines had to be stripped and cleaned, as well as the radar equipment and anything else with moving parts.   Sand would penetrate anything, anywhere.   I remember that one night the pilot tried three times to get airborne.   Then, just before the fourth try, the navigator announced on the intercom that three tries was enough for him and if the pilot proposed trying again, he wouldn't be on the plane.   With that, the navigator opened the hatch and left the aircraft.   That ended that night's flight, the likely cause of our repeated failures being sand getting into one or both engines.

'If sandstorms are ignored, spending one's time on a camp such as ours was no particular hardship.   We had our fun – and living in a tent in the desert was never lonely... the tents were always full of sand fleas, sand

[*] The initial letters 'RO' stood for Radio Observer; as time went on and 'RDF' became 'Radar', there was a common understanding that the wearer of an 'RO' half-wing brevet was a Radar Observer or Radar Operator.

flies, many scorpions and a variety of spiders.   One never went to bed without checking it; and one never got dressed before checking all one's clothing, especially shoes, to ensure that there were no intruders.

'Later, when we'd moved forward from LG 109 in step with the 8th Army's advance and there were two squadrons of us at Benghazi, tents became a source of great fun.   Pranks abounded, like driving up in a Jeep, connecting one of the guy ropes to the vehicle and driving off, the collapsed tent fluttering along in its wake.   I can also enlighten you as to the exacting and thrilling art of tent-running...   that's when you run full pelt at a tent as fast as you can, the object of the exercise being to go up the side, over the top and down the other side.   Of course it's even better if someone is inside the tent, fast asleep, during the run... [3].'

Active service in the Western Desert was not confined to installing, operating and maintaining the various forms of radar systems, though obviously this was the main reason for so many being posted there in a radar capacity.   Craig Cooper recalled a period when in command of AMES 221, a mobile unit with 'an antique array on 105 ft towers, located 20 miles west of the Mena-Fayoum road, where living was not too uncomfortable, apart from the odd sand-storm, as the tents were mostly EPIPs, well dug in on this 600 ft desert plateau where the days were hot and the nights very cool'.   He goes on:

'There wasn't much operational interest, as I remember, but we did go out into the desert on a couple of search and rescue missions, the most noteworthy being to locate part of a Wellington crew, newly arrived in the Middle East and returning from a bombing operation at Benghazi.   While descending gently to see where they were, they found themselves sliding, in a stable upright position, on a patch of hard gravel.   The plane caught fire and the crew abandoned ship, to consider their position.   No food, no water and location unknown.   Four set out eastward, which was correct, and by chance investigated a stray Jerrican – unbelievably, it was full of water!   A small Arab caravan came across these four and brought them to our camp some 30 hours later.   The other two crew members had chosen a different direction, south east, and didn't stumble on any water anywhere. When we found them they were quite "magoon" [4].'

An assignment of temporary duty at AHQ Western Desert saw Doug Crozier, another of the 'Class of September '41 at Trenton' (24 of the 30 overseas postings all went to the Middle East), carrying out what was probably a unique if short-lived function.   It appears that 'some bright spark in Intelligence' decided that if a small group of specialists were to follow the 8th Army closely in the El Alamein breakthrough, it could recover abandoned German radar equipment for subsequent examination at Headquarters.   Put in charge, Doug was supplied with two 15 cwt trucks, an eight-man team including cook and nursing orderly, and ordered on his way with instructions 'to stay close to the front-line troops, anything we found to be shipped back with the Ordnance Corps in empty ration trucks'.   It was impossible to identify most of the salvaged gear but all was dutifully returned to HQ, though 'I doubt if it ever was of any use or was ever examined'.   In a bomb attack one night, when an ammunition dump was hit and there was 'a fireworks display better than the

Toronto Exhibition', two of Doug's men were hit by shrapnel, fortunately escaping serious injury. By then, with the front line beyond 'Marble Arch', it was decided to disband the unit. Posted in the following January (1943) to take over AMES 522 – 'a CHL station so mobile that we could move in 12 minutes from being operational to being ready to transfer to our next location' – Doug stayed with this unit right through to Tunis and until the Germans were expelled from Africa [5].

A classmate of Doug Crozier from Administrative Course # 21 at Trenton in the late summer of 1941, Bruce Stewart, joined AMES 216 in that January of 1943 when it made a journey of more than 2,000 miles from Syria to Tunisia in a convoy of some nine or ten vehicles which arrived at Rear AHQ, Desert Air Force, on 16 February, soon after the 8th Army had crossed into Tunisia and taken up its position in front of the Mareth Line. He recalls tragedy and turmoil, evidenced when RCAF radar officer Bill Scotland lost his life when the station wagon he was in ran over a land mine, and a succession of unit moves occasioned by the Allied advance. Bruce said:

> 'Our task was to follow the fighter bombers as they flew between their bases and their targets just beyond artillery range. The station shut down during hours of darkness since enemy air activity was minimal. During this time we were within sound of the artillery but we depended on the BBC short wave broadcasts from London to hear the news of what was happening nearby. After the breakthrough at the Mareth Line, we followed the 8th Army north and set up at a site near Sousse. With the enemy driven out of Bizerte and Tunis, fighting ended on 12 May. The war in Africa was over and the invasion of Europe was about to begin [6].'

Memories of the Middle East are as varied as the events which recall them... like Charles Larose, ignoring a quarantine restriction imposed because of suspected bubonic plague while with AMES 523 at Port Tewfik, breaking camp to hitchhike to Bethlehem for Midnight Mass, Christmas 1943, and hitchflying with an RAF padre, thanks to the helpful (on this occasion!) intervention of the Service Police... and Vern Turner, with AMES 239 at El Arish, 'a site remembered for the excellent swimming and the town itself, which provided an interesting window on the day-to-day life of the Egyptian peasant. Besides the RAF bodies, 50 East African troops under a British officer graced the site for guard duty. Fortnightly trips to Ismailia, across the Sinai, traversed much desert as often depicted in the movies. Quite unlike the stony scrub of the Western Desert [7]'.

Not everyone traveled to the Middle East by ship – on occasions, from the UK, there was air transportation for the fortunate few; indeed, one radar technician, Jay Christensen, flew all the way from the Bahamas to Cairo by way of South America and West Africa, a mammoth trip that was not without its perils. Jay graduated from Clinton in July 1943 and spent six weeks at the US Naval Air Station Corpus Christi learning about ASG, ASD and the Radio Altimeter – 'Tyrone Power, the actor, was on the base at the same time', he recalls. On the first leg of the journey from Nassau, riding the co-pilot's seat in a Ventura, there was a nasty moment when the fuel supply was being switched from the main cabin tanks to the auxiliary tank in the bomb bay, causing an immediate loss of power in both engines. Prompt action by the pilot saved all on board from a Caribbean baptism. A minor problem, perhaps, but it was an indicator that these inter-continental posting flights were not without danger; in fact, two of Jay's group of 28 lost their lives in separate aircraft accidents going overseas from Canada to take up their first operational duties [8].

Leaving Cairo to join # 454 RAAF Squadron in Libya, Jay had his first sight of towns which had been ravaged by war, among them Tobruk, Derna, Barce and Benghazi, and his first taste of night stops which 'featured bed spaces on concrete floors, where I realized what a comfort my bed without a mattress was in Nassau. Even the sand could be shaped to fit the body but not so the cement floor in a grim transit camp'. With 454 Squadron, for a short period he operated a radar beacon at Derna, the closest point in North Africa to German-held Crete. Looking back on those days in Derna, he remembered the beacon as being a battery-operated modified IFF set, meals being taken with 278 AMES, 'which was responsible for rearranging a squadron of dummy Spitfires after each German reconnaissance flight over the airfield' and building a radio set from spare parts. This enabled those in Jay's tent to listen to the BBC and to German broadcasts which 'included all of the current musical hits of US dance bands plus an avalanche of slanted war news and propaganda presented in a sexy voice by Axis Sal'.

On camp with 454, where the accommodation was in a 'typical tent city'...

> 'It was hot and cold, windy and sandy; and it was loaded with sand fleas and Libyan flies. A purple or blue powder dusted into the blanket each night seemed to discourage the fleas, while a mosquito net over the bed was the only escape from the sticky flies. Our letters home were always written inside the net. Our food was minimal and monotonous, consisting of corned beef, cheese, dried eggs, soya links and sometimes bread and mutton. We supplemented our diet each evening with scrambled eggs cooked on a stove in our tent. The eggs were obtained from the natives in a trade deal for Woodbine cigarettes – we were issued "V" cigarettes from India but even the natives refused to smoke them [9].'

There must have been many ground personnel who had a craving to become aircrew and been forced to give up the idea for reasons of their medical condition, their age or for some other form of unsuitability. Among them, however, Jim Ritchie is surely unique; trying to enlist in the RCAF at the outbreak of war, when he was in his 30th year and rejected for flying because he was too old, Jim subsequently joined to become a radar technician and won one of the very, very few DFCs awarded to a non-flyer.

Turned down for flying in 1939, it was another year and a half before he was in uniform, the work that he was doing as a civilian being considered essential to the war effort; he was working for Northern Electric at the time and involved in degaussing ships in Montreal harbour – a process intended to reduce the possibility of the magnetic field of the ship's steel hull triggering the firing mechanism of a 'magnetic' mine. The big publicity drive in Canada in the spring of 1941 had more pulling power than this work, the result being Jim's acceptance for training in the new and hush-hush activity known as RDF. Basic instruction came at McGill University where, the professor in charge being so impressed with Jim's knowledge of radio, he was given some lecturing to do for six to eight weeks. This elevation from pupil to part-time teacher wasn't too surprising; having tinkered around with radio from its inception, Jim was by then far beyond the mere basics in this fast-developing science.   The course over at McGill, Jim exchanged student life for an embarkation posting and sea transportation to Britain in November, a 'terrible trip, cold, wet and part of a 60-ship convoy'.

While some of the new arrivals were posted to radar stations, others were chosen to serve on operational squadrons in Coastal Command, Bomber Command or Fighter Command.   Jim remembers the senior officer telling him that he 'looked like a fighter' – his build suggesting that he could hold his own if it came to a scrap.   The paperwork was initiated that would take him into one of the best-known fighter squadrons in pre-war days, # 600 (City of London) Squadron, which was flying AI-equipped Beaufighters. from RAF Station, Predannack, on night-time raid-interception duties in late 1941 and most of 1942 until its departure for North Africa.

Jim recalls the selecting officer giving him the impression that...

> 'I must have been the best of the lot and that there was so much I could do by way of research to figure out a way to diminish the strength of the enemy's air attacks against Britain.   At that time the German planes were coming in low over the English Channel and would increase height as they came inland.   I was put into several 'squads', as they called us, to see if we could figure out a way to get our fighters into the air more quickly and by so doing reduce the numbers of bombers getting through the coastal defenses. I never did learn to what extent, if any, the research that we carried out was successful; because by then, in 1942, with 600 Squadron in North Africa, I was summoned to join them.'

Thus came an unforgettable episode in Jim Ritchie's life which began with little involvement in enemy action of any sort and mushroomed to a point when, virtually unknown for anyone in a non-flying category, he would sometimes 'do a double shift, working by day in my role as the squadron's radar technical officer and, by night, occupy the radio/navigator's seat behind the pilot in one of our twin-engined, two-seater Beaufighter night fighters – doing this job because we were so damned short of aircrew at that time'.   Initially, Jim was busy testing equipment to allow planes to patrol at a certain height and developing equipment enabling them to detect the enemy while carrying out this function; soon, though, his role evolved into one where his understanding of the equipment and his ability to get the maximum benefit from it, encouraged consideration of allowing him to substitute on occasions when there was an aircraft and pilot available to carry out an air test or an operational patrol in circumstances when there was no radio/navigator to complete the crew.   Squadrons always had an 'establishment' which consisted of a certain number of aircrew members – a number that was judged both necessary and adequate to maintain its operational status under normal conditions.   This magic number was seldom achieved when the squadron was under pressure, as most of them were, most of the time; and the situation could rapidly worsen when, for example, aircraft were lost, anticipated replacement crews failed to turn up, injuries were sustained or there was illness affecting perhaps more than just one individual at any one time.

Shortages such as those were the reason why Jim was able to wage a personal war against the German air force during the Mediterranean campaign in 1943/44...

For 600 Squadron, having moved from North Africa to Malta and now in Italy with its base at Monte Corvino and detachments at Gaudo and Tortorella, Christmas 1943 and New Year 1944 were memorable for two pleasurable yet rather different reasons: the traditional celebrations which warmed them physically and the message from the Honorary Air Commodore, Sir Archibald Sinclair, which no doubt warmed their hearts.   During this period the weather was mainly non-operational although the squadron maintained a rota system so that someone was always ready in case of instructions to 'scramble' and have planes airborne to respond to the threat of an enemy attack.   It was the squadron's role to fly under the control of a GCI station (Ground Control Interception units whose formal designations such as AMES 15051 and AMES 8015 were substituted by a more easily recognized code name – in this instance, Mature and Flametree respectively).   A combination of skilled application of the radar equipment in the air and on the ground would provide the means for the radio/navigator to achieve a 'contact' with an enemy aircraft and, now being in close proximity, hopefully to facilitate a 'visual' sighting enabling the pilot to line-up his gunsight on the 'bandit' and either destroy or damage it.

On Christmas Day, in any event, there would have been an excusable lack of enthusiasm for operational flying; the fact that bad weather effectively put an end to such activity was welcome relief which provided the opportunity for the customary celebrations to take place without everyone being 'on edge' about the possibility of a call-out.   The squadron diary would report that after a meal in the Airmen's Mess which ended with rum and the issue of 50 cigarettes and three bottles of beer apiece, the men 'generally discarded their worries and spent the remainder of the day in pleasant festivity' – and that 'revelry was not less in the other Messes' 10 .   At Gaudo, food was prepared and part-cooked at Monte Corvino, then rushed to this detachment by the MT section in hay boxes and the cooking completed on site; at Tortorella, personnel in this detachment were divided into four parties and became guests of # 3 SAAF Wing and the three squadrons comprising it.   The first post-Christmas patrols were flown on 28 December 1943 and the first of 1944 were flown on 2 January, by which time 600 Squadron had 'brought in the New Year with its appropriate inter-visiting and first footing' 11 .   The 94 enemy aircraft that the squadron had brought down at night in 1943 was 'a shining proof' of its 'superb efficiency and spirit', to quote Sir Archibald Sinclair in his message of congratulations wishing 'good luck to you all' in 1944 12 .

One of those 94 'kills' was the work of a Beaufighter crew partnership in which Jim Ritchie was the radio/navigator [*see page 2*]; and before January was out, an even more remarkable success was achieved with two German bombers brought down within the space of five minutes in one night – his first operational flight of the New Year.   Flying with Flight Lieutenant R W Hilken, radar contact and visual sighting was achieved on four Do 217 bombers and then quickly lost when the formation peeled off and dived towards the beaches in the Anzio region.   A 'visual' was regained on one of the Dorniers and four bursts from dead astern ended any threat that it may have posed to the Allied troops in this beachhead.   Strikes were seen on the fuselage and starboard wing, causing the Beaufighter's crew to claim that it was damaged, though AMES 871 later confirmed it as having been destroyed.   A second Do 217 was destroyed two miles south of the mouth of the river Tiber and in a further night patrol, eight days later, another bomber of the same type was attacked 30 miles north of Rome and seen with one engine on fire and diving steeply to continue burning on the ground [13].

The records confirm the position in which 600 Squadron found itself during the Italian campaign. The day after that fourth 'kill', four crews were put up for disposal, their tour of operations being expired. Furthermore, 'owing to the slowness of the arrival of new crews, the fact that they have not flown for some time and the heavy commitments of the squadron, some difficulty was being experienced in getting these crews fully operational at night'. Unfortunately, it was a situation which did not show signs of improving: in the space of a week, Hilken (Ritchie's pilot) finished his tour and left for Tunis; Wing Commander C P Green DSO DFC, Commanding Officer for the past 14 months, moved out on a posting to # 1 MORU; a flight commander, too, left on a posting; and despite the arrival of three new crews, 600 Squadron was short by 2 pilots and 5 radio/navigators when compared with its establishment of 23 pilots and 23 radio/navigators [14]. When the replacement CO arrived, Wing Commander L H Styles DFC, it was 'spare' radio/navigator Jim Ritchie who was teamed with him. On one of their first operational flights together, on 17 March 1944, a Ju 88 was dispatched earthwards to bring Jim's 'tally' to five enemy bombers... 'too old to enlist for flying duties' and 'of non-aircrew category' he had reportedly shown himself 'competent to fly as observer and has always availed himself of every opportunity of flying'.

An award of the Distinguished Flying Cross effective 15 May 1944, which began its recommendation process before this fifth and final 'kill' while a member of an operational air crew, makes him a rarity among radar specialists; those who put his name and his actions forward for the DFC commenting upon Jim 'having always shown outstanding courage and coolness' [15]. Courageous, without doubt; but reticent too... and here's why... It is well known that, whenever practical, it was the practice for the winners of a DFC in Britain to receive their medal and its blue-and-white striped ribbon personally from a member of the Royal Family – King George VI himself attended many such investitures; in Jim's case he received the award by registered post... In fact this quite astonishing method of delivery for something so prized came at Jim's own request. Although he was invited to Ottawa to receive his DFC from the Governor-General of Canada, by that time 'I was back at work and the war with its many reminders was behind me. There's something else, too. Having been bound by the Official Secrets Act for so long and feeling concerned that, on such a public occasion, I might find myself placed in a situation where inadvertently I might breach the Act, I thought it best to ask for the medal to be mailed to me'. For more than 40 years, he says, he didn't once discuss his WW2 activities with anyone – not even in his own family.

If ever it were needed, surely that is proof indeed that so many of the radar technical officers and radar technicians, party to countless secrets during times of war, continued to keep their silence for so long, even well into the enduring years of peace and on towards the new Millennium...

In fact, Jim Ritchie was not alone in earning a DFC as a squadron radar officer in the Mediterranean theatre of operations; Flight Lieutenant G A Muir is another... and with this pair there are more coincidences yet to come. The records show that both were in the Royal Canadian Air Force and both flew as a member of a Beaufighter crew in action against German aircraft – though the events which prompted their award were dissimilar. To stretch those coincidences, both men were 'Gazetted' with their award in the same month of the same year, May 1944.

It can be said that everyone is entitled to a moment of glory and that Flight Lieutenant Muir's came in March 1944, while serving on # 46 (Uganda) Squadron. One night he is flying as observer with the squadron's CO, a Wing Commander, their Beaufighter carrying out intruder operations over the islands of Rhodes and Cos and failing to see any enemy aircraft, the next night he is performing the same task over Crete, this time with a group CO, a Group Captain, and their score is two aircraft destroyed, one probably destroyed and one damaged, all in the space of 25 minutes! Certainly those night intruder activities must have contributed significantly to the Distinguished Flying Cross awarded to him on 12 May 1944 – an extremely rare award for a squadron radar officer – the citation adding that 'Flight Lieutenant Muir's technical knowledge and experience have been invaluable to his squadron, while his keenness and devotion to duty have been an inspiring example to all [16] '.

That night of triumph, that 'moment of glory', occurred while flying with Group Captain Max Aitken, DSO, DFC, with whom he had flown as observer in the UK. The four aircraft which crumpled beneath their Beaufighter's armament were all Ju 52 transport planes; one was damaged at 2015 hours, one destroyed at 2020 and another at 2030, the last being probably destroyed at 2040 [17] . It was his last op as squadron radar officer; on 18 March 1944 he was posted to AHQ Eastern Mediterranean – for staff duties.

To focus on the extraordinary airborne activities of radar specialists serving on an operational squadron is not to downgrade the 'ordinary' ground-based duties that officers, non-commissioned officers and airmen were required to perform – and did perform with diligence, enthusiasm and efficiency. It is a matter of record that # 219 Squadron's radar officer, Flight Lieutenant J O Camden, while this unit was in North Africa, 'was instrumental in effecting a high percentage of serviceability of radar equipment' and that there was 'an almost complete absence of failures during the subsequent operations' – to quote the documentation put forward in support of a recommendation for the award of the MBE which he received in the 1945 New Year Honours List. As well as doing 'much flying' to test equipment and to train aircrew members in the use of their radar aids, he trained the mechanics of three American night fighter squadrons in the use of radar equipment [18] . To have done 'much flying' is understandable, as are his technical capabilities, given his pre-war inclinations. Chief engineer and 'one-man technical staff' at the CJCS radio station in Stratford, Ontario, in 1939/40, earning $15 a week, he decided he could afford to buy 30 minutes of flying instruction two weekends out of three. He logged some five hours in the air and went solo – though he failed his medical because of a color vision problem (surprising, isn't it, when he had been earning a living for several years working with color coded resistors, capacitors and wires [19]). When, in October 1940, there was a recruitment drive 'to try and enlist as many knowledgeable radio people as possible for some very secret radio work with the Airforce', he mentioned that apparent defect right away because he knew that an aircrew medical would be required. It would be interesting, he thought, 'to see how they could get around the color vision problem when they wanted something'. Four 'lantern tests' and several weeks later, the recruiting people were satisfied; he joined up in January 1941, spent four weeks 'learning to be an Officer and a Gentleman' in Canada and most of his first seven weeks in Britain working on a CH station at Drone Hill. Eight weeks at Yatesbury and he was ready for almost anything...

Of course radar mechs whose feet stayed firmly on the ground were not without exposure to danger, their duties around the world including service on mobile units, their locations possibly on or near the front line and the hazards facing them ranging from bullets to bombs, cannons to captivity and sandstorms to strafing. Death was in their midst... its presence not to be ignored, nor feared.

Pacifico 'Puss' Valeriote, who crossed the Atlantic from his Canadian homeland on the troopship *Leopoldville* among some 160 embryo radar technicians newly recruited into the RCAF, wondered what would happen next when, now that he was at Renscombe Downs, he was going through the various stages of a pre-embarkation process. Radar personnel were being brought into Renscombe Downs from across Britain to form mobile units to perform a COL/GCI (Chain Overseas Low/Ground Control Interception) role in conjunction with fighter squadrons in forward military areas. He says:

> 'In the formation stage we were known as "G" Crew, with a complement of some 50 officers and men comprising technical and administrative staff, motor transport, medical, cooks and even a detachment from the RAF Regiment for perimeter security. The technical staff included Aircraft Interception Controllers, Radar Technicians and Operators, W/T (Wireless Telegraphy) Operators and Ground to Air Telephony Operators. We became AMES 894 and our CO was Flight Lieutenant Marshall Killen, who had come to Canada from the Azores where he was working with Western Union on the transatlantic cable; the Senior Technical NCO being Flight Sergeant Andy Maxim, who had been in Russia instructing their military personnel on the use of RAF radar [*].

> 'During training, we practised moving our mobile radar vehicles and equipment onto a designated location, erecting the antenna and seeing how quickly we could become operational. We had to achieve this status in less than an hour. Eventually we became proficient in this task and our equipment was prepared for shipment to some overseas destination, we knew not where. Later, during which time we were at Drytree in Cornwall and at Wilmslow, near Manchester, we learned of the invasion of North Africa and guessed, rightly, that this would be our new posting. On a tender going up the Clyde towards a huge flotilla of ships which was to be our convoy, "Maxie" Maxim pointed at the one directly ahead of us and began shouting excitedly, "It's the *Leopoldville*! It's the *Leopoldville*!" The ship which had brought us to the UK was now to take us to Algiers – an eight-day voyage which, and you've got to believe it, turned out to be even more uncomfortable than our first [20].'

---

[*] While Russia as a country was a comparatively unusual posting for radar personnel, a posting to its capital was without doubt rare. The author is aware of one Clinton-trained radar technician who spent time there, though he was 'wearing another hat' at the time; a Russian-speaker, he remustered to Intelligence, gained a commission and was posted to Moscow.

Arriving in the port of Algiers on 22 November 1942, AMES 894 formed up for a full-kit route march to cover the four or five miles to a French Air Force camp at Hussein Dey until the time came to board the armed assault craft *Princess Beatrix* to take the unit to Bone, 'the front-line port for General Alexander's First Army, of which we were now a part'. There, spending this first night in a building recently used as a tobacco factory, with a group of German POWs in the cellar below, 'Puss' and his colleagues had to keep raising their voices to counter 'Deutschland Über Alles' with 'Land of Hope and Glory' until a crescendo of falling bombs and the bursting shells of the responsive anti-aircraft defenses eventually overpowered even those vociferous and nationalistically-minded singers.

During the period December 1942/January 1943, while a member of the technical team with AMES 894, operational on a site near the village of Morris, 'Puss' recalls that, though the GCI unit was ready for action, the Beaufighters under their control were not able to fly due to wet weather and soggy landing field conditions at Souk-el-Arba, just over the Tunisian border. He says...

'While we were waiting for conditions to improve, the enemy bombers were coming in and blasting the port of Bone and an airport to the west of us. All we could do was to report this activity to Sector Operations at North West African Air Force Command. It was our fourth night in position before the Beaufighters were airborne. Then, three of them were each given a target by our Controller, Squadron Leader Brown, with the result that three enemy bombers were shot down in flames. On the second day of operations we netted ten German bombers, two of the Beaufighters each getting three of them. You will understand our feeling of elation at this initial success, but it was tempered by the loss of one of the Beaufighters (which had shot down one of those ten in the one night), when it overshot the airfield and crashed, killing the pilot.

'In the first month AMES 894 was successful in claiming a total of 30 enemy aircraft shot down due to controlled night interceptions, with the loss of another of the Beaufighters, again for reasons unrelated with enemy action – it crashed due to engine failure and both members of the crew lost their lives. Towards the end of the next month, January 1943, the war in Libya was coming to an end with General Montgomery's 8th Army pushing Rommel's Desert Army into Tunisia. The unit's tally increased when 7 enemy aircraft were shot down during that second month at Morris, during which time came the arrival of two more mobile radar units from England to further strengthen our ground-controlled interception capabilities and marine/aerial monitoring activities in this part of the battle zone [21].'

An enemy breakthrough towards the end of February 1943 caught 'Puss' himself in a tricky situation when, having been sent with two wireless operators to set up a W/T station in the lighthouse tower on a position occupied by the newly-arrived AMES 8009 and 8010 at Cap Serrat (by then the north-western end of 'no-man's land'), capture or a worse fate became a distinct possibility [*]. The trio's own unit, AMES

---

[*] Six months earlier, a lone radar officer, Doug Thompson, did fall into enemy hands; the intention was a raid on a radar installation at Tobruk, part of a much larger operation involving the Long Range Desert

894, arranged for a motor torpedo boat from Bone to pick them up on a beach near the lighthouse; the radio equipment was to be blown up before leaving, as were whatever radar parts could not be carried on the MTB, and rescue was achieved. The see-saw consequences of those desert operations is well illustrated by the fact that some radar equipment and vehicles left behind when the Germans seized Cap Serrat were found in good condition and put back into service when the area was recaptured.

June 1943, which saw 'Puss' Valeriote's GCI unit celebrating its 50th successful interception with a dinner missed only by the unfortunates who had to man the equipment, brought the Allies closer to the invasion of Sicily, on 10 July, and that of the Italian mainland on 3 September, when the initial landings took place at a spot some 30 miles from the hilltop town of San Giorgio Morgeto where his parents lived pre-war. Still the home of various uncles, aunts and cousins, it would not see 'Puss' before the following summer. By then, military pressures had eased and extended leave became possible, facilitating a visit to exchange news with relatives of both parents, including his maternal grandfather, an alert 97-year-old who had started the liquor and perfume manufacturing plant then still functioning under the watchful eye of family members.

In the year between, when AMES 894 personnel were switched with those of AMES 895, 'Puss' re-located at the isolated Cap Rosa, which had long lacked a proper road link with the nearest highway. Given permission to start making improvements, he told a US Army engineering unit in Bone that he wanted a better road bulldozed through to Cap Rosa. No problem – until arrangements were scuppered by Wing HQ 'because the Lease Lend Board was going to charge the RAF with the cost of building a 10-mile stretch of new road'. Having now displayed latent talents in this direction and shown his prowess at turning his technical skills to those of management, 'Puss' Valeriote, with the benefit of knowing the language, encouraged the best endeavors out of Italian POWs whom he used to repair the highway link road and to build an accommodation block and shower facilities, 'all the materials to do the job being taken with or without permission from military stockpiles in Bone'.

In May 1944 came orders to leave North Africa for Italy where, on a mountain pass between two staging posts on the way to their prescribed location along the Adriatic coastal road, one of the unit's three-tonners lost its brakes and slammed into a bridge. Three men lost their lives in this tragic accident, which 'stunned us, but we had to gather our damaged equipment and keep going' [22]. The airmen were taken to Avellino for burial and when the unit reached Foggia a memorial service was held for these dead comrades. At their ultimate location on a farmer's field on a high point overlooking the seaside town of Grottamare some 10 miles distant, AMES 894 was then stripped and packed, ready to be disbanded at Sorrento by Christmas 1944, the team having been together for more than two years.

In readiness for service in that same Mediterranean theatre of operations, which would be with Type 6 mobile radar units, Roy Taylor was first trained in the use of

Group and a seaborne assault. It failed and there were heavy losses. Doug 'got one in the leg' and spent five weeks in a field hospital before being shipped to Italy and into a POW camp [23].

machine guns and hand grenades and then sent to a Combined Operations school in Scotland to practise going ashore from an invasion landing craft, before familiarization with the new equipment at units scattered around the coast. Four Type 6 units were being formed: AMES 6060, 6061, 6062 and 'my odd-ball number which was 6109'. Each consisted of 2 radar mechanics, 3 NCO radar operators, 3 aircraftmen radar operators; 2 wireless operators; 1 wireless operator/mechanic; 1 cook and 1 driver mechanic, the position of Senior NCO in charge (Sergeant, Flight Sergeant or Warrant Officer) usually going to one of the radar mechanics although sometimes it was filled by a radar operator. These units proved

> 'very effective in North Africa, in the see-saw action on that front, because the crews were able to move forward with the troops and if necessary withdraw just as quickly. Since they were quite a bit forward of the airfields, they could give a more effective early warning of enemy approach. In Sicily, where I joined the campaign on arrival by troopship out of Gourock on 29 June 1943, they also proved their worth in the slower forward movement. In the later part of the campaign, their function was to plot our own damaged aircraft coming back from a raid. We also guided amphibious aircraft to sites where downed flyers were located. These AMES crews were often subjected to enemy action and there was one in North Africa which was strafed by supposedly friendly aircraft, losing several members of the unit killed or wounded. It turned out these were captured Allied fighters, which were soon put out of action [24]'.

Roy's unit was intended to leave the ship at Catania and to set up on the airfield. The enemy was disinclined to give up such a prize, however, so the disembarkation point was switched to Augusta, their arrival aboard one of three troopships escorted by three destroyers coinciding with an attack by the Italian Air Force which resulted in 6 out of the 10 aircraft being shot down without damage to the convoy. Roy's group was on deck when the bombers were approaching and failed to hear the alarm signal which required them to go below. Watertight doors were hastily prised open, leaving just enough room to squeeze through, compelling the group to stay put for several hours, without air-conditioning or access to the deck – 'They expected a further attack, which didn't happen. I hate to think what would have happened if the ship had been holed.' He continues:

> 'We were given some compo rations and told to take our units as far as we could from the port. That night more enemy planes arrived, though I believe that this time they were German. The ack-ack guns opened up on them and the falling shrapnel was almost as bad as the bombing. One bomb landed so close that we received some of the earth on our sleeping blankets. Fortunately we were near a lumber yard and the crew climbed inside the wood piles for protection. It was fortunate we had some shelter – I found a nose cone in my bed when I returned to our accommodation! The merchant ship alongside the one with our vehicles was hit and small-arms ammunition was exploding all night long as firefighters tried to extinguish the flames. Next morning we greeted some pretty scared drivers who had brought our vehicles.'

When the Sicily campaign came to an end, Roy was posted to another Type 6, AMES 6039, a unit from North Africa which had become depleted and its crew dispirited during and after an incident in which one of the radar operators was killed by a rifle shot in the head, presumably the victim of a keen-eyed sniper. Understandably, such a tragedy is all the more poignant in a small unit like these Type 6s. Now in charge and needing to restore confidence within the crew and to regain efficiency, Roy and a Corporal who was the most senior member talked to each individual in what these days would be called a 'counseling session', to appreciate their feelings about the situation. Roy told the group that it could be run 'by the book' but, if everyone would turn their hand to producing a really efficient unit, he was prepared to get them to ENSA shows and to obtain as many additional 'perks' as was humanly possible. As a result, he says, 'the unit did just that and saw more shows than larger outfits'.

Bill Lower: his was one of the first names that sprang to mind to the powers-that-be when someone was needed to land a mobile radar unit 'up front' in a planned invasion of enemy territory. Bill's unit, AMES 871, which in approximately a year and a half moved from Cairo to southern France, took pride in its ability 'to move on a moment's notice and yet not lose a night's operations', this mobility being honoured by a commendation from the Commander-in-Chief, Royal Air Forces, Mediterranean and Middle East [*].

Formed to fill part of the radar commitment of the Middle East for the invasion of Sicily and placed under Bill's command, AMES 871 was given the latest equipment to arrive in this theatre of operations, including 'the only power-turning gear of the Desert Air Force'; its personnel, chosen carefully and coming from experienced desert units, gained experience in waterproofing at a special training camp. Towards the end of May 1943 it was loaded on flat cars to travel by rail from Alexandria to Tobruk, receiving operators from AMES 845 in an *en masse* transfer. Invasion # 1 was Sicily where, on 10 July, in a quiet field some distance from the landing place, the unit began de-waterproofing while inquiries were being made as to the local situation. During the first night's operations, on a poor site with an anti-aircraft gun within 20 yards of the antenna, two Ju 88s were downed by aircraft under their control. A report in a detailed history of the RAF during WWII refers to the operations of squadrons of Beaufighters and intruder Mosquitoes being made 'much easier by the putting ashore of a Ground Controlled Interception Unit on the evening of 10 July, and the subsequent speedy extension of warning systems' [25].

Invasion # 2 took place following the unit's transfer to the US Air Force in preparation for the landings at Salerno. After waiting at assembly areas in Sicily and additional waterproofing, AMES 871 was shipped aboard an LCT which arrived off the invasion beach after nightfall, during a heavy air attack, and went ashore at H+12 on

---

[*] Bill Lower was among 19 Canadians (members of the previously-mentioned 32-strong group which came together for the first time on the parade square at Trenton on 17 September 1941) who left the UK on 20 March 1942 for service in the Middle East. This account of his exploits during four successive invasions of enemy territory has its foundation in a privately produced compilation, *WWII Radar, The Story of One Group, Royal Canadian Air Force, 1941-1945*, which the author is pleased to acknowledge as having been an invaluable source of material when recounting the experiences of Bill and others in that group.

D-Day, 9 September 1943.   Inactive for three days and its transmitter damaged by shell splinters, the unit set up a temporary site on what became Asa airfield, operating despite continuing bombing when several bombs fell close to the equipment.   As the technical site lay on the proposed aircraft dispersal area of the new airstrip, another location was adopted to the west of Monte Corvino airfield where unfortunately one member was injured by splinters from heavy mortar fire.

Invasion # 3 was Anzio, the LST   arriving offshore on 22 January 1944 at its appointed section at H-1.   At H-Hour, diesels were started and communications checked, but the radar could not get into full operation until the cargo was unloaded at H+2.   Operations were 'decidedly inferior to shore work, as bearings and pinpoints lacked complete accuracy'.   Coming under increasing heavy gunfire, which crippled one vehicle, felled a 75 ft VHF mast and sprayed shrapnel over the camp, AMES 871 took up a new position, continuing to operate under 'most difficult' conditions not helped by enemy jamming.   Everyone in the unit was personally commended by General Hawkins of the 64th Fighter Wing for the work done on the beachhead.

Invasion # 4 was in the area of St Tropez in southern France, the unit arriving at H+6 on D-Day, 15 August 1944, and finding a significant improvement over Anzio in that bearing compensation devices were available, materially altering the technical set-up.   The first phase was a race with another radar group for one of two sites, Montelimar and Valence.   If Valence had fallen, the winning unit was to set up there, if not it was to set up at Montelimar while the losing unit waited until the town fell and set up at Valence.   Valence had not been taken so Bill Lower's unit installed itself at Montelimar.   After operating for several days at the new site, AMES 871 was relieved by more modern American radar and sent back to Salon en Provence on coastal work – and Bill was posted home [26].

Bill Lower's work brought him a Mention in Despatches effective 1 January 1945, one of the five MIDs awarded to a member of the Trenton 17 September 1941 group of 32 newly-commissioned Pilot Officers who were there between their basic training in one of the Canadian universities and going to Clinton for radar training before their first posting, when 30 were shipped to the UK and 2 were retained to train subsequent courses at Clinton.   On 14 June 1945 Bill Lower was awarded an MBE (Member of the Order of the British Empire) which surely echoed such phrases as 'an extremely high standard of technical skill and excellent qualifications of leadership and initiative' and 'unfailing enthusiasm and example' which appear in the recommendation documentation associated with his earlier MID [27].

Stationed in Corsica during that summer of 1944, Jack Bishop, courtesy of an American radar unit, managed to get a grandstand view of the invasion of southern France by means of one of their MEWs – 'Very modern for its time and generating extremely short waves.   From this site, on the northern tip of Corsica, which is like a fist with the finger pointing north, we could see the line of ships approaching the coast.   They stopped and the landing craft left them to head for the shore [28].'

Usually, he reported, 'we got along very well with the Americans, but in Corsica there was one little corporal who tried to get under my skin.   He was about five feet six and about 120 lbs; and he insisted on letting me know that he had been Golden Gloves Champion of his area.

'This was at a local café where there were girls to dance with and lots of wine to drink. He couldn't get any of the former and so had lots of the latter. One night we got into a shoving match but I backed down – I figured that if I hit him, OK, but if I missed, all six feet of me could be lying on the ground. It wasn't worth it.

'Next time, before going to the café, I put my 38 revolver in the inside pocket of my battledress jacket. So when he shoved me, he felt the gun. I've never seen such a change – he immediately backed off and I never saw him again. Americans have fantastic respect for guns. He never did find out that I didn't carry my gun loaded this far back from the front.'

Jack Bishop sailed from the UK to Suez via Durban and Aden, spent several months as Technical Officer with AMES 295 in Benghazi, followed by service in Algiers and Oran before going to Corsica. In November 1944, the unit was broken up and he returned to Canada in January 1945, becoming a civilian in October the same year.

Wally Tanner, who was with AMES 102 in Corsica in the summer of 1944, provides an indication of the problems that had to be overcome when setting up a mobile radar unit in mountainous countryside. Newly-arrived from the UK, the instructions were to position their unit on the top of the 4,281 ft high Mount Cipolla, with a mule train waiting, together with native drivers under the charge of a corporal, all from the French Foreign Legion. He said:

'We loaded up the mules by strapping a pack on either side of their backs and set off up the mountain. As the track was very narrow we had to travel in single file most of the way. After about two hours we stopped at a very welcome spring for a rest and a drink, then off again to find the route getting steeper all the time. At one point one of the mules slipped off the mountain path and rolled over and over down the hillside, ending up in a valley far below. On climbing down to it we unloaded the packs and much to our amazement the mule stood up and was ready to carry on as though nothing had happened. After this event we had the greatest respect for the mules as they would carry on until exhausted.

'Many weary miles further on, the track ended at the foot of a near vertical cliff several hundred feet high. It was obvious that the mules could go no further so we unloaded them and, strapping the packs of equipment on our own backs, started the climb to get to the top of the mountain. It was simply the hardest physical work I had ever done – and there were occasions when we thought the task was beyond us. However, with much encouragement from each other and especially from our CO [Flying Officer Phil Macdonald, RCAF], we eventually reached the top to find there was a plateau about 100 ft across. After removing the packs we lay down absolutely exhausted for a while. However, with a drink and some food we had brought with us, we set to putting up the tents for our equipment. The heaviest item was the petrol/electric generator and this, somehow, we had managed to transport. We were now on the highest point of Cap Corse, the northern tip of Corsica [29].'

With equipment still being carried on the final stretch when orders came through for it to be operational that night, AMES 102 was 'live' on time and so provided radar cover for the ships and planes used for the invasion of Southern France on 15 August 1944. At a later date, however, it emerged that apparently the original plan was to send in this unit by glider, ahead of the landings, so that, with the help of the French Resistance, their equipment could be used to guide in the air and sea invasion forces. Wally took the view that 'on reflection it was just as well that the plan was changed'; later 'we were to receive official recognition and congratulations for a job that we all felt had been well worthwhile'.

By early September, AMES 102's job was finished and the unit returned to the UK, its next and final series of adventures being in North West Europe.

It might be assumed that newly-arrived radar officers would need only to complete a quick check to determine that everything was in place in readiness for a smooth transfer of responsibilities. Perhaps that was the case where there was merely a change in the incumbent; it was certainly not the case when # 205 Group converted to heavy bombers based on the Foggia plain in Italy in 1943 when the North African campaign neared its successful conclusion. Its six Wellington squadrons, later converted to Liberator squadrons, each mustered into three wings, with a target-marking Halifax squadron, would continue to support the British 8th Army and the US 5th Army and assist the Balkan Air Force in supporting and supplying the partisan units in South East Europe.

Bob Linden takes up the story, having arrived at # 236 Wing in April 1944, in tandem with the radar officers of the two other wings and a month after the Group Staff Radar Officer took up his post – his appearance being 'most welcome since the work involved by the use of radar had increased beyond all proportion' [30]. Bob's initial task being to take stock of what men, materials and facilities were available to fulfil his assignment to install, service and maintain radar equipment in the aircraft of # 40 Squadron and # 104 Squadron, he found that there was in fact 'nothing, absolutely nothing'. He explains:

> 'The radar technicians were on the strength of the squadrons and reported to the squadron engineering officers (aeronautical), placing me in an advisory role to them. This type of organization went back to the days of biplanes, wooden propellers, goggles and white scarves, but it was a dodo in the age of electronic warfare. There was no workshop; I had no service transport. Tools and general purpose test equipment intended for the radar sections had been issued to other tradesmen and workshops (engineering, signals, electrical etc) and to cap it all, the Wing Signals Officer was under the impression that I was to be his assistant [31].'

If that wasn't bad enough, next day he had a run-in with the Base Commander. It occurred when Bob, aghast at hearing the Base Commander's instructions for his aircrews on the use of 'Chaff' – strips of aluminum similar to tinsel on a Christmas tree and known in the RAF as 'Window'. They were to disperse Chaff continuously after crossing the Adriatic Sea until reaching their target, Budapest. Bob tried to interrupt to contest this edict; it was Bob's contention that Chaff was only effective close-in, its purpose being to blanket the enemy radar. As he would put it later, by dropping Chaff as soon as the Adriatic coast was reached, 'you might as well have sent the enemy a telegram that you were coming'.

The briefing over, Bob tried once more to communicate his views to the Base Commander; and again without success. So he drove to Group Headquarters to inform the Group Staff Radar Officer, Flight Lieutenant W J Bell, who in turn raised this concern with the Senior Air Staff Officer (SASO); the outcome was SASO countermanding the Chaff directive. The following morning, as he might well have expected, Bob was ordered to report to the Base Commander, whose first statement was that Bob had gone over his head. 'Yes', Bob replied, 'and in similar circumstances I would do it again. You added unnecessary additional risk to your aircrews.' Bob's explanation for contesting the Chaff directive was accepted and his offer to request a transfer was declined, the Base Commander telling him: 'I'll keep you, young man.' From then on, until leaving 236 Wing after VE-Day, Bob had his 'unqualified and often unquestioned support' [32].

That unfortunate episode over, Bob Linden quickly turned his attention to the wider aspects of his responsibilities as 236 Wing's Radar Officer. The evident shortage of facilities, equipment and materials made it impracticable to establish a radar workshop for each squadron, so he suggested a central workshop under his direct control. The radar personnel would remain on their respective squadron's strength for pay, rations, quarters, medical, administration and like matters but Bob would be responsible for their performance, promotion, discipline, welfare and leave. The Base Commander agreed and the Squadron Engineering Officers heartily concurred; not a single item concerning this reorganization was put in writing or placed in orders, yet it came into being 'and worked without a glitch for the next 15 months'.

He explains some of the early problems:

'Apart from the two NCOs, the airmen technicians were recent graduates from the training schools and none had seen the inside of an aircraft, let alone serviced one. The NCOs and I started an on-job technical training program and instituted a system of supervision and quality control in the practice of inspection and servicing airborne radar equipment [*].

'We turned a vermin-infested stone stable into a workshop; we searched every nook and cranny, every toolbox and every workbench in both squadrons to recover the tools and the test equipment that had been intended for the radar sections; we recovered the servicing vehicles from the motor pools and installed generators, equipment racks and tool boxes in the new workshop.

---

[*] Sergeant N Smith, 104 Squadron, and Sergeant R Galbraith, 40 Squadron, were RCAF members too, as were the Group Staff Radar Officer, the two other Radar Officers in 205 Group and, soon afterwards, the Radar Officer on 614 Squadron.

'With a GEE simulator, we trained the navigators and when the whip-type antennae were late arriving we rigged a lash-up antenna from the now superseded Mk II IFF equipment, enabling the aircrew to use GEE some five weeks before the proper antennae were received.   By the autumn of 1944 we had re-installed the GEE equipment in the Liberator bombers as the squadrons converted.   And we went on to install Loran, for navigating at much greater range than GEE, as well as the Monica countermeasure equipment and Mandrel to jam the enemy's Freya search radar [33] .'

It appears that Bob Linden was not alone in having almost to start from scratch when joining a Wing Headquarters as its Radar Officer.   In later years he would find, duly recorded in 205 Group's Summary of Events which all such organizations were required to maintain as their day-to-day diary, an item for the month of April 1944 referring to his posting to 236 Wing and those of Pilot Officers R T Henry and A Laprade to 231 Wing and 330 Wing respectively.   The entry noted their arrival at Group Headquarters on the 13th and then, after being given a brief survey of the radar situation, joining their respective Wings on the 14th; they were, the record shows, 'a little surprised at the lack of equipment compared with their previous home under Bomber Command, but never the less keen'.

Posted to that same group and doing the first leg of the flight from Montreal in 'a war-weary Liberator which was now being used for transport work', Orv Marshall reached Algiers not knowing – since nobody in Canada seemed able to tell him – whether 205 Group was based somewhere in Africa or somewhere in Italy.   He recalls:

'After landing at Algiers I tried to find the location of 205 Group.   There were very few RAF personnel there – mostly American.   Eventually I learned that I was supposed to go to Italy but there would be a delay of several days before a seat on a flight would be available.   In the meantime I was to stay at an hotel in downtown Algiers operated by the RAF and was free to see the local sights.   As I wandered around, intrigued by my new surroundings, I was approached by an elderly gentleman who claimed to be a former employee of Cooks Travel and he would be my guide for a fee. This seemed reasonable and he took me to many interesting places.   Later I found out that some of them were out of bounds to Allied personnel as possibly too dangerous [34] .'

Eventually reaching 205 Group at its headquarters near Foggia in Italy, and meeting Flight Lieutenant Bell, the Group Radar Officer, it was decided that Orv would be more useful at # 614 Squadron, the group's Pathfinder squadron, rather than at Group HQ.   It was 614's job to find the targets, mainly at night, and to mark them with flares, the aircraft being equipped with extra electronics and flown by carefully selected and trained crews.

Orv's arrival at 614's base in Italy coincided with the squadron being converted from Halifaxes to Liberators.   To accelerate the rate of delivery, a crew would take an old Halifax back to Algiers and bring back a new Liberator.   Making one of those trips and flying with a pilot who was experienced on Liberators but a little rusty on Halifaxes, Orv wasn't inspired to hear his pilot say to the flight engineer: 'I wonder how you start one of these things!'   He probably wasn't joking because the Halifax swung badly during take-off and ran off the runway. It bounced around until finally coming to a stop, at which point a number of those on board had difficulty in effecting a swift escape because the handle of the escape hatch broke. A subsequent flight was fortunately less eventful...

Crews found the Liberator to be much more comfortable than the Halifax although there was skepticism about its ruggedness. Indeed, Orv cites two incidents which proved that latter point in dramatic fashion. He says:

> 'On a mission, with aircraft attacking from different levels, there was always the possibility of one plane being hit by bombs dropped by another that was flying at a greater height. One of the Liberators on our base returned with the top of the fuselage full of holes where a number of small incendiary bombs from a higher aircraft had gone through, the crew having to throw them overboard before they ignited. In another instance, which involved a Liberator on a nearby base, this unfortunate aircraft was hit by a heavy bomb which then bounced off. Somehow the pilot brought back his aircraft and when I took a look at it I could not believe how such a badly damaged aircraft could still fly. It was in such a state that no attempt was made to repair it [35].'

Orv comments that Liberators, with their complement of electronic equipment, performed well in their operational Pathfinder role and fortunately the losses were fairly light in the months that remained to the war in Europe coming to an end. In mid-May 1945, with others in 205 Group, 614 Squadron took on a transport role, its many and varied loads ranging from tins of gasoline to freed French POWs being repatriated and South African troops being flown to Cairo on their way home. Recalling his time on 614, Orv notes:

> 'Life on an RAF squadron in the Mediterranean theatre was not easy and particularly for airmen. It was lonely and uncomfortable – and all of us worked hard to find ways to make life easier and more comfortable. The ingenuity displayed at times was quite remarkable. For example, I remember that we had several electrical generating sets powered by a little gas engine to supply power to the electronic equipment during test. One of them appeared near the tents of the radar mechanics and provided electric light. Soon afterwards it was discovered that some bulbs were missing from aircraft. Whether connected with the lights in the tents or not, the CO decreed that the generator was to be removed immediately... [36].'

Reference has been made to the heavy bombers in # 205 Group in Italy being fitted with the radar navigational system GEE [*see page 87*], where the airborne equipment relied on signals from three ground stations. GEE had been used progressively from early 1942 in the air war against Germany but, since all the ground stations were in the UK and there was a range limitation of some 230 miles, its use by aircraft attacking targets more distant from the UK would require additional ground stations – and, necessarily, mobile units for maximum benefit. For Italy, AMES 7600 was formed as early as October 1943, comprising a master station, AMES 7611, and two slave stations, AMES 7612 and AMES 7622, but it was May 1944 before it became operational [37]. Even then, with the lack of spares, to extend the life of the large transmitter valves, power output was at a reduced level with a corresponding loss of air-operation effectiveness.   There were problems over transportation priorities, difficulties in accessing selected sites, the need to produce new lattice charts and a shortage of spares for the transmitters.   At one point, the 205 Group radar officer, Flight Lieutenant Bell, with top-level authority to 'seek and find', returned with a Wellington bomber 'filled to capacity', having found all the required items for the ground stations, including the sorely needed transmitting valves, in various parts of North Africa [38].

By the time that the aforementioned GEE station was operational in Italy, GEE cover in the southern half of Britain had been expanded considerably in readiness for the Allied invasion of Northern Europe, now due to take place in a matter of days.   The build-up to D-Day would evoke different memories to different people: circumstances changed whether working on a unit destined to remain in Britain or to cross the Channel; whether due to go across on some future date, specified or unspecified, or – as would be the lot of certain radar mechs – to be part of the D-Day operations themselves... on land, at sea or in the air.

CHAPTER 7: GEE-DAY, 6 JUNE 1944

To the world at large, 6 June 1944 was D-Day... but to people working at the Telecommunications Research Establishment (TRE) it was 'GEE-Day'! This was a term both apt and justified: the radar-based navigational system named GEE * was arguably the best-known product to come out of TRE and the one most widely-used that day, the day the Allies invaded Normandy.

It was used to get bombers to their targets and ships to the landing beaches; D-Day was as much a successful large-scale application of radar for navigational purposes as was the Battle of Britain for aircraft detection purposes. Of course GEE was by no means the only form of radar in use on D-Day; the veteran IFF device was still there, safeguarding Allied planes from possible 'friendly' fire, Oboe provided the means to achieve precision bombing of critical objectives, GCI and AI facilitated the protection of troops and shipping from enemy bombing and strafing, while no doubt there were dedicated requirements for other radars less familiar but nonetheless important in a specialist application.

As for the radar technicians who were members of the Allied air forces or providing a service on their behalf, some were seeing action for the first time – and experiencing it where the fighting was at its toughest... in the front-line. For there were radar units landing on the beaches in both the British and the American sectors; and there were radar crews on key vessels positioned close in to the shoreline. And there was even one man, a member of the RCAF, trained in radar though by now doing an entirely different job, who literally had a bird's eye view of the D-Day landings...

A farm commentator for the Canadian Broadcasting Corporation during the first three years of the war, Corporal D B Fairbain enlisted in June 1942, training at Queen's University and at McGill before undertaking further training at Clinton during the first half of 1943. He was taken on the strength of the RCAF Overseas Headquarters in the UK in February 1944 and became a member of the field radio recording unit at its inception [1]. On D-Day it was his assignment to accompany Mitchell bombers into aerial action to broadcast over leading international networks and to describe RCAF operations contributing to the Allied invasion * .

---

* A pre-war concept that came to reality to satisfy wartime needs, the GEE system comprised continuous transmissions from one Master and two Slave ground stations, enabling navigators to obtain an instantaneous fix anywhere within the area in which those signals could be received. Its D-Day uses were described by Walter F Blanchard in *The History of Navigational Aids, Proceedings of the IEE/CHiDE-sponsored third annual colloquium held at Bournemouth University, 12 September 1997.* He noted that 'by D-Day there were four operational GEE chains', that 'at least 860 ships were fitted for the Normandy landings' and that the southern UK GEE Chain remained operational until the late 1960s.
* Awarded the BEM on 14 June 1945, Corporal Fairbain's citation noted his 'extraordinarily productive job far beyond the line of ordinary duty' and paid tribute to his 'concise, accurate and so authoritative' daily reports to Canada, 'bringing to millions of listeners the feats of the Royal Canadian Air Force' [2] .

The activities of the Mitchell bombers and all the other aircraft busy overhead meant little to people like Geoff Harpur, a radar technical officer; he needed to concentrate all his endeavors on taking a GCI unit into Normandy by way of Juno Beach.   This he did, ensuring that his team (AMES 15083, # 85 Group, 2nd Tactical Air Force) was operational before midnight above the beachhead and beyond the village of Meuvaines; it was an accomplishment that brought him a Mention in Despatches in the New Year Honours List, 1945.   Those are the basic details, the bones without the flesh.   To establish more precisely what he did and how he did it, it would be necessary to delve more deeply into the circumstances – as was done by the three-man team of Hugh A Halliday, Douglas A Swanson and Robert F Linden when researching and producing, in time for Canada's first radar reunion in 1996 in Calgary, a limited private edition entitled *Honours and Awards granted during the Second World War to RCAF Radar Personnel.*   Geoff Harpur is one of the 193 individuals named in that publication; in which it is recorded that besides his MID, he was honoured post-war by the French Government with the Croix de Guerre.

The citation shows that:

> 'He led a reconnaissance to the pre-planned site of the GCI in order to reconnoiter the proposed site of the radar convoy and the detailed positioning of the units.   This work was done in an extremely exposed position under close range fire from a variety of enemy weapons.   The assembling of the radar equipment was achieved with remarkable speed and was operational on the night of D-Day.   This officer worked unceasingly for several days and nights and the good work of the unit has resulted in the destruction of many enemy aircraft since D-Day.   Flight Lieutenant Harpur, by his zeal and untiring work, has set a very fine example to the airmen of the unit.'

The Royal Air Force Signals History provides further details, noting that technical difficulties had rendered this unit's Type 15 GCI equipment unserviceable and only the Type 11 and 13 were used during the first night on French soil.   However the Type 15 was repaired during the day so, 'during the night of 7 June, control of RAF night fighter aircraft was effected using Type 11, Type 15 and Type 21 equipment, all of which worked extremely well' [3].

In a more personal account, Squadron Leader R H McCall, who was in command of AMES 15083, recalls the approach to 'King Red' Beach, seeing lines of tanks and other vehicles 'moving slowly, very slowly, up the hills' and feeling 'how small we were in this gigantic mass of movement'.   When the point of disembarkation was reached, it was his function to go forward with a measured pole and if the depth of the water was over two and a half feet, he must require the LCT landing craft to move in closer.   He wrote later:

Another who began in radar and made a 'career move' in which he went on to distinguish himself in an unrelated field is George Avery. He joined the RCAF in 1941, trained as a radar officer and in 1943, in the UK, volunteered to become a frogman. In Burma, on the night of 24/25 February 1945, he led the first assault party across the Irrawaddy River in the Myittha area and guided craft to the landing beaches under heavy fire, his 'remarkable achievements' earning him the Military Cross [4].

'In fact, the Navy had done a good job and my rod measured an inch or two under the mark. We drove off through the water and up the beach in quite good order but the beach was still mined in part. However, the Jeep in which sat our two Group Staff Officers (Wing Commanders Brown and Mawhood) led off our second LCT a little ardently and driving over a low spot only the heads and shoulders of the occupants showed above the sea. The amusement thus caused eased the tension! I reported to Beach Control, our landing time being approximately 15.45. There were casualties still lying on the beach in mine fields, some certainly dead being men who had joined us in the pre-invasion exercises [5] .'

By dark, one operations room was working but with faults still on the other aerials or sets. Squadron Leader McCall recalled his unit taking over its first night fighter and 'at about or just after midnight, our second frequency came on the air in fairly reasonable conditions and able to control. We were not able to find the fault on the third frequency until next day. At one point, Sergeant Bews climbed the Type 15 aerial, in the pitch dark, to make adjustments and was nearly run over by an FW190 which came over a few feet above him and nearly swept him from his perch [6] .'

Coincidentally, at the opposite end of the Normandy invasion beaches where Geoff Harpur was occupied with the British forces, a fellow member of the RCAF was with another mobile GCI unit; this time it was Muir Adair with AMES 15082, the landing craft carrying Muir and his men about to go ashore with the Americans in the thick of the action on Omaha Beach. The plan was to be inland, the equipment in operation to help protect the advancing troops from air attack, with the minimum delay; indeed, the crossing was without interference and the LCT was all set to race for the shore just before midday. However, out of the five beaches (Utah and Omaha designated to the Americans; Gold, Juno and Sword to the British), the one which Muir's group faced turned out to be the toughest nut to crack: 'Most things that could go wrong did, and the beach became known as "Bloody Omaha" with good reason' [7] . Survivors tell of German defenses having escaped the attention of advance bombing intended to put them out of action and the presence of tougher than expected German troops, the combination resulting in fierce shelling while the landing craft were approaching and accurate small-arms fire awaiting those aboard them when it was their turn to storm ashore.

Muir recalls that…

'There were five landing craft which carried our GCI unit and other equipment forming part of an advance party from # 21 Base Defense Sector in # 85 Group and we crossed the Channel without incident, reaching the Normandy coast just after daybreak. Half an hour or so before midday, it became our turn to go ashore, although it was obvious that this was going to be far more difficult than we had been led to believe in the final days of training when we were given an indication of the composition of the invasion beaches and the nature of the defenses.

'Heading towards the shore, the area where we were due to land was seen to be under enemy machine-gun fire as well as heavy shell-fire, so there was no way that a unit like ours was going to be put at such risk.

Consequently the instructions were that we were to withdraw while steps could be taken to make conditions less threatening, not just to us but to all those whose job was to hit the shore, to secure the beachhead and then press inland as their contribution to the overall strategy.

'At 1700 hours our convoy went in once more, though the beach was still under enemy fire and there were vehicles lined up with nowhere to go because the way forward remained impassable.   As best we could, we effected what is perhaps best described as a wet-shod landing, our LCTs having stopped in water that was deeper than anticipated.   The vehicles on board four of them had to cope with a drop of more than four feet, rendering two in three of the vehicles unserviceable, while the fifth came to an abrupt halt on a sandbank.   Being still further from the shore, the situation there was even more serious; one by one each of those vehicles was lost when trying to reach land in ever-deepening water, their occupants having to clamber on the roof and then try to swim ashore.   In all, in the course of this premature landing forced upon us by those unforeseen circumstances, this convoy lost most of its equipment – though perhaps more by luck than planning we did get our Type 15 ashore in a semi-operational state and, when supplemented with the equipment that had been held back in reserve in the UK, we were able to become completely operational a short time later 8 .'

When the Normandy landings began, AMES 15082 personnel knew the precise spot where it would be required to set up all their equipment to start work detecting the presence of enemy aircraft and directing Allied fighters to intercept and attack them. The ferocious defensive measures taken by the Germans at Omaha Beach, however, forced a four-day delay during which time the Fighter Direction Tenders (FDTs) offshore were employed in this same manner to help safeguard shipping in the Channel and troops on the beaches – FDT 216 covering Utah and Omaha, FDT 217 covering Gold, Juno and Sword, with FDT 13 operating in the main shipping route.   It was not until 9 June that orders came for Muir Adair and his team to go next morning to the location intended to have been made secure for them on D-Day. By the evening of 10 June, though, AMES 15082 was 'in business', notching-up the first 'kill' by the night fighters under its control during that very first night.   In 20 days, 21 enemy aircraft were destroyed and 4 more claimed as damaged – 'a very creditable performance in view of the light enemy night activity' 9 .

Although some other units were given Combined Operations training in only the last month or so before D-Day, Muir Adair and others in this GCI unit were engaged in combat simulation, wet landing practice, physical development, integration with other branches of the armed forces, convoy leading etc for a much longer time.   He says:

'We had become welded together as a unit for over a year with continuous and vigorous training.   I'm sure that this worked to our considerable advantage, not only during D-Day itself but in everything that occurred later on.   Our unit, with a Type 15, Types 13, 14 and 11 supplemented by other assorted night fighter control equipment, remained in the forefront of the battle until the fall of Paris in the last week of August.   I can't vouch for it, though I do reckon that we were the first British contingent into the French capital, a couple of days before the "official" entry, when we attempted to go operational there on the Longchamps race track (and regrettably got chased out!). Normandy landings onwards, we were credited with over 50 enemy aircraft – and that's surely a figure which would have been hard to equal in this theatre of operations.

'In the UK, before the landings, AMES 15082 was on continual training and operational night fighter control duties, so we were at "fever pitch" when we sailed for Normandy. We wore khaki and Combined Operations badges until shortly before D-Day, when some obscure officer in some equally obscure HQ somewhere in never-never land ordered that we must go ashore in Air Force blues. Believe me, when those "blues" suffered the indignities of swimming in the English Channel, crawling over a mine-infested beach, diving into water-filled depressions with every shell burst and rolling around in other undignified positions, our uniform very shortly took on the appearance of the German gray/green, particularly in the eyes of American Rangers who had never before seen an Air Force type. Finally I found a discarded flying jacket that disguised the "blues" sufficiently to ensure a degree of safety from friendly carbines. This clash of uniforms created other problems of a less life-threatening nature – like our Technical Officer, a former Polish Air Force pilot whose English left a lot to be desired, been taken a prisoner-of-war and temporarily incarcerated in an American POW compound.

'Looking back on D-Day and the immediate aftermath, with the detail clouded by all that chaos, confusion and general disorganized mayhem, I cannot quarrel with the definition "disastrous landing" which I came across in an official record of our activities $_{10}$. For my part, I had taken the first echelon off an LCT, seen our vehicles drowned and had to swim ashore with gear that included a strange combination of gas mask and flotation device issued by the Americans. Having waded ashore some considerable distance from the planned landfall on the beach, I spent the rest of D-Day, that night and most of D+1 with equally bewildered US Rangers and other strays, my personal ragtag company hunkered around me because I was the only one in the immediate area with stripes and metal crowns shining out for all to see.

'With close on 60,000 American troops and more than 75,000 British and Canadian troops going ashore on D-Day, something just had to go wrong... certainly I wasn't alone in being spewed out on a beach that was constantly under fire, considerably east of the planned landfall, with a motley assortment of Rangers with no place to range, Navy types without boats, engineers with nothing to engineer, all of us shooting and being shot at until D+1 when ultimately our gaggle of misfits came upon what was left of AMES 15082 [*] .'

---

[*] In charge of the major part of the men and equipment of AMES 15082 from D-Day until the fall of Paris, Muir Adair received from the French Government the Croix de Guerre in recognition of his 'skill and devotion to duty, his coolness and judgement in the face of many difficult situations' which was 'a fine example to all those who worked with him'.

At sea was an armada of vessels – battleships and hospital ships down to tiny tugs – among them three Fighter Direction Tenders (FDT 13, FDT 216 and FDT 217), their use off the Normandy beaches on and after D-Day coming about as a result of the operational successes achieved with a GCI unit installed aboard a tank landing craft in the Mediterranean in the previous June. Without doubt this initial application of shipborne radar for interception purposes was indeed a success, two enemy aircraft being destroyed and two others damaged during just two hours of active use, this unit having detected their presence and made their positions known to the fighters under their control. In other respects, however, this episode was not altogether the accomplishment that it appeared to be; there were other factors which quite clearly must have put a damper on the spirits of those who were among this particular GCI crew.

First, or so it seems from a subsequent report which HQ Mediterranean Air Command sent to Air Ministry – the installation of AMES 15076 having been completed on 9 June 1943 and followed by calibration and VHF tests in Liverpool Bay and northwards to the Clyde – LST 305 set sail with no real understanding of the role which it was expected to play in whatever operations it had been chosen to participate… there were, apparently, no sealed documents and no operational details [11] . The Army contingent on board LST 305 was better served when being given its orders: two days before the operation was due to commence – the invasion of Sicily no less – and it became time for their sealed documents to be opened, these did at any rate provide some details regarding the GCI unit. Nevertheless, having arrived at Cap Passero on the appointed day, AMES 15076 was at least provided with a call sign of its own, together with those of other vessels and shore bases; even so, it still lacked what might be termed 'the complete picture' of what was expected of the equipment and those handling it.

Despite these and other operational and technical problems which were highlighted in that report, LST 305's activities were judged to offer 'great possibilities', although particular reference was made to the affect of seasickness on the way that the GCI unit was able to function. As many as 9 in 10 of the personnel succumbed and operational efficiency was jeopardized – a disturbing state of affairs which sensibly prompted a warning that due consideration MUST [*the word was in fact capitalized in the report*] be given to seasickness.

Although it was LST 305's operational achievements which led senior officers to take this as the prime example when pressing for the provision of seaborne fighter-direction facilities in the forthcoming invasion of Normandy, the Desert Air Force too had employed two GCIs on LSTs and again with encouraging results. Some 10 enemy aircraft were reportedly destroyed by those two stations while operating from aboard ship. Both were judged to have 'worked satisfactorily', though here again matters did not get off to a particularly beneficial start – this time because of what was termed 'conflicting requirements' [12] . The problem appears to have been the two-fold role which the vessel had to fulfil, that of tank-carrier as well as a floating radar post. Consequently, no doubt being eager to begin work without undue delay, the GCI crews found themselves in competition with others on board whose responsibility was to deposit on the beaches, in double quick time, the much-needed cargo of fighting tanks which the LST had carried from its embarkation point.

For Normandy, the intention was to have four vessels converted for fighter-direction purposes, the reduction to three coming about because of the matter of supply and demand. This meant that, whilst their application was to save ships in the operation, this had to be balanced against their diversion from their normal function. Conversion would prove a weighty problem, the GCI aerial with rotating gear being calculated at three and a half tons, plus any additional supporting structure to obtain the required position, with some twelve tons of further gear, most of which could be placed low in the vessels. Eight operational rooms and offices were envisaged, the fighter direction office occupying some 20 ft by 18 ft while the smallest, the cipher office, still needed some 6 ft by 6 ft. Add two diesel power vehicles, each weighing about three tons, and allowing for an RAF contingent of perhaps 15 officers and 60 other ranks supplementing the ship's own complement, this would certainly call for a sizeable vessel – maybe a coaster or, as used in the Mediterranean, a tank-carrying landing craft.

In the frantic months of planning, the radar specialists at the Air Ministry were becoming more and more concerned that little seemed to be happening to produce their vessels in time for Normandy. They had been pressing for ships to carry fighter control equipment since the beginning of the year, 1943, and 'even if we get three ships today there would be no time to fit them up as fully equipped fighter direction ships before they are required for operation. It is quite possible that all we can do now for *Overlord* is to provide some LSTs fitted with GCI and a very elementary form of Control Operations Room' [13].

Though this was a far from satisfactory state of affairs, it was by then early November 1943, the Normandy landings were scarcely more than six months away and circumstances forced the inevitable compromises. Coasters were out of the question – they provided the only means of carrying cased petrol and landing craft and would take about twice as long to convert – so LSTs were now the designated fighter-direction vessels for Normandy... and just the three, not four. Both the application itself and the choice of vessel were seen however as matters demanding discussion and eventual sanction at the highest levels in the planning hierarchy. It is interesting to note that the 'essential' requirement for a seaborne fighter control facility for Normandy was recognized by the Supreme Commander and stressed consistently by the Commander-in-Chief of the Allied Expeditionary Air Force [14]; that the subject was discussed at the level of the Vice Chiefs of Staff; and that even Prime Minister Churchill himself was required to become involved in its authorization. He had directed that 'there should be no diversion of landing craft from their normal roles without reference to him' [15].

The plans and specifications were produced within two weeks of the go-ahead and the conversions from LST (Landing Ship, Tank) to FDT (Fighter Direction Tender) were completed in eight weeks. The radar crews were specially selected by HQ Allied Expeditionary Air Force and underwent training at a Combined Operations Centre in January 1944, a crew being picked for each of the three vessels and remaining together as a team. By mid-March 1944 the technical trials were done and towards the end of April all three vessels had moved round to the Humber and were carrying out interception exercises under the direction of HQ Air Defense of Great Britain and HQ # 12 Group. Exercises continued daily until they sailed for south coast ports for final 'working up' under HQ # 11 Group.

At one point during fighter control exercises arranged by # 11 Group, with the co-operation of the naval authorities in Portsmouth and Portland, FDT 217, one of the three vessels, found herself in a situation where quite possibly the vessel, equipment and crew could all have been lost to enemy action when D-Day was still some six weeks ahead.

John Glen, Flight Sergeant and Senior NCO within the complement of nine radar technical personnel aboard (the others being a Flight Lieutenant in charge, three Corporals and four Leading Aircraftmen), recalls a signal ordering FDT 217 to sail from Cowes to Portland to join an American Task Force in Exercise *Tiger*, a full-scale mock landing with live ammunition employed, to simulate various aspects of the planned invasion of the Normandy beaches.   He goes on [16] :

> 'Ours was the only British ship sailing out of Portland and we moved out into the Channel in eager anticipation of obtaining a taste of what the eventual landings would be like, knowing that this would be close enough to the "real thing" but minus enemy action.   There we were, heading in the direction of France, when the exercise disintegrated into a calamity.   What had happened was that a pack of German E-boats had swept into this unsuspecting gathering of some 100-plus vessels, which were fully loaded with troops and all the miscellaneous equipment necessary for a landing on enemy soil.

> 'We didn't pick up much information about what had occurred and it was many years after the war before the public learned anything at all about what happened that tragic night.   Exercise *Tiger* involved the concentration, marshalling and embarkation of troops in the Torbay-Plymouth area and disembarkation at Slapton Sands.   So far as FDT 217 was concerned, fortunately we withdrew from the area before any harm could occur.   The exercise was abandoned and we lost no time at all when responding to a signal to us to make PORT ALL HASTE.

> 'In that surprise attack and elsewhere in Exercise *Tiger*, it appears that nearly 1,000 American soldiers and sailors "died needlessly" in what the author of one of the several books on this subject described in the late 1980s as "one of the great fiascoes of World War II" [17] .   The E-boats picked on landing craft similar in size to ours so I suppose all of us on board FDT 217 can think ourselves lucky that we were not positioned where our presence could have attracted the enemy's attention.'

Although the area chosen for the invasion was obviously kept from the crews, FDT 216 was to be positioned off the two American beaches in the western half of the assault area, its job being to control the British and American fighter squadrons detailed to operate in that area; FDT 217 was given a similar role off the three British beaches in the eastern half of the assault area; and FDT 13 was to be operating in the main shipping route. Each vessel would be conspicuous by its aerial arrays and highly vulnerable both to sea and air attacks because of the long periods to be spent in the vicinity of the invasion coastline.   In an ideal world these vessels would operate some 20 miles offshore and clear of anchorages in order to avoid permanent echoes from land and large ships respectively; in the event, however, seaborne protection was not possible at such a distance so, when the time came, the two FDTs covering the assault areas moved closer to the beaches and varied their positions from 5 to 15 miles offshore [18] . The aircraft under their control were tasked with preventing the enemy from attacking firstly the shipping and secondly the beaches, this seaborne form of fighter-direction to continue until a shore-based radar station could be set up to undertake these duties.

Six Spitfire squadrons, each with 12 aircraft, maintained low cover over the beaches and shipping continuously throughout daylight hours, 1 squadron to each of the American beaches and 1 squadron on the western flank, 2 squadrons over the entire length of the British beaches and 1 on the eastern flank. Three Thunderbolt squadrons, with 16 aircraft apiece, maintained high cover – 1 disposed centrally, 1 over the eastern area and 1 positioned midway between the two areas; this latter squadron was operating some 8 to 10 miles landward of the beach area, under FDT 217 which, besides its own role, co-ordinated the activities of all three FDTs. Adding to the aerial umbrella in the daylight hours were 4 squadrons of Lightnings, 16 aircraft in each squadron, which maintained a continuous patrol over the assault forces and shipping proceeding along the main shipping route.

Although attacks on the beachhead and shipping were minimal, with none at all for almost 12 hours of the first troops going ashore, the FDTs nonetheless had their work cut out because of the sheer volume of aerial activity despite the often atrocious weather conditions.   Aircraft identification both by day and by night presented a difficult problem in the filter rooms, there being such a large number of friendly aircraft in the area.   All three FDTs were in continuous employment for up to 17 days, the fighters under the control of FDT 217 destroying 39 enemy aircraft by day and 9 by night, plus 1 probable by night; those controlled by FDT 216 destroyed 13 by day and 3 by night; and those controlled by FDT 13 destroyed 12 by night plus 1 probable by night – a total of 76 destroyed plus 2 probables.

FDT 13 was the first to move away from the invasion scene, returning to port for refueling and revictualing on 13 June; FDT 217 had spent the most time there when withdrawn on 23 June; and FDT 216 was the most unfortunate, being forced to return to port on 15 June for repairs to damage sustained in a collision and then, on 7 July at one minute before one o'clock in the morning, being torpedoed by an enemy aircraft at the cost of the ship itself and the lives of five among those on board.   The RAF group suffered most in this tragic incident – two were known to have been killed, three more were missing presumed killed, all five believed to have been near the spot where the torpedo struck, while there were a further four who were slightly hurt and classed as walking cases.   The casualty figures show the Navy with one 'walking wounded' and no doubt it will come as a measure of comfort to some survivors and to others that among those snatched from the sea was... the ship's dog.

In graphic terms which are worth recalling for posterity, FDT 216's commanding officer refers to a 'great explosion shaking and shuddering the ship' and then, some half an hour later, when the survivors were still being gathered from the water, 'we saw our ship and home heel over, slowly, majestically, with an air of defiance, down by the head and stern in the air, ensign flying, her lights still burning and pumps working' [19] .

The results achieved with FDTs in the Normandy invasion prompted a decision to earmark both surviving vessels for a similar role in the Far East, when suitably converted to include considerably improved ventilation and increased space made available for recreation and exercise, although the war ended before either vessel was needed. Their success can be gauged by the fact that only one ship was lost by bombing and attacks on the beaches were reduced to tip and run raids. In fact, 'greater numbers of enemy aircraft could easily have been destroyed if the primary object of the fighter cover had been ignored' [20]. It was further noted that the GCI worked particularly well, giving ranges of over 120 miles at height and providing all that could be desired for plan position. There was, however, a 'very real and urgent need for a good heightfinding set with a range of 50/60 miles' to help counter fast and easily maneuverable small formations which were difficult to intercept in daylight and almost impossible by night.

A particular tribute to the crews of the three FDTs came in another much later report [21] which concluded that their use in the Normandy landings was 'a great success and that they amply fulfilled all that was expected of them'. It remarked upon the continuous employment of the FDTs for a period of about a fortnight having imposed 'a very severe strain' on their personnel; they were living in 'conditions of great discomfort'. It was recalled that the officers and men were carefully selected for this work and that 'many were tried and discarded during the training period'. In the event, this was a policy which 'amply justified itself and the way that everyone stood up to working under conditions foreign to them was beyond praise'.

One of the seven RCAF radar technicians on FDT 217 was Karl Work – 'Chiefy' John Glen, a Scot, and Len Betts, an Englishman, making up the complement of nine. Karl came into FDTs under what might well be described as a misapprehension; he explains that towards the end of November 1943, when he was an AI radar mech on a Beaufighter night fighter OTU, he saw a signal asking for people in his trade to volunteer to go on ships 'under some danger, with hard times and periods at sea'. He responded 'thinking that this would be an aircraft carrier with night fighters [22]'. Len became involved through the work he was doing on modifying GCI equipment for use at sea; an LAC as was Karl, Len had spent the bulk of his time in the RAF on ground-based radar systems.

Karl remembers FDT 217 doing her sea trials in the Firth of Clyde between the last week of February and the first week of April, when the RAF had only an advance party of some 40 airmen and 2 officers. This group did include all the radar technicians, however, the other Canadians being their officer, Hugh Tracey, the three corporals, Lionel 'Cookie' Cook, Ted Parfitt and Charlie Pinnell, and Karl's fellow LACs, Bennie Howe and Bob Stalker. The others in the RAF contingent were radar operators, radio and communication operators and diesel mechanics, the RAF's electrical requirements being separate from those of the Royal Navy.

To put some dates to FDT 217's activities before and after D-Day, Karl notes that when she moved off on 1 June 1944, the area bounded by Cowes, Portsmouth and Southampton 'was literally filled with ships'; on June 3, the weather was 'getting bad' and on June 5, when it was 'very bad', the belief was that FDT 217 should have sailed the previous night [*History records that the D-Day landings had to be delayed because of unsuitable weather conditions*]. In fact the sailing was at 2200 hours on

June 5 'and H-Hour for us was 0400 hours to be off the French coast'.   All three FDTs were 'in position at 0430 hours' and the traffic of aircraft and vessels 'unbelievable'.   Its work done, FDT 217 was back at Cowes at 2300 hours on June 23, sailing on November 22 for her 'winter port', which turned out to be Inveraray on Loch Fyne.   Aside from a few days when Air Ministry had a film crew on board to show RAF personnel operating the radar equipment 'as though we were in action', FDT 217's spell on active duty was over, that momentous D-Day period remaining a memory that would stay with its crew for the rest of their lives.

Not everyone could be 'in the frontline' either on or close to the Normandy beaches on 6 June 1944.   Some may have wished to be nearer the action; many more were surely thankful that their own essential duties distanced them from it.   For WAAF member Pat Parker, on the 0800 to 1600 hours Watch at Tilly Whim, which was one of a number of ground stations giving the bomb-release signal to Oboe-equipped aircraft of the RAF and USAAF, D-Day was 'the busiest and most exciting day' in the three and a half years that she spent as a radar operator.   She recalls:

> 'The weather was fairly clear and our targets, as they had been for several days before, were the German heavy gun emplacements and other military targets along the coastline of Occupied France. As soon as we had given the signal to "Release" on a "Run In", we would quickly dash out of the Ops Trailer to see the plumes of smoke rising from the explosions of the bombs on the German positions. We would then rush back to our "Tubes" to begin the next run [23].'

Already there were mobile ground stations in prospect for use on the Continent, to enable Allied bombers to use Oboe against targets further afield than those within the range of ground stations in the UK.   It was, said Pat, 'a great disappointment to most of the WAAF Oboe operators when we were told we would not be allowed to go to the Continent with our mobile Oboe trailers even though we had volunteered.   All that we could do was to write good luck messages on the back of the plotting board when our trailers were taken away and sent to France and we were sent either to Hawkshill Down or Winterton'.   On the Continent, their male counterparts took the Oboe ground-controlled precision bombing system further and further forward while the WAAFs remained on those fixed-position ground stations, 'from where we continued controlling aircraft by Oboe till the end of the war in Europe' [*].

Radar technical officers such as Sydney Goldstein, who was on a GCI station near Eastbourne, retain random memories of D-Day... 'The disappointment to learn that we would not have a very active part because most of the action would be taking place further west...   Seeing weird floating shapes out in the Channel, moving

---

[*] In *Beam Bombers: The Secret War of No 109 Squadron*, Michael Cumming notes that Tilly Whim, on 2 May 1944 and paired with Beachy Head, handled an Oboe 'first' when two aircraft from # 109 Squadron took part in an experimental operation where, for the first time, an automatic release was triggered from the ground station instead of the navigator releasing on a signal received from the ground station.   In the same book, it is noted that between 2315 hours on 5 June 1944 and 0617 hours on 6 June 1944, the Tilly Whim-Beachy Head partnership controlled 32 aircraft (27 successful Mosquito runs and 4 successful Marauder runs), the USAAF Marauder bombers taking over from the RAF's Pathfinder Mosquitoes at daybreak on D-Day.

westwards, which turned out later to be components to form the Mulberry artificial harbour... Our tubes a solid white at the western end from before first light... Sector, of course, keeping asking us to try and identify "bogeys" in the stream of bombers going and coming (an impossible task!)... And, later on, finding ourselves more than making up for our small part in the invasion when we began taking the brunt of the V1 attacks...

'One afternoon we were asked to track a "bogey" leaving France and coming straight at us, flying at a considerable speed, the echo too small to be a conventional aircraft but maybe it was a small one unknown to us. We continued tracking and then, on losing it amid our radar ground clutter, some of us went outside to have a look at this mystery object. It putt-putted right over our station and we could see that it looked more like a horizontal bomb with wings than an aircraft. There was what appeared to be a tube over the rear end, which we could see was emitting fire when this 'thing' had over-flown us.

'I distinctly remember our CO laughing derisively, when it had passed, and making some comment about us not having much to worry about if that was the best that the Germans could do. He was soon to eat his words when those V1s began falling in greater numbers, even in his own village and forcing him to move his family to a safer location. We started scrambling our fighters, which would try to tip the wing of a V1 so that it fell into the sea before being able to do much harm – and there were times when we would see a dozen Typhoons chasing one little "Doodle Bug", giving the appearance of a pack of hounds chasing the hare. Things soon got organized, however, and there was a battle plan to deal with this challenge, the first point of contact occurring when aircraft under our control, patrolling about 20 miles out to sea, had a zone in which to try to intercept before giving way to successive belts of anti-aircraft guns [24].'

The Oboe mobile ground stations were soon to cross to the Continent of Europe where some crews would see and be threatened by those V1 flying bombs and others even be imperiled by an enemy counter-attack. First, though, the focus in this narrative switches from the war on land to the war at sea... where radar's targets were on and under its surface.

CHAPTER 8: HUNTING U-BOATS

I t is on record that one version alone of the ASV radar system was probably the most widely manufactured radar of the Second World War, the Mark II being produced in Canada, the United States and Australia, as well as in Britain [1] . While some may regard the term 'Air-to-Surface Vessels' radar as an understatement of its application capabilities, there is no question that to most people ASV was *an* airborne radar system and '*the* airborne radar system' in RAF Coastal Command.

Although air-to-surface vessels radar has long been best known and rightly hailed for its war-winning accomplishments in the Atlantic, its introduction and use robbing the U-boats of their element of surprise, it must also be acknowledged that ASV 'was operated on both Atlantic and Pacific coasts of Canada, on such coasts as those around Gibraltar, Malta, the UK, New Zealand and many other countries and territories such as the Orkney Islands' [2].

Post-war, when radar technical officers and radar technicians talk amongst themselves about those long-gone days, the considered view remains that few knew much about the equipment and the uses in radar other than in their own domain. Initial training touched upon the principal systems and gave, in the current phraseology, an 'overview'; but once into ground radar or airborne radar, that view became blinkered. It was unnecessary to learn too much and to know too much. The situation has been explained thus:

> 'Most of us went off to war not appreciating the complex nature of radar operations and without being briefed on what one would expect to see and do if posted to a different phase of the armed forces. Airborne equipment folks knew a great deal about the nine or so radar receivers, transmitters and protective machines under their purview. They usually knew almost nothing about what Coastal Command had responsibility for in the radar line...' [3].

ASV began proving its value in 'sub-hunting' in the winter of 1941/42; and when the war was over, Germany's naval chief, Admiral Doenitz, conceded that radar had 'conquered the U-boat menace' [4] . That was airborne ASV, of course, which deprived his submarines of their 'essential feature – namely the element of surprise'. Its assets were not solely aimed in this direction and the personal experiences of just one radar technician reveal just how versatile was the ASV system...

Having spent the majority of his war years working with ASV, it is none too surprising to find that Les Card became particularly adept at adopting this basically airborne submarine- and ship-spotting radar system to perform an interesting variety of far from basic roles, one such variant gaining acceptance from the powers-that-be and even going onto the production lines. He said:

'In Malta, where I began operational flying [*see page 68*], taking spare equipment and carrying out in-flight maintenance besides working the radar set, Fred Few and I built an ASV ground station at the fort overlooking the harbour, to detect E-boats and other enemy vessels trying to sneak in. We used bits and pieces from bombed aircraft.

'A lot of our flying was firstly in conjunction with the Fleet Air Arm. We would hunt down shipping, then radio-in their planes for torpedo runs, illuminating the target with flares. On occasions we would make our own attacks, the task of the radar operator being to find the target, position the plane for a flare-drop and then re-position either to release bombs or torpedoes, depending what we were carrying that night.

'Later our role changed and we did some liaison work with our own submarines. There was a requirement to communicate with them, which meant that there was a need to be able to tell a 'friendly' from a 'foe', the Med being full of enemy subs in those days. So we modified an IFF Mk II to an IFF Mk IIG, added a Morse key to both the ASV transmitter and the IFF, enabling identification to be achieved and information to be passed between the aircraft and the submarine.

'I, personally, worked on the IFF modifications and on the early tests of what was known as "Rooster". Our prototype was flown back to England and more IFF sets were manufactured and returned to us in Malta – sets which came straight off the production line without change to what we had done. When we received those sets, 12 submarines were fitted with IFF. Although I was transferred from Malta to Egypt in October 1942 [*Les Card was posted to 201 Naval Co-operation Group*], I continued to work with ASV and did the first air testing on "Vin", a device that diverted the output power to a dummy load on approaching an enemy submarine, causing the target to assume that the aircraft was going away and that an attack was no longer in prospect.

'In Egypt, while Radar Officer at Shallufa, we modified the ASV to range down to 400 yards for rocket firing. At this distance, which was the optimum range for best effect, the radar operator would call out and the pilot would know when to press the firing button. It was most successful, so we decided that it would be an easy job to build up the circuitry to achieve automatic fire at 400 yards. This modification worked very well… except that the crew of one aircraft inadvertently left the ASV to fire on automatic, the consequence being that the rockets were released by accident not by design. This ended the auto-version.

'It was at Shallufa, incidentally, that I had the privilege of going up with a former Battle of Britain pilot who, having turned his hand to tank-busting in rocket-firing Hurricanes during the desert war, wanted to do a shipping strike in one of our Beaufighters while he was visiting our station. I flew as his navigator and radar operator, the strike turning out to be rather too successful – we hit a boat that was loaded with ammunition! While turning away from the unexpected blast we lost about five feet off our wingspan and suffered other damage which caused the pilot considerable difficulty keeping the plane level. Besides giving him encouragement and instructions about the course to follow to get us back home, I was anticipating every minute to have to join him at the controls to use our combined strength to hold ourselves level.

'It was fair game for us to attack that ship, of course, but it seemed decidedly unfair when, on another occasion, I found myself on a frigate heading for Italy, with monitoring equipment on board, where deliberately we were to get ourselves bombed. Why an ASV specialist should have been called to join the crew, I know not; maybe (as was my habit) I just volunteered for this "suicide mission"! Anyway, my job was to see whether the enemy had developed a radio-controlled bomb. We out-maneuvered the bombing of our ship, fortunately, and I found no radio frequencies; however we ran across wire while we were maneuvering and this provided the vital clue. Putting two and two together later, we came up with the idea that a length of wire was spooled out behind the bomb and that control signals from the aircraft were transmitted down that wire to change the course of the bomb to make a hit [5] .'

Mention has been made of ASV being converted to ground use and employed with singular effect in the Faroes, when Earl Moore picked up the presence of a U-boat on the surface of the water [*see page 45*]. Although, as the acronym implies, the prime purpose of ASV radar was the detection of surface vessels from the air, Earl would later explain that his experience 'showed a lobe pattern which did cover the surface and from our location on top of a 400 ft cliff we plotted surface vessels as far away as 24 miles' [6] . In its customary employment, ASV was the harbinger of death for many a U-boat crew; if this occasion in the Faroes was not unique, it must certainly have been rare for a U-boat to have been sunk as a result of being spotted first by ground-based ASV.

Mark I ASV was installed first in land-based Hudson aircraft of Coastal Command, then in their Sunderland flying boats. By the end of 1940, up to 50 aircraft carried this system, which was succeeded by the ASV Mk II, developed at the Royal Aircraft Establishment at Farnborough in early 1940 and becoming 'probably the most widely produced radar of the whole war' [7] . Although called a 1.5 m radar, it actually used 1.7m (176MHz); its range was up to 36 miles, the minimum being about 1 mile [8] .

Joe Lusina was a radar technician with # 502 Squadron, which pioneered the use of ASV. This was the squadron that carried out the first successful attack on a U-boat by a Coastal Command aircraft using ASV, when U-206 was sunk on 30 November 1941 in the Bay of Biscay [9] . He recalls that while ASV radar 'was very good equipment, the U-boats learned to identify us, listen for us, crash dive and be nowhere in sight' [10] . However, when the means were found to overcome that problem, 'Coastal Command had a field day with many sightings and many sinkings'. Joe goes on:

'At the outset the crews had trouble using this later equipment so they asked for volunteers to show them how to use it. On our first trip we sighted a U-boat, homed in on it and when the pilot got visual contact I left my radar post and went to watch the attack. He spotted us early enough so that when we got to him he had already gone under – you could see the bubbles of the escaping air. We dropped depth charges and when we circled we saw all sorts of debris coming up to the surface. The Air Force would say that that one was just a "probable" because the U-boats had a trick of loading their torpedo tubes with debris and shooting that out to make you think that you've got them and leave them alone.

'Several flights later we spotted another one and this one was really caught cold. He was charging his batteries; there was nobody on deck – they thought they were safe. We dove from 3,000 feet, dropped the charges and got 'em good. He sunk at an angle of about 60 degrees so that meant that one end of the U-boat got flooded and we got pictures of it. This was 1942 and it was a low ebb in the British struggle against the Germans. The picture was published in all the British newspapers so it gave a big morale boost to the people.'

Contemporary reports made by aircrew members of 502 Squadron, flying twin-engined Whitley aircraft out of St Eval in Cornwall, show that even the most ferocious aerial pounding did not always secure a sinking capable of confirmation. One crew, dropping six 250 lb depth charges from 50 ft on a U-boat sighted on the surface at less than half a mile distant, reported that the third exploded 'abaft the conning tower, sending up flat shower yellow white sparks and fountain of water to height of 150 ft' [11]. When the explosions subsided there was 'a white patch of foam and bubbles equal in diameter to length of U-boat' with 'a further convulsion' three minutes later. Another's fate was beyond doubt; crippled by depth charges and caught in a hail of machine gun bullets, it was 'finally attacked and destroyed an hour later by a Lancaster of 61 Squadron' thanks to that earlier 'severe mauling' [12].

Within Coastal Command, naturally enough the use of ASV was not confined to 'sub-hunting'. By terminology 'Air-to-Surface Vessels' radar, ASV was in the hands of its crews to benefit their searches for any worthwhile shipping targets; equally, Coastal Command had other targets – and sometimes it would be imperative for its aircraft actually to leave behind their radar equipment...

When Andrew Kennedy arrived on # 42 Squadron (of RAF Coastal Command) at Leuchars in Scotland in mid-January 1942, bringing the strength of the radar section to 11 – 6 RAF and 5 RCAF – the squadron's Beaufort torpedo bombers were still in the process of being fitted with ASV equipment; the expectation was that the job would be completed in the next month or so. Meanwhile, his duties, once he had 'learned the ropes and got to know the personnel', would be to assist with the DIs (Daily Inspections), first on the aircraft IFF sets and later on the ASV equipment.

It wasn't long before there was a taste of high-profile action, 14 of the squadron's aircraft leaving for Coltishall in Norfolk to refuel and join the desperate attack on the German naval fleet scurrying homewards through the Strait of Dover – the infamous 'Channel Dash' by two battleships, *Scharnhorst* and *Gneisenau*, a battlecruiser,

Prinz Eugen, five destroyers and more than a dozen motor torpedo boats. Nine of 42 Squadron's Beauforts were airborne that murky afternoon of 12 February 1942, seven launching their torpedoes at the *Scharnhorst*, one failing to release his torpedo while the other failed to find the enemy ships [13] . There were further sorties, none achieving contact, but already there were casualties among the squadron's crews and damage to its aircraft. Beaufort 'V', its torpedo dropped from 60 ft and seen 'running strongly for the second ship, believed to be the *Scharnhorst*', took considerable flak, the hail of heavy calibre shells engulfing this aircraft and some even striking the water, so low was it when making the attack. The top of the turret was blown off, there were four holes in the port wing, near the engine, and another in the tailplane. The rear gunner took a bullet in his arm and sustained facial lacerations while the wireless operator, who delayed reporting back to base to attend to his colleague's injuries, suffered a grazed leg [14] . The Fleet Air Arm lost all 6 Swordfish aircraft which carried out the initial aerial attack and in total the RAF lost 20 bombers and 16 fighters. Reconnaissance on 3 May 1942 revealed the *Scharnhorst* at Kiel, *Gneisenau* at Gdynia and *Prinz Eugen* at Trondheim, all badly damaged [15] .

It is not recorded whether ASV was used on that occasion – ASV was, of course, the means to detect the presence of shipping by radar – and by the time 42 Squadron's Beauforts were sent in, the enemy naval force had already revealed itself. Although invaluable in certain operational sorties, the most obvious being a patrol with the express intention of searching for enemy submarines, the unnecessary inclusion of such sensitive gear was a security risk. This meant that there were times when it was prudent for an aircraft not to carry ASV, as Andrew Kennedy explains:

> 'When the unfortunate "Channel Dash" episode was gone from our minds, there was a situation early one afternoon in mid-May when panic hit the radar section. All our kites were "torped up", all the DIs were re-checked to make sure that all the ASV gear was in proper working order and the aircraft were ready to take off on an hour's notice. In fact none was required for what we assumed would be another strike against some German ships. Next day, though, the squadron was still on alert and in the afternoon there was a fresh panic. This time all the ASV equipment had to be stripped out of each Beaufort and stacked in our workshop; we didn't know where our kites would be going but we did know the reason for leaving the radar gear behind – which was to prevent it from falling into the hands of the enemy in the event of an aircraft crashing onto the deck of the target ship during a torpedo-dropping run [16] .'

At 8.20 pm that day, 17 May 1942, a special strike force of 12 Beauforts of # 42 Squadron, escorted by four Beaufighters and six Blenheim fighters, sighted and attacked the *Prinz Eugen*, some four miles off the Norwegian coast near Lista. The German battlecruiser was protected by four or five destroyers and more than 20 fighters. The attacking aircraft encountered 'very stiff opposition but torpedoes were dropped (2 hits and a probable are the official figures)' [17] . Combat with enemy aircraft resulted in 'at least five hits'. However the crews of three of 42 Squadron's Beauforts did not return and were posted missing, among them the squadron commander and his crew. A fourth aircraft, partially disabled by enemy flak, managed to reach Leuchars where it made a crash-landing, the crew escaping unhurt [18].

Andrew recalls:

> 'Our aircraft started arriving back around 10.30 pm and continued through to midnight. When we got back to the Section at midnight it was pouring rain and we were greeted by the news that all aircraft had to have their ASV equipment re-installed, tested and ready by dawn. After a late supper my working partner and I began our share of the work load. We pushed our petrol genny around to various aircraft in blackness and heavy rain – we had our big gum-boots and slickers on but the latter didn't help very much. All kites except "T" were completed by 3.30 am and we were all played out; everything went wrong with "T" and we didn't finish until 7.00 am. We went back to our barracks soaking wet, washed up, changed our clothes and had breakfast, then we got to bed at 8.30 am, sleeping until 4.00 pm [19].'

As with the earlier strike against the battle fleet sailing up the English Channel, on their return the aircrews were tight-lipped so far as communication with the ground personnel was concerned. Ground crews on duty would see which aircraft were home and it would be plain to see if any had been 'shot up'; others, though, might be back safe but on another airfield. In Andrew's experience, information about the operation itself and the squadron's participation was invariably nil or minimal. In the case of the "Channel Dash", he heard about it on the radio; this time, as he noted in a diary, 'some said it was the *Prinz Eugen* they went after and seeing how their torpedoes were missing, there must have been some truth in it [20]'. Any reticence to dwell on the circumstances was perhaps understandable, given the severity of the enemy resistance and the losses sustained in this attack. It transpired that during the strike, at least two of the squadron's Beauforts made their attack from as low as 50 ft and one of them, seeing a clear run and turning in, came under cannon fire from three Me 109F fighters – one from port, one from starboard and one from astern [21]. The squadron's target, *Prinz Eugen*, did more than just stay afloat throughout this attack, it survived the entire war [*].

For every aircrew member pursuing an active role like those of # 42 Squadron and all others in Coastal Command, many more were involved totally on ground duties or doing work which gave them a mix of airborne and ground-based activities. In the 'paperwork' presented in support of a recommendation for the award of the Air Force Cross – in each case it was to a member of the RCAF – it is clear that while both were in a non-flying category among radar-trained personnel, both were hardened flying members.

Flight Lieutenant C K Burlingham, whose AFC came through on 1 September 1944, joined Coastal Command Development Unit as a radar officer in October 1943, logging some 845 hours in an aircraft and surviving two serious crashes while working on the development of airborne radar operating techniques. The point was made that, although a technical officer, 'he has flown as many hours as a normal

---

[*] This German battlecruiser was sunk ignominiously in 1947 during an atomic bomb test in the Pacific [22].

crew member in addition to evincing administrative abilities'. One result of his endeavors was that 'the efficiency of general reconnaissance squadrons in all theatres of war has been increased as a result of his researches' [23].

Flying Officer H D Davy, who was with HQ Coastal Command, received his AFC on 14 June 1945. Born in London, England, he enlisted as a radar mechanic in Toronto in April 1941, received his commission in July 1943 and by the time the war in Europe was over he had put in some 450 hours of flying time. He had been employed on radar experimental and instructional duties since February 1942. Not only did he 'play an important part in experimenting with, and developing, new equipment but he has devoted much time and energy to training crews in the use of the complicated equipment'. Two of his 19 operational sorties 'resulted in the probable sinking and severe damaging of two U-boats, the detection of which was due in both cases to the extreme skill of Flying Officer Davy'. Twice Mentioned in Despatches – the first on the day that his AFC came through, the second on New Year's Day 1946 – 'by his untiring efforts he materially contributed to the high standard of efficiency attained by many crews' [24].

Not all ASV-equipped aircraft of Coastal Command were based on the mainland of Britain, nor were all its squadrons equally adept at maintaining this gear at peak efficiency. At Ballykelly in Northern Ireland, LAC H Parfitt was with # 8086 Servicing Echelon, employed on major inspections of radar equipment. He was responsible for detecting faults and submitting modifications which, when put into effect, 'often resulted in the higher serviceability of equipment'. When recommended for the BEM he received on 14 June 1945, the phrase used was that 'it is largely due to his untiring efforts that the anti-submarine radar equipment at this station during the last six months has shown the highest serviceability of any in the Command'. It is also significant to see noted that on several occasions he was 'entrusted with initiating work of the highest importance beyond the normal scope of a radar mechanic' and that 'each time he has completed the work most successfully and speedily' [25]. He received, too, a Mention in Despatches on 1 January 1946. Coincidentally, Corporal E H Kassie, a member of the radar section on a squadron based at Ballykelly, # 59 Squadron, received a BEM as did LAC Parfitt – and on the same day – his 'outstanding efficiency, zeal and leadership' playing a large part in what was described as a 'remarkable performance'. This related to the radar serviceability at Ballykelly which, during 1944, 'rose from a position near the bottom of the list of stations in Coastal Command to the top', the rate of serviceability being 'very nearly double the average for the Command' [26].

As noted, Air Force Cross recipient C K Burlingham was a member of CCDU – Coastal Command Development Unit; this was an organization that, in Steve Flinders' time with them at Ballykelly and Tain, had him working aboard a submarine! As a radar technician, in this he must have been extremely rare if not unique. He recounts how it happened:

> 'When the Battle of the Atlantic was in full swing we were using Wellingtons equipped with Leigh Lights, which were used to catch U-boats on the surface and bomb them. It didn't take long for the Germans to figure out a device that picked up the radar waves and, as they became stronger, to submerge before the aircraft could switch on the Leigh Light and bomb.

Our outfit figured out a way that would reduce the power from the ¼ wave diapoles as the aircraft approached the U-boat. This necessitated one of us being in a submarine, the other being in the aircraft, which meant that I was on board one of two training subs for 24-hour stretches.

'When one shift comes off, the other uses their bunks; and space is at a premium. I was in the wireless room with the operator – a room as large as a telephone booth. Once on the 500-ton sub and once on the 750-tonner was more than enough. I can say with feeling that anyone volunteering for submarine duty should get a medal – simply for volunteering. Our gadget worked very well and there were a few decorations awarded for this effort [27].'

Others served further afield than the UK, sometimes working on radar equipment carried in land-based aircraft, such as the Hudsons, Liberators and Fortresses flown in its time by # 59 Squadron, on flying boats like the Sunderland and on amphibians which included the Catalina.

Having volunteered for duty outside Britain, Keith Knox was 'most disappointed' to find himself at Gibraltar when others were being posted to West Africa, the Far East and the Middle East. He was on # 202 Squadron, with Catalina flying boats, and he remembers there being a huge hangar able to hold three of these amphibious craft. He goes on:

'Right in front of the hangar was a slip to haul these Cats out of the water. When one was coming in for maintenance a whistle went up and anyone that could went over to the slip. One of the fitters would go out in the water, attach the wheels and pulling ropes, then we would grab the ropes and haul it up. What a job! These guys got an extra sixpence for going in the water. The Americans, who used the same aircraft, had a crane to do all that.

'The sea wall had a break in it to bring the aircraft through and this break had a net in it to prevent the enemy from coming through. This net could be put aside for our needs, but at night, when you couldn't see, a depth charge was discharged every fifteen minutes in front of the net on the outside to discourage unwanted entry. Sometimes one would fail to explode and people would wake up and say, "What was that?" [28].'

On Gibraltar there was a radar beacon at the top of the famous Rock and it was Keith's wish to have a spell up there, a wish that came true to give him a break from working on the Catalinas' radar systems. It was a tough ride, the truck driver having to 'back up' when negotiating the succession of hairpin turns. There was no guard rail and, as Keith says, 'you just hoped he didn't back too far'. He says of those two weeks on top of the Rock:

'There were just two of us on duty and we could look out our back window at the thousand foot drop right down to the concrete casements. The building was small, just room for the beacon and for us to live in and do our cooking.

'Every four days we had to walk down to town for supplies. The nine hundred steps would take us to the sloping narrow streets of Gibraltar where we would get our supplies, put them on our backs and hike back up. At least it was preferable to riding the truck! It was an interesting place to be for those two weeks, although it was only thirteen feet wide at the top.'

Coastal Command had set up a base in Gibraltar a week after war began, to cover the southern part of the Bay of Biscay and the waters closest to this entry into the Mediterranean. Operations in Iceland began in May 1940; and in late 1943, after a British-Portuguese agreement, Coastal Command put aircraft of # 247 Group on the Azores, beginning operations in October with two B-17 Fortress squadrons supported by two Leigh Light detachments from Gibraltar [*].

In terms of range of duties, where the Sunderland squadrons were concerned, # 204 Squadron would take some beating in respect of its time in Gambia, West Africa, with Flying Officer J G Gow its radar specialist. In October 1942, for example, its aircraft and their crews were on anti-submarine patrols, escorting convoys, reconnaissance, searching for survivors from sunken ships and on one occasion trying to locate an aircraft missing on transit – the successful outcome of this trip being to locate and pick up those on board and to take them to a place of safety [29]. The base itself had additional duties, that of handling the arrival and departure of BOAC and Pan-American flying boats which were providing a trans-ocean service via West Africa.

For his work on 204 Squadron, Flying Officer Gow was awarded the MBE in the New Year Honours List 1943, the citation noting that he had 'devised and constructed a radio beam far in advance of any other in West Africa enabling aircrews to find convoys and return to base under the worst weather conditions [30]'. He worked night and day, personally supervising the construction of the set and training operators, and during the past 12 months, by his personal example, 'has built up a radio section that would be hard to equal, let alone surpass in the RAF'.

Another radar technician, Jay Christensen, transferring from North Africa to East Africa in September 1944, was assigned to # 209 Squadron in Mombasa, Kenya. It was equipped initially with Catalina flying boats and employed on anti-submarine patrol and convoy work, its area including the western side of the Indian Ocean from Mombasa to the Seychelles, around Madagascar Island, to Mauritius and the Mozambique Channel. He recalled that

> 'The ground trades were all aboard on the operational patrols to detached bases and were responsible for maintenance on these extended operations. I participated on missions to Pamanzi Island, Seychelles, Mauritius and Tulear. Often the flights would last for 12 to 13 hours on anti-submarine patrols during which I would take my turn in operating the radar [31].'

---

[*] Named after Squadron Leader H de Vere Leigh, the Leigh Light was an airborne searchlight with upwards of five million candlepower, carried under the wing or in the nose, which ASV-equipped aircraft used to illuminate surfaced U-boats or suspicious radar contacts.

There were 'real beds in thatch-roofed barracks' though it was necessary to sleep in mosquito nets because of the malaria threat, many squadron personnel going down with malaria despite a daily dosage of mepacrine. Those nets, Jay wrote, 'also kept us safe from snakes which often roamed through our barracks. A world record 33 ft python was killed between our camp and the air base'.

His squadron converted to Sunderland flying boats in March 1945 for assignment to the Far East, the radar personnel on 209 being trained on H_2S and finally saying goodbye to ASV Mark II. VE-Day was celebrated with a squadron victory parade down the rain-soaked streets of Mombasa and shortly afterwards, when 209 was due to transfer to its new theatre of war, Jay was moved to Egypt. Assigned to an RAF Maintenance Unit before repatriation to Canada via England, where he celebrated VJ-Day in London, he worked in a radar repair section located in caves that had been excavated to provide stone for the Pyramids in Cairo.

Some stayed longer on a squadron than did Jay Christensen in East Africa... and some moved with their squadron from one country to another, as did Dave Roumieu...

As Dave recalls, there was a pronounced cosmopolitan feeling within # 86 Squadron, with whom he remained throughout his overseas service from June 1943 to September 1945. One of the most successful of the RAF's U-boat hunting squadrons, with more than a dozen 'kills' to its credit when the war ended, its aircrew members included – in Dave's time with them – Britons, the Southern Irish, Canadians, Australians, New Zealanders and one or two South Africans. Equally, there was a broad mix of radar equipment which required his attention: vertical time base Mk II, IFF, radar altimeter, FM sonar buoys and then the arrival of the flux gate compass – 'which I remember required me to devise a bench set to connect this equipment to an ASV 10cm search radar set'. It was around this time that the squadron lost two aircraft in a relatively short period, both of them – to Dave's certain knowledge – simply disappearing without trace. Such losses, where the crew members were acquaintances if not close friends, hit hard; less so, perhaps, when a lost aircraft belonged to another squadron, as also happened while at Tain, a Liberator with a Czech unit crashing on take-off and Dave having to help in the removal of all the radar equipment from this aircraft.

It was one of those not infrequent mix-ups when Dave was posted to 86 Squadron. He had arrived at Liverpool on 24 May 1943 and taken the train down to Bournemouth, reaching this seaside resort soon after enemy raiders had attacked it with machine guns and bombs, killing some 117 civilians and military personnel [*].

There was a delay before his movement orders were ready, requiring him to report to Thorney Island, a little way along the coast, where his group of half a dozen airmen were to join 86 Squadron.

---

[*] Gerry Franklyne, writing about # 3 Personnel Reception Centre, Bournemouth, in *Airforce*, April-May-June 1987, notes that during the 23 May 1943 attack by 24 FW 190s, which came in low over the cliffs in sixes, the Metropole Hotel was hit and 33 people killed, including 13 RAF, 10 Canadians and 4 RAAF personnel.

He says that...

> 'On arrival we were informed that the squadron had moved to Aldergrove in Northern Ireland, a couple of months previously, so we had to take a train to Stranraer next day, cross by ferry to Larne, go by train to Belfast and thence find our own means of transport to reach the airfield. Thus began my 28 months with 86 Squadron. We shared Aldergrove with another RAF squadron, # 59 Squadron, and the radar section was manned by officers, NCOs and airmen from the two squadrons. Virtually all of us were Canadian RCAF members, perhaps as much as 95 per cent Canadian RCAF radar mechanics. Both squadrons moved from Aldergrove to Ballykelly, near Londonderry, in September, the winter months on our new base being dreary and wet and our Nissen hut cold. To add to our despondency, one of 59 Squadron's Liberators took off early one evening, its tanks full and depth charges for the anti-submarine patrol in place, when it blew up in sight of those who were in our hut at the time... I became one of the pallbearers at the funeral of the Canadian air gunner in that crew, all of whom were killed. Occasions like this gave us time to contemplate our own fate – and often I have reflected what might have been my lot if, as a fellow radar chum Paul Bourdeau and I had done, volunteering for what was described on the bulletin board at Aldergrove as 'a dangerous mission on the coast of France' had materialized. Nothing, fortunately, came of our eagerness – or was it, perhaps, our irresponsibility [32] .'

A detachment with 86 Squadron to Iceland for some three months during the spring of 1944 was 'an interesting stay', perhaps all the more so because of two sets of cultural relationships which were formed in that country – one with his fellow Canadians, the other with the people of Iceland.

Flying there in a Liberator and filling-in as a radar operator on the trip from Ballykelly to Reykjavik, those in his squadron, which was RAF, found that there was already an RCAF squadron, # 162 Squadron,. on this air base, though located at Camp Maple Leaf some distance away. Strangely enough, as he remembers it, personnel from the two squadrons seldom saw each other and made no effort to fraternize – 'Those of us who were Canadians and serving with the RAF were not considered to be Canadians; we were regarded as Britons who had lived in Canada before the war and returned to the "home country" to join the RAF, which allowed us the privilege of wearing the "Canada" flash on our uniforms [33] .'

While that was one cultural surprise that surfaced in Iceland, another came in contact with the people in whose home country Dave was now based. It was 'mildly fascinating' though the people were 'none too friendly', which some put down to the substitution of a military presence for the pre-war economic assistance provided by the Germans, who had harnessed the hot water springs to provide central heating to the citizens of Reykjavik. Historically, the period while these two squadrons were there was one of transition and encouragement for the future: a Viking conquest, Iceland was then, in 1944, in the process of becoming an independent republic having been under Danish rule from 1380. Although acquiring independence in 1918, Iceland still shared its king with Denmark until 1943.

Dave has random memories of his time in Iceland:

> 'There was a super American Red Cross facility where one could have a bath and a swim and enjoy lots of other comforts which went a long way towards making us forget the irksome side of our work duties – like those seemingly interminable dusk until dawn patrols around the airfield that made DIs [daily inspections] and mods [equipment modifications] in the radar section welcome relief.   There was an occasional air raid siren signaling the approach of what was maybe a German aircraft from Norway come to snoop on us and on the movements of shipping.   Come mid-May and the movements were all in the air, rather than at sea, with a daily procession of some 75 to 100 Liberator and Fortress four-engined bombers touching down for a short say, presumably on their way to the British Isles in readiness for the invasion of Northern Europe.   Around 4 am on 6 June 1944, I was in a Sunderland flying boat heading for Scotland as a member of the advance party to establish 86 Squadron at Tain.   We arrived at Invergordon to learn that the D-Day landings were in progress while we were airborne.'

Towards the end of 1944, Coastal Command was being supplied with more precise radar in the form of ASV 3 cm with wave guides, an innovation which required Dave and a radar sergeant from another squadron to attend Cranwell for a course of instruction on this 3 cm gear with the sea-return discriminator.   It is not difficult to understand why, instead of recalling the complexities of ASV, he has retained two particular and unrelated memories of the Cranwell classes: the bunks shaking with the explosions caused by enemy attacks in the Grimsby area and a contingent of WAAF girls winding up their Christmas Eve revelry by 'invading the men's barracks while we were still in bed... it was just as well they didn't stay too long...'

Dave Roumieu's time in Iceland with one of the top-flight U-boat hunting squadrons contrasts significantly with fellow Canadian Aime Colonval's tropical posting to Takoradi in the Gold Coast, subsequently named Ghana and known in those days as the 'white man's grave' because of its climate, insects, poisonous creatures, diseases and kindred forms of killer unpleasantness.   It began with a necessarily circuitous voyage, aboard the *Highland Princess* for some 30 days in July/August 1942, the convoys from UK ports to Takoradi suffering many losses due to U-boat attacks.   Aime recalls in these words the scene that was set for the one-year-plus that he would spend in West Africa:

> 'We knew that we were to build a COL station, but our equipment had not arrived. A previous convoy had lost at least one ship to the submarines and others were to follow * .   We bided our time, helping out on the local radar station, still known at that time as an RDF station.   The RAF combated the

---

* Albert Cumming, uncle of the author and an RAF radar technician, sailed for West Africa on the *Anselm*, surviving, as did most of those on board, a U-boat torpedo attack which sank this vessel on 5 July 1941.   A chaplain, Squadron Leader H C Pugh, chose to be lowered into a hold below the water line, where he was seen kneeling to pray with trapped airmen, the water already reaching his shoulders. Never seen again, he was awarded a posthumous George Cross.

U-boat menace by the use of Wellingtons, flown mainly by South African air crews. They monitored their end of the shipping lanes for enemy submarines and dropped depth charges on or around them. The overseas radar chain was needed to help protect those bombers from possible attack by German fighters in the future and to guard the shoreline west towards Freetown and north towards Gibraltar. Our station was going to be one more link in that chain, the team comprising Flight Lieutenant H D MacGregor, an RAF sergeant who was a radar whiz and four radar mechs, all of us being Canadians – Terry Nervick, Jim Scott, Jim Proudfoot and myself. As our station construction reached completion, we were joined by about 10 RAF airmen, radar operators, administration and security.

'Life in equatorial Africa is unique – no doubt about it – and frankly I'm astonished and perhaps even angry that while wartime service in other parts of the globe has been recognized post-war by the authorities, in places such as West Africa it has been overlooked, leaving those of us who had to endure those special hardships to feel that we were forgotten folk.

'The memories of my time in and around Takoradi will never leave me... especially those hot, savagely hot days when, at noon, quite literally you stood on your own shadow, the sun straight up above your head. You had to mind what you drank and ate, you had to check your shoes for scorpions every morning and for ever you were watching out for mosquitoes and snakes, particularly the mamba, which in each of its stages as green or black was fast, poisonous, and known to attack!

'Wherever you were stationed, I suppose, there were culture shocks which produced experiences of their own, experiences which were hardly hardships but ones that certainly provided a fresh perspective on life. The culture clash I found the most striking came from the practice of people lying down and sleeping on the side walks at night – so many of them that you had to be careful where you stepped – and the constant pestering, on the streets, when kids no more than 10 years of age or so would be pimping their sisters. Still more disturbing was the sight of so many young adults who had a hand missing because of punishment for stealing, in accordance with Muslim law [34].'

Early September saw Aime's group leaving Takoradi for Accra to build the planned Chain Overseas Low radar station, AMES 5050, on a rise of land called Achimota Mountain. A building was erected to house transmitter, receiver and diesel generator, using 'sandcretes', which were blocks of sand made by placing the moist mix in demountable wooden moulds and laid in the sun to dry. The woodwork was made from local mahogany, cut laboriously by hand by native carpenters; the gantry comprised mahogany timbers more than a foot across; and the beams were all bored by hand, using augers with bits over two feet long, then bolted together. The gantry was comparatively low, being no more than twenty feet, there being a good location for the lobe.

Aime explains that the unskilled work was done by local 'bushmen', controlled by a 'headman', the radar mechs living in individual native-built, village-style mud huts about ten feet in diameter with palm thatched roofs, an entry door and a shuttered window.   The walls were some two feet thick and the floor was Mother Earth, pounded smooth by bare feet.   The huts were, he says, 'great! – cool during the heat of the day and with the temperature remaining constant during the night.   The roof let the hut breathe while remaining waterproof in the torrential rain that was another feature of West African life'.

Young, strong and well adjusted to the heat, some of the group suffered from one or more of the tropical diseases, Aime becoming extremely ill with a form of dysentery in February 1943 and spending 16 days in the civilian hospital in Accra.   Within four months he was back under medical care, this time in the RAF Hospital at Takoradi, with malaria.

Changes in the fortunes of war brought about a decision to close the station, to pack up the equipment and to return to Takoradi for relocation on a temporary basis while awaiting new postings.   Aime switched to a wireless station 'where there must have been about twenty transmitters in the one building, mostly 1087s plus three very large ones, including a Marconi and an RCA'.   The CO introduced the newcomers in 'embarrassingly glowing terms', asking his men 'to give us their equipment problems to solve'.   A 25 kw transmitter was the first challenge – it was new but no-one could get it to work.   He teamed-up with a Corporal Wireless Mech, checking every wire and component against the appropriate diagrams, eventually finding over twenty manufacturer's errors.   These were corrected and the transmitter 'worked like a charm', giving its operators no further trouble.   A subsequent problem, prompted by an operator's complaints about low or absent transmitter output in the receiver building, produced a solution unrelated either to manufacture or breakdown.   He notes that 'we usually found the transmitter fine but the aerial either down or badly drooped, only a few guy wires in place to hold it up'.   What was happening was that the natives were cutting the guy wires for use on their fishing nets – a surprising discovery matched only by the surprising nature of the remedy...   'We booby-trapped all aerial guy wires by insulating them and feeding them with AC voltage, so when word got around we had no more trouble with aerial sabotage', Aime reports with a barely suppressed chuckle.

On 30 September 1943, Aime's unit left for the UK, returning by way of Freetown where the *Queen Mary* was among countless ships at anchor, and from mid-November he was on a CHL station in Devon as a base while taking Yatesbury courses in Basic Centimeter and in Oboe.   The successful conclusion of this training period resulted in the prelude to a further spell overseas, this time the posting being to an Oboe unit at Beachy Head the following April in the run-up to D-Day.   The tropical heat associated with one overseas tour was to give way to the heat of battle with a mobile Oboe station in a part of the world, North Western Europe, where wartime service has been more consciously recognized during post-war years.

CHAPTER 9: SOUTH EAST ASIA

What was life like for radar technical officers and radar technicians serving in South East Asia, which many will no doubt regard as an often forgotten theatre of operations? There probably won't be identical answers but the certainty is that everyone would come up with one or more of these nasties: 'Poor food, the pests, the tropical diseases and especially the monastic lifestyles' [1] .

With hindsight, maybe some of the misfortunes that were occasioned by the more obvious hazards to health might well have been avoided. In hospital four times with tropical diseases, Angus Hamilton recalls that when the authorities were setting up one of the first stations on which he served in India – it was at Baigachi, some 25 miles from Calcutta, on the road to Dacca – the risk of Japanese air attack was real. He explains that...

> 'The prevailing wisdom at that time was to build billets, cook houses etc several miles from the airstrip and amongst the densest grove of trees available. This may have been successful camouflage but it caused a medical disaster in a place that has several months with 100 per cent humidity at temperatures in the 80s Fahrenheit. The Japs didn't inflict any casualties but sickness did. At a time when I was in hospital with jaundice, half of the squadron personnel were suffering from one ailment or another. When new billets, hot showers and a new cook house were built in the open on high dry ground at the end of the year, the incidence of ailments dropped dramatically [2] .'

A fellow Canadian, Bill Barrie, who was in this theatre of operations from 18 October 1942 until 25 January 1945, reckoned that in most places in that part of the world the RAF was fighting on two fronts – the Axis Powers and health; to stay healthy was 'a constant struggle requiring alertness and concentration [3]'. He continues:

> 'At first it was dysentery. Almost everyone had tummy troubles while an immunity was being built up. On the parade ground it was not unusual for a newcomer to let out a groan, double up, and disgrace himself on the spot. The house fly was the cause of much of the trouble. At Korangi Creek [Karachi], when the wind changed and blew from the direction of the rotting fish fertilizer on the coast, the flies all left the mess hall. Next day they would be back.
>
> 'Malaria was endemic after a rainfall brought out the mosquitoes. Though we all used netting to sleep under, there was still quite a bit of malaria and dengue – another disease transmitted by mosquitoes. Dengue fever was what got me. All I can remember is waking up in the hospital with a very high temperature that took about 48 hours to get down to normal.

'Bed bugs were everywhere, in the movie houses, in chairs and even in polished dining room tables. When I wrote home to mother for sympathy all she could say was, "Be sure to shake out your clothes before you come home!" '

As regards the war on the 'other' front, the struggle against the Axis Powers, this can be brought into focus by acknowledging that just as there was a radar watch in Britain before the war began with Germany, ready to spot approaching raiders should hostilities commence, so there was a radar watch too in some of the more vulnerable areas of South East Asia before Japan came into the conflict. In the event, of course, the surprise and the sheer strength of the Japanese onslaught overwhelmed whatever lines of defense were in existence on that fateful day, 7 December 1941. With virtually simultaneous air raids on Hawaii, Northern Malaya, the Philippines, Guam, Wake Island and Hong Kong, Japan stormed dramatically into World War II and began relentlessly to overrun South East Asia. It was, said President Roosevelt in a speech next day denouncing the sudden and deliberate attack on the US bases at Pearl Harbour, 'a date that will live in infamy'.

American ships and planes were not alone in crumpling beneath the aerial assault. On the British colony of Hong Kong, the RAF base at Kai Tak was an early target for Japanese bombers. Those attacks were followed by further and heavier air raids, then by artillery bombardments and finally, ten days later, by troops landing from their assault boats in increasing numbers sufficient to crush even the most determined resistance. Within 24 hours, half the island was occupied. Isolated and with no hope of relief, Hong Kong surrendered on Christmas Day. It would be Malaya's turn next to submit to occupation, bringing the key commercial centre and port of Singapore under immediate threat. And in the ultimate, perhaps Australia and New Zealand too?

A transportable radar station on the east coast of Malaya, sited some 100 miles north of Singapore before war came to South East Asia, plotted the first enemy air raid on Singapore, 'thereby giving almost an hour's warning of its approach' [4]. The technical officer commanding this unit was the then Flying Officer B W ('Stan') Martin; he would be awarded an OBE for his initiative and leadership keeping his station on the air prior to the fall of Singapore. In the words of the citation, Stan Martin rendered 'gallant and distinguished services during the period of operations against the Japanese in Malaya and the Netherlands East Indies, terminating in March 1942'. The unit escaped by the skin of its teeth in the face of the rapid Japanese advance through Malaya, the personnel, their vehicles and their equipment managing always to keep one step ahead; at one point, when the enemy was no more than a river's width away, Stan Martin's team hurriedly dismantled the tower and carried out a hasty evacuation. They made it down to Singapore, however, setting up their station and operating from successive sites while enemy troops massed for the assault which everyone knew would come within days. Eventually ordered to leave, the unit escaped by boat to Sumatra where, with the Japanese already beginning to occupy the island, British warships moved in to evacuate the Singapore survivors and take them to Ceylon.

On 15 February 1942, no more than 48 hours after Stan Martin was told that it was time for his radar unit to go, Singapore was surrendered to General Yamashita, some 70,000 British, Indian and Australian troops being taken prisoner. The fall of Singapore was 'one of the greatest Japanese victories in World War II' and 'a significant milestone in the ending of British imperial interests in South East Asia' [5] .

Where Stan Martin made his way to Sumatra (and thence to Ceylon to join a newly-forming Radio Installation and Maintenance Unit in Colombo), one of his fellow Canadians, Oss Luce fled to the smaller and more distant island of Java. Oss, who had trained at Yatesbury and served briefly at TRE before leaving the UK, arrived in Singapore just ten days before the surrender. Although unable to make any contribution there to the radar scene, in Java he and others were posted to a naval base to set up radar equipment. As he put it later:

> 'The only problem was that we didn't have any radar equipment. When we got there we found American gear which looked similar to gun-laying equipment and was nothing at all compared with the English stuff with which we had been working. It was very amateurish and certainly not the sophisticated stuff that we had known. But we tried to range the thing in optically and sort of calibrate it from what we could see. However, that didn't last very long because the Japs had invaded the island. So we headed south for the coast, trying to find some way to get into Australia [6] .'

It was a goal beyond their reach. With a price on their heads, Oss Luce and the others in that small group of would-be escapers were, not surprisingly, handed over by the natives to the newly-arrived Japanese and put into working parties. After a year or so, with their clothes and their shoes worn out, Oss and his comrades were reduced to wearing a loin cloth and going around bare-footed, their heads cropped so short that if a guard was able to get any hair between his fingernails 'you would get a beating and it was generally a good beating'. It was advisable 'to become grey – to try to merge into the background.

> 'The bigger you were the more they would pick on you, because they were of small stature themselves and they hated anyone bigger. I guess that it was sort of an inferiority complex. Some of the torture was mild. They would have you kneel in front of the guardhouse and underneath your knees they would put a stick about the size of a broom handle. You try kneeling for about three or four hours with a broom handle under your knees. If you moved or tried to get off that stick, they would beat the devil out of you. That was one of the milder forms of torture. At other times they would give you two stones weighing about one pound each and you would hold them in your hands in front of you without dropping them. That is a thing you can try easily enough for yourself. Take a pound of butter and try and hold it in each hand and see how long you can hold it there before you have to drop it. But remember that if you drop it you will get a beating.'

Oss was a prisoner-of-war from March 1942 until August 1945. Returning to the UK from Singapore, he recalls being handed a pink slip of paper before landing at Liverpool – 'That is the Official Secrets Act and you must not speak, write or divulge of any information on anything you have learned during your time in prison', he was told. There was no alternative: he had to sign before he could disembark. Many years later, in Ottawa with the National Prisoners of War Association, the Official Secrets Act came up. Oss asked the Veterans' Minister for how long he had to abide by that Act. The answer was that he was in fact 'free' – the Minister adding, 'No-one would believe you anyway!'

Casting his mind back to his time as a POW, during which period his weight all but halved – it dropped from 190 lbs to 105 lbs – Oss noted that 'we endured a bad enough time in prison knowing about radar and trying to keep it to ourselves'. It was a predicament that many radar personnel would have wished to avoid. Oss, well aware of the seriousness of being placed in such an agonizing situation, notes:

> 'Everything we learned about radar had to be memorized and we were always afraid that someone would find out that we knew the secrets of radar. Of course, if the Japanese had decided to torture us or anything like that, I know we couldn't have stood up to it. We had no means of suicide – no pills, no nothing. Our group decided that our only hope in such an event was to try to take on a guard in hopes that they would kill us. That was the only way we felt it might be possible not to divulge those secrets because we wouldn't trust ourselves.'

Of seven RCAF radar technicians captured by the Japanese, Oss was the sole survivor at the time of AFTA's 60th Birthday in 1994; Ron Neal and Ed Goodchild died while prisoners-of-war, the others 'mainly due to the lasting effects of malnutrition, beatings and torture'. Ron's death was attributed to dysentery, malnutrition and beatings; Ed's death was recorded on the Japanese death certificate as being caused by bacillary dysentery though 'there is little doubt that death was brought on by the injuries he received at the hands of his captors' [7] [*see page 38*].

With Malaya, Singapore, the Netherlands East Indies and much of Burma gone by March 1942, the Allied front now stabilized along a great arc stretching from the southern Chinese province of Yunnan, along the Indo-Burmese border, through the Bay of Bengal to Ceylon, and then out across the Indian Ocean to Papua-New Guinea. Besides exercising air superiority along the whole of this arc, the Japanese also enjoyed a decisive naval superiority over the maritime portions of it. Recognizing this, Admiral Sir James Somerville 'handled his motley and mostly outdated fleet very cautiously and accepted that Ceylon, the key to the Indian Ocean, could best be defended by land-based air power' [8] .

A prime requirement for this form of defense to be effected was an adequate air reconnaissance capability to give early warning of any attack. To meet this need, # 413 Squadron, which had been employed on convoy protection duties off the Scottish coast, was ordered to Ceylon. The arrival of its first Catalinas at Koggala was fortuitous. On 4 April 1942, on their first patrol in this new theatre of operations and after a 12-hour flight, a crew with Squadron Leader L J Birchall its captain and pilot spotted Japanese ships on the southern horizon while returning to base. Closing in to try to identify the types and numbers, the flying boat was attacked by Japanese carrier-borne fighters and forced to put down on the sea. The crew managed to get a signal through to alert the Ceylon defenses and give Admiral Somerville time to get most of his ships out of the way [9] . As a result of the warning, when Japanese aircraft launched Pearl Harbour-style attacks on the naval bases at Colombo and Trincomalee the toll inflicted on the British Fleet was much less than if it had been caught unawares * . Those raids were the first and the last that the Japanese carried out against Ceylon.

In Burma, the fall of Rangoon had closed the only overland supply line to General Chiang Kai-Shek's Chinese Nationalist Army and paved the way for the Japanese to make a rapid advance which enabled them to occupy virtually the entire country by the end of March 1942. For the next two years the Allies' task would be to keep them from moving into India and this, coupled with the necessity to safeguard Ceylon, key to the Indian Ocean, created a Battle of Britain-like situation where there was a vital role for radar in warning of all enemy air activity. As Canadian radar technician Angus Hamilton notes in his book *Canadians on Radar in South East Asia, 1941-1945*, 'keeping dozens of radar stations on the air 24 hours a day, 7 days a week was not glamorous, but it was essential'. At one time or another, he states, there were Canadians on nearly all the ground radar stations in India and Ceylon.

It was March 1943 when Les Wood, 'along with a few hundred RAF types and three army regiments' reached Bombay, via Freetown and Durban, to serve as a radar technical officer on a number of ground stations. In fact his first assignment of all was quite unrelated to the war effort – it was 'to participate in welcoming the new Viceroy by lining the parade route to hold back the crowds'. He notes that everyone had 'issue' tropical kit with what he calls 'the customary tailored fit!' It was indeed, Les noted subsequently, 'a sorry-looking turnout' [10] .

In the same manner as Les Wood, personnel who were sourced from the UK to install and maintain those stations were mostly transported there by ship, initially involving an 11,000-mile voyage via West Africa and South Africa to Bombay and up to eight weeks at sea. However by mid-1943, when the Allies had trounced Rommel in North Africa, the shorter route via the Mediterranean was opened – though this was an option that put the convoys at considerable risk from air attacks. This was a hazard that was well demonstrated when, on 6 November 1943, the troopship *Marnix von Sint Aldegande* became the target for air-launched torpedoes. Don Reid recalled that when the ship righted itself after being struck by two torpedoes and the attackers were gone, 'the order came to proceed to boat stations.

> 'It was night and the sea looked black. While we were waiting for the order to abandon ship, one soldier decided to do it his way and jumped overboard. In due course, we each slid down a rope to a lifeboat and on to a destroyer. On the destroyer no-one mentioned our night out. One of their crew, still in his teens, on that strategic run to Malta, was listed as a survivor three times in one day [11] .'

---

* The toll was serious enough, Japanese bombers finding and sinking two cruisers which were at sea on 5 April and, four days later, an aircraft carrier also at sea. Squadron Leader Birchall was subsequently awarded the Distinguished Flying Cross for his 'timely warning', he and his crew having been hailed as the 'saviours of Ceylon' [12] .

Some weeks later, on Christmas Day 1943 to be exact, Mediterranean convoys were still under attack. Joe Brigham, putting his experiences on record for the Canadian Radar History Project, wrote:

> 'I sailed from Liverpool on the *Strathaird* and the convoy was torpedo-bombed by Luftwaffe aircraft from the south of France. They ignored the three troopships and went after the oil tankers, sinking three. RAF fighters from North Africa drove them off. The troops were all below decks during the attacks and were allowed on deck after the all clear. The oil tankers were sinking on the horizon behind us [13].'

Priority for ground radar stations to give early warning of incoming enemy bombers was accorded to Ceylon, which was strategically important, and to Calcutta, the main logistic and communication base for the support of the front line along the Burma border. However these stations could only demonstrate their real value when there were defending fighter aircraft to respond – more particularly during the hours of darkness – and it was not until the early days of 1943 that radar-equipped night fighters began reaching this theatre of operations. Then, on the night of 15 January 1943, with 'everything working according to the book', there took place 'the most dramatic accomplishment of radar in South East Asia [14]'.

Enemy raiders were detected approaching Calcutta, their presence revealed by blips on the radar screens of COL (Chain Overseas Low) stations. The GCI controller at Deganga vectored Beaufighters newly arrived at Dum Dum airport from Egypt, and one of these night fighters was responsible for the destruction of three of the four incoming Sally bombers in the space of four minutes, the fourth managing to escape though damaged [*] .

Four nights later there was another raid and again the detection and ground-controlled interception procedures worked without a hitch – the proof, if any were needed, that 'the warning network, the GCI unit and the radar-equipped night fighters could collaborate and make the investment in radar worthwhile. It would be months before the Japanese had the courage to mount another attack on Calcutta [15]'.

Eric Inch, who took over 224 AMES, installed it at Bhadrak, on the east coast of India, about 100 air miles south west of Calcutta, and had it operational in the closing weeks of 1942, remembers his unit being there 'just in time to be somewhat useful' during that short series of Japanese attacks on Calcutta around the New Year. Shortly after those raids there was a 'substantial exodus from Calcutta for a few weeks, as the terrified populace ran for cover.

> 'The trains through Bhadrak were jammed with people. One day, when some of the staff from my unit were at the railway station to meet the evening train, they saw a child of perhaps two clinging to the outside of the

---

[*] Radar technician Angus Hamilton, who had checked in at Dum Dum just two days earlier to join # 176 Squadron, notes that a flight of fully equipped Beaufighters 'with their well trained air and ground crews from 89 Squadron literally got 176 off to a flying start' with that hat trick performance [16]. It was a little over three weeks later that Angus moved with 176 from Dum Dum, the civilian airport at Calcutta, to Baigachi [see page 116].

train.   There was no evidence of parents, so the lads took him back to the unit and adopted him.   He was named Jackie Ames.   When I left the unit a year or so later, he was speaking well in a broad Scots accent.   Later I heard that when 224 AMES was decommissioned at the end of the war, the men took up a collection and had him admitted to an orphanage in Calcutta [17].'

With the immediate threat to Calcutta seemingly reduced, radar technicians Bob Young and Clive Roberts were transferred from Deganga, on the Ganges delta, eastwards to Kattali, outside Chittagong, expecting the posting to be to a similar GCI unit.   It turned out that the pair were the sole mechanics for a smaller and portable unit in a paddy field some distance from the main unit, linked to it by a land line. This was a posting not without its dramas: too close to enemy action for comfort, Clive once found himself a 'sitting duck' in the middle of that paddy field, a dozen or so fighters circling overhead, and nowhere to hide but a trench dug earlier to drain the water.   In less than no time he was in that trench, desperately trying to make it ever-deeper with his fingernails and staying there until all was quiet again.

Like Bob and Clive, many radar technicians in South East Asia were associated with these portable units; this pair knew them as 'Wigwams', because the equipment was set up in a special wigwam-like tent, though there were various other synonymous terms such as Portable RDF, Light Warning and Light Early Warning.   Some of these portable radar stations were set up ahead of, or complementary to, the permanent stations; more often, others were used in temporary situations where there was a particular requirement for mobility and improvisation, perhaps at short notice.

While Light Warning units were employed in other theatres of war, one form of theoretically mobile radar station that seems to have been used exclusively in South East Asia was the radar barge.   There were four operating as either GCI or COL stations and proved effective when in sheltered waters close to a supply base.   The 'down side' was their lack of propulsion, as a consequence of which radar technician Geoff Marples, when posted to one of them while it was still being fitted out at a shipyard in Calcutta, found that he was in for a 150-mile tow between the low-lying islands of the Ganges delta before reaching his operating site at Chittagong. Geoff's new floating home 'defied description'; it resembled a double-ended coal barge some 90 ft long and 20 ft wide, the crew's living quarters being reached by a vertical ladder through a manhole roughly 2 ft in diameter.   He explains:

'Here slept 22 men in double-decker bunks around the perimeter.   The boys in the top bunks had the occasional porthole which supplied the only air we had.   This sounds better than it really was in practice.

'We often thought you could have poked your thumbnail through the bottom of our ship but nobody ever had the nerve to try it.   It was obviously very thin, not much more than a layer of rust.   There was no way for 22 men to get up that ladder if the hull was punctured!   We left well enough alone. So, thankfully, did the Japs! [18].'

Geoff notes that presumably the idea of the radar barges was to give advance warning of air raids on India near their point of departure, as opposed to a point near their destination. The logic was never explained but, he muses, perhaps this earlier warning would 'give the RAF more time to scramble its ancient Hurricane fighters to fly them away from danger of attack by the faster Zeros, or give the Yanks time to break up the parade ground wingtip-to-wingtip parking pattern of their B-29s. We never knew.' It is nearer the truth (and doubtless rather more charitable!) to take the view that from Chittagong south along the Arakan coast, the mountains were so close to the shoreline that, without those barge-borne radar stations, it would have been impossible to pick up the presence of Japanese aircraft until they were almost over British bases such as Chittagong and Cox's Bazaar [19].

Certainly life on a radar barge seems not to have been lacking in drama...

Harold Northover, at 47 'probably the daddy of all Canadian radio mechanics' and in command of a radar barge which was for three months 'the most advanced unit on the whole Arakan front', nearly drifted ashore one night where certain capture awaited him, the Japanese being only four miles away [20].

It appears that Harold and some of his men were in a small supply boat, returning to the barge, when a break occurred in their engine's feed system. The problem was fixed by siphoning petrol from the tank into a can, puncturing the bottom of the can and placing it directly over the carburetor. Though the boat was almost aground by this time, they nonetheless managed to get back to the barge undetected.

For those on board another of these radar barges, AMES 8514, two incidents were prominent: a hurricane that forced the crew to evacuate – the barge dragging its anchor for some five miles – and picking up their first 'hostile' at 75 miles on the radar, a Spitfire being directed towards it and claiming a 'kill'.

Radar stations that were sited on dry land could sometimes find themselves in the very midst of battle, being put in such a plight because the nearer the frontline, the more productive their function. A classic example is what happened to AMES 857, a mobile GCI in the Imphal Valley in March 1944 during the period when the Japanese were making a determined effort to trap and seize the British forces. As a turning point in the war in South East Asia, the bitter struggle to control the Imphal Valley has been likened in significance to that of the Battle of El Alamein in the Middle East campaign and to the Battle of the Bulge in North West Europe.

In a graphic and exhaustive account for the Canadian Radar History Project, Jack Wadham, who was posted to AMES 857 at Buri Bazar, some eight miles from Imphal in November 1943, highlights nine successful interceptions controlled by this unit during the battle, the compulsion to re-locate from one site because 'the Army couldn't stop Jap patrols breaking through and they couldn't give protection' and the knowledge that some of the fighting was 'not more than half a mile away'. Then, in a diary note for 23 May 1944...

'Stood-to all night; some shelling and machine gun fire at intervals throughout the night. Off duty 0730; went to bed. Air alert 1230. Heavy mortar, machine gun and artillery fire at the hill half mile down the road

continued all afternoon.   Some tanks went into action – watched them
through my telescope – the reports echoing and re-echoing through the
valley.   Had another snooze in pm; did two hours guard, 2130 to 2330, and
to bed.   Some mortar and machine gun fire and a few flares.   We received
a company of Army and three tanks for reinforcements [21].'

Elsewhere the war was proceeding apace: the Italian capital was in Allied hands on
4 June 1944 and two days later Allied troops were landing in Normandy; the safety of
Leningrad and the opening of the Gulf of Finland to the Russian Fleet were assured;
and on 21 June the US 8th Air Force made its first 'shuttle raid' between Britain and
bases in Russia, bombing oil refineries south of Berlin.   In India, though, despite
encouraging progress, on 23 June 1944 there came orders to close down the GCI
unit on which Jack Wadham was serving and to get ready to move.   Jack was 'pretty
busy as I was the senior mech on station at the time'.   The new site was about four
miles away and near the Tulihal air strip.   There was, he wrote, 'quite a
concentration of Japs around now, over 1,000 in the hills'.   In this new fast-changing
situation, it was by early July 'very quiet here, hard to realize there is a war on'.
There was even a liberty run to a mobile cinema at Tulihal strip – 'the first show of
any kind we have had a chance to see for six months', though he does not indicate
what was showing.

Airborne supplies had sustained the British forces until the supply road could be
opened on 22 June 1944 and the Japanese were 'forced to speed up their
withdrawal in the difficult conditions of the monsoon rains.   In the long campaign to
penetrate into India they have lost 30,000 men [22] '.   The battle was over – the first
major Allied victory in South East Asia – and for AMES 857 there was a
congratulatory message from Lord Louis Mountbatten, Supreme Commander, in
recognition of the unit's good work.   For the men and the equipment of AMES 857 it
must have been the narrowest of shaves...

Where Jack Wadham was in the thick of the action and at times just a few hundred
yards from the enemy, a fellow Canadian radar technician, Neil Turnbull, spent two
months in charge of a Light Warning unit, AMES 6181, which was sited in a jungle
clearing in the heart of enemy-held territory.   Having been flown into an improvised
landing strip named 'Broadway', from which Major-General Orde Wingate's Chindits
conducted their guerrilla warfare expeditions, it was Neil's job on arrival to erect new
gear to replace American equipment that had been destroyed by fire as a result of an
air raid.

The recommendation documentation for the BEM awarded to Neil on 1 January
1945 points to the results obtained when the replacement Light Warning equipment
was first sited falling short of the standard that he and his four operators expected.
So the equipment was dismantled and moved to a new site – a location which then
came under heavy attack, to the extent that the Gurkha guard was overwhelmed and
the unit compelled to evacuate.

When surrounded, for about a week, in Neil's own words 'the Army called in some
British dive-bombers and I was afraid they were going to hit us because there were
only a hundred yards between the Japs and us – but it chased the Japs out.   When I
got my equipment back I expected it to be destroyed.   The Japs had occupied the

site the radar was on – they slashed the seats the operators sat on and bent some dipoles and left the rest of it. I guess they didn't know what they had [23] '.

Neil Turnbull's award recommendation states that, when able to reconnoiter the area and inspect the equipment, he decided that the chosen site was good from a technical point of view, afforded good camouflage cover from the air and was in a location ensuring greater protection from enemy ground forces. It was 'to his credit that the equipment remained operational until the airstrip was abandoned', the radar unit being loaded on the last aircraft to be flown out from this behind-the-lines hotspot.

Radar technicians responsible for installing and maintaining airborne equipment were often able to travel to their South East Asia posting in the aircraft of the squadron on which they served; Joe Soper, for instance, arrived at Koggala, Ceylon, in the first of # 413 Squadron's Catalinas to leave the UK, complete with a skeleton ground crew. Another was Les Tozer, who joined # 240 Squadron, also equipped with Catalinas, when it was based in Northern Ireland; he moved with the squadron to Madras in the same month as Joe did with his squadron, March 1942. Les says of those early days:

> 'At times we would be very busy and have to work long hours when there was a panic on, but most of the time we were waiting for something to happen.

> 'Our other main duty was acting as guards for our equipment 24 hours a day and at times we'd have to guard it in shipment to other locations. Radar equipment had to be guarded by radar personnel; to guard our repair section one of us would sleep there all night. The other sections of the squadron were guarded by Indian troops.

> 'At times we would have a chance to fly as radar operators, especially during a panic or when testing new ideas or new equipment [24] .'

South East Asia-bound, Doug Gooderham flew only part-way in a Liberator, for which he was probably grateful. This was the first leg of his journey and when he was on the tarmac, in a group walking out to the aircraft, 'it was clear that our status was somewhere between "General Cargo" and "Jettisonable Cargo". In the bomb bay we were carefully stowed on some wide shelves with three small mattresses, sleeping bags, some blankets and a few chocolate bars. As the doors folded up to entomb us I tried not to think about the possibility of a wheels-up landing [25] '. After a day of rest in Cairo, he continued in an Imperial Airways flying boat to Karachi and Gwalior, thence by train to New Delhi to report to the Command Radar Officer at Air HQ India. He would become one of the most senior radar men in this theatre of war…

Flying boats such as the Catalina and the Sunderland obviously required maintenance staff to go out to them by boat. This was not the only difference, though, between them and land-based aircraft such as the Liberator, which was used in South East Asia for activities as diverse as long-range bombing, mine-laying and supply-drops to guerrilla forces, one such sortie entering the record books as the longest undertaken by a Liberator in South East Asia during the war. It was flown from Ceylon on 31 July 1945 by a largely Canadian crew of # 160 Squadron and lasted 24 hours and 10 minutes [26] .

Ed Bastedo, who was on Catalina and Liberator squadrons while stationed in South East Asia, makes some interesting comparisons between the radar servicing aspect of the Catalinas, which were his responsibility on 240 Squadron in Madras, and the Liberators of 160 Squadron in Ceylon. In Madras, a reservoir/lake provided the necessary water area for the Catalinas; it was 'not as corrosive as salt water but, arriving as I did right at the beginning of the monsoon season, we immediately encountered the problems that high humidity and high temperatures inevitably cause with electronic equipment [27] '. Referring to flying boats in general, Ed said:

> 'Aerials required close checking and care since splashing water, especially salt water, was always present; heat and humidity, especially in the tropics, affected not only aerials but also cables which we had to megger daily to ensure there were no electrical or signal leaks. Also with flying boats, which were almost always moving in the water, it was next to impossible to have any fixed target to check that the target distances were correct, hence the need for us to go on test flights.

> 'We had much more sophisticated sets on the Liberator, the radar antenna being located in a blister, or radome. The set had a much improved magnetron as a signal generator. It also continually rotated through 360 degrees so that the targets could be picked up in any direction. The tilt, up and down, of the antenna was also controllable by the operator so that a very definite "fix" could be made and relative bearing given to the pilot.

> 'Maintenance on these sets was more frequent and time-consuming than the old ASV. There were more component breakdowns and much more failure in the wiring systems running between the antenna set location; this latter was generally due to breakdown between wires due to the humidity of the tropics. Multiple wires were carried in one conduit and the daily megger test between lines was necessary.'

In his final posting, Ed Bastedo could have been judged as now having 'the best of both worlds'... it was to # 321 Squadron, a Dutch squadron based at China Bay, Trincomalee, which had been flying amphibious Catalinas and was then in the process of converting to Liberators.

Bill Barrie, Senior NCO at the radar workshops at Korangi Creek, near Karachi, from November 1942 to July 1944, recalls Catalina flying boats from that base carrying out convoy escort duties into the Persian Gulf; surveillance duties in the Arabian Gulf and the northern Indian Ocean; air-sea rescue work; and, due to this aircraft's extreme range capability, dropping supplies and agents into enemy-held territories. He describes one patrol where 'we took off from the blistering hot dusty desert and headed out into the Arabian Gulf...

> 'Normal altitude was about 3,000 feet but along the coastline we stayed at about 100 feet above some of the most barren rocky ground in the world.

The purpose of low flying was to look for signs of ships or submarine supply activity.   So low were we over one of the small native boats that the startled crew jumped overboard like frogs from a log.   Further on, a goatherd threw a stone at us for scattering his herd.   He missed! [28]'

A refueling stop on the coast of Oman provided the crew with a break of a few hours before the return flight.   Bill noted that 'not every flight enjoyed as successful a working radar but having personally made up the beacon and its antenna I was pleased that the Yagi antennas on this particular Catalina were able to guide us directly back to Korangi Creek after an absence of 17 hours'.

Besides ASV, which enabled the flying boats to pick up the presence of enemy shipping, and AI, a means of helping night fighters to hunt down enemy bombers, South East Asia radar technicians were concerned in the main with IFF, to identify friend from foe when an aircraft trace appeared on a radar screen, and with the combination airborne Rebecca/ground-based Eureka system.   This was a beacon facility for pinpoint navigation and to ensure the accurate location of dropping zones when personnel and supplies were to be landed by parachute; drops like this were critical when so often there was no other way to send vital provisions over great distances.

There were times when the unquestionably beneficial attributes of the Rebecca/Eureka combination were ignored even though available and intended for use: the Rebecca equipment installed and functioning in the aircraft, Eureka beacons positioned on the ground and all set to respond.   For a while in the winter of 1944/45, Angus Hamilton served with # 52 Squadron, a transport squadron with Rebecca-equipped DC-3s, flying out of Dum Dum, where his billet was in Lord Clive's old summer house.   It was once his job to go over 'The Hump' in one of those DC-3s to Kunming [then the Chinese Nationalist Headquarters] to 'check the beacon', his conclusion being that 'so far as we could determine the air crew on 52 Squadron never used the Rebecca receivers'. All their flights were between well-established airports and the crews were comfortable 'flying the beam'.   On another occasion Angus went on one of their 'skeds' [scheduled flights] to Bombay and 'despite my entreaties they never looked at the Rebecca equipment [29] '.   Certainly Rebecca/Eureka had its uses, being at times indispensable for the squadrons dropping supplies to the Chindits and other 'behind-the-lines' units in Burma, but in that particular theatre of war, in Angus's view, 'it was of no interest to other crews'.

Asset or otherwise, it is easy to overlook the commitment necessary for positioning those Eureka transponder homing beacons.   On occasions the beacon would be in use for merely a brief period, perhaps to guide-in an aircraft on a lone mission, but there were times when a more lasting location was essential, maybe for a repetitive application.   One of the radar technicians responsible for placing a number of them, Bill Hilborn, recalls that each installation presented its own unique problems and local laborers were hired as required.   He remembers:

'At one site the beacon was to be installed in a bomb-proof reinforced concrete building.   A mason was hired to drill a hole in the wall for the aerial leads.   He, in turn, produced a large star drill, a large hammer and a small labourer to do the work   The concrete was over a foot thick and reinforced with very hard crushed gravel. The poor laborer pounded away for hours before breaking through.

'In another case, on an aerodrome, we decided to install the beacon in the control tower building. We consulted with the Indian "Works and Bricks" officer, who agreed to lay on a crew to do the work. I was a little surprised the next morning when about a dozen laborers and tradesmen showed up. There was a man to dig holes and about three women to carry the dirt away in pans on their heads. There was a carpenter, a mason, an electrician, an iron worker and, of course, a foreman. We must have doubled the local payroll for the day. But the work was beautifully done, a joy to behold and I got a big smile from each worker as they passed me [30]'.

Despite the fact that radar technicians posted to units in this theatre of operations had undergone their specialist training beforehand on the appropriate radar or radars and that facilities existed for further training on the ground stations and on the squadrons, eventually a South East Asia radar school came into being at Bangalore in the autumn of 1943. Al Brown, formerly an instructor at Yatesbury and Cranwell, arrived to find construction in progress and an 'army of coolies swarming about the place'. They were, he noted, 'a typical lot consisting of almost equal numbers of men and women doing the same work, carrying the same loads and equally industrious'.

Paying tribute to the strength and stamina of Indian laborers, he recalled an incident at his first stop in India when the new arrivals were told to carry their kitbags the half-mile or so to the camp from the point where a lorry had dropped them. He noted that...

'A little man, barely five feet tall and weighing not more than 100 lbs offered to carry the bag for me for two annas, about four cents at that time. I agreed happily and he lifted the bag effortlessly to his shoulder. But then he asked for another bag, which one of my buddies supplied. He now had a bag on each shoulder, the total probably equal to his body weight. By this time we were all sure he was over-estimating his strength and endurance, but someone supplied a third bag that was put on his head. He then started off for the distant camp at a dog trot and we unladen bag owners had a hard time keeping up with him. That was the first and only time I questioned anyone's ability to perform any physical task he volunteered to do [31].'

Once the new school was functioning, Al recalls that the classes varied widely in both numbers and type of students, averaging perhaps 50 per cent Indian with a majority of the non-Indians being officers on refresher courses. It was his view that many of the Indian students 'seemed to be entering a completely unfamiliar field'. That, plus working in a second language, must have made the classes very difficult for them. Nevertheless, he said, 'many did well'.

A radar servicing and maintenance organization in India became imperative too and this included Base Signals Depots (BSDs); these evolved from Base Signals Units via Radio Installation and Maintenance Units. Len Tozer, having been posted from

240 Squadron to # 5 BSD in Calcutta in May 1944, makes a striking comparison between the RAF's and the Americans' approach to coping with the inescapable 'hiccups' that occurred with IFF sets. He said that...

'We had the opportunity to meet American airmen through softball and other contacts. The Americans too had a radar repair depot in Calcutta but one American pilot who was concerned with the efficiency of his IFF asked if I would check it if he brought it to our section. Permission was easily obtained. A short time later he was back with another set to check and I asked why he didn't take it to his own service depot; he said "There is too much red tape in getting it checked".

'Sometime later I was asked to do some instructing on IFFs at the American depot; when I went to take the cans off the gear the sergeant told me I wasn't allowed to do that because it was secret equipment. My response was "How do you repair it?"; his answer was that he didn't – they were only supposed to change sets and adjust them. No wonder their sets were not being triggered! Here was a pilot walking around with a set under his arm and the mechanics weren't allowed to open it!

'I might add that I found the American sets very unstable and harder to adjust for maximum range than the English sets. The English sets were more reliable too [32].'

By 1943, air operations had improved as 'more up-to-date aircraft, better equipment and maintenance, and increased experience, enabled the Allied air forces to fly more regularly and maintain a greater intensity of effort, despite the monsoon weather' [33] . Nevertheless, logistics would pose one of the greatest problems confronting the planners charged with instituting an effective Allied counter-offensive to recover Burma.

When, in early 1943, a concerted British and American offensive started in South East Asia, there was a gradual change in the RAF's needs in keeping with the heartening switch in emphasis from defense to attack. Heavy bomber squadrons came on the scene and in time, particularly in 1944, the turning tide brought about some movement of radar technicians from one role to another, for instance from night fighter and submarine patrol squadrons to the transport squadrons. The role of the radar ground stations altered too in the course of time, becoming 'somewhat like a modern air traffic control system. Many more Allied aircraft would have been lost had not the radar network been there to guide them to a serviceable airfield [34] '.

Although the significance is not to be exaggerated, on one occasion a number of radar technicians were taken right away from their specialist activities. It became a prerequisite to undertake an ingenious scheme aimed at tackling chronic unserviceability in COL and GCI equipment; this was being put down to the high temperatures and humidity. Doug Gooderham [*] , head of Radar Staff on the RAF and USAAF formations that provided air defense in Bengal, Assam and the Burma

---

[*] The highest ranking Canadian officer on radar in Eastern Air Command, Douglas Gooderham received the OBE in April 1945 and six months later the US Bronze Star.

Front, tells this story, recounting how the problem was solved first by a 'quick-fix' and then by lowering the humidity of the environment by means of window-type air conditioners. Therein, though, lay the snag...

> 'Very few of these [*air conditioners*] could be purchased in Calcutta and it became necessary to requisition from affluent citizens. Selection of suitable machines and their subsequent installation and maintenance required skills not taught to any RAF tradesman at that time. Fortunately we found a number of radar mechs who had had experience with air conditioners in their civil vocations – all of them turned out to be RCAF. Flight Sergeant Bud Porter was one of those who were involved in this project from its inception. The need for these special skills remained even after the troublesome items of equipment were modified; the stifling conditions that otherwise prevailed in crowded GCI vans called for at least some air conditioning if controllers and their supporting operators were to be efficient. These vans retained and used their air conditioners as long as the radar unit remained in service [35].'

For all who served there, India was a country of startling contrasts. Don Munro, based in Calcutta from November 1943 to March 1945, provides a vivid illustration when, touching upon the then squalor of that city, he observes that there was indeed remarkable beauty to be seen in India. There was in Calcutta 'the enormity of the Banyan trees in the Botanical Gardens – a sight to behold', in Darjeeling 'the tea plantations rising from the plains for 6,000 feet' and 'from Tiger Hill, the sight of Kanchenjunga rising 28,208 feet like a blue diamond as the tropical moon rose over the Burmese Hills. Travel and leaves like that still flash back in one's mind [36]'. Don was another, though, who would never forget the calamitous impact of 'the ever-present dysentery, malaria, dengue fever, skin diseases and a hundred other plagues running rampant' among Allied servicemen in India. In June 1944, in a unit with 528 personnel, in excess of 400 were, he said, in hospital with dysentery, malaria or dengue.

Some spending time in India, like Jim Partridge, took the trouble to try to learn the Urdu language – 'the military patois used to communicate with the native people of all races and religions in the sub continent [37]'. Sometimes, however, actual or feigned ignorance of a means of verbal communication was perhaps a wiser course. For example, Jim was travelling across country in an ancient train for hours on end 'when we came to a halt in the middle of nowhere.

> 'As we peered out at the desolate landscape, there arose from the ditches and out of the scrub desert hillocks the scruffiest band of savages I'd ever seen. They were Pathans wearing multi-layers of raggedy clothes and carrying long, old-fashioned rifles, home-made swords and staves six feet long. One of them broke away and approached our carriage asking for alms, money, food or what have you. I tried to tell him, in my limited Urdu, that some urchins had already been to us and we had given them all our change. .

> 'I explained that we were not Burrah Sahibs [*important people*] but there would be some on the next train. He ran to the leader of this band of

brigands, a tall, fierce-looking, hawk-like man, who – upon hearing this story – turned to his men and, waving his huge rifle, urged them all towards our carriage.

'I thought we had had it! With that, the train whistle blew and we started to move. They, too, started to move, running alongside us until we gained speed. What did I do wrong to irritate these characters? I guess the lesson was to keep my mouth shut unless I knew what I was saying and to whom I was saying it. This was just one of the many lessons I learned in my tour of duty in India...'

By the time the atomic bomb had brought about the Japanese surrender and with it the end of WWII, radar-based aids had had a part to play in a range of functions in the metamorphosis from the dark days when this was an imperiled region to those when there was, at last, the scent of victory. In one way or another, radar was seen to be an indispensable tool: detecting incoming bombers, ground-controlled fighter-interception, submarine-spotting, confirming that an aircraft was friend and not foe, as well as employment as a homing device for any number of applications. Angus Hamilton [*], who has made a considerable and greatly detailed study of the subject for the Canadian Radar History Project, answers his own question as to whether or not radar was 'worthwhile' in South East Asia. He points out that radar is most useful in defense against attack from the air; in this theatre of operations, however, after the battle lines were drawn in mid-1942, there were no air attacks comparable to those during the Battle of Britain, thus a similar opportunity for radar to prove its value did not present itself. In South East Asia, in time, the Allies were able to achieve almost complete control of the air and here radar did make 'a significant contribution' towards that achievement. Air superiority, in turn, helped the Army to win its battles on the ground and hence to drive the Japanese forces out of Burma. So, 'yes, radar in South East Asia *was* worthwhile' [38].

---

[*] Accepted as a radar mechanic in the RCAF in April 1941, Angus Hamilton spent most of his time in South East Asia on # 176 Squadron, which flew Beaufighters (and even, for a short time, AI-equipped Hurricanes); post-war he became chairman of the Department of Surveying Engineering at the University of New Brunswick and a Professor Emeritus there from 1987. Since retiring from full-time employment in 1986 he has pursued 'a long-suppressed interest' in history.

CHAPTER 10: ON THE CONTINENT

In the countdown to the Allied invasion of Europe and in the south-east corner of Britain especially, # 60 Group found itself once more in the front line against the forces of Nazi Germany; first there was a return to a much earlier form of weaponry, then a taste of newer ones that were more sophisticated in their concept and more ruthless in their intent.   Using the last of his big-gun ammunition in vicious cross-Channel artillery barrages against the Dover area, the enemy endangered several of the Group's installations; while the appearance of the V1 'flying bomb' and the menace of the V2 supersonic rocket posed new problems for operational personnel and others inside and outside the Group who were working to combat these latest threats.   In January 1944, Swingate suffered RAF and WAAF casualties, some of them fatal, with further shelling taking place in February, March and September; several other stations were attacked by aircraft and in one particularly tragic incident, 1 airman was killed and 5 airmen and 4 airwomen injured at Rye when a Bofors shell from British guns fell in B Site, damaging the barrack hut and guard room [1] .   Swingate's ordeal was relieved only when the enemy gun emplacements were captured by advancing Allied troops in September 1944... but then came the unwelcome novelty of V1s launched from the air, above the North Sea, bringing the east coast chain an added challenge that was successfully met [2] .

It might have been assumed that the influx of radar personnel which began early in 1941 would have been enough, by mid-1944, to have eased the manpower situation. This was not so: the records show that, in fact, 60 Group was still in dire need of more radar mechanics and – since it appeared that sufficient numbers were unavailable elsewhere – the only alternative would be to find them within its own ranks.   In a Memorandum to the Headquarters of 70, 73, 75 and 78 Wings, the Air Officer Commanding 60 Group wrote on 16 June 1944 that 'if this Group is fully to implement its responsibilities both   in connection with the manning of the Home Chain and in the formation of crews for overseas, *it is of paramount importance that 360 operators be remustered to mechanics within this group by 31 August 1944.* From the training point of view this is unquestionably the greatest contribution to the war effort that Wings can make at the present time [3] [*],.

As occurred in most branches of the armed services, changes in the method of training tradesmen and women were proposed and introduced from time to time. For example in April 1944, in respect of radar mechanics, TRE put forward some ideas to the Director-General of Signals that proceeded up the chain of command to Air Ministry with a recommendation for their implementation.   It was suggested that radar mechanics should be trained 'not in one or two specific equipments but in such a way that they could reasonably be expected to work on any equipment'.   The

---

[*] For added emphasis, this document used capital letters for each word in the entire phrase printed here in italics.

trained mechanic 'should be able to find his way about a new radar set, if given a circuit diagram and a few setting up instructions. He should be able to make it work, test it on daily inspection and diagnose, locate and repair straightforward faults. He need not understand the detailed working of the set [4] '. The proposed aim should be to turn out radar mechanics with a sound basic knowledge who would then be readily capable of assimilating the detailed knowledge of individual equipments, 'perhaps with the assistance of some form of instruction in Commands'. There was agreement that the then 24-week *ab initio* course was desirable, with a radar principles course for all radar mechanics of 10 weeks' duration; on its completion, mechanics would be divided into RM (Ground) and RM (Air) and to do a further period on the practical aspect using representative equipments. In a later stage of those proposals, the 10-week course was replaced by one of 8 weeks with subsequent additional training of 1 to 2 weeks for selected persons. A training procedure of that sort would 'greatly facilitate manning and posting problems' -to quote a letter to Air Ministry from the Director-General of Signals on 27 April 1944.

With the Oboe ground-controlled bombing system particularly, much effort was directed towards the creation of mobile equipment and the training of personnel to use it.

Transferring from Treen to Bawdsey shortly after D-Day, to work on an Oboe mobile station on a cliff outside the gates of Bawdsey Manor, where much of Britain's early work on radar had taken place, Harry Carlyle notes that 'our arrival was coincidental with two events: the huge CH aerial towers being lit with red lights to warn returning bombers to keep a safe distance and the arrival of V1 flying bombs, which prompted an anti-aircraft battery being situated behind us to shoot them down. Our station was thus in a very precarious position. The locals blamed the whole scenario on us, reckoning it was our warning lights that were attracting Jerry's new weapon in our direction, and for a while we seemed to be distinctly unwelcome – particularly in the local pub [5] '.

An incident unrelated either to the warning lights or to the ack-ack guns may well have been responsible for making the arrival of this Oboe mobile station equally unwelcome to the RAF and civilian occupants of Bawdsey Manor. Harry explains that this being a mobile station, it was necessary for crew members to be able to drive, adding that 'for those who couldn't drive, the British School of Motoring was engaged to train them. As a consequence of one of the driving lessons, where one of our airmen was under instruction in a three-ton Bedford lorry, he managed to knock down the pillared gates of Bawdsey Manor... whereupon I was reprimanded and informed that in some seven or eight years, every conceivable type of RAF vehicle had entered those gates yet in no more than two weeks we had managed to knock them down!'

Wally Tanner, an RAF Corporal proud to claim founder membership of AMES 102, which he joined at Worth Matravers on 1 March 1944, staying with them until 6 June 1946, gives an insight into those early days before this unit launched into what he describes as 'some very exciting adventures in many countries'. He notes:

'It was quite a small unit in the beginning, only 11 of us, the others being the CO, known to us as 'Mac' [Phil Macdonald, a Canadian and a Flying Officer at that time]; Dave, the Sergeant Mechanic, who was Welsh; Sam, the Corporal, a Londoner; three other mechanics – Jim from Canada and two Scots, Bill and Gordon; my fellow radar operators, Alan and Cliff, both of them English; an MT Fitter, another 'Mac'; and our cook, Frankie, who came from Wakefield, complete with a broad Yorkshire accent.   All the radar personnel had come from various stations on the Home Chain and some had several years' service.   As the equipment would be in vans and we were to be highly mobile, the purpose of sending us to Worth Matravers was to teach us to drive.   One morning, without much ado, I am seated behind the wheel of a three-ton lorry with a Corporal Instructor alongside me.   Although able to ride motorcycles and drive cars, handling a bigger vehicle was a new experience.   We set off round the Dorset roads but soon ran into a problem, to be precise a Canadian Armored Division, with some of the biggest tanks I had ever seen.   To say that I was apprehensive would be a gross understatement and on one occasion the Corporal was so nervous that he leaned across and took over the steering of the lorry, which did nothing for my confidence.   However I managed to avoid hitting the tanks, and vice versa, but time ran out before I could finish the course [6] .'

One incident stood out while doing final training and their technical site was a field alongside the road from Much Wenlock to Broseley in Shropshire.   With the help of a civilian scientist from TRE, AMES 102 duly tested its radar equipment once again, only to find an indignant RAF Group Captain arriving to complain that their radar transmissions were affecting the blind landing system at his airfield some miles away.   Wally recalls his CO saying that 'we were acting under Air Ministry orders' and somehow, it seems, 'the matter was resolved amicably'.   Shortly afterwards, while at Cardington in the knowledge that the unit would be going abroad – 'but to where, nobody knew' – Wally's CO was given special leave to get married on 6 July 1944.   The couple had met at Rame Head, near Plymouth, when Phil was Technical Officer there and Janet was i/c Ops.   She remained there up to and after D-Day 'but Phil wasn't allowed to enter our zone because of the continuing D-Day movement restrictions, so we went home to North Wales to be married on a 48-hour pass [7] '.

The posting took AMES 102 by air to Gibraltar – a bitterly cold flight lasting eight hours through the night with the RAF Dakota transport plane so tightly packed with their equipment that there was room only for four members of the radar crew (the CO, Alan, Cliff and Wally), all having to position themselves on top of the crates where a minimal amount of space remained between them and the roof.   Next day the aircraft and crew, with their load and their passengers, continued to an airfield near Rome for an overnight stop before the two aircraft designated to carry all the equipment and all the crew completed their final leg, taking them to the Mediterranean island of Corsica [*see page 84*].

Where Phil Macdonald and his unit were off to the Mediterranean, Fred Mullen and his unit were off to Normandy…

Postings were a 'lottery' in the Services in wartime, with an airman or an NCO who was expecting to go to such-and-such an outpost in, say, the Outer Hebrides, finding himself island-hopping by the fastest available means to take up the same duties in another equally remote bastion of Britain's radar chain.   Rank made no difference:

Fred, who was introduced to radar when sent to join RCAF Radio Course # 2 at the University of Saskatchewan in January 1942, was 'slated' for North Africa when at Renscombe Downs as a technical officer in March 1943 (following service on the CH station at Staxton Wold, near Scarborough) and he finished up with a mobile CHL unit at Chigwell in Essex. His eventual overseas posting from the UK came when he joined the 2nd Tactical Air Force's holding area at Old Sarum in the wake of D-Day, landing on Omaha Beach (by now well cleared of the enemy!) in July 1944 in an LST operated by the Royal Navy. That arrival on French soil was to be one of Fred's lasting memories – 'waiting for the tide to go out and driving off the landing craft down the steep ramp of two narrow LJ channels'.

Like many who were there, Fred can recount a series of 'almosts' occurring while on the Continent of Europe: times when his radar unit was almost hit by a crash-landing aircraft on a French airfield near Lille, almost hit by a V1 flying bomb intended for Antwerp and almost hit by a V2 rocket, also while at Lille. This latter incident was 'unnerving, this first encounter with what we knew by the code name "Big Ben" during our briefings, feeling the explosive force before the sound arrived'. There was no 'almost' about one episode where, undoubtedly un-typical among radar people, he took a German prisoner one night... He explains:

> 'I had moved my radar unit off the airfield at Lille because it seemed too dangerous and there was no operational need for us to be there; we were in transit up north. Astutely I posted a guard to secure our convoy and later that night he saw a suspicious individual checking one of the vehicles. Our guard yelled out just the one word "Halt" in a deep voice which confused the intruder. He then took this unknown as a prisoner, only to be attacked with a knife. Smartly he was able to disarm the prisoner without shooting.

> 'This unknown turned out to be a German soldier who had been left behind and was looking for transportation. The single command "Halt" had sounded like the German *"Halt"*, which confused the prisoner in those precious first seconds. This was certainly an excellent performance on the part of the security guard, for he was an airman trained as a radar mechanic not as a specialist in security. The prisoner was hand-tied and delivered to the local British Army, who could hardly believe this incident [8] .'

Fred's 75-man CHL unit included a Type 15, a Type 11 and a Type 14, plus the customary diesel power units and so on, which comprised as many as 30 vehicles and required 3 LSTs from the Royal Navy to convey the entire radar unit to the shores of Normandy. The vehicles had been waterproofed to cope with transit through four or five feet of sea water between disembarking and reaching dry land; however there was less urgency than would have been the case in the earlier stages of the invasion so the unit could afford to wait for the tide to go out in order to give a relatively dry landing, thereby preserving their vehicles.

To help secure the bridges taken by the airborne landings at Nijmegen and Arnhem, in September 1944 Fred's radar unit was quickly assigned to Nijmegen, travelling up a narrow corridor that British armored units had punched through, setting up their equipment on a site between the Grave bridge and the Nijmegen bridge. While operating there to protect those bridges, a Type 13 (radar height finder) was added to the unit to radar-control the RAF's night fighters more efficiently when patrolling the sector.

An occasion in late October 1944 illustrates the sort of situation which could develop so quickly and become so dangerous in wartime. Darkness was falling when Fred was returning to the radar site near Nijmegen from a visit to HQ and the time had come for a rest stop. He goes on:

> 'It was pitch black and quiet when I heard clicking noises and rustling in the ditch beside the road. In split-second thinking, I feared I must have made a mistake, managed to take a wrong turning and I was now in German territory – an understandable error with only very limited headlights on our vehicle. I was desperately considering what to do – make a run for it, surrender or what. But no one shot at us so I waited a little longer and then decided that this was the moment to identify ourselves. After what seemed like an eternity, an English voice replied, torchlights were beamed on us and we found ourselves surrounded. After checking us, the British Army lieutenant in charge explained that his unit had heard people talking in a strange accent – obviously my Canadian accent – and this had alerted them to what was assumed to be an infiltrating group of Germans. They were about to fire on the three of us but then they heard a Scottish accent so they relaxed. They knew that no German could imitate *that* accent so fortunately we had been saved by the presence of a Scot among us.
> . Whew!'

One evening in late November 1944, while Fred's unit was still at Nijmegen, its Type 13 radar height finder failed one evening, the flexible wave guide having burned out and there was no spare. This was a critical component and the unit's consequent inability to operate its equipment had a demoralizing effect on the crew. HQ was put in the picture immediately, by radio, and the crew sloped off to bed 'feeling down', amid mutterings about how the war could be won with such a shortage of spares. Next morning, bright and early, a motor cycle roared up, its rider handing an astonished Fred a replacement flexible wave guide! Evidently a spare had been flown over from England during the night, Fred explaining that 'we had been rated # 1 priority, due to our strategic position'. How was that for a morale booster?

The months of November and December, 1944, were bitterly cold with the temperature plummeting to minus 15 degrees Centigrade – 'There was a four-inch thickness of ice on a nearby pond; we were living in tents, sleeping with our clothes on, using blow torches to thaw the water tanker and eating our meals wearing gloves – but at least we avoided sickness and frostbite'. The New Year brought a move into Belgium where, with the unit located on the airport at Brussels and controlling night fighters, there was 'some comfort at last' when billets were found 'in a real building'.

In February '45, with the Allies going all-out to build-up supplies via the port of Antwerp, Fred was transferred to another radar unit at Breda; this put him in 'Doodle Bug Alley', the pathway to Antwerp for a saturated approach by the Germans to overwhelm the port defenses. He goes on:

'Our radar unit was able to plot these V1s (and identify them as propellerless planes) sometimes 20 or 30 at a wave. We would then pass on the flight path and altitude to anti-aircraft units which by now had accurate short range radar to aim their guns. These ack-ack guns were shooting down almost every one of those "Doodle Bugs" – very, very few got through to the outskirts of Antwerp. Unfortunately for me, one of them came down around 6:00 am, close to our unit, and I awoke with the explosion. Plaster and glass were falling around me and I felt my face bleeding – but I could wiggle my toes and fingers so I got up and scrambled outside.   Luckily my facial cuts were not serious and the blankets had protected the remainder of my body.'

Returning to the UK, Fred served out his time at places as far north as Stromness, Scapa Flow and Ronaldsay.   That spring and summer, he says, rather than their opposite numbers in the RAF, RCAF personnel were manning an increasing number of radar stations 'because the RAF were sending their people to the Pacific war zone whereas many Canadians were due for repatriation and therefore became ideal candidates to be moved around Britain willy-nilly in the interim period'.

For people in the UK, V1s were by then 'old hat'; the first to be directed against England were launched just one week after D-Day, in the early hours of 13 June 1944.   One carried on as far as London, where the distinctive 'putt-putt' of its engine ceased and the two-ton, 26 ft long cigar-shaped missile began its silent earthwards glide, claiming the first 6 of the eventual 6,000 lives lost to this initial 'vengeance weapon'.

For Allan Paull, Signals Officer at # 15 Maintenance Unit, RAF Station, Wroughton, near Swindon, where the Royal Navy's Barracuda bomber was being fitted-out for service on aircraft carriers in the summer and autumn of 1944, this work required a once-a-month visit to London…

'I had to attend a meeting at the Air Ministry offices in Lower Regent Street to discuss with the Navy "brass" which pieces of radio and radar equipment they wanted installed in their Barracudas.   They usually wanted everything, the standard joke at the time being that if the Navy asked to have one more piece of equipment added, the Barracuda would not be able to keep up with the aircraft carrier. I recall at these monthly meetings in mid-1944 that on a few occasions, when we were all sitting around the conference table talking business, the distinctive putt-putt sound of a V1 flying bomb would be heard approaching. Everyone would try to be nonchalant and continue with the business of the meeting even as the noise grew louder; but if the noise should suddenly stop, all of us would dive for shelter under the conference table until the explosion was heard.   Fortunately it was never too close [9] .'

The V1 flying bomb caught most people unawares the first time one came into sight, none more so than one of the Oboe Controllers at Hawkshill Down during 'Mac' McNarry's spell there as a TO.   He recalls that, while preparing for the customary evening of operational activity…

'The equipment had been checked out and the target ranges set. It was a pleasant evening so we gathered outside for a breath of fresh air. Just at dusk, one of the Controllers spotted a red light proceeding rapidly towards the Dover coast, coming in from France, and immediately he assumed that it was a German aircraft with one of its lights left on. He commented on the pilot's stupidity, then, when crossing the coast, all hell broke loose. The sky was filled with tracers from anti-aircraft guns and salvoes of rockets roared into the sky. The red light just kept on its heading without the slightest deviation. At one point one of the Controllers remarked: "He deserves the DFC and Bar for that performance, even if he is a Jerry!" We didn't know then that this was a V1. When one came over our area a little later and we heard the diesel-like rumble of its engine, we knew that it was something new and different. None landed near us, but they were to keep us busy for some time as we attacked the launching ramps with 4,000 lb bombs dropped by Mosquitoes under Oboe control [10] .'

Some radar mechs were among the first to plot the course of a V1. 'Mac' McCallum, due to have gone into Normandy on D+6 with a mobile radar unit, landed dry-shod with the gunners asleep, via the Mulberry artificial harbour, pressing ahead through France, into Belgium and then into Holland which was, he said, 'a waste of time... there were too many aircraft. We spent some time at Valliancourt, near Amiens, which the locals said we liberated, before we moved on to a location just west of Gilze-Rijen airport close to Germany. We'd been in "Buzz Bomb Alley" in England, having operated at Beachy Head where we plotted the first of the V1s to come across, and on the Continent we were in the path of still more of them. Then came the Ardennes breakthrough in December 1944... where the Germans themselves, rather than their "V-for-vengeance" weapons, almost got us [11] '.

Back from Corsica, AMES 102 crossed to France on 14 November 1944 and was in the American zone of operations when the following month the Germans made their counter-attack in the Ardennes. Wally Tanner recalls:

'We were heading west towards Metz when I drove ahead to try to find a place for our convoy to stay for the night – and was duly arrested by the Yanks! It wasn't really surprising as the Germans had penetrated the area with troops in Allied uniforms. I was wearing khaki battledress with RAF badges and over this I had an RAF greatcoat which was not so different from the German gray uniform. Fortunately our CO [Flying Officer Phil Macdonald, RCAF] caught up with me and persuaded my captors to release me – the fact that he was a Canadian probably helping [12] .'

A hazard in those frequent changes of site was the danger posed by unmarked landmines. Wally explained that 'we had no mine detector so when we arrived at a new site we would draw lots and the person who lost would drive our heaviest vehicle round and round the field. Fortunately we never hit anything explosive...'

Where Wally Tanner was in Corsica in the summer of 1944, his unit ready for whatever task it might be required to undertake in preparations for the invasion of Southern France, Oboe radar mechs in the UK were contemplating their role now that the Allies had landed in Normandy. The system required both the continuation of ground stations on the east, south-east and south coasts of Britain and the placing of mobile units in France, which could then move forward as and when needed.

For Will Robson, a mobile unit operating on Beachy Head was his first assignment on completion of his training as a radar technician specializing in the ground station equipment associated with the Oboe ground-controlled, blind-bombing system.   He was aware that, once the Allies had secured a foothold on the Continent, mobile Oboe stations like his would be needed first in France, then in Belgium and Holland and ultimately in Germany.   Oboe had a range limitation, wherever the ground stations were located, so the use of transportable equipment on the Continent would enable the RAF and the USAAF to benefit from this precision-bombing aid when attacking targets which otherwise would be beyond the signal transmission capability of Oboe ground stations in England.   Having arrived on the Continent, Will recalls the area around the Dutch town of Arnhem being mentioned as the likely initial setting-up point for his particular unit but the failure of the Allied paratroop and glider drops behind enemy lines put paid to that plan.   He explains:

> 'We were stalled for a couple of weeks in Mons, eventually moving on through Brussels and into southern Holland to Eindhoven.   Our instructions were to find a suitable site in this area near the front line.   An Oboe controller and I headed out in a Jeep in search of such a location.   Most of the area east of Eindhoven was relatively flat and much of it was flooded as a result of destructive action by the Germans on the intricate canal system. We were about to "call it a day" when we came across a well-constructed road disappearing into what appeared to be a re-forested area.   At the end of it, the road emerged into wide-open flat countryside with an unobstructed view towards Germany in an arc of more than 180 degrees.   Along the tree line was a system of electric wiring suspended on insulators above the ground and not far from this area we found a partially destroyed 50 cm radar antenna mounted on a concrete base, later identified as having been part of the enemy's Wurzburg radar system.   It took no more than a couple of minutes for us to agree that the Germans had kindly provided us with our first Oboe site in Occupied Europe!   Next day we directed our whole convoy onto this site, the Oboe vehicles being positioned in front of the trees and immediately camouflaged to blend in with them.   The nearest village was named Rips, so Rips became the name for our station [13] .'

At Rips, some 15 miles north east of Eindhoven as the crow flies and no more than 2 or 3 miles short of the German border, tents were set up in the protective cover of the woods and the Oboe equipment was soon ready for operation.   Discarded German switch gear, blower motors and so on were used to replace less efficient items that had been brought over from the UK and some of their electric cables were brought into play to supply generator-fed lighting within the tents.

From October until late December 1944, Rips was a vital part of the Oboe system in benefiting numerous Allied bombing raids throughout north western Germany, particularly affecting the supply lines of the retreating enemy forces.   Will Robson notes that 'these successful Oboe operations were curtailed only when the Germans mounted their counter-offensive in the Ardennes.   It was their aim to re-take the port of Antwerp and to cut off the Allied army units in Holland – and this would have included us'.

While the mobile Oboe unit at Rips was able to stay put, the one at La Roche was forced to move out – fast...

Bob Steel, who was on the Oboe station at Tilly Whim in the build-up to D-Day, recalls the streets of Swanage being crowded on June 3 and 4 with American troops preparing their equipment for embarkation. He recalls that 'we had been watching the ships gather along the coast and then, during the night of June 4, all the soldiers were gone. We guessed that this must be the long-awaited invasion because our Oboe operations were now largely concerned with guiding the bombers to the German gun emplacements along the French coast. These turned out to be precisely where the landings were to take place' 14 .

In late August/early September the mobile unit AMES 9442 was formed in Cardington where their vehicles were waterproofed in case it became necessary to make a 'wet' landing in France. He notes that 'we drove to Gosport, boarded an LST and landed in Normandy. The road from the beach had a line of white tapes on each side and when we inquired, we were told that mines had been cleared to the tapes. For many of us, war had come closer'. The eventual location for Bob's unit was La Roche, where the crew's quarters were in a chateau.

Where Bob Steel was an RCAF radar technician with AMES 9442, Tom Hatcher was an RAF radar operator, also with AMES 9442. In his recollections of his time with this unit, Tom came up with a piece of doggerel that was produced round about the time the unit was 'on air' at La Roche. It went like this:

> '*They stuck us in a chateau, we suffered there from chills,*
> *We'd nowhere we could put our kit, 'twas on the window sills.*
> *We couldn't go into town at night –*
> *There's Bosche in them there hills.*'

Tom has described some of the differences between working as an operator on the radar chain and doing the same job on an Oboe station. He said:

> 'When on duty on the chain one was on constant watch for aircraft activity which was continuously plotted and reported. Operational conditions varied considerably in intensity and there was no means of knowing what might come about or from what quarter. One was constantly on the alert and ready to react promptly. The Oboe operator on the other hand would know in advance the timing of the operations in which he was to be involved. There were the pre-operation duties of setting up and testing the equipment, all to be done with meticulous care. Then came the anxious minutes of the operation itself – it was quite a different matter 15 .'

Bob Steel, recalling their quarters in that chateau, notes:

> 'One of the rooms was occupied by a New Zealander and three Canadians (of which I was one) and it was given the name "Dominion Dive". By the

time we arrived, in October, the British rations were fully used up; we were in the American sector so we had to replenish from the American commissary in Bastogne. The change in rations was so great that some RAF stomachs could not handle the richness of the new food – though we RCAF members, having had parcels from home, were better prepared for it. We Canadians were lumberjacks in RAF eyes, which probably explains why I was earmarked to chop wood for the cook. Although we were busy with our Oboe ops, when Christmas was approaching we put on a party on December 5 for the children in a nearby village – which took our minds off the war for a while. Then, middle of the month, we began hearing the thunder of guns. The cook, who had been increasing his food stocks for a bang-up Christmas, took a butcher's cleaver and began punching holes in the quart cans of grapefruit he had collected, going on to treat everything else in much the same way. It was time to leave – and he wasn't going to leave anything for the Germans...'

It will be remembered that, despite being well settled on the Continent of Europe, the problems of the early days and the Arnhem setback behind them, the Allies' thrust towards Germany was not always 'plain sailing'.

In that mid-December of 1944, in the Ardennes region of Belgium, where Bob Steel was located, the comparative peace of a Sunday morning was broken when German artillery opened-up on US 1st Army positions with 'a shattering effect on the Americans, who are completely taken by surprise' for 'until now the initiative has always rested with the Allies [16] '. It wasn't only the American troops who were caught unawares: Bob's unit, AMES 9442, a radar unit some 180-strong, under the command of Flight Lieutenant Art Craig, RCAF, operational for the past couple of months at La Roche – in the American sector and enjoying excellent co-operation from them – found itself inextricably mixed up in their fast-changing fortunes. Art recalls:

'Having moved out from HQ # 72 Wing at Mons on 8 October 1944, at La Roche we were a very busy and successful site. We used tents where required, then requisitioned suitable civilian accommodation. The local civilians were most co-operative and helpful and we did whatever we could to repay their generosity. Then, on 15 December, we detected a certain uneasiness regarding the possibility of German military action and I advised my men to pack up all their personal belongings in the event of a move. Then came a phone call from the Americans in the early hours, saying that they were preparing to withdraw and advising me to leave our site without delay. I told Wing HQ of our intentions, the men were all out of their billets within an hour and we were all hard at it, working through the rest of the night and into the morning, dismantling and preparing our Oboe gear ready to get on the road. Much to our dismay we discovered that, because of the mud and the snow, our large Matador diesel unit couldn't shift our Oboe trailers, either conventionally by winch or by any make-shift methods that we tried. All was not lost: I knew that the Americans had a couple of caterpillar tractors and I was successful (after much discussion with them) in commandeering one which was dispatched to us with two operators, both sergeants and highly skilled. One of our Technical Officers, Adam ('Pop')

Pohoreski, was successful in flagging them down on the now very busy retreat road [17].'

Fifty years and more later, Pop was still sensing the disappointments and the frustrations of having 'to pull up roots and retreat with the US troops who were streaming down the road past our site'. What happened was this:

'I talked the US sergeants into unloading their vehicle and pulling our vans off the field. The alternative would have been to blow up those vans and, thereby, lose our equipment . A couple of US military policemen soon arrived on the scene and demanded to know what we were doing holding up the retreat. They threatened to push the transporter off the road and blow it up if need be. After some pleading with them, they allowed us to haul off the remainder of our radar vans and we were able to join the retreat. Just in the nick of time, for we heard some heavy cannon fire, coming from German tanks about a mile away. Afterwards the Belgians told us that a tank column had bypassed our location an hour or so before we left the site! It was a close call... [18].'

Art Craig notified Wing HQ that he had shut down AMES 9442, made a final inspection of the site and left with Pop Pohereski in the unit's water bowser, in the certain knowledge that without the Americans' help it would have been impossible to get the important main units out of La Roche. There were enemy tanks and gunfire 'which appeared to be not very far away' and 'straggled on' to reach Mons, suffering neither any casualties to personnel nor damage to the radar equipment [*].

On 26 December, AMES 9442 was sent to a new site in France, near Selvigney, some 60 miles distant, where the unit was refitted and successfully tested in readiness for a return to operational duty. This was able to come about when, on 3 February 1945, the unit set out for La Roche – the site it had left to the oncoming Germans on 16 December. As it was dark when the convoy reached La Roche, it was the following morning before the extent of the devastation became evident. Art remembers that sorry scene:

'We could see what a mess the whole area was, burned out tanks, trucks and German and American bodies all over the place, most of them frozen. We also discovered that there were mines here and there. Nonetheless, after a mammoth job of site clearance, preparation and setting up, remarkably we were able to get back on the air within 24 hours or so. I informed Wing HQ and soon there was a secret cipher message for me from the CO saying: 'F/LT CRAIG FROM PHILLIPS. GOOD SHOW' – a message that I was pleased to accept as being his personal tribute to my hard working men. It was recognition by Wing HQ that La Roche was back in business – having learned a few lessons in the meantime! Unfortunately we were not entirely unscathed during our time at La Roche: we did lose one airman in a German minefield near the site and in a night-

---

[*] # 72 Wing records indicate that the advancing German troops had in mind capturing the radar units located at La Roche; the enemy was 'in full possession' of the pinpoints of the sites and the mobility of the convoys into which they were formed [19].

time vehicle ambush near Vielsalm, one of our MT drivers was killed and our catering officer was wounded [20] .'

Readjusting to operational life on their former site was difficult, cold and uncomfortable but the welcome by the unit's civilian friends was, he says, both warm and touching. When a little order had been restored from a lot of chaos, Group Captain R L Phillips, accompanied by Air Vice-Marshal W E Theak, # 60 Group's AOC, visited La Roche to enjoy 'a spread that we had put on for them in our extremely pleasant Officers' Mess in the Chateau St Marie near Vielsalm – "best blues", a lovely dinner, cigars (courtesy of our American colleagues), port and all the trimmings. Our illustrious visitors loved it!' By late spring 'we had done about all we could do from La Roche and we were moved to a site not far from Wurzburg in Germany'. Then came VE-Day and this brought what would be Art Craig's last move with AMES 9442, re-locating at Wilhelmshaven where he remained until posted to Canada on 22 October 1945. It had been 'quite an experience [21] '.

In their different ways, others had 'quite an experience', for instance Ron Staughton, who joined the RAF from his home town of Plymouth, much of which lay in ruins from enemy raids at that time. Serving on the Continent in the second half of 1944, he saw how countries there, too, had suffered beneath aerial assault. And on New Year's Day 1945, on shift on a radar station north of Brussels, he saw first hand how the enemy was still well able to inflict death and destruction by means of a still-determined if reduced-strength Luftwaffe. He recalls:

'I was on the tube about 9 am and picked up echoes of 10-plus aircraft, then 20-plus aircraft and reported their presence to the Controller, who wouldn't believe it. He claimed these must have been spurious echoes... saying that the Germans didn't have that number of aircraft. The echoes now indicated 50-plus, the numbers continuing to mount and all these aircraft coming directly for us. With three years' experience, I knew exactly what I was plotting. The CO tried to convince that Controller but even he wasn't believed.

'Soon we had the living proof: above us came a mixed bag of Heinkels, Dorniers, Focke Wulfs and Messerschmitts at maybe 4,000 feet, which worried us no end because we had big trucks on our site, each with those huge RAF roundels on the roof. The Germans were on their way to attack Brussels Airport where, later, we nearly wept to see Dakotas and other aircraft, wing tip to wing tip, which were now burned-out shells. That Controller should have been strung up by the thumbs [22] .'

Charles Larose, who had charge of a mobile Oboe station which crossed to the Continent in early 1945, tells a salutary tale of what might have happened if caution had not prevailed. This incident occurred some time after his unit entered Germany and Charles was 'riding my motorcycle ahead of my convoy with hundreds of armed German soldiers lining the road. As I approached, they would stand up, raise their arms, then sit down again after I had passed. Then, nearing Munster to find our new site of operations and riding through a wood on a small country road, I found the area full of dead American and German paratroopers.

'Nearby in a ditch, facing north there was a German soldier. On the other side of the road, facing south and about 60 degrees diagonally, there was an American paratrooper. Both had one bullet hole in the forehead. They must have shot each other simultaneously. That's not all, though. The American soldier had some nice binoculars under his arm and strapped around his neck. As I reached to take them, my brain flashed a booby-trap warning. Sure enough, there was a hand grenade, pin out, under his arm. You could never, ever be too careful [23] .'

Danger was ever present and not every risk was avoidable. Fred Watters, having been among personnel assembling to form mobile Oboe unit AMES 9431 in the September/October of 1944, embarked at Tilbury, LST 405 to be the means of transportation to the Continent. He notes that 'rough Channel weather and minefields, which caused the loss of an accompanying LST * , delayed by several days the arrival and disembarkation of the unit at Ostend' [24] . Fred's nine months' service in Belgium and Germany, which included La Roche, comprised a second overseas tour while away from his homeland, Canada, the first being 'a thoroughly unpleasant, unhealthy and unproductive' posting to West Africa.

In March 1945, with a course at Yatesbury on updated Oboe equipment now behind him, fellow Canadian 'Mac' McNarry was also on his way to the Continent. He took the same route via Tilbury and Ostend to join a different mobile unit, AMES 9422, at Mutzig in Alsace, on a site overlooking the Rhine valley towards Strasbourg. Several operations were with the US Air Force and one of the strong impressions remaining was what 'Mac' calls 'the sheer futility of trying to move a mass of aircraft in formation onto an Oboe ground station's tracking signal. The enormous inertia of the aircraft ensured failure, because they still tried to fly in formation on the Master Bomber. I know that all of us on the ground station were frustrated to see the transponder signal suddenly switch off as the target area was approached – and we would know that the Master Bomber was going to make a visual identification and rely on his Nordern bomb sight. To the Americans, so it seemed to us, Oboe was no more than a handy navigation device to get them to the target area [25] '.

Aside from that 'bone of contention', AMES 9422 personnel had some cause to appreciate the Americans' contribution to the progress of the war effort; looking after the 'inner man' was less troublesome than it might otherwise have been because American rations were supplied. Everyone ate well, one of the letters 'Mac' wrote home recording that 'for breakfast there is porridge or corn flakes, fried egg with either bacon or tomato, toast, marmalade and coffee. And for dinner, a variety of meat, vegetables and tinned fruit for dessert. Tomato juice and fruit juices stand on the sideboard and are there for the taking... So, don't send any food, *please!*'

Where the Oboe mobile ground stations were concerned, the site structure of # 72 Wing was similar to that of December 1944 ahead of the Ardennes counter-offensive, with units at Florennes, La Roche, Rips and Commercy. There was also an Oboe unit operational at Molsheim (Convoy # 1/9000) before the year was out, having endured three. days and nights *en route* in extremely cold weather with snow

---

* LST 420 hit a mine off the Belgian coast with the loss of 231 RAF personnel; more radar mechs were lost in that tragedy, on 7 November 1944, than probably in any other single incident throughout WWII.

and rain, opening for business on 27 December after experiencing 'great difficulty' in getting its vehicles sited and participating, on New Year's Eve, in a successful bombing of Mannheim. It was an interrupted sojourn, Wing HQ ordering the station to be dismantled and moved to Commercy owing to the advance of enemy forces, the absence lasting into the second week of February [26]. However the pattern of Oboe stations started to change in March as the Allied armies penetrated the Reich more deeply, Convoy # 3 being the first to arrive on German soil and becoming operational at Kempenich on 24 March 1945. It is recorded that...

'Convoy # 6 crossed the Rhine on 7 April 1945 at Wesel and became sited at Horstmar. Convoy # 2, retained at La Roche to cover the Ruhr, moved forward to Rottingen for the special benefit of the USAAF on 16 April. Convoy # 5 was moved to Barntrup from Rips, where it became operational from 15 April. Convoy # 4 left Commercy on 2 April and crossed the Rhine at Worms. Thus, on 5 April, Convoy # 4 became the first 72 Wing unit to cross the Rhine, on a pontoon bridge. Convoy # 4 was moved from Bad Homburg on 26 April to travel to Erbendorf, near Weiden, on the Czech border. The station was declared operational by 30 April but did not operate as the war was effectively over by then.

'It was just as well that 4/9000 [Convoy # 4] was not needed at Erbendorf as its hardware had taken a battering on the journey from Bad Homburg. Its advance party had followed a Third Army main military route where it met a railway bridge under which the Oboe trailers would not pass. Several hours were lost in bridging a ditch, crossing a field, climbing an embankment, crossing two railway lines, etc, by stripping a farm of every brick, stone, piece of timber, to make a relatively smooth track for the trailers but they didn't like it. The delayed US troops didn't like it either, but got their own back the following day when a small US tank struck the rear of one of our two trailers and effectively broke every valve in it.

'By VE-Day, Convoy # 1 was at Molsheim, # 2 at Rottingen, # 3 at Gotha, # 4 at Erbendorf, # 5 at Barntrup and # 6 at Horstmar [27].'

When a bridge was built across the Rhine and Allied troops had advanced to eastern Germany, Harry Carlyle's mobile station set up at Gotha and was active in the Oboe-led operations against Berlin. One day, when returning to this mountain site at the head of a motor convoy after a visit to the town, 'a group of displaced persons stopped us and warned that there were German soldiers ahead of us.

'We left our vehicles and spread out to investigate. Ahead, I saw a group of six soldiers in a small clearing, having a smoke. I signaled to the other officers, indicating what I had seen, then realized that I had to act. So I ran in amongst them, shouting and brandishing my revolver. Single handed, I took all six captive before the others came on the scene. We disarmed my prisoners and put them into the hands of the RAF Regiment. I thought we had all done pretty well – and then I came in for some sharp criticism... for allowing them a smoke [28].'

Travelling through Germany, eventually being located on the Wasserkuppe, near Fulda, which had been a favorite spot for gliding pre-war, the AMES 102 crew once pulled into a village appearing to be populated by dozens of obviously pregnant German girls. Wally Tanner noted that this 'turned out to be one of their human stud farms for breeding the so-called pure German race. Apparently the girls were kept by the State until able to resume work, each being given a signed copy of Hitler's book, *Mein Kampf.* I must confess that for some reason we thought it was a very funny business and the jokes were endless'.

For AMES 102, VE-Day was spent on a site near the Buchenwald concentration camp – 'truly the most horrific sight I would ever see, where one could get the smell of death for miles around'; among countless unit celebrations to mark the end of the war in Europe, theirs was most certainly one of the more low-key occasions on account of the isolation and the locality. Those 'celebrations' did have an amusing side, though; a bonfire was built outside the radar tower and cans of petrol thrown on it to stoke up the blaze, this being followed by Nature helping out by providing a summer storm in the mountains to the south, a feature of this being some spectacular lightning. Wally remarked that 'at one point we thought the war had started all over again!'

In Germany in those final weeks of WWII, as was Tom Hatcher, an RAF radar operator with the Oboe mobile unit AMES 9442, 'we continued to see as much as we possibly could of the country', going on to cite 'particularly interesting visits to Heidelberg and Rothenburg and to Nuremberg', the countryside being 'quite beautiful'. Able to enjoy plenty of swimming, cricket and other pastimes, AMES 9442 was situated well inside the American Sector and able to share in some 'lavish entertainment', noting that on 28 July there was 'a show in a large open-air natural amphitheatre with Jack Benny, Ingrid Bergman, Martha Tilton, Larry Adler and Dave Le Winter'; and on another occasion 'a concert by the Boston Pops orchestra in nearby Bad Mergentheim [29] '. Tom was posted from AMES 9442 to 72 Wing Headquarters in October 1945, joining AMES 7911 on the Jutland G-H chain at Horsens in Denmark which finally went off the air at 23.59 hours on 31 March 1946.

Those 'particularly interesting visits to Heidelberg and Rothenburg and to Nuremberg' diverge dramatically from an obviously sickening tour which a number of the members of AMES 9442 made in June 1945, being allowed to go inside a former concentration camp during the unit's deployment at Mutzig, in Alsace-Lorraine. The camp was reportedly used by Nazi Germany for experimental purposes on political and military prisoners; and post-occupation, at the time of the visit by the Oboe crew members, the French authorities were using it to accommodate political prisoners who were predominantly Alsacians and Germans, together with military prisoners consisting of SS and Hitler Youth. It is appropriate to warn that the following description is as AMES 9442 crew member Findley Macdonald experienced that visit; the words are those that he wrote at the time, pulling no punches, and they are but a brief extract:

> 'In the furnace room on the ground floor the bodies were shoved into the furnace by means of rollers which carried the steel stretcher. Some of these poor souls were not even dead. Beside the furnace was a large tank possibly 500 gallons in capacity and held hot water maintained by the

burning of human bodies in the furnace. This hot water was used for other devilish tortures and other uses. Each body had a fireproof identification disc, when entering the furnace in the event any kin of the dead wished the ashes for home burial. If such was the case the ashes were placed in urns, keep in mind possibly five bodies in the furnace at one time. There were two types of urns, clay and metal, and cost the kinfolk of the victim 75 marks ($20) for clay and 200 marks ($50) metal, and were shipped after payment was received, the ashes of other dead mixed in. If not claimed and payment was not received the ashes were dumped outside at the back in a huge pit. I visited this spot and, although leveled off, the stench of the dead hung like a pallor about the place; flies and bugs in swarms, and pieces of bone to be seen. This piece of land has been consecrated and upon which stands a large wooden cross, a cairn with a cask containing ashes of two victims, in memorial for the 32,000 murdered [30].'

Radar equipment mobility was by no means confined to the Oboe system, which was used to particular advantage in 72 Wing – not forgetting, of course, that memorable reversal of forward movement necessitated by von Rundstedt's determined tanks and troops in mid-December 1944. There was always going to be a requirement for permanent ground stations, as evidenced by the RDF home chain in the early days and later by the Oboe installations set up to facilitate the bombing of important targets in the Ruhr. Yet in some respects mobility would be more vital – a point which emerged as the forms of radar and their potential applications widened. In time, the manner of mobility became as diverse as the uses made of the principles of radar. Motors and mule trains, landing craft and even gliders became the means to transport the men and the machines in radar-based warfare…

CHAPTER 11: GLIDING INTO BATTLE

Where WWII radar systems were concerned, how mobile was 'mobile'?   As Canadian radar technician Fred Hunt explains, one on which he worked was reckoned to be so transportable that a string of packhorses was all that was needed to move this system from, say, a remote airfield staging post to a distant and even more isolated operational site.   Referring to the Light Warning Set, a small ground radar set which saw service in North Africa, Italy, South East Asia and North West Europe, providing early warning of approaching aircraft, Fred says that…

'They came in two versions where the same radar equipment was mounted either in a specially constructed tent or in a 15 cwt signals van.   During transit, the tent-mounted equipment could be dismantled and transported in about 15 wooden boxes, each capable of being carried by a maximum of 4 men.   In most cases these boxes were taken from Point A to Point B in a 3-ton truck, though theoretically there was nothing to stop the boxes going on a camel caravan or even a mule train.   In both versions, the antenna turning gear was the central piece of equipment, either in the centre of the tent or the centre of the forward end of the van's interior.   The antenna array could be dis-assembled for transport in both versions [1] .'

His first experience of the Light Warning Set (LW) came in the spring of 1943 when LW 6096, comprising two radar mechanics, six radar operators, one   wireless mechanic, two wireless operators, a motor transport mechanic and a cook, formed with five other LWs at Renscombe Downs, a training station for mobile radars near Swanage, Dorset.   The first week was spent on a 'backers-up' course including unarmed combat, learning field-cooking, first aid, use of firearms and so on, with the next two weeks devoted to training on the radar itself.

After a fortnight's leave, LW 6096 re-assembled at High Street Darsham, a CH station near Yoxford, Suffolk, quartered in bell tents in the receiver compound and spending 'most of our time on route marches, nominally for physical conditioning, but we always seemed to end up at a pub!   Some of us also tried to learn a bit of Morse code in order to substitute for the WOPs in an emergency, while others continued with their driving instruction'.   There were a number of moves which included Longcross, 'a hole-in-the-ground run by the RAF Regiment as a training centre'; Chigwell, where the men 'lived in hangars with cement floors and the poor-quality food was typical of these transient establishments'; and Stoke Holy Cross, near Norwich, 'where, having started a 24-hour watch system, due to interference with a nearby GCI we had to close down during the nights'.

Back at Chigwell, when by now it was early July, LW 6096 crew members were told that the Middle East was to be their new home and of course rumors abounded, the strongest being that with three other LWs and a mobile GCI unit grouped together on this former balloon barrage centre, the destination was to be a Greek island soon to be captured.   Fred Hunt wasn't convinced: later it was his belief 'that we were involved in a giant British Intelligence hoax to divert attention from the landings in Sicily, which took place that month, and Italy.   Since these mobile radars were not required immediately for operations, for a small cost in movements about Britain, tropical inoculations etc, any misleading intelligence leaks could very well have disrupted German thinking on future Allied landings'.

With other LWs, 6096 was then engaged on further training, including participation in a Combined Operations course, before joining what was known as '130 Airfield', situated first at Odiham in Hampshire and then at North Weald in Essex.   It saw in the New Year, 1944, at the Air Forces Tactical Development Unit at Tarrant Rushton in Dorset, a test centre for airborne troops, mostly dedicated to working with troop- and equipment-carrying gliders.   There were the tiny Hotspurs, which held 7 fully-equipped men plus the pilot; Horsas, capable of taking about three times that number; and the massive Hamilcars, designed to transport a 3-man tank. He says:

> 'We tried to fit our tented version LW into the Hotspur but it became obvious that at least five of these gliders would be needed to take the equipment plus the men to operate and maintain.   We voiced our disapproval, pressing our case by pointing out that the failure of the arrival of only one of the five gliders would mean that there would be no operational radar. Wouldn't it be far better, we suggested, if a single Horsa was used, because this could carry the equipment and the men.   In fact, while trying to maneuver the radar equipment inside a Hotspur, someone managed to put his foot through the side – and that was enough to make the authorities appreciate our difficulties.   All was forgiven and our glider-transport was switched to Horsas.'

The first time airborne proved to be an eventful occasion.   It turned out that the Horsa had an unserviceable air-speed indicator, which led its pilot to think that the glider was travelling too fast, whereas the pilot of the tug, a four-engined Stirling, feared that reducing his air-speed could cause a fatal stall.   There was much shouting over the intercom between the two pilots and then, after making just one circuit of the airfield, the exercise was ended and the towrope released.   Both the glider and its tug landed safely but, as Fred remarked later, 'so much for the first flight of glider-borne radar'.

Within three months, LW 6096 had disbanded and some of the crew, Fred among them, found themselves posted to form Eureka-H beacon crews; other LWs however, specifically 6080 and 6341, continued a relationship with gliders, a number of the officers and men losing their lives at Arnhem, the Allies' leapfrog operation in September 1944 which became the subject of countless articles, several books and the film *A Bridge Too Far*.   It will be remembered that British, American and Polish parachute troops belonging to the 1st Allied Airborne Division were dropped in Holland with the aim of seizing key bridges over the Lower Rhine in a bid to speed-up the advance into Germany. Interestingly, the role of glider-borne radar, an innovative application, attracted scant attention – though surely, as can now be shown, it must rank as one of the most tragic episodes in radar history.

There had been no call for glider-borne radar in the Normandy operations because all troop movements were under a fighter umbrella controlled first from only the FDTs and then also by radar units landed with advance units of the invading armies so as to move forward when their pre-determined operational sites were cleared of the enemy.   In the event, even making glider-borne radar a part of the Arnhem operation was an on-off-on situation.

In anticipation that, in future operations, airborne forces might be landed considerably forward of the main field forces and require effective fighter cover, the groundwork was done to design and produce air transportable Light Warning Sets and air transportable Ground Controlled Interception units, the subsequent crewing-up and technical training being done by HQ 60 Group ahead of the transfer of two LWs and one GCI to HQ 38 Group for operational training.   Then, so it appeared, with the début operation just days away, there wasn't a need for them after all...

The on-off-on circumstances are documented in once-secret records.   At a meeting at Bentley Priory on 15 September 'it was stated by a representative of the 1st Allied Airborne Division that air transportable radar equipment would not be required for the operation.   Subsequently this decision was over-ruled and on the morning of the 18th, Light Warning Units # 6341 and # 6080 were airborne in four gliders destined for Arnhem, to take part in what has since been described as "the bloodiest battle of the war" [2].

When, eventually, Fred Hunt learned of the fate of those gliders and members of the unit crews transported in them, a number of whom were known to him, he felt a personal compulsion to build up as clear a picture as was possible, given the restraints of the passage of time.   Initially, he says [3], the two LWs were to fly in the first lift to Nijmegen but this was subsequently changed to the second lift as there was a shortage of tug aircraft.   A lack of tugs is understandable: 'between 1025 hours and 1155 hours on Sunday morning 17 September, there took off the greatest troop carrier fleet in history. The total force was 1,544 planes and 478 gliders' [4].   The LWs' destination was also changed, from Nijmegen to Arnhem, the radar-quartet of gliders becoming part of a total force of 1,360 planes and 1,200 gliders on this second day of the campaign, all but 58 planes and 57 gliders reaching the drop and landing zones; D+1 was 'a day of building-up of forces on both sides, the second lift going in as planned but the Germans too were increasing in strength' [5].

Taking up the story, Fred says that at the last turning point at s'Hertogenbosh there was heavy flak and one of the tugs spun into the ground, the glider pilot pulling away successfully and landing on the wrong side of the Rhine [6].   The LW crew destroyed their equipment with Sten gun fire to prevent its seizure by enemy troops not then in the immediate neighborhood.   A second glider, with its tail shot off and therefore impossible to handle, crashed with the loss of all on board, leaving two remaining gliders which successfully reached the intended landing zone.   In the process, however, both encountered machine gunfire, some of it incendiary, and one was on fire even before touch-down, the occupants escaping though their equipment was lost.   There was but a single glider remaining and the landing zone was under mortar and machine gunfire.   It was obvious that there could be no radar operations so the order was given to demolish the surviving glider's load with Sten gun fire and explosives.

The equipment was now gone but what was the fate of the LW crews? Fred's research puts the casualties at 2 officers and 8 men killed, with 11 men, one of them injured, taken prisoner, and 4 officers escaping, one of whom was wounded*. Those figures are not entirely consistent with a report among the War Office documentation on this operation, which states that 'the evacuation of Arnhem took place on the 25/26 September, and the survivors of the Radar Section of the First Allied Airborne Army, which originally comprised 5 officers and 40 ORs returned to the UK, this party consisting of 3 officers and 1 OR'. A close study of reports made by those survivors 'proved invaluable in formulating the requirements of air transportable radar for any future airborne operations' ₇ .

It is certainly worth placing on record that whereas Fred Hunt and others in training were pressing for an entire radar unit to be accommodated in a single glider and that this was not the case at Arnhem, the documentation cited above is seen to be wholeheartedly behind the concept of a complete radar equipment henceforth travelling with its crew in one glider – it 'must' do so * . Furthermore, that equipment and its crew 'must be able to move swiftly from the glider to cover on a pre-selected site immediately upon making land-fall'. In fact there were no more such operations, though other radar units were trained for that eventuality. Here, again, there was an unfortunate loss of life. It occurred during Exercise *Conway*, which 38 Group was conducting at RAF Stations Cranfield, Acklington, Coltishall and Bentwaters during the period between April 17 and 30, 1945, when 'owing to accident, one AMES Type 6 Mk IX was lost, two of the crew being killed and others injured' ₈ .

Charlie Young, another Canadian and a radar technical officer, trained for post-Arnhem operations with the British 6th Airborne Division out of Tarrant Rushton, the intent being to convey two radar sets in a Horsa glider and to become a fully operational GCI within minutes of touch-down, the record being a remarkable eight minutes though not, of course, when under fire. He says of those days in training:

> 'There were three crews, each consisting of 4 officers and 34 men, each crew additionally having a van-mounted LW set with a six-man crew attached to it, the van being carried in a Hamilcar and the LW crew both reporting-in to the glider-borne "mother station" and covering its blind spots. Our uniform was unique. We wore khaki battledress, boots and web belt, with an RAF Regiment blue beret, while on our sleeves we carried our Air Force badges of rank and the 6th Airborne Division badge, which was a silver Pegasus on a purple patch. In my own case, I wore my "Canada" badge too, being one of only three Canadians involved, each of us a Flight Lieutenant radar officer ₉ '.

---

* Flight Sergeant Semon Lievense was among the fatalities; 'Blondie' Lievense (LW 6080 crew member}, a radar mechanic from St. Boniface, Manitoba, killed in action on 22 September 1944, apparently lost his life while under artillery fire.ᐟ Post-war, Fred Hunt gained an Honours BSc, MSc and PhD in Physics at the University of Western Ontario, joining the National Research Council of Canada in 1955 where he spent the first 10 years on research and development of 'quick-fixes' to Canadian military radars. The final period of his 31-year career with the NRC was a study of the compatibility of electronic devices – the effects of mutual interference – while at the same time being the Scientific Secretary for the Electrical Engineering Committee, which was responsible for government grants for research at Canadian universities.

In training, besides the April 1945 fatality, where apparently the two victims were in a vehicle with insufficient space to open the doors to get out when a Hamilcar made a rough landing that resulted in a fire, there were a number of potentially fatal accidents where crews who worked with radar equipment carried in gliders had a lucky escape.

One such occasion involved Charlie Young's crew, which was the only one of three identical crews with the radar-equipped Horsa glider known as AMES 65 * . Although the radar glider carrying Charlie and the OC successfully released from its tow-plane and landed without incident – as did the glider carrying the tents, blankets, rations, kit and so on – this crew's other glider unfortunately ran into trouble.   As there were the two controllers and the 34 ORs on board, anything that put this one in jeopardy would clearly have the most serious consequences in human terms.   What happened was this: when releasing from the tow-plane, the heavy metal fixture on each end of the tow rope swung inwards dangerously instead of falling away safely, clear of the glider, punching a foot-wide hole in each side of the fuselage – a matter of inches away from the heads of two airmen sitting just behind the cockpit.   As Charlie remarks: 'Their guardian angels were awake and all landed safely.'

In another incident, one of the other two crews was involved this time.   It happened while carrying out the standard procedure when the tow-plane blows a tire part-way down the runway with the glider already airborne, the Horsa making a safe landing in a valley at the end of the runway but coming to rest with a power pole having sliced through the cockpit.   Charlie commented:

> 'Here was a packed glider, carrying up to three dozen men, which could have been cut right down the length of the fuselage, but luck was with them. Even the pilot and co-pilot, who sit beside each other, escaped without a scratch.   Weren't they lucky – the pole that the Horsa hit as it slowed to a halt was right between the two of them!
>
> 'I saw one accident in training which was more serious, again when the tow-plane, which was a Halifax, burst a tire while towing a Hamilcar.   The glider pilot broke the rules and tried to do a 360 degree turn back to the airfield, but he lost air speed over the aircraft dispersal area and fell on a parked Halifax, both going up in flames.   Meanwhile, adding to this tragedy, the tow-plane with the blown tire lost control when trying to land and this, too, caught fire.   There were no radar personnel involved in this incident [10] .'

In WWII, gliders were considerably more often used to transport fighting troops to the battlefield than to carry radar equipment.   That having been said, it is equally important to acknowledge the contribution made by the use of radar equipment for navigation purposes on squadrons whose aircraft were dedicated to glider-towing or to transportation duties, sometimes in a mass landing by glider-borne or parachute troops, sometimes in covert operations.

---

* The other two crews had their radar packed in crates which in turn were stowed in specific locations in a Horsa for load balancing; each individual crate was weighed and its location recorded for future use.

By the middle of 1942, ideas in the melting pot to make use of radar in military operations which would involve glider-borne troops and/or parachute troops included equipment to be carried on board leading formations of tug and parachute aircraft for accurate navigation and the use of some form of Rebecca, carried in gliders and as well as in tug and parachute aircraft, to facilitate identification of the landing zone. This would need ground beacons on whose signals the troop-carrying formations could home-in; these beacons, with the personnel to operate them, would have landed from leading formations engaged in the particular operation.   It was, however, 'long term policy' [11] .

The first positive move came with the allocation of Rebecca equipment to # 38 Wing, arrangements to fit '1 Horsa and 1 Hamilcar or 2 Horsa gliders' with Rebecca, the allotment of suitably-equipped aircraft to carry parachute troops or to tow gliders and the posting of personnel to operate and maintain this equipment, the aim being to enable trials to be carried out without delay and techniques to be developed [12] . The emphasis would be on providing the airborne forces with homing facilities and assuring the accuracy of navigation for their aircraft.   As for the glider-borne equipment, by the autumn of 1942 there were test flights with Horsas, which showed that the aerials of an experimental Rebecca set were 'completely satisfactory' [13] and on 9 February, at RAE Stonehenge, came the flight tests on the first production model of Rebecca Mk III in a Horsa.

No RDF equipment having hitherto been fitted in gliders, no establishment therefore existed at that time for RDF personnel to maintain glider-borne equipment.   The outcome was agreement among those concerned that this should approximate 1 Flying Officer RDF officer at Glider Squadron HQ, 1 Sergeant, 2 Corporals and 7 Aircraftmen RDF Mechanics (Air) for major maintenance for the Maintenance Squadron and 3 flying flights, each with 1 Corporal and 2 Aircraftmen RDF Mechanics (Air) for daily maintenance [14] .

38 Wing would start with some 20 Horsas and 7 Hamilcars modified for Rebecca, some 20 Eurekas and a suggested 50 crews to be trained to fly those gliders.   Early flight trials and aerial measurements during May/June 1943 gave a Eureka Mark II beacon a maximum range of 35 miles at 5,000 ft and a minimum range of 12 miles at 500 ft [15] .   The time for these gliders, those crews and their equipment to see action was now fast approaching, instructions being given for 25 Horsas to be dispatched to North West Africa during August and September 1943 with a further 8 ready for towing by end-September and the possibility of an additional 20 Horsas per month from October onwards [16] .

For security purposes, should there be a risk that either a Rebecca set or a Eureka beacon might find its way into enemy possession, their relative importance was established in a memo from the Director of Radar at Air Ministry, writing to the Air C-in-C at the Allied Expeditionary Air Force HQ on 28 January 1944, with reference to what he called 'the projected use of Eureka Mk II by Airborne Division in the Western European war theatre' [17] .   There was provision for a detonator to be fitted, so that in the event of such a beacon having to be abandoned, it could be destroyed.   It was considered 'highly important that Eureka Mk II should not fall into enemy hands' and full detonation instructions should be given to all units likely to use those beacons. Rebecca Mk II and Mk III had the necessary space for a detonator too, though fitting was no longer necessary because it had been decided that 'no disastrous results are likely to ensue if this equipment falls into enemy hands intact.'

Meanwhile for the forthcoming invasion of Europe, it seems that while the need was for only 50 Rebecca-equipped Horsas out of the 850 being prepared for those operations in early spring 1944, eventually as many as one in three Horsas were to be similarly equipped, though this proportion dropped substantially in the next six months, causing the radar specialists at Air Ministry to seek guidance on 'the policy for equipping gliders with Rebecca Mk III in all theatres, in order that provisioning action may be taken at the earliest possible date' [18]. The consequence was a decision that 'only Hadrian II gliders shall be used in the Far Eastern theatre', that the total numbers of gliders involved would be 1,400, the Rebecca requirement being similar to the one-in-ten proportion applied to the Horsas and Hamilcars in Britain [19].

Meanwhile the Allies' use of parachute troops and gliders in Operation *Dragoon*, a key component in the invasion of southern France, would go down as being 'without doubt the most successful airborne operation of its kind yet undertaken by Allied forces in this theatre', in the words contained in a 14-page report produced by the Assistant Adjutant General, Allied Force HQ, on 25 October 1944 [20]. The plan called for a night drop using airborne pathfinder crews, a main parachute lift of 396 plane loads to follow, with subsequent glider landings by 38 Waco and Horsa gliders and then, later in the day, 42 paratroop plane loads to be dropped with the subsequent use of 335 Waco gliders.

Once the target date for that operation had been set [D-Day for Operation *Dragoon* was 15 August 1944], it could not be changed to suit the airborne troops even though it necessitated a drop without the assistance of moonlight. At their stations at ten airfields extending some 150 miles along the Italian peninsula, the troop carrier units assembled... then it was time for the three pathfinder units to be airborne, their take-off being followed by that of the main parachute lift about an hour later.

In so far as the contribution made by radar-based navigational aids was concerned, the relevant paragraph of the Assistant Adjutant General's report begins with high commendation indeed for the radio, radar and other marker installations; they were 'undoubtedly, responsible for the accuracy achieved in carrying out the flight mission'. It goes on to define their location, purpose and achievement; however, since there then emerges a rather disturbing sting in the tail, it is appropriate to quote this part of the report in full [21]. So...

> 'The radio, radar and other marker installations were, undoubtedly, responsible for the accuracy achieved in carrying out the flight mission. Eurekas had been installed at each wing departure point, the command departure point, the north east tip of Elba, Giroglia Island (North Corsica) and on three marker beacon boats spaced 30 miles apart on the course from Corsica to the first landfall checkpoint at Agay, France. These worked exceedingly well, with an average reception of 25 miles. Holophane lights had also been placed at three positions and aided the navigators in correcting their courses against the contrary wind currents. Their reception averaged 8 miles until the DZs were reached, at which time they became

invisible because of the haze and ground fog. MF beacons (the radio compass homing devices) were installed at Elba, North Corsica, and on the centre marker beacon boat, and were also dropped on the DZs along with the Eurekas and Holophane lights. Many pilots reported that they received these signals up to 30 miles. The MF beacons often kept the aircraft on beam when they occasionally lost the Rebecca signal on their Eurekas. In too many cases [*those words are underlined in the report*], the Rebecca signals exhibited a tendency to drift off the frequency despite constant operational checking. It should be emphasized again that the entire parachute drop was accomplished in an absolutely "blind" state by the troop carrier pilots who had to depend entirely on the MF beacons and Eureka sets for their signal to drop the paratroopers. Such evident functional defects in the Eureka-Rebecca sets should not and must not be accepted in future airborne operations. Brigadier Pritchard, Officer Commanding, 2nd Parachute Brigade, felt that this single deficiency could have jeopardized the complete operation.'

In the Far East theatre of operations, radar-based navigation aids were said to have provided 'generally very satisfactory results' in Operation *Dracula*, a Rangoon paradrop on 30 April 1945. A report on this, which calls it 'one of the most successful paratroop operations of this war' [22], refers to 800 paratroops, 18 door bundles and 221 parapacks being put down by the initial serial. It was 'very nearly 100 per cent successful', with only eight minor injuries reported among the paratroops and 'every returning pilot enthusiastically stated upon interrogation that this mission was the most perfect they had flown'. The RAF Chief Intelligence Officer concluded that…

'The results in the use of the special navigational aids were generally very satisfactory. Loran provided excellent over-water fixes in doubtful weather conditions. The SCR-717-C in the Pathfinder provided island and coast line presentation and inland navigation was aided by the use of hills and rivers as other check points. The equipment also provided an excellent means of checking Loran fixes and of accurate navigation through inclement weather encountered *en route*. The Rebecca-Eureka proved accurate in identifying the turning point at Ngayok Bay, the average range obtained being 22 miles. Of the four Mk II British Eurekas dropped on the DZ, one was working by the time the main serial arrived. Average range obtained with this beacon was 11 miles.'

Radar technician Flavio Botari's 20-month sojourn in Britain from April 1944 was a 'hands-on' function from start to finish, even to the point of having to vacate one of the trains taking him from his arrival port in Scotland to Bournemouth and add muscle-power to locomotive-power; it was 'so loaded with bods that we actually had to get off and push it around a curve! [23] '. In Canada, Flavio was with # 1 RDF, Eastern Air Command, 'probably the most powerful unit in Canada at the time, an RM3A with its 100 ft wooden tower and 100-mile range, patrolling the approaches to Halifax'; in Britain, he was working on very different equipment doing a very different job, looking after GEE and Rebecca installed in Stirlings – the first of the RAF's four-engined bombers, now fulfilling a new role to drop people and supplies covertly into the occupied countries and overtly to tow troop-carrying Horsa gliders in airborne operations that included Normandy and Arnhem.

A member of # 299 Squadron and serving alongside # 196 Squadron, initially at Steeple Ashton in Wiltshire, then at Wethersfield in Essex and finally at Shepherds Grove in Suffolk, he speaks fondly of the Stirling, which both squadrons were flying throughout his time with them. He notes that...

'When the Stirling was retired from bombing operations, because the rugged old girl couldn't fly high enough, she was stripped of all arms except for the four-gun tail turret and supplied with GEE, to help navigate to and from the target area, and with Rebecca for the final precision-approach to the target. In our case, since we weren't bombing, the term "target" meant the location where the Stirlings would drop their load or, if used as a tug, release their gliders. The Stirling was huge – you could walk upright for most of the length of the fuselage – which was ideal; and its engines could take all kinds of punishment – the air-cooled Hercules would even run with missing cylinders, which was a great advantage over the Merlin where it needed only a ruptured glycol line to seize-up.

'For what we called "night intruder raids", the Stirlings would usually fly at a low level to avoid enemy radar and to take advantage of the sleeve-valve Hercules engine's low noise level. Sometimes the squadron would be dropping someone by parachute; sometimes it would be containers the size of a 500 lb bomb and filled with all kinds of supplies which would have created useful mayhem when the requests came in from across the Channel. Whether these flights were carried out to transport "special delivery" supplies, or to drop individuals secretly and silently into enemy territory by parachute or to take groups of paratroops to the battlefield to form into a fighting unit, the exit point was a hatch in the fuselage floor.

'Let's imagine the situation in the aircraft on such a mission. With the GEE set having helped him most of the way, the navigator watches the target signal appear on his Rebecca cathode ray tube as two "arms", one on each side of a vertical trace. A shorter arm means a weaker signal, a longer arm a stronger signal, so the necessary adjustment is made to equalize the arms. Now the aircraft is going straight in; the increasing movement of the arms down the tube indicating that the target is getting closer. The Rebecca CRT has three range settings – Long, Medium and Close – and the final setting (Close) pinpoints the target. Then, when the arms reach the bottom of the final trace, you're there! In all probability a resistance group is waiting to collect those badly-needed supplies so the crew in the Stirling will have wanted to drop them as close as possible so as to reduce the risks to those on the ground.

'With the combined use of GEE and Rebecca, very accurate positioning could be achieved without the need for visual contact. For still greater accuracy, the response signal picked up in the aircraft would come from a transponder on the ground – a portable unit with a whip antenna and powered by a string of batteries strapped around the waist of its operator.

This person, trained in the use of this equipment, would have parachuted in for this very purpose. To make detection difficult for the enemy, the transponder's portability made it easy to change the drop point; and to increase that difficulty, the triggering burst of energy from the aircraft would go out on one radio frequency and the response on a different frequency. The GEE antenna was in the form of a slim whip hanging under the Stirling's nose while the Rebecca antennae stuck out on either side of the nose. There was a switch-motor inside the receiver to switch the incoming signal from one antenna to the other in rapid succession.

'The navigators loved Rebecca, not only because it simplified their task in getting to the drop point, it was also something which could be used to get them back home again. There must have been a great temptation, sometimes, to rely on this radar aid when you were supposed to be using conventional methods of navigation – a bit like school kids these days who use a calculator for their sums. I do know, though, that on certain practice runs, the CO would give orders to cover the CRTs so that the navigators could brush up on their dead reckoning! [24] '

Envisaged as early as the summer of 1942 for troop-carrying operations and so used in the Mediterranean and Far East theatres of war as has been described earlier in this chapter, the airborne Rebecca and ground-based Eureka partnership was used in an entirely different manner throughout the campaign in North West Europe. Modified for the purpose, the Rebecca/Eureka combination was employed as navigational aid by aircraft of the Second Tactical Air Force whose role was to take pictures of target areas during darkness with the help of photo-flares. Although used to considerable advantage, daylight aerial photography wasn't always sufficiently up to date to make effective tactical judgements on a fast-changing battlefield. A crucial element in night photo-reconnaissance, the 'excellence' of the work of the Eureka-H units was commended in a message of congratulations and thanks to all crew members which the AOC-in-C, 2nd TAF, addressed to # 34 Wing HQ on 8 June 1945 [25]. He noted that there had been Eureka-H cover over substantially the whole Army operational area at all times. To achieve this, he stated, 'it has been necessary for beacons to move often for long distances and at short notice'. The AOC-in-C continued:

'The service given by Eureka-H beacons has been exemplary. This has only been so because of the keenness and efficiency of the crews. These small units have often worked under uncomfortable conditions, sometimes well within shell fire range of the enemy. The work itself has not been spectacular, but the obtaining of photographs by night has been a vital requirement, and to a very large extent it could not have been done without the aid of Eureka-H beacons.'

In 34 Wing there were three long-range photographic-reconnaissance squadrons – # 16 Squadron with Spitfires, # 69 Squadron with Wellingtons and # 140 Squadron with Mosquitoes; in addition there was a meteorological flight with high-altitude Spitfires. Eight Eureka-H beacon units were formed, trained and used in Normandy, from the early days of the invasion right through to the end of hostilities in Europe, the first four five-man crews assembling at Renscombe Downs in mid-April 1944 (numbered 5320-5323) and the second group (5324-5327) following the same itinerary some few weeks behind them.   Both the Mosquitoes and the Wellingtons carried Rebecca-H, the smaller and faster Mosquitoes being the main beacon users.

Each beacon crew comprised two radar mechanics, one of them being the NCO in charge, a radar operator, a motor transport mechanic and a dispatch rider.   Fred Hunt, an RCAF Leading Aircraftman who was in RAMSU [standing for Radar and Mobile Signals Unit] 5320, 'Two-Zero', remembers meeting his fellow radar mechanics in the first four crews at 34 Wing HQ at RAF Station Hartfordbridge in Hampshire [later to become Blackbushe Airport].   The majority of the RMs were, as was Fred, crew members from disbanded Light Warning units which had been in existence since early 1943 and therefore well experienced in mobile radar.   He recalls the RMs' first move together, to the Telecommunications Research Establishment (TRE) for a two-week course on the circuitry and operation of Eureka-H, before joining the ROs and MTMs at Renscombe Downs.   Being billeted in civilian homes in West Malvern necessitated a hike over the Malvern Hills to reach TRE, though 'this was alleviated by a pub crawl on the circuitous route around the base of the hills on the return trip in the evening'.

A description of the equipment for a Eureka-H beacon shows that...

> 'It was mounted in a 15 cwt signals van with the antenna on top, hinged so that it could be lowered when we were on the road, though this did tend to make the van top-heavy and therefore called for care when driving into curves at high speed!   The antenna consisted of four vertical dipoles in a vertical line and behind them was a parabolic-shaped reflector made of chicken-wire on a 10 ft high framework comprising three-quarter-inch pipe. The array produced a horizontal beam width of 90 degrees.   Power for the equipment was provided by Douglas twin-cylinder petrol engines driving electrical generators' [26].

A description of the application of the Rebecca-H equipment shows that...

> 'The aircraft's navigator knew, from a pre-flight briefing, the ranges of the targets from two beacons.   Depending upon the geography of the area to be photographed, he would decide on which beacon he would use to fly at a constant distance.   Using Rebecca, he would direct his pilot to fly to a point on this constant range line; then the pilot would fly along that line until the Rebecca display showed the navigator that they had reached the desired range from the second beacon.   The navigator would then press the button to initiate the release of flares and the start of photography' [27].

On 2 July 1944, Two-Zero was on its first operational site, six kilometers from the frontline and on the southern slope of a hill facing Caen, where the living area was in the midst of some 200 guns ranging from 75 mms to anti-aircraft guns.   These 'appeared to all fire simultaneously every hour, supplemented by 16-inch shells from a warship lying offshore; these passed overhead periodically, sounding much like a freight train in the sky'.   The fatal effect of an artillery bombardment became evident to the crew of Two-Zero when, three weeks later on a site north-east of Caen, the very first enemy shell hit a Wireless Observer Unit attached to them for communication purposes.   Two were killed, two were injured badly enough to require evacuation to England while the fifth member of this unit escaped with a scratch on the head.   They had been sitting down to afternoon tea when the shell struck their post...

For the crews of 34 Wing aircraft using these ground beacons for pinpoint accuracy in navigation, the night tasks at that time 'were mainly concerned with trying to watch for German movement of reinforcements in the areas immediately behind their forward troops, so detraining stations were the principal targets'.   It must have been heartening to aircrew and ground personnel alike to learn later that when a report was subsequently published about the activities of the Panzer Lehr Division, it paid 'a fine tribute to the night work of RAF squadrons dropping flares, flashes and bombs as a result of which movements were severely hampered and much sleep was lost' 28 .   During the early weeks of the Normandy campaign 'many excellent reconnaissances were carried out by 140 and 69 Squadrons, who were quickly developing their technique'.   Their role was not entirely confined to photo-reconnaissance however; on one occasion four of 34 Wing's aircraft were given the task of dropping flares to illuminate an area near Caudebec so that pilots who were skilled in the role of what might be termed airborne spotting posts could continue to direct artillery fire even at night.   It was 'a great success, a message of congratulation being received from the Canadian Army 29 '.

Moving on from the area of Caen and operating in the American sector with a new Wireless Observer Unit, Fred Hunt and his colleagues found themselves close to an American hospital unit where most of the patients were survivors of tank battles and suffering from shell shock.   A number of German prisoners were looking after them and other prisoners were offered to Two-Zero 'to look after our housekeeping chores.   However we refused as the difficulty in providing guards for them far outweighed their potential use'.   A subsequent transfer of beacon location saw the unit having to struggle through a 'wildly cheering Saturday afternoon crowd in the streets in newly-liberated Brussels'.   One 'perk' of their brief stay in the vicinity of the Belgian capital was the privilege of free tram rides – 'The German military hadn't paid and the Belgian authorities granted their allies the same freedom!'

It must have seemed as if for Two-Zero the horrors of war were now far behind... Fred describes the unit's arrival at Boschgot in Eastern Flanders:

> 'It seemed that the entire village turned out and sat by the roadside to watch us set up camp and prepare the technical vehicle for the night's operations. Our antenna was pointed almost due north as we were to cover the area of the Schelde Estuary over the next month and a half.   The local people were very friendly and I considered the time spent at this site as the high point in the beacon's lifetime.   There were no other troops in the immediate neighborhood and life was very peaceful.   No artillery, bombs or other signs of war.   The children used to stop on their way to school in the morning and trade eggs for hard-tack biscuits.   Some nuns from a nearby convent even baked we "liberators" some custard pies and we never lacked invitations to nearby homes.'

Although not directly affected by the German offensive in the Ardennes in December 1944, Two-Zero being in southern Holland and on the outskirts of the airfield at Gilze-Rijen, New Year's Day 1945 provided visible and dramatic confirmation that the war was still much in being when the airfield was attacked by some 16 enemy aircraft.   Fred and his colleagues, sleeping in a nearby farmhouse, were rudely awakened by the commotion.   Still in their night attire, they grabbed their rifles and optimistically commenced firing at the assortment of Me 109s, FW 190s and Me 262s screaming overhead.   Fred notes that 'most of us were in our pajamas so were probably breaking the rules of war by not being in uniform when firing on the enemy'.

A similar raid the same day on Melsbroek, on the outskirts of Brussels, where 34 Wing was headquartered, proved more serious.   Six of the Wing's Spitfires, six of its Mosquitoes and 11 of its Wellingtons were destroyed and its personnel suffered 25 casualties, 6 of them fatal, in an attack at 0900 hours by about 40 FW 190s and Me 109s.   The enemy planes 'fired off all their ammunition in the course of 25 minutes, during which they were almost unopposed, as our Bofors guns had been converted to their anti-tank role in deference to the Hun Ardennes offensive and were loaded with anti-tank shells' [30] .

On 24 March 1945, with Two-Zero back at Boschgot after various repositioning moves and a short spell of UK leave for its crew, an order was received early that morning to point the antenna to the west, an unusual direction when setting-up for the day's operations.   Around 9 am, when Fred was taking the first watch of the day, 'the beacon's earphones began to emit a queer sound and it was obvious that the equipment was either unserviceable or being interrogated not by the customary single aircraft but by a large number of aircraft'.   Quick checks showed that the equipment appeared serviceable so what was going on?   Within some 15 minutes Two-Zero knew the answer: there was the familiar sound of approaching aero-engines and the sky began to darken with the presence of several hundred Dakotas over-flying the beacon.   Later, it emerged that these were carrying paratroops bound for their landing sites east of the Rhine and north of the German town of Wesel.   It was this beacon's final function in support of operations against the enemy.

CHAPTER 12: OSWALD AND THE V2

I f anyone could always be relied upon to produce just the right word or a suitably descriptive passage, it was surely Winston Churchill in his wartime days as an Allied leader and Britain's prime minister. The tiniest amount of imagination is all that is needed to visualize his Service commanders and others who had a dominant role to play, desperately gathering from all possible sources the facts and the judgements with which to respond to his probing questions.

Aware that Germany had created a means of rocket-bombing Britain was enough to have him composing, swiftly and succinctly, a series of questions which he addressed to his government's Secretary of State for Air on 28 July 1944 in order to obtain a better understanding of this new vengeance weapon, successor to the V1 flying bomb which had been directed against London since shortly after D-Day. Where the V1 was visible, audible, low-flying and increasingly able to be destroyed by fighters in the air and gunfire from the ground, the V2 posed a much more serious threat because it would attain speeds and heights far beyond the capability of aircraft – and hit the ground before anyone heard it.

Churchill, signing his questioning personal Minute from 10 Downing Street, Whitehall, in his customary manner with the initials W S C, began simply [1] : 'Pray let me have a report on the various countermeasures against rocket attack.' He could not have been more precise in his approach or more positive in making his requirements known, then going on to demand information in such detail about what was being done that it seemed he was telling the recipient and others having sight of it, what he himself proposed should be done.

With its succession of pertinent questions, it was a message that ended with what was perhaps a typical Churchillian rallying call, on the lines of victory over the rocket-bomb being all that was needed to dash one of the enemy's last hopes of continuing the fight.   He asked: 'Is sufficient effort being directed to the bombing of the liquid oxygen installations, and other key points in the enemy's preparations?   What are the arrangements for locating and reporting the discharge of the rockets?   What plans have been made to bring down instant air attacks on the vulnerable train of vehicles which will be collected at the firing points when rockets are being fired? Have such attacks been practiced? We must be sure that heavy and immediate counter-attack falls on every point of the enemy's rocket organization as soon as it takes shape. The defeat of the rocket attack will be a victory calculated to remove one of the enemy's last hopes.'

The use of radar equipment, together with the skills of the personnel manning Britain's coastal defense chain who faced the Netherlands, Belgium and France from which direction the rocket-bombs would come, would be vital participants in their potential detection and destruction.   A meeting at the Air Ministry, just over a fortnight before Churchill began asking questions about countermeasures, discussed the 'imminent threat' of the rocket-bomb, then code-named 'Big Ben' and generally known as the V2 only after the first ones hit London on 8 September 1944. There was, so those attending the Air Ministry meeting on 11 July 1944 were told, 'a possibility' that the rocket-bomb would be used against Britain 'in a matter of weeks, three weeks has been mentioned' 2 .

The background was that information had reached Britain from Sweden, where radio equipment from one of these rocket-bombs had been recovered, and from Poland, which was a testing area, indicating the existence of this new and threatening weapon.   It was judged that the radio equipment was not only complicated, the rocket-bombs carried within them a high standard of anti-jamming technique.   It was considered essential for the Telecommunications Research Establishment (TRE) at Malvern to form a team to determine how best to cope with the various requirements; for steps to be taken to develop special high power transmitters, receivers and aerials at high speed and to anticipate rapid modifications 'and even fresh starts' at short notice; for the 'Y' Service, which monitored enemy transmissions for intelligence purposes, to have additional listening posts with scanning receivers operating uninterruptedly; and for # 80 Wing – the organization responsible for undertaking radio countermeasures against enemy radio systems employed against the UK – to have facilities for listening on the frequencies indicated by the 'Y' posts and to determine modulations etc to apply to the transmitters.   One indication of the extreme urgency of the situation came with a new priority grading, that of 'absolute', which the Ministry of Aircraft Production was to institute when meeting requirements relative to 'Big Ben'; another and more visible sign was the introduction of a 'Big Ben Watch', utilizing special equipment at five CH stations from Swingate to Ventnor in anticipation of detecting the new missiles during part of their flight, this information to be passed to a 'Big Ben' computation unit at # 11 Group Filter Room at Stanmore.

Air Ministry's own signals specialists considered that 'at present the available information is vague and insufficient to be able to allow any opinion being formed as to whether effective radio countermeasures can be taken' 3 .   Given that this new weapon was an explosives-carrying rocket designed to rise from Point A on the Continent and to fall at Point B in Britain, a more positive attitude than this could be adopted with regards to detecting its departure and flight.   There were the more obvious measures, all of which were considered and some brought into play: patrolling aircraft to try and intercept radio control transmissions during experimental firing at the ranges; aerial patrols to watch for a launch and to establish the firing point, loosely traceable from the tell-tale vapor trail rising vertically to around 50,000 ft; increased use of existing airborne jammers; ground-based flash-spotting stations and search receivers suspended in the air by balloons; and sound-ranging equipment, all of these additional to the role of the radar stations. These would have a dual purpose: to provide data regarding the location of the firing points and to warn, within the short flight time, that a missile was on its way 4 .   A dim memory, maybe, to those who served on those stations is photographic equipment which went by the name of Oswald and Willie: Oswald recorded continuously, Willie proceeding only for a two-minute period and having to be started by pressing a push-button.   It must have placed an unnerving responsibility upon those engaged in this function, because the camera known as Willie would only be activated if the echo-signal was recognized sufficiently quickly as being due to a 'Big Ben' launch.   Two-minute Willie was the more critical of the two cameras because it provided a full record of the CRDF data for later examination, with stored information about range, bearing and time, whereas non-stop Oswald recorded only range and time.

Where detection was concerned there would always be a use for radar. It was immaterial whether the missile was controlled by radio, as first intimated, or merely fired as if by a gun and allowed to free-fall; but if the missile was not controlled by radio, there would be no call for radio countermeasures activities. In early August, radio-control was 'confirmed' and the 'most likely attack on this control by radio countermeasures must be by jammers carried in aircraft' [5]. The following month, when this form of attack had begun, 'most of the information concerning rockets' was being obtained from photographic records at Type 1 stations. Useful data had come from radar stations in the UK to assist in locating areas from which the rockets were fired but, 'as was expected' these stations could not be relied upon to give early warning [6].

By October, despite a continuous watch on all frequency bands on which rocket control signals were likely to be heard, none was intercepted which could be associated with rocket launches and no radio countermeasures had been applied; and in December it was now 'definitely established' that radio was no longer installed in rockets launched against Allied targets, authorization being given for the cancellation of all anti-rocket radio listening stations and radio countermeasures in Britain [7].

The first two V2s to land in Britain (early evening on 8 September 1944 at Chiswick and Epping) were estimated to have come from Holland, one from the Amsterdam area and the other from the Rotterdam area. Unlike the V1s, which were fired from fixed sites on the ground in the main, the V2s could be launched from mobile sites. As their range was limited, London was soon no longer threatened but Belgium and Holland became target areas as a result of the Allied advance. In fact, Intelligence sources indicated that a 'limited number' of rockets launched against Antwerp were under radio control – beam control was a supposition – but the listening watches, with some indication of the radio frequency, had not recognized any such signal [8].

Radar mechs in Britain and on the Continent were in the forefront of the campaign against the V2s; it would seem that there was nothing that the Allies could do to stop one of those supersonic rockets once it had been launched... but surely there was something that could be done to minimize the effect of the V2 on the civilian population – like stopping so many from being launched and, more of a problem, warning responsible authorities who might then be able to take appropriate safeguards?

Charlie Mills, who had already served in the Pacific as a radar specialist during 1942/44, subsequently turned down an RCAF HQ offer of repatriation and went instead to Yatesbury for a microwave radar course with the result that he stayed in the UK for the remainder of the war, based on the East Coast on Final GCI stations.

He recalls...

'Three months as supernumerary Technical Officer at Neatishead in Norfolk, covering part of the northern approaches to London, produced my two and only claims to fame, both of them associated with Germany's two "vengeance weapons", the V1 and the V2.   We tracked the first air-launched V1 (Buzz Bomb) to be directed against the UK; it was a really weird sight on the screen with one blip splitting into two going in opposite directions.   As for the V2 rocket, we were on the receiving end of a dozen or so which landed in two circles around the station.   These were close enough to rattle things but not do any harm.   This resulted in photo-tracking equipment that recorded every sweep of the day' [9].

Bob Jones, a member of the RAF, whose first radar station posting was to Kete in Pembrokeshire – 'The place was simply over-run with Canadians, with as few as perhaps only three or so of us poor Britishers to maintain a balance of sorts!' – remembered that 'to avoid undue alarm among the populace just when it seemed we were getting the European affair completely under control, the authorities passed off the first several V2 explosions as being gas mains blowing up' [10].

He was among several radar technicians from across the UK who were sent on 'a special highly-secret course quite a few months before these rockets began to arrive' and noted that...

'The British Government knew all about them, both from their spy network and from members of the "underground" in Europe, plus of course their own decoding of Nazi radio communications traffic.   To counteract this threat, "Oswald" was created, whereby certain CH stations were modified, so that the tube was under constant camera observation.   Then, when an operator caught sight of the all-too-brief flash which signaled that a rocket had possibly been detected, she'd shout into her headset the code message "Big Ben at Bawdsey!" – or whatever the station was called.   By this time, the rocket itself had probably landed somewhere, confirming that the flash was indeed that of a V2!   Then Filter Room would pass back the code "Change Oswald!" to a few adjacent stations, indicating that specially-trained operators at these sites were to remove the photographic film and develop it with all speed in a close-by dark room.

'The recorded data from a few stations made it possible to back-track and compute the spot from which the rocket had been launched, and without further delay a small fleet of bombers or fighter-bombers would be dispatched to blast the hell out of the launch site.   Unfortunately these countermeasures proved effective for only a brief period; the Germans responded by developing high-speed mobile launchers which could fire off a rocket or two, then quickly scoot off somewhere else before the bombers arrived.   Reliable sources have said that if the V2 had been used on a sufficiently large scale before D-Day, it could very well have changed the entire course of the war, even resulting in the cancellation of D-Day, but fortunately for us the Nazis left it too late [11].'

RAF radar technician Roger Richards, commissioned in 1943 and posted some time later to Bawdsey, an original CH station, where 'Camera Oswald' was being installed, goes into more detail about this equipment.   He notes its range display as being 'intensity-modulated only, so that a target would appear as a bright dot at the indicated range.   The range trace was moved vertically down the tube very slowly, taking perhaps 30 to 90 seconds to complete its scan from top to bottom'.

Recalling the use of 'Oswald' when tracking V2 launches, he said:

> 'The track of a very fast moving target would differ greatly from that of a normal aircraft, which would be a nearly vertical line.   On the contrary, a V2 could be seen to go straight up through the lower lobe of the antenna, the range rate of change increasing as the missile trajectory tilted towards the target, giving a curve to the track on the CRT.   It would fade out as it reached the gap between the antenna lobes, then reappear in the next lobe, decreasing in range more rapidly as it reached its apex and began to descend.

> 'By comparing the shape of some of these curves with those recorded from missiles which had hit London, it was possible to make a fair estimate of the probability of a landfall in the London area.   The great fear of the Civil Defense authorities was the admittedly extremely small chance that a strike into the Thames between the underground railway system flood gates might breach the river bed, flooding the stations which were used as air raid shelters and causing heavy loss of life.   We were told by the senior technical officer at 60 Group who had special responsibility for this V2 work that our information was useful and that it was acted upon by closure of the watertight doors [12] .'

The London Passenger Transport Board (LPTB) was alone in being given these 'Big Ben' advance warnings.   Its control centre at Leicester Square was linked directly with # 11 Group Filter Room by telephone and when a warning came, the flood gates were closed immediately as a safety precaution.   According to a passage on page 499 of *The Second World War, 1939-1945, Royal Air Force, Signals*, Volume IV, Radar in Raid Reporting, while radar proved 'very valuable' as a means of locating firing points and launching sites, 'it did not achieve its secondary purpose of giving adequate early warning to the general public in the United Kingdom'.

Surprisingly perhaps, V2 rocket spotting activities were carried out even by Oboe ground station personnel.   Will Robson was on the mobile unit near Rips in Holland during a time that V2 rockets were being fired from Germany against targets in England.   He recalls that there was a period of down time during January 1945 until La Roche became fully operational again 'so our technical staff modified the Oboe equipment to operate as a radar station'.   This action was taken to enable his unit to help pinpoint rocket launching sites, the vapor trails of the V2 having been seen on a number of occasions.   He says:

> 'As I recall it, our technicians rotated the microwave antennas to the bearing at which we had observed the vapor trails.   They adjusted the Oboe set so that it produced the normal horizontal radar display, to determine the range as the rocket passed through our beam.   With the exact position of our mobile station, identified as map co-ordinates, both range and bearing

could be communicated to Bomber Command.   Our objective was to get a fix on the location of the rocket launchers, working independently of whatever may have been going on in England to identify those sites.   Of course there was no possibility of determining the path of the rocket, merely the range and bearing from our Oboe station, which I recall as being approximately 25 miles from Rips.   Nevertheless, we assumed that this would have been useful to Bomber Command when their people were working out the targets [13]'.

There were other lesser-known applications of radar in the air war, for example its use to assist searchlight crews working alongside anti-aircraft batteries.   This seems not to have been one of the more successful uses, however, and ground radar specialist Sydney Goldstein summarizes his own experience in this activity by noting that to the best of his knowledge 'very few "bogeys" were shot down but many of our night fighters had some scary moments when illuminated by our searchlights'.

At Wartling, one of the cabins facing onto the main plotting room was designated as the Searchlight Control Room.   It was manned by an Army officer with land-line communication to the searchlight batteries and had direct control over when the battery could 'Illuminate'.   The equipment...

'was a special type of radar display – a five-inch CRT with rotating yoke to act as a PPI and surrounded by a circle of mercury vapor lamps that illuminated the tube.   Through a lens system, this projected the image on the tube onto a mirror and then onto a flat ground glass screen about 36 inches in diameter.   A map of the area was drawn on the screen, with the position of the searchlights marked on it, enabling the officer to know where his searchlights were in relation to the radar blip, or blips, created by aircraft.   Co-ordination between our aircraft chasing a "bogey" and the searchlights was not always perfect and many a night I heard a pilot screaming to "take the candles off me" when it was the "friendly" not the "hostile" which was in the searchlight's beam.

'One major problem was the instability of those mercury vapor lamps.   It only needed a momentary drop in voltage, perhaps caused by a bomb affecting the country's electricity grid, and the lamps would fail.   They would stay out until, having cooled sufficiently for the internal pressure to drop and allow an internal arc to strike, they would light up again.   When this happened the searchlight controller was "in the dark" in more ways than one; furthermore, he couldn't control the batteries at such times so they would light-up independently and most of the time find our fighters instead of the enemy.   We radar specialists did what we could, such as trying to increase the speed of the cooling fans, but all anyone could do was just to wait to resume operations [14].'

Much scientific effort was behind radar-based applications which seemed worthwhile at the time and then disappeared, perhaps because to continue with the idea wasn't judged to be cost- or time-effective or maybe on account of the reason for its conception and development no longer being as pressing.

A member of the Electronics Training Group, US Army Signal Corps, Jerry Stover arrived in England in October 1941.   With a colleague, Ed Usher, he was attached to the RAF for training on airborne radar at Cranwell and Prestwick.   After Pearl Harbour, they were assigned to # 233 Squadron, Coastal Command, at Thorney Island.   Then, after a brief tour as Radar Observers flying in Hudsons and looking for U-boats, they were transferred in February 1942 to Hurn, where the RAF was carrying out experimental work [*] .

Hurn, where Ed, a pre-war private pilot, was able to get in a few hours 'stick-time' as co-pilot in both civilian and military aircraft, provided a change of pace from long sea patrols to short, sharp bursts of activity to sort out what was going right and what was going wrong in a particular series of experiments.   He explains one project which relied on radar equipment in an ambitious bid to recycle high explosives...

'The scheme was to lay a beam across a bombing range so that RAF bombers aborting a mission could bring back their bombs over land and, instead of wasting them in the sea, as was customary, the bombs could be dropped on the range, unarmed and able to be salvaged.   It seemed a great idea – providing that a sufficiently precise method could be devised to get the bombers and their bombs to the right place.

'We mounted two 212 Mc/sec Yagi antennas on a small van, which was driven to the range, carefully aligned and leveled.   Ed and I then made runs in a Wellington bomber with cameras to check accuracy of simulated "drops".   The film showed surprising accuracy in the first day's runs and we were pretty excited.   The next test was flown on what the British call a "showery" day and this time the photos showed very uneven results.   We began to discuss wet antenna fittings, impedance changes and other possible causes.

'Then Ed, using a magnifying glass, made an intriguing discovery.   He detected that, on the good runs, the driver was outside and away from the van, as instructed; on bad runs, though, he was nowhere to be seen.   You can probably guess what was happening: when the rain started, he nipped back into the van to stay dry... and his weight tilted the van enough to throw the beam off!

'There's a lesson for all of us in what happened during those quite critical experiments at Hurn.   Shortly afterwards, I was back in the States and testing radars for the Air Force Board in Orlando, Florida.   There, also in business later, I too often forgot the Hurn lesson and frequently overlooked a simple solution to a complex problem [15] .'

Ed Usher, who stayed in England doing research work for the US Embassy, provided the sequel to those experiments to lay a beam across a bombing range. He told Jerry that finally consistent results were achieved at Hurn but that the bomb-

---

[*] When the Telecommunications Research Establishment (TRE) moved from Dundee to Worth Matravers in April 1940, its flying activities were carried out at Hurn. In May 1942, when TRE moved from Worth Matravers to Malvern, these were switched to Defford [*see page 53*].

recycling project was abandoned. H_2S and other radar navigational aids were coming along and Bomber Command had fewer aborted missions, thus the original requirement was no longer worth pursuing.

One radar-based device which came into being much earlier than H_2S and remained in operational use throughout WWII was IFF – Identification Friend or Foe. Besides its longevity, its widespread usage is noteworthy, though there could well be problems with IFF equipment in aircraft or on the ground that one radar mech or another would be called upon to resolve…

Having traveled from the UK to India by air in December 1943, wearing civilian clothes as a security measure in the event of the plane being forced down in a neutral country – he was on 'a high priority assignment' to install a special type of IFF interrogator unit at ground stations in South East Asia Command – Canadian radar technician Murdock ('Smitty') Smith, a Warrant Officer, and an RAF colleague, Jack Spivey, a Flying Officer, traveled across India four times, were into Burma twice, were cut off by the Japanese in Imphal and were three times around the island of Ceylon. Their job was to install those special units because 'their IFF did not respond on our radar frequencies [16]'.

He explains that the officially approved unit had its shortcomings, being able to indicate an aircraft's range but not its bearing, and with time to spare during one installation visit he and Jack 'made up a directional antenna from pieces of packing crates, some wire and a few pieces from our kit'; they tested it, confirmed to their satisfaction that it was 'far superior', then de-installed it and left the approved version in place. However, back in Calcutta, the pair were reprimanded 'for unauthorized work on an RAF radar unit' and banished to the Chittagong area with instructions to keep themselves out of trouble.

On their second day at 182 Wing HQ, Smitty was summoned into the CO's office to take a phone call from Douglas Gooderham, then the senior radar officer with the 3rd Tactical Air Force, who queried whether he had installed a directional IFF antenna at the Dimapur radar station. To Smitty's surprise, Gooderham asked whether he could do it again, Smitty's affirmative response leading to his own CO saying that he could get what he wanted from stores, he could have a vehicle and a driver, but 'whatever you said you could do in one week, you had better make sure it is done, because Gooderham is going to be here in one week to check it out'.

When the anticipated visit took place, Wing Commander Gooderham stood behind Smitty, who was directing a mock interception involving three USAAF Lightning fighters whose blips showed up at 100 miles even after the main radar contact had been lost. A few days later, the person who had reprimanded Smitty and Spivey instructed them to do an IFF installation at # 4 BSD, adding that if there was anything the pair did not understand about the blueprints, 'we could ask him and he would explain'. As Smitty recalls: 'Spivey looked at the blueprints and with a casual shrug said "I don't think we will have any trouble with these, I drew them" [17]'.

Where the airborne 'end' of IFF equipment was concerned, Angus Hamilton was the 'gen' man on # 176 Squadron for much the biggest part of its sojourn in South East Asia; this dubious distinction came about in much the same manner as many

Servicemen became specialists in a given field. He would have been the first to admit that 'I didn't know much about IFF, but neither did anyone else [18] '. Most of the reported faults on this equipment on board the Beaufighters on his squadron were due to failure of one of the big 'condensers' – subsequently known as 'capacitors'. Sometimes, he says, new ones were available but most of the replacements were salvaged from 'detonated' sets, rarely a month going by without at least one IFF set being detonated. Angus came to the conclusion that 'judging by the reaction of "the brass", losing a few IFFs by detonation was preferable to having one fall into enemy hands!'

Roy Taylor, an instructor in IFF equipment for a while, recalls that every effort possible was made to prevent information about this radar system from becoming known to the enemy. An explosive charge was fitted so that the airborne equipment could be triggered in the event of a crash in hostile territory; and even the wiring was in a single color, green, so that the circuit could not be traced by conventional color coding.

Besides working with radar-based equipment and systems, radar specialists in the Allied air forces would sometimes become involved with radar countermeasures (RCM) activities, one of the best-known of these RCM products being 'Window', the aluminum strips that fluttered down to 'blind' enemy radar.

In late 1944, back in Europe following a tour of duty in the USA and now Radar Officer for the US 9th Air Force, Jerry Stover found himself with a problem concerning Window.   Both the US 8th and 9th Air Forces were making wide use of Window, as was the RAF, and this created a shortage which saw the 9th starting to run out. As he describes it, 'the 8th was getting priority because they were doing deep penetration raids into Germany, but we needed the protection of Window because our B26 mediums were doing short bridge-busting runs and still getting hurt [19] .' There had to be a way around the problem – but what was it?

To appreciate Jerry's eventual solution requires an awareness of the fact that Britain and Germany both had 'Window', the opposing sides holding off using it so as not to give away to the other this 'secret' radar-beating application [*] .   There were, he explains, differences in the size of these aluminum strips: the Allies' Window, used against a 600 MHz gun-laying radar system, measured about a quarter of an inch in width and was some ten inches in length, whereas the Germans' countermeasures against the 212 MHz GCI radar system required a strip about three times that length. Jerry takes up this story, which is one of useful intelligence, resourcefulness and justifiable bribery...

> 'We were in Verdun when I learned that US troops had captured a warehouse full of German "Window". Here was our salvation! Being three times the length of ours, it would need to be cut and then packaged for automatic release.   Clearly this was a task for our ever-resourceful Chief Warrant Officer, so I gave him some trucks, a pass to get him to Paris with

---

[*] The British finally decided it would help them more than it would hurt. Bomber Command used it with great success in a raid on Hamburg on the night of 24 July 1943. The Germans' radar-controlled guns and searchlights were jammed and the RAF had light casualties.

his vehicles, explaining what was needed.   Three days later we had our Window.   When I asked how he did it, the CWO, looking beat but happy, answered that it had been easy; he had collected the strips, taken them to a bookbinder in Paris and given him five cartons of cigarettes and two cans of gasoline. Apparently he worked all night but he reckoned that the reward was worth it when cigarettes and gasoline were as scarce to him as Window was to us!'

That episode occurred round about the time that radar technical officer Roy Cuthbert was with RAF Fighter Command and on the staff of a unique training unit known as # 584 Squadron – '584' for a reason that will soon become obvious.   Arriving in the UK from Canada in 1941, Roy worked first on IFF while a member of a Wellington squadron based at Molesworth and the following year joined 60 Group, going on to serve in Northern Ireland on CH and CHL, a COL unit (AMES 5001) in North West Africa and finally, when back in the UK, at Dimlington and then at Swingate during the 'Big Ben' V2 back-tracking period during 1944.

Events then came about that saw him engaged in a much less documented aspect of radar history when moving out of 60 Group and into 584 Squadron.   Located initially at Drem, a few miles from Edinburgh, the squadron transferred soon to RAF Manston which, being one of the nearest fighter bases to the coast of France, played an important part in the Battle of Britain in the summer of 1940.   The distinctive factor about 584 was the type of radar equipment in use on the squadron, SCR 584, hence the squadron's numerical identification.   The SCR 584 was a mobile system that had been modified from its more customary gun-laying role for anti-aircraft defense to that of controlling bomb-carrying aircraft engaged on close-support operations on the battlefield.   The much-used and widely-employed SCR 584 originated on the other side of the Atlantic, though it was Roy's understanding that the British Branch of the MIT Radiation Lab had assisted with the design and supply of components to effect this quite remarkable transformation.

RAF squadrons were accustomed to possessing upwards of a dozen aircraft though 584 had only three – they were Spitfire fighters adapted to carry bombs – and on 584's books there were three pilots to fly them, three flight controllers and two radar officers – Roy, a Canadian, and Ed Joce, who was in the RAF – the responsibility of these two technical officers being to provide operator skill training.   The unit itself was employed on hands-on close support demonstrations for pilots, flight controllers and radar operators.   Roy recalls:

'For the trainees to learn the skills of VHF radio communication between the flight controller on the ground and the pilot in the air was most important. When the time came for them to put into practice what they had been taught about the principle and the application of radar-directed tactical bombing, the way I remember it working was for the flight controllers to "navigate" the pilots to targets in the area of the Thames estuary where there were observers in place to record the accuracy of their bombing.

'Trainees generally came from active RAF Tactical Air Force and US Tactical Air Corps units, the Free French, the Poles and the Czechs among them, and often they would fly directly to Manston to join us for three days for their hands-on instruction.

'The radar set was magnetron-based, 10 cm, with an operator seated at the left position handling range and the one at the right position handling azimuth and elevation. The equipment occupied a single 19 ft 6 ins long semi-trailer, the 6 ft diameter parabolic dish being inside for stowage and travel, then rising on jack screws on the roof, making the SCR 584 a highly mobile, self-contained unit.

'Deployment of the parabola in this manner gave room in the trailer for the flight controller and for his close-support plotting table, its servos driving the pen that recorded the course of the aircraft being tracked. Since the servo elements showed strain under the auto-tracking mode, I made it my job as Technical Officer in charge of radar maintenance to monitor servo strain and to attempt preventive maintenance.

'The SCR 584 was both a pioneer and a winner on all fronts in its anti-aircraft role and with the formation of our training school we were hoping that, in the hands of those who had gone through our unit, this specially-modified version would achieve a similar success as an offensive weapon by providing precision guidance in directing tactical bombers *en route* to their target.

'All of us recognized that this was an application promising extreme versatility, being the means to benefit strike and photo-reconnaissance missions that called for speedy action with minimum briefing – for instance harassment, interdiction against enemy ground forces to reduce their positions and to isolate them from their resources, whatever might suggest itself as being tactically helpful to our own ground forces. Furthermore, personal experience in the role of flight controller on several SCR 584 bombing runs confirmed the accuracy achievable by this method, the reported displacement on one of those runs being just 35 yards.

'However, as can easily happen with all the best ideas in wartime, this one was destined for delay and to produce the inevitable frustrations. The first kit arrived in late 1944; however VE-Day came towards the middle of the following year and still there were no signs of the promised factory models. We were hard-pressed ourselves, being short of the necessary resources for maintenance and modifications and to train the crews in the manner we would have wished. We had no squadron test equipment for the SCR 584 – and we didn't even have a spare set for test or maintenance training! Unfortunate though it all was, 584 Squadron was nonetheless able to carry out the intended training program which enabled many pilots of single-engined fighter-bombers and the crews of twin-engined medium bombers to use this equipment in action in the closing stages of the war in Europe.

'There is probably no better justification for the introduction of SCR 584 as a "blind" bombing system than the fact that, as I understand it, in the "Battle of the Bulge" in the Ardennes, mid-December of '44, the only planes to fly in the days of near-zero visibility were SCR 584-directed tactical aircraft [20].'

An operational research team working with the British 21st Army Group made a detailed examination of the results obtained through the use of a mobile radar control post equipped with SCR 584 for air support activities, the flight controller seeing on a plotting table (scale 1:100,000) the immediate plan position of his aircraft within plus or minus 100 yards in range and plus or minus one tenth of one degree in bearing [21].   Using two-way RT communication, he would notify any necessary changes in height, course or airspeed on the way to the target, warn the pilot that he was approaching the bomb-release point and then tell him when to drop his bomb load.   Meanwhile, of course, the equipment had been calculating the exact point over which the bombs must be released, making due allowance for speed, height, wind and terminal velocity of bombs.

The team's report   showed that operations could be carried out on days when, without the assistance of the SCR 584, they would be impossible; that with the pilot flying on instructions received from the flight controller, personal errors of navigation were eliminated; that the accuracy was such 'that targets can be accepted much closer to our own troops by this system than any other radar means'; and that 'unlike any other radar sets the SCR 584 is not very exacting in its siting requirements' [22]. The obvious disadvantage – shades of Oboe! – centred on the necessity for the aircraft to fly straight and level for the final several miles to its target, thereby becoming easy prey for the enemy's ack-ack batteries.   This was countered by the fact that in every case examined by the operational research section, the attacks had always been carried out from between 8,000 and 10,000 feet, which put them beyond the range of light flak, and that most were flown above thick cloud in situations where the heavy AA guns were visually controlled.

During the period 8 February 1945 to 5 March 1945, operating first at Hatert and then further forward at Materborn, # 1 Mobile Radar Control Post (MRCP) controlled 409 planes – medium and fighter bombers – which dropped 1,478 bombs (348 tons) on targets requested by the Army.   Those 54 missions, in which the number of aircraft ranged from 6 to 42, 'were flown in conditions when, without radar aid, they would not have been attempted. On at least two days the radar-controlled sorties were the only ones flown, so bad was the weather' [23].   According to this report, the average displacement of the Mean Point of Impact (MPI) from the aiming point was found to be 340 yards and no single bomb was found to be more than 550 yards from the aiming point.

It was noted that 'owing to the very close formations kept by planes under MRCP control the spread of bombs on the ground is small.   A formation of 12 Spitfires have dropped 24 bombs in an area 150 yards long by 75 yards wide and a box of 6 medium bombers have dropped 48 bombs in an area about 300 yards by 150 yards'. From 'the limited number of operations' studied, it was concluded that bombing accuracies were 'already comparable with those obtained by visual methods in level bombing' and that 'the accuracy is such that targets can safely be engaged closer to our own troops than by any other existing radar means' [24].

Rather than a number, products in the radar war were often given a name. Sometimes these were easy to appreciate, for example IFF, which was simply an acronym, and Oboe, where the sound in the crew's headphones was likened to that of the musical instrument; more often than not, the name bore no relationship, for instance Lucero – apparatus enabling an aircraft to position itself and to home onto one and a half meter AI beacons. And how about some of these, which were to be found in the Minutes of a meeting at Air Ministry on 25 May 1944 to decide on the 'agreed future policy regarding airborne equipments for homing' [25] ... Abdulla, which 'performed satisfactorily but showed up badly against the enemy'; Greenbottle, which it was 'generally agreed' was not satisfactory and some replacement was required; as well as Serrate, Macaboy, Meerschaum and Opposition – which 'would be rendered obsolete' when homing equipment undergoing development at TRE was proven. This was a 'universal aerial which could be fitted quickly to an aircraft' – and it was going under a name which, arguably, could not be faulted... Universal!

CHAPTER 13: 'CASUAL' COLONIALS

For radar mechs in Europe, unlike those in the South East Asia theatre of operations, VE-Day itself was a time for celebration and the several weeks before VJ-Day a period that was for some a 'winding-down', for others personal concern that an overseas posting would introduce new risks and renewed anxieties.

By chance, Dave Roumieu was in London on leave when the European war came to an end. He said:

> 'The events of those few days are unforgettable. Churchill's voice over the Tannoy system addressing the crowds – I'm certain he had been partaking of his favorite brandy; and walking down the Mall towards Buckingham Palace, with thousands of others, to see the King and Queen on the balcony with the two Princesses and the Prime Minister.

> 'Tain, where we were still based, seemed so different on my return from leave. Life in our hut had changed, now that the emphasis of the war was turning from Europe to the Far East. Two of my radar colleagues, Jim Holden and Dudley Searson, were posted to Ceylon and other RAF personnel were posted elsewhere by degrees. I don't recall how we occupied ourselves in those few weeks in May and June before we flew down to Oakington to our new Transport Command station. It seems that probably we did little more than play the occasional softball game – flying from one station to another for this purpose – or cycling around the countryside passing time with acquaintances we had made in Tain and bidding our farewells. I had indicated that I would volunteer for the South Pacific but certain events in certain locations called Hiroshima and Nagasaki made my further services unnecessary ₁.'

At Oakington, with the squadron converting from its Coastal Command role to a new one in Transport Command, there was little to keep its radar technicians busy so several leaves in London and a six-hour 'Cook's Tour' flight over the Continent were the highspots. Accompanied by a colleague from the radar section, Arnold Liddle, Dave used his camera to advantage to take aerial shots of Holland, Belgium and the devastation visible in the heavily bombed German cities of Aachen and Cologne. Then, with six weeks of such inactivity, he was posted to the Repat Depot at Torquay – with which came the opportunity to earn some pocket money by clipping hedges and, more of a major project, clearing a hillside of timber with axes and hand saws. The daily grind completed, the journey back to the Torquay billets was always amusing – 'It was a routine which required us to stop at a pub to sample their cider and, often along the way, passing a group of Italian POWs in another transport and, of course, exchanging greetings and waving at each other.' War service ended for

Dave Roumieu when he returned to Canada on the same ship as he had arrived some two and a half years earlier – the *Empress of Scotland.*

At Jordan River radar station on Vancouver Island, to which Roy Taylor had been posted on his return from Italy, VE-Day was 'just a working day for us, so we missed the activity and celebrations in Victoria. Japanese submarines had shelled several coastal points so we had to keep looking for "hostiles" 2 '. Aircraft plots were passed to the Observer Corps, enabling them to carry out their procedures if those aircraft turned into visible sightings, and 'they gave us a Certificate of Thanks for that service'. The June and July of 1945 saw an influx of radar mechanics who were returning from Europe – 'We had more NCOs than airmen' – and then came The Bomb. Gradually that surfeit of staff diminished as more and more were discharged, the role of the radar station itself minimizing to the point when, shortly after VJ-Day, orders came for it to be dismantled.

At Wartley, Sydney Goldstein helped organize a VE-Day fireworks display for which he took apart rounds of ammunition for a Very pistol – the only form of ammunition on the station – and glued the powder on a large 'V' made out of wood. Having first advised the local Observer Corps unit that Very pistols were to substitute for fireworks, a liberal amount of food and drink was followed by the lighting of the 'V', seen only by those gathered around it, and the firing of Very pistols whose colorful fiery trails into the night sky were watched for miles around the station. It was, Sydney says, 'not too much of a show to mark the end of the war in Europe but one that we enjoyed... and next morning we discovered drinking glasses in the most impossible places in the Ops Block, proof if it were needed that everyone had found somewhere for some private celebration' 3 .

When Sydney's 'number came up' for repatriation to Canada, he went first to the reception depot at Bournemouth and then to the embarkation depot at Torquay where, he remembers, 'we never changed the sheets, instead we changed hotels'. It was 'as if we were moving along a line to a point where, ultimately, there would be a ship to take us back home'. He too returned as he had come, aboard the liner *Queen Elizabeth,* by now under American control with improved accommodation and other amenities lacking on the inward trip. Four days later the ship was in Halifax, with everyone gathered on the side closest to the dock – 'I swear she was leaning over'. An overnight train journey came next, the highlight for many being 'fresh real eggs and bacon with, joy of all joys, ketchup with our eggs'. It is said that there wasn't a bottle of ketchup to be found when the train reached its destination and a 'tired, none too clean group' marched into the main hall at Lachine Manning Depot in Quebec. Lachine was where he received basic training starting in April 1942 ... and where, too, he ended his service in November 1945.

For Julien Olson, a member of 109 Squadron's radar section, VE-Day was distinctly unlike that of the vast majority of the personnel at Little Staughton where his squadron and another one in Pathfinder Force, # 582 Squadron with Lancaster bombers, had their base. He recalls that, 'presumably to reduce the risk of excess celebration', everyone was confined to camp that special day. Undaunted, 'three of us Canadian mechanics, as well as some Canadian aircrew, went down to London for the celebration. Nothing was said upon our return – being that the RAF were prone to believe that the "Colonials" were quite casual about orders. The memory of the crowds and being among them in front of Buckingham Palace to greet the Royal Family will remain with me for ever 4 .'

Bob Warner was on a 10 cm Type 52 radar training course at Yatesbury when the war finished in Europe. There was a speaker system in the barracks room, where BBC radio broadcasts could be heard, and with others he listened to Churchill announcing the end of hostilities. Everyone received the day off from classes to celebrate VE-Day but 'we were not to leave the immediate area so as not to overload the railway system. Some of us went to a nearby country pub and had a few pints with the few locals who took time away from their farming duties to celebrate' 5 .

Completing the course, Bob returned to Kingswear and he was there for VJ-Day. He recalls that 'there was a special issue of pay in the forenoon for those wishing some extra cash. I think that the local pubs had been setting aside extra supplies of ale for the celebration that would occur with the end of the war. There was music and there were street dances for those celebrating, in contrast to the quiet celebration in the small country pub near Yatesbury for VE-Day'.

One among a draft of radar technical personnel awaiting repatriation from India towards the end of January 1945, having been away from home for four years and with Service life 'wearing thin', Bill Barrie was somewhat philosophical about what would come next. There was a certain amount of information from the RCAF liaison office in New Delhi about veterans' benefits 'but you had to get home first! Christmas had come and gone; still no snow and no tree. Some RAF people were actually making plans to stay in India, or to return at war's end. The second front had been opened in June [1944] and the Burma road was open but the Japanese were fighting on fiercely. By now we knew we would win the war, but when would it end? 6 '.

Even with the war in Europe at an end, UK-based radar personnel were not allowed to slacken off too much, as Janet Macdonald confirmed in an article in *West Coast Radar News* recalling her time in the WAAF between January 1941, when she volunteered to become a driver and was told she would be in RDF, and demobilization in December 1945. Referring to her time on a CHL station at Anstruther in mid-1945, she explained that...

> 'On one watch, an operator told me there were 100 aircraft coming in. I'd seen enough "Windows" while serving on radar stations down south to know that what she thought was a huge formation was in fact the result of "Windows" being dropped to confuse us. The Duty Officer came on and tried to tell the operator that this wasn't possible. I kept to my "Windows" report, fortunately as it turned out, though I too was beginning to wonder, just a little, as the others were so sure that the radar was showing the presence of a large number of incoming aircraft. A few days later, it was reported to us that this had been a "Windows" practice to keep us on our toes as the war was nearly over. They also told us that we were the only station in the area that didn't report aircraft' 7 .

During the period between VE-Day and VJ-Day, Fred Mullen was recalled to Holland, the reason being that he was summoned to appear before a Court of

Inquiry... He explains that during his time with AMES 15092 in Holland, it was said that the Type 13 for which he was responsible was in a 'poor condition' when inspected [*] . Disgusted with having to defend such an allegation, Fred argued that the equipment had been in a far worse condition when he received it second-hand at Nijmegen and that his men 'had kept the delicate electronics working in abnormal conditions of driving rain, mud, freezing temperatures and a shortage of spare parts' [8] . No doubt there were other such Courts of Inquiry where someone in charge became a 'fall guy' for those for whom he was responsible for reasons of rank – and no doubt also there were proceedings where guilt was proven and the punishment deserved; be that as it may, Fred Mullen, a Flight Lieutenant at the time, won the day. Cleared of any blame for the alleged state of that Type 13, he left the courtroom wondering why (as he continued to do for many more years), with a war going on and no equipment failure having occurred which was in any remote way prejudicial to the war effort, there should have been any necessity for such a large amount of time to be taken up initiating and pursuing such procedures for matters of little consequence.

Like many other Canadians, Fred sailed back home on the *Queen Elizabeth*, arriving at Halifax, Nova Scotia, in November 1945 and receiving his discharge early in the following month.

It is heartening to find instances of wartime romances on radar stations blossoming into a long-lasting marriage, for example that of RCAF radar technician Alf Cassidy and WAAF radar operator Pat Parker, who met while serving at Great Ormes Head, a CHL station overlooking the North Wales seaside resort of Llandudno. Though this was Pat's first station after training at Yatesbury, she was already there when Alf and a fellow Canadian, George ('Red') Cunningham, arrived in mid-October 1942 on their first posting in the UK. The two men were 'bushed after a day's travelling in a succession of crowded trains and then having to hike up to the top of the Orme because there was no transport for us from the station'. Pat remembers that...

> 'The weather was misty, it was beginning to get dark and into the Common Room came these two bedraggled, tired-looking airmen, their backpacks, side packs, helmets, tin hats and web belts seemingly draped all over them. Not a very prepossessing pair! However, when they had showered and came back a short time later with chocolate bars and cigarettes to hand around, they did look a little more presentable [9] .'

Typical of the CHL stations of that time, Great Ormes Head was small both in its physical size and in the number of personnel necessary for its round-the-clock operation, so it didn't take long for newcomers to know just about everyone by their first names. Operators and mechanics were assigned to a particular 'Watch', their shifts being 0800 to 1600 hours, 1600 to 2300 hours and 2300 to 0800 hours, Alf being put into the same Watch as Pat. He recalls that their friendship grew 'quite naturally' because...

---

[*] This was the equipment where the flexible wave guide burned out and there was no spare, a replacement for this critical part being ordered that evening from England and reaching him by motor cycle next morning. It was the kind of technical problem, Fred told the author, 'that was so common for radar people and neither understood nor appreciated by outdated "spit and polish" Courts of Inquiry'.

'Most of the time, our Watch, like the others, spent a lot of our off-duty time together, playing table tennis in the Common Room, listening to the radio, reading, going into Llandudno for shopping in the daytime or to the pubs, dances and the cinema in the evening or visiting the many interesting and pretty villages in the surrounding area. Such was the camaraderie that I am sure was common to all radar stations.

'When the weather warmed up, Pat introduced me to tennis and to field hockey. I wasn't too popular on the hockey field because, being left handed as an ice hockey player, my stick had a habit of being on the wrong side a lot of the time. Nevertheless, the other players put up with me. The local swimming pool was another great way to spend an afternoon off. So, the months passed quickly and as they did our friendship grew. Our first 'date' was, I think, going to see the movie *Gone With The Wind*.

'By D-Day, both of us had been posted away from Great Ormes Head, Pat to one of the Oboe ground stations, Tilly Whim [*see page 100*], followed by Hawkshill Down, while I was sent on an Oboe course, eventually joining an Oboe mobile station, AMES 9432, which moved across to the Continent in August 1944.'

The couple kept in touch by letter and some of their time on leave was spent together at Pat's home in Addiscombe, Croydon. Once, while on the Oboe course at Yatesbury, Alf 'took off one Saturday morning and hitch-hiked to Swanage to visit Pat. There wasn't usually a bed check at Yatesbury but they did one that Saturday night and I was listed AWOL for the first and only time in my Air Force career. I was given just one week's CB (Confined to Barracks). It really didn't mean much – there was no place to go in the evenings anyway – but without doubt the visit was well worth that minor inconvenience'.

Interestingly, Alf and Pat Cassidy, who celebrated 55 years of married life on 18 June 2000, might never have met but for what Alf calls 'one of those pivotal points that most of us experience at some time in our life when we make a decision to go one way or another'. He was on parade at the RCAF Transit Depot in Bournemouth when the Duty Officer asked if any of Alf's group of new arrivals from Canada wished to go to Bomber Command rather than to a CH or CHL station. Alf admits that he did ponder that option very seriously but, despite having been trained on airborne equipment and attracted by the proposition, 'I decided to remain with the much more complex ground radar equipment and I have not regretted it one iota' 10.

As did Alf and Pat Cassidy, Muir and Chrissie Adair also met for the first time while serving together on the same radar station – in this instance, Aberleri in the Cardigan Bay area of Wales. Muir was there from October 1942 to August 1943, a radar technician working on Type 15 (209 megacycles) ground-controlled interception equipment; his wife-to-be, the then Chrissie Ferguson, spent from February 1943 until September of the same year as a radar operator on the same GCI unit. After the seven months that their time at Aberleri overlapped, Muir was moved away; much earlier, while based in Northern Ireland, he had volunteered for Combined Operations and this was the posting which now came through – a belated posting that would take him, eventually, into the frontline of the North West European campaign via Omaha Beach on D-Day [*see page 92*]. Chrissie, meanwhile, served out the rest of her time in the WAAF at a second GCI unit, this one being at Fullarton in Scotland. At least this brought some compensation for their separation: Fullarton was much closer to Chrissie's home town of Dunfermline, which is where she and Muir were married on 23 December 1943, in Dunfermline Abbey. She was given a compassionate discharge in June 1944 and a year later, when their firstborn was little more than six months old, Chrissie arrived to set up home in Canada – two months ahead of Muir, however, whose repatriation came through only in August 1945 after his four and a half years in the RCAF.

To a certain extent, Chrissie's own time in uniform is indicative of the manner in which some of the radar operators in those days came into their specialized and highly demanding jobs. When the time came for her call-up, which was delayed for a couple of years because she was in a reserved occupation, Chrissie requested entry into the WRNS – the women's branch of the Royal Navy. In 'true military fashion', though, she was put into the WAAF. After taking what she recalls as being 'a multiplicity of aptitude tests', Chrissie was selected to be a GCI radar operator, which carried with it the Grade 1 trade classification, the highest in the Service 11 . After training at Nantwich, Aberleri was her first operational station. She recalls:

> 'Aberleri was a mobile station with all the equipment mounted on lorries and it controlled a Beaufighter night fighter squadron, based at Valley for the protection of Liverpool. Typically, for more adequate distance control, GCI units were located many miles away from RAF stations with whose squadrons they were working as a team, the consequence for us being zero personal contact with anyone on "our" Beaufighter squadron – we saw its members only as blips or deflections on the radar tubes.

> 'The WAAF operators were billeted in two private homes that had been requisitioned in the tiny seaside village of Borth. During inclement weather and on night shifts there was motor transport to take us to the technical site, though at other times we used standard-issue bicycles which also came in useful for exploring the nearby Mount Snowdon area. The men on the station were billeted in twos and threes throughout the village and they seemed to fare rather better in gaining acceptance by the local civilians – there being still a distinct feeling that women should be in the kitchen rather than in uniform.'

In contrast, Fullarton, being a camp of a more lasting nature and in an area with other RAF, Army and Royal Navy establishments in the immediate vicinity, offered more organized activities than did Aberleri – leisure facilities such as sport, dances, theatres and other forms of entertainment. There, the WAAFs were housed on a golf course and the Operations Block was located in a building rather than a Crossley truck as was the case at Aberleri. At both locations, typical of service on a GCI unit, the radar operators were rotated constantly through four jobs while on duty – Distance & Bearing Tube (PPI), Height Finding Tube, Plotting Table and Switchboard. Chrissie notes that the tubes required a great deal of concentration and could not be worked on for too long a period without a break, hence the rotation. Depending upon the assignment, both radio and line communication was necessary with Sector or other connected units.

Charlie Mills is another Canadian who met his future wife on a radar station, in this instance RAF Orby in Lincolnshire, a Final GCI station which was his last active station in the UK before going to Germany. He recalled:

> 'The most important incident at Orby was to meet a very pretty WAAF whose trade classification was Clerk Special Duties, the lady who later became my wife. We became engaged the evening before VE-Day so the next day the country celebrated. We were married in September 1945 just prior to the station being disbanded. The next couple of months were spent on a variety of postings around the country until I signed-on for the Occupation Forces and a return to the RCAF. I had taken this posting to Germany in preference to repatriation to delay returning to Canada until my wife was able to follow soon after. In May 1946 the Canadian Government decided to pull the Air Force out of Germany and ours was the last RCAF station to close in BAOR (British Army of the Rhine). After leave in the UK, I returned home in late June, arriving at the Montreal demobilization centre in the morning and was on my way by mid-afternoon as a civilian. So endeth nearly six years of world tour at His Majesty's pleasure [12].'

Charlie Mills was one of 32 newly-commissioned Pilot Officers, their basic training at university behind them, who met when posted to Trenton for early instruction in radar and were assembled together on the parade square on 17 September 1941. Another was Les Wood, whose astonishment can be well understood on finding, four years later to the month, two others from that very same group, Al Revill and Bill Lower, in his line-up when enrolling for an Eng Phys course at the University of Toronto. He had not seen either of them since January 1942. Coincidences didn't end there, however; group members Alf Houlgrave and 'Harpo' Baldwin were in the same class at the U of T!

Servicemen and women around the world would draw on humor to keep the realities of war in the background and to concentrate their hearts and their minds on the peace that must surely lie ahead. Radar technician Don Tilley, who served at various stations in the UK and in Sierra Leone, wrote for a concert party while on a COL site in West Africa and one of his ditties (a joint effort with Jak Dean) ran like this:

> *I want to remuster civilian,*
> *I want to put on a soft hat*
>   *A shirt that's not blue,*
>   *Not a boot but a shoe,*
> *And say 'No, I shan't – and that's that!'*
> *For I am so sick of my uniform,*
> *I'm fed up with being so poor,*
> *So I want to remuster civilian –*
>   *But not till we've finished the war!* [13]

Don's and Jak's verses were written in 1941 – when a return to the days of peace must have seemed almost beyond hope; no-one could have known it, but for those who would survive, it would be another four years before the opportunity came to 'remuster civilian'... to change into 'a shirt that's not blue' with 'not a boot but a shoe'.

Some form of light relief was essential in wartime, especially when you knew full well that you were doing your best and then someone or something comes along and you find yourself in hot water...

While a flight sergeant and in charge of a Light Warning unit, LW 6066, Ted Beckstead found not once but twice that it was possible to get into serious trouble for turning in a performance that was above and beyond what was expected of him. The first time was when on duty at the time the German warships *Scharnhorst* and *Gneisenau* were making their dash up the Channel in February 1942. It was an epic escape from their refuge in harbour at Brest to the safety of home waters that left egg on many faces. Ted, having newly completed a course on the effect of German jamming at the time, surmized that what he was seeing on the radar screen was the movement of those two vessels – though initially this supposition was met with disbelief by others up the reporting chain. When the tumult died down, an astonishing sequel occurred where Ted was hauled over the coals and challenged that the only way he could have been right was 'if he had received his information direct from Germany!' He argued his case, making it clear that instead of reporting the movement of the German warships, he could have done as other stations had apparently done and blamed faulty equipment for not spotting them. He heard no more...

The second time he was in the wrong for being in the right, Ted found himself under close arrest as a suspected saboteur. This incredible episode occurred during the period when certain CHL stations in south and south-east England were hurriedly adapted to make them capable of jamming back-looking radar equipment in enemy bombers. It was a rush assignment with the tightest of deadlines to complete this critical work; Churchill himself, it was said, demanded that it be done [*see page 49*]. When Ted and his crew reached the second station, the CO there refused to accept their credentials and ordered the men to be confined to the guardroom, while he himself cleared off to bed. A helpful WAAF on duty in an adjacent room listened sympathetically and she was persuaded to make it possible for Ted to call a special telephone number where he could explain the situation and enable the crew's presence and purpose on that station to be verified. Ted, privileged to be able to listen-in to the conversation that his contact was having with the CO, reckoned that he'd 'never before heard a balling-out like it!' The work duly carried out, the team moved on to the third and final station, not only completing all that had to be done but doing so within the allotted 48 hours. And when the enemy planes came, the successful use of the ground stations' newly-installed jamming equipment gave the fighters a clear run which sent bomber after bomber tumbling out of the skies [14].

Mind you, as radar mechs were among the first to concede, there were occasions that brought their rewards...

Thanks for a job well done come in different ways – the appreciative supply of drinks from a crew whose aircraft was lost until tracked home by radar, for example – though sometimes it is merely the expressions on the faces of an excited pilot and navigator, who have just downed an enemy bomber, that is sufficient recognition...

which is what happened to Harold Wolverton while on # 157 Squadron, then operating out of Colerne, near Bath, with radar-equipped Mosquito night fighters. That particular night the weather was absolutely foul, it didn't seem worth while going into Bath for the evening so he volunteered to put in night duty at the section. He goes on:

> 'About the time I considered putting my head down, the ground crew began running-up one of our Mosquitoes. Shortly thereafter, the aircraft made its way along the perimeter track in the heavy rain, passed the section and before long was airborne into the dark, the gloom and a threatening storm. The crew hadn't been gone for more than 10 minutes when my phone rang and a rather angry flight sergeant announced that there was an aircraft returning any minute with a "bent weapon" [*failed equipment, in this case the AI – Air Interception*]. The crew, he warned me, didn't have nice things to say about my "gear".

> 'I piled one of each piece of the equipment into the section's van, hustled over to the Flight Office to wait unobtrusively until the aircraft was back in its "Bay" and then, the instant the pilot was out, I plugged the "genny" in and scrambled up the ladder like a monkey. No ground crew was going to get in my way – and I let them know it! The problem was in the receiver but in the shortest time ever recorded I had a new receiver in place. I'd left the "genny" running so all I had to do was switch on. Lovely, a picture came on; I went through the usual routine of tests and was confident in the fresh equipment; unplugged the "genny", rushed back to the Flight Office and reported everything OK.

> 'Anyway, the crew decided to have another go, wasting no time in getting back into the Mosquito and taking off right across the field – out over the trees on the far side, gadzooks! Some time later, when I was back in the section, the phone rang and there were excited voices at the other end. "My" Mosquito had got an enemy bomber, a Ju 88 – and the crew was coming over to thank me 'for replacing the "bent weapon" with one that had worked to perfection. The GCI team had vectored them in behind the enemy aircraft, which was above the cloud base and looking for a hole to locate a target. The Mosquito was in cloud cover beneath the Ju 88, which they followed with their radar until reaching a suitable position from which to emerge and to "do the necessary". This they did, applying the full force of their 20 mm cannons at the ideal range and making quite a mess of the enemy, which banked over and went down, the Mosquito's crew confirming the general area in which it crashed. No medals for me, obviously, but the jubilation on the faces of that crew and the excitement in their voices made me feel that I was part of that operation – and that was thanks enough [15] !'

Radar technician Gordon Burniston tells a similar story of unexpectedly receiving a Mosquito crew's gratitude for a job well done, though this time it was a case of radar saving their lives in a situation where the aircraft was not the hunter but the hunted...

Gordon, an LAC, and an RAF Corporal, Joe Rose, were on attachment at Manston in Kent during the last winter of the war, their job being to install the first backward-

Lancaster four-engined aircraft,a mainstay of RAF Bomber Command for much of WWII, with its H₂S radar cupola prominent under the fuselage; this equipment provided a TV-like image of the ground below and early Pathfinder Force crews especially found its introduction invaluable to locate target areas and aiming points.[Douglas Fisher Collection].

Left: *The cover removed on this occasion, this was a sight familiar to many radar mechs on night fighter airfields but seldom to less privileged individuals; the AI equipment carried in the nose of a Beaufighter to help quide its crew to an interception and hopefully to a successful conclusion.*
[Douglas Fisher Collection].

Photographed at Hurn in March 1942, this is the Halifax aircraft used by TRE in the development of the H₂S radar system; within three months and then based at Defford, it caught fire in the air and crashed with the loss of 6 Scientists and other associated with the program, the 5 crew members and the only H₂S then operative.[Douglas Fisher Collection].

Antennae highly visible here, above the fuselage at its nose, this is AMES 6563 photographed while on a training exercise at Tarrant Rushton. The first glider-installed radar for raid reporting and ground-controlled interceptions, the purpose of an AMES 65 was to facilitate radar cover rapidly over an area that could not be reached by means of conventional mobile radar convoys. Documentation displayed during a 1997 radar reunion in Ottawa, Canada, indicates that the AMES 65 Horsa glider carried Type 6 and AN/TPS-3 plan position radar systems, IFF, homing beacons, VHF and HF communications equipment and MF receivers, the centre section of the fuselage being equipped as an ops room .[Via Charlie Young].

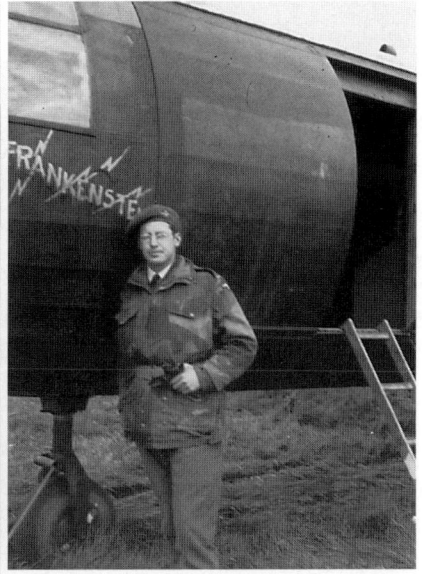

Above, left: *Antenna protruding from its nose, this AI-equipped Beaufighter was no novice in the art of locating and downing enemy aircraft, as evidenced by the 'kills' shown below the cockpit.* [Douglas Fisher Collection]. Above, right: *Whatever horror stories surrounded 'Frankenstein's Monster' before its conversion to the radar-carrying AMES 6563 were fortunately unknown to Charlie Young, seen here beside this Horsa.* [Via Charlie Young].

Air Vice-Marshal W. E. Theak, AOC, 60 Group, second from left, and Air Commodore R. L. Phillips, CO, 72 Wing, on his right, pictured during a visit to AMES 9442. [Via Art Craig].

Middle and lower photos: *A US Army bulldozer was instrumental in enabling the last remaining equipment belonging to AMES 9442 to be withdrawn from La Roche, leaving the site empty, when the enemy counter-attacked in December 1944. Pausing briefly in front of the Oboe equipment then in tow are two radar personnel from AMES 9442, in the foreground being Flight Lieutenant 'Taffy' Evans, one of the TOs.* [Both photos via Art Craig].

Air Vice-Marshal Don Bennett, centre, commanding RAF Pathfinder Force (PFF), on a visit to AMES 9442 – one of the mobile Oboe units which controlled tracking and bomb-release for PFF planes spearheading Bomber Command raids deep into Germany.[Via Art Craig].

Before a mobile Oboe ground station could operate, a survey crew had to ensure that its equipment was positioned exactly to requirements; this was vital to assure the in-built accuracy achievable with this ground-controlled blind-bombing system. [Via Art Craig].

For AMES 9442, some of whose members are seen here, Art Craig, their CO being on the extreme right, the drama of the enforced evacuation of La Roche is now behind them. In a more relaxed situation, with the personnel safe and the Oboe equipment secure, AMES 9442 was able to prepare to resume its duties. [Via Art Craig].

Home from the Normandy battleground and pictured in tranquil Loch Fyne: FDT 217, longest-serving of the three fighter-direction tenders on duty off the invasion beaches, having been on station for a period of 18 consecutive days on and after D-Day. [Via John Glen].

Resembling a battleground itself, a bomb-battered Cologne was one German city that radar technician Dave Roumieu saw on a 'Cook's Tour' facility flight organized for ground staff at the war's end. Here, the famous cathedral seems barely touched. [Photo by Dave Roumieu].

Honorary Life Membership certificate from the Air Force Telecom Association (AFTA) for Air Commodore Douglas Gooderham (left), *who spent much of the war in South East Asia and became one of the highest-ranking among the radar specialists. Harry Huggins made the presentation to him at Kingston on 5 June 1999.* [Photo: Crystal Sweeney, AFTA Newsletter, July 1999].

Flight Sergeant Oss Luce, prisoner of the Japanese for 3½ years, received his certificate the same month, from Charlie Brunger. [Photo: Joyce Kingsford, AFTA Newsletter, July 1999].

Calgary Radar Reunion '96 organizing stalwarts Les Card, left, 'ham' radio operator, and Bob McNarry, long-time computer user, called on those hobby activities to spread the message that helped draw a 792-strong attendance – 490 radar vets (including 9 deceased represented by family members) and 302 spouses and friends.[Still from the reunion video].

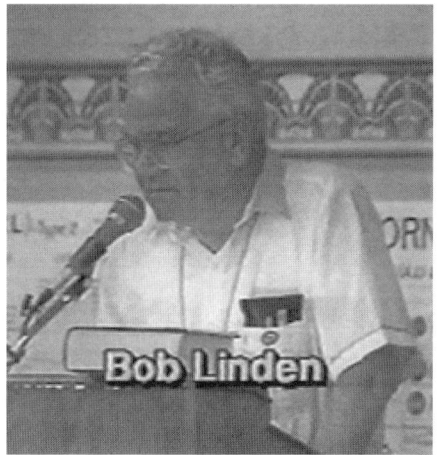

Lloyd Francis, left, took up the cudgels with the Minister of National Defense to get Canada's radar mechs their long-overdue Certificate of Appreciation. Bob Linden had contacted him, thus launching a tough campaign that resulted in some 450 of these certificates being presented at Calgary Radar Reunion '96 . [Still from the reunion video].

Cyril Lloyd Francis
Can R132837

was One of those who, in the hour of England's greatest need, came forth voluntarily to man the vital Radar stations upon which the air defence of Great Britain so signally depended.

By their selfless and devoted services these men not only had an indispensable share in the defence of this country but also contributed in great part to the development of this new branch of science, to the general benefit of the Allied cause.

Air Ministry, 1946

Secretary of State for Air

Researching in the National Archives in Ottawa, Bob Linden came across 'the sole survivor' of some 5,000 of these Certificates of Appreciation that had apparently been issued at the request of the Director General of Signals in the British Air Ministry and forwarded, in March 1946, from RCAF Headquarters in *London to the Department of National Defense for Air in Ottawa. Bob concluded that none was ever issued. When Calgary Radar Reunion '96 was being planned, it was thought that this was the time to remedy the situation.

looking radar into Mosquitoes flying intruder missions.   As Gord recalls it, obsolete Mk IV and Mk V AI equipment was married to Mk X forward-looking radar, the use of a selector switch enabling the Mosquito's two-man crew to benefit from an instant rear-view picture, when circumstances required it, at the touch of that switch.   He explains that the morning after the pair finished their first 'Mossie' and were busy on the next, 'a Canadian pilot came into the hanger yelling for the radar guys'.   Gord continues:

> 'When he found us he almost shook our arms off!   It turned out that he had been on a night intruder mission, using the very aircraft on which we had been working, and while he was chasing a contact over a Jerry airfield something prompted him to use our little switch.   There was a Jerry night fighter on his tail so he took off out of there like the proverbial bat out of hell. This pilot reckoned that we had saved his bacon – and naturally enough we were quite pleased about it too.   Joe and I finished a couple more Mossies before we returned to our base at # 63 OTU, at Ouston, near Newcastle upon Tyne, but nothing could have given us greater satisfaction than learning how successful had been our very first installation of backward-looking radar [16].'

Nor was it all work, work, work for radar mechs in WWII...

Serving with the RCAF as a radar technician in Italy, Roy Taylor saw the extremes of a pleasant informality in rural areas and irksome 'spit and polish' when on leave in a big town.   He cites an instance when the local mayor invited a group of airmen to a dinner of spaghetti and wine, apparently because he wanted his radio set repaired. The Italian government had fixed it so that he could only listen to the Italian stations so it became Roy's task to 'unfix' it... a simple task that he was happy to perform, though one that was rendered rather more difficult by the host's no doubt worthy intention to keep pushing the wine.   In Bari, however, which was then a leave centre, informality was replaced by the need to wear 'best blues' – in Roy's case, tunic and forage cap with brass buttons deliberately left unpolished because, as he had to explain when one of the   SPs (Service Police) stopped him, 'where I come from shined brass makes a good target'.   Having just about convinced the SP but adamant that his brass must retain its dull appearance, he opted for a khaki outfit next day.   He notes that 'they picked on you for anything that was not militarily correct. At the station we were only interested in doing a job, but here everything had to be spick and span, never mind the war. Once I was told to keep my hands out of my pockets when actually I was going for a handkerchief! [17] '.

Of course London was the hub when on leave in the UK.   In the opinion of Allan Paull and some of his RCAF friends in radar, the 'hotel of choice' in London for them tended to be the Strand Palace; 'I think it was Bill Stovin and I who did try the Savoy across the street one time but we were made to feel not welcome when they did such things as add corkage to our bill and object to our having guests in our room'. Allan recalls that...

> 'In general, London was good to us, with its concerts, plays and Service clubs. We went to the Royal Albert Hall and heard the London Philhar-monic play Beethoven's Fifth, which had become the V-for-Victory

symphony with its dit-dit-dit-dah motif. We went to the West End theatres to see the new plays of Noel Coward and others. The Lord Tweedsmuir Canadian Officers' Club in Winfield House on the Outer Circle at Regent's Park was one of the better Service clubs: Winfield House, with its gold-plated plumbing fixtures, was owned at the time by Barbara Hutton, the Woolworth heiress, becoming the residence of the United States ambassador post-war. There were also the Balfour Service Club on Portland Place and the Jewish Service Club in Woburn House, near Russell Square, all providing general hospitality and tea dances for Servicemen and Servicewomen on leave [18].'

Being an air force officer in the UK carried with it privileges; it was, says Allan, 'like belonging to a national club with branches everywhere'. He recalls meeting a friend during the period between the end of the war in Europe and the end of the war against Japan...

'An army captain and I were to board a train north to catch a boat to the Isle of Man for a brief vacation. On the train we shared a compartment with an RAF pilot who was going up to Manchester to pick up an Anson at Ringway aerodrome to deliver it to another location. Learning that we were on our way to the Isle of Man, he suggested he could fly us there and drop us off at the RAF Station. Needless to say we accepted gladly. The most exciting part of the trip was taking off from Ringway when the pilot asked me to hurry and pump up the undercarriage because there were no hydraulics. Next he proceeded to buzz his girlfriend's house in Manchester before we headed west. Our hotel reservation at the Isle of Man was not until the next day so we requested accommodation on the RAF Station. We were welcomed with open arms and the two of us spent a pleasant evening in the Officers' Mess enjoying the camaraderie of the RAF officers there [19].'

At Wartling, one of the South Coast GCI stations, where Sydney Goldstein was an RCAF radar technical officer, a visit from a mobile Type 11 proved intriguing because not only was it 'made and manned by the Canadians, it was extremely interesting because this Canadian-built CRT had a display which was sharper and brighter than our own'. It was, he says, a copy of the British tube but in this case an improvement on the original. This led to speculation, naturally, and 'we reckoned that possibly it was better because the water used in Canada was purer than that used in the manufacture of the British tube. In any case, I was very proud to show off this display to all the British controllers on our station and to those who came to see us. This showpiece was soon gone, however... on its way to France when the invasion took place [20]'.

In times of comparative inactivity at Wartling, Sydney came up with a neat idea for a training exercise to try and reduce the monotony of being on duty but not having anything to do. He says...

'I rigged up a pair of "Crabs" [three-legged/motored instruments that were used to teach navigation to pilots] to act as a fighter on patrol and a "bogey". As they moved, blips were produced on the screens in the Operations Block cabin and the fighter was moved according to instructions issued by the Controller.   Two operators controlled the movement of the "Crabs" on a table we built for this purpose in the basement .   It was quite a task to set all this up but the "radar tecks" on the station were very happy to pitch in and to make it work.   It was a challenge which all of us enjoyed.'

Whether or not prompted by the occasional (!) period of inactivity, there are always those who can be relied upon to come up with an ode to amuse colleagues with time on their hands, their offerings often finding grateful acceptance in a camp newspaper or, sometimes, in a more serious form of communication.

Over the years, radar-based 'odes' must have appeared in many publications – and then been repeated again and again until the original source can no longer be attributed (if, indeed, its source was ever a matter for public record).   Can anyone, perhaps, substantiate the derivation of 'Installation Day' [21] which surely captures so vividly a situation that must have exercised the patience of countless radar personnel, wherever their location and whatever their function, irrespective of rank or civilian status.   What's more, you don't need a Clinton, Corpus Christi, Yatesbury or Cranwell graduation certificate to appreciate its humor!

Our station's in an uproar –
Installation's in full swing,
And running around the Ops Room
Are bags of bods from Wing.

The station mechs are busy
Running to and fro with tea;
Resplendent in their corduroys
Come types from TRE.

The Rx is in pieces,
It will surely work no more,
And all the bods with all their mods
Lie scattered on the floor.

Ops and Mechs and CMEs,
Rings and tapes and LACs,
Sergeants playing with a scope,
Giving ACs all the dope;
Squadron Leaders use sig gennies,
Flight Lieutenants toss for pennies.

Louder grows the noise and din –
But here's the TO squeezing in;
With sickly mien and palsied hand
He tries to quell the busy band.

His voice comes weakly without tone.
'I've just had Group upon the 'phone…'
(He swallows hard, his face turns white)
'You're working on the wrong damn site!'

For Angus Hamilton in India, 21 January 1945 brought the magic word: Repat! He docked at Liverpool on 13 March, spent a week in Bournemouth getting acclimatized, kitted-out, paid etc before going on three weeks' leave. He spent much of his 23rd birthday, 18 April, travelling between Bournemouth and Warrington; it was a day he would long remember, not because of the celebrations that generally come with birthdays but for the rather disturbing fact that this was 'the only day in two months in England that I didn't get to a pub! [22] '

Back to Canada on the liner *Ile de France*, Angus began his disembarkation leave and returned to form the opinion that...

> 'We were somewhat of an embarrassment to the authorities. It was obvious they didn't know what to do with us. To their credit they did give us postings in our home province. Most of us from Ontario were first posted to # 1 Repair Depot in Toronto [near Bay and Front Streets] but we were soon dispersed. I remember being at Hagersville and Mount Hope, Saint Thomas and Trenton. It's not surprising that we weren't welcome at these training stations. For several years, we had all been on operational units where "bullshine" was minimal; the only parade we were ever on was "pay parade". We made no effort to conceal our lack of respect for Flight Sergeants and Station Warrant Officers who had not been overseas. We had put up our Sergeant's stripes as soon as we came under RCAF jurisdiction at the Repat depot in England and the last thing the cozy Sergeants' Mess regulars wanted was a group of disrespectful repats who got into the bar as soon as it opened and drank most of the daily quota of beer.
>
> 'Some of us were still restless and inquired about service in the Pacific but Hiroshima ended that possibility. Forced to face reality, many of us registered for university and were given leave to start classes in September even though our formal discharge from the service did not come through until mid-October.'

It is appropriate to mention the 'Shadow' rank system that was adopted in the RCAF. Angus Hamilton noted that 'many' radar technicians held 'Shadow' ranks, which in his case began on 1 July 1942 when he became a Corporal in the RCAF while remaining a Leading Aircraftman in the RAF. He explains that...

> 'The benefit of having a "Shadow" rank was that our pay was increased although we couldn't draw it... We had to assign our pay differential to someone in Canada, in my case it was to an aunt of mine, who arranged for it to be put in a separate bank account. As long as we were attached to the RAF we couldn't draw more than the RAF rate for our RAF rank, the rationale being that those of us who were a long way from where promotions were handed out by the RCAF were disadvantaged... Specifically, our classmates who remained in Canada as instructors or were the first to be posted to a Canadian squadron were promoted rapidly whereas we, who were attached to the RAF, had virtually no chance of promotion – the RAF had many technicians senior to us.

'Some noble senior officer, no doubt a victim of similar circumstances in World War I, initiated these "Shadow" ranks whereby we got promoted – on paper. Eventually most of us did become RAF Corporals – a non-event if there ever was one. We did the same jobs we'd done as LACs; we lived in the same billets; and we ate in the same mess... The only difference was that those of us who were in India were permitted to draw a few more rupees on pay day; however most of us preferred to see our savings building up a little bit faster * .'

To what extent did luck, fortune, fate or what-have-you play a part in personal survival during wartime service?   Les Card, whose five years overseas included more than three years spent in the Mediterranean theatre of operations, much of this time being spent under the constant threat of air or ground attacks and on an aircrew tour of 30 sorties against enemy targets, worked out the chances of coming through unscathed. He said:

'I was university-trained in physics and maths, among other things, and all my time I've been working out probabilities – especially, during wartime, my probability of survival.   The way I worked it out, the odds were always in my favor; so I took chances.   I volunteered for anything going – and I was always available to do something foolish or to go somewhere stupid.

'Once, though, it did seem that the end was nigh!

'A colleague [*RAF radar technician Tom Rogers*] and I, caught in an air raid in Malta while we were doing daily maintenance on one of the Wellingtons, ran to the back of the plane and lay there throughout the bombing, believing we were reasonably safe because this was the lowest part and offered the best protection.   When we came out, however, we saw one more aircraft approaching, a Ju 88 obviously on its bombing run.   I called out to Tom to head for the roadway, which had a stone wall on either side to shelter us from bomb fragments.   As we ran, we came across a slit trench and dived inside.   It was meant for two people but besides us there were two soldiers who had been caught in the same predicament and followed on our heels.

'We watched that Ju 88 heading directly towards us, bomb-bay doors open and two good-sized bombs coming straight at us.   Mesmerized, I suppose, we watched until the last minute, certain that this would be curtains for the four of us.   I remember saying to Tom: "Well, it was a good war up to now. Looks like this is it.   Goodbye."

'The bombs exploded on either side of the slit trench, both of them within 10 meters of us, which caused one of the soldiers, while we were dusting off the dirt and the rubble, to say that it was "a good thing you guys knew

---

* For the record, RCAF Corporal Angus Hamilton (an LAC in the RAF) became an RCAF Sergeant on 1 April 1943 but, in the RAF's eyes, he was a Corporal. For him (and the many like him) the door of the Sergeants' Mess was still closed, the key to that privileged establishment and its accompanying 'perks' being something that the money earned by the three stripes awarded on paper by the RCAF HQ in Ottawa couldn't buy.

where this trench was!" To which Tom and I responded in all honesty that "we didn't know, we just stumbled on it". Incidentally our Wellington, having served us well by being our first bolt hole, now looked rather like a sieve – having suffered more than 100 holes from bomb splinters [23] * .'

Service personnel returning home from overseas service were required to make an HM Customs declaration in Britain in the same manner as holidaymakers pre- and post-war. Roy Taylor, who came back by sea after his time with AMES units in Sicily and Italy, remembers what happened on his arrival in Scotland...

'I got the job of having a crew bring up the belongings of the ENSA girls who had been entertaining the troops in the Mediterranean. The Customs officer had one of the girls make a declaration and immediately chose to go through her stuff, passing what she declared but making her pay duty, plus a penalty payment, on what he found which was not on her list . I asked her what she wanted to be done with her luggage; she said I should throw it overboard! Customs officers were pretty good to the troops, except on cigarettes and liquor. We were allowed one bottle of "booze" and where some guys would be carrying two bottles the Customs officer would say: "You are only allowed one, so why don't you open the other and celebrate your arrival". If you agreed to do so, he would let you go but didn't watch to see if you were going to open it. One guy, though, was adamant; he was going to keep that second bottle to celebrate at home. He was allowed to do so... but only after he was made to pay the duty on it [24] .'

Service records that were lost or mislaid were not entirely rare (!) but what happened to J Vic Davies does certainly merit inclusion among such stories. A Canadian, Vic worked first on airborne radar on Catalina and Sunderland flying boats, then on Lancaster bombers and finally on automatic gun-laying turrets. The war ended and, as he put it, 'I heard that some of my Radar Group were being sent home.

'I inquired about it and was told that they didn't have my records. I was getting a little bit tired of having my own pay parade, no shadow promotions etc, so I got some of the fellows who were posted to the UK with me to go to Lincoln's Inn Fields in London to swear that I was who I said I was. I guess they were convinced, so I got home on the "Lizzie" * with the rest, otherwise I'd be a Limey by now [25] !'

For Canadian radar technician Bob Warner, the voyage home was memorable in that it was on board the *Queen Elizabeth*, it spanned the 1945 Christmas period and... Oh boy was it a rough crossing! Assigned to a stateroom on 'C' Deck with

---

* While on a radar station in the UK [School Hill, near Aberdeen], Craig Knudsen had a similar experience when a Junkers 88 came heading straight for him, its bomb doors open, causing him to dive for cover amid gunfire and the clear threat of an imminent bombing – 'The two HE [high explosive)]bombs from that Ju 88 fell no more than 40 or 50 feet from our shelter but neither of them went off. They had been made prior to the beginning of the war, the dates being clearly visible on them [26] .'

* The liner *Queen Elizabeth* on which he had travelled to Britain in January 1943. Lincoln's Inn Fields was where the RCAF had its headquarters in the UK.

nine other RCAF sergeants and two privates from Le Régiment de la Chaudière, he had an early indication of what was to come when one of the NCOs sharing this accommodation was sick before the liner had even cleared the harbour at Southampton. He goes on:

'When she was rolling, I felt a bit "queasy" but was not sick. We had two meals a day served in dining rooms cafeteria style; these were excellent, including items like roast beef, steaks and pork chops. There was no shortage of food with extra helpings available, probably partly due to the fact that only about half of the 12,000 on board showed up for meals. On Christmas Day we were in mid-Atlantic. Everyone received the traditional two pints of beer and a full Christmas Dinner with turkey and all the trimmings, as well as a printed souvenir menu with a photograph of the *Queen Elizabeth* on its front. The entire crossing was very stormy but the day before Christmas had been particularly bad. The open decks were out of bounds, there were waves breaking over the bow of the ship and a spruce tree that had been lashed to the mast was blown away. A lifeboat and several life rafts were also lost on the trip. The chief engineer told a group of us that he had been sailing the north Atlantic for over 30 years and this was one of the roughest crossings he had ever encountered. He also told us that the Cunard Line had hoped to have the *Queen Elizabeth* set a new speed record for the crossing from Southampton to New York. In fact we reached New York about 24 hours behind the regularly scheduled arrival time [27] .'

There must have been many occasions where, post-war, Servicemen from opposing sides have come across each other in business life or on holiday and discovered that there was some chance affinity between them. Perhaps, by reason of their age group, it would emerge that they had fought against each other; maybe it would transpire that there were common circumstances, for example both having been a member of aircrew in the same theatre of operations, or sailors on ships in the same ocean, or maybe even riding a tank in the same desert battle. For Murdock Smith, the link turned out to be particularly close when, working on a project which brought him in touch with a number of Japanese, it turned out that both he and one of their electrical engineers had been in India during the war – 'and that he had been in Imphal on exactly the same date, when we'd been cut off there by the Japanese. So I'd been in slit-trenches on one side and he'd been in slit-trenches on the other! We had to have a drink on that one, at which point a young Japanese in his party came up and said to him: "You're crazy, not so many years ago you were shooting at each other; now you're drinking together and you're the best of friends!" [28] '

In this connection it is certainly relevant to note an incident in the final hours of WWII which reveals a perhaps totally unexpected response from the Japanese. From 2 July until 6 September in the last year of the war, 1945, Cliff Lee was a member of the radar section of # 321 Squadron, Royal Netherlands Naval Air Force, based on the Cocos (Keeling) Islands in the Indian Ocean, whose Liberators were on missions over Java and Sumatra, as well as Singapore, all held by the Japanese. The incident that he relates occurred early in August 1945 and this is it:

'On this particular day, a reconnaissance Mosquito from our base was on a mission over Singapore when it developed engine trouble. It was forced to land on the airdrome at Singapore with its crew fearing the worst. The atom bombs had been dropped and the war appeared to be just about over, but no official peace terms had been arrived at.

'After they landed, the crew got out of the plane not knowing what to expect. A Japanese officer arrived, asked, in perfect English, what the trouble was and then reassured them that their technicians would have the plane operational in very short order... which they did.

'While waiting for the job to be completed, a large number of English and Australian prisoners-of-war who had been working on the base came to the crew and asked if they had any treats for them. They did not, but what they did was fly back to our base on the Cocos Islands and hit us all up for donations of food, clothing etc, for the POWs. They then flew back to Singapore where the Japanese helped them unload the plane and distribute the gifts to the POWs. All this well before the official end of the war! [29]'

CHAPTER 14: DEFENSE OF A NATION

A s shown with regard to air force applications alone, the Allies' use of radar in WWII was wide-ranging; just as there was variety in its operation – the principle of radar attracting continual consideration – so there came increasing breadth in its geographical usage. Where the British Empire was concerned, countries like Australia, Canada, New Zealand and South Africa had the chance to be quick off the mark because Great Britain had already recognized the value of radar as a means of better protecting herself against aerial attack from a potential aggressor on the Continent of Europe.

With the imperative growth of coastal radar chains for national defense, it clearly made more sense to employ indigenous personnel to install, operate and maintain the specialist equipment in these stations than bringing in others from distant parts. So, Australians generally provided the technical muscle on stations in the fast-expanding chain in Australia, Canadians in Canada, South Africans in South Africa and so on. Britain was the exception because of her hub position in a major theatre of operations, particularly in the early days of WWII when there was such an acute manpower shortage in radar and in many other areas necessary to combat the on-grinding German war machine.

Why, then, did the intriguing situation arise where a pair of Canadians, both members of the Royal Canadian Air Force and both of them radar technicians who trained and served in the UK, found themselves installing radar stations right around Australia? Furthermore, how come these two 'Canucks' were in charge of installation parties where all the members were Royal Australian Air Force personnel? To understand, it means going back to February 1942 when the pair, Corporals Charlie Cheshire and Doug Wiltshire, received orders to leave their posts in Britain and to prepare to go overseas, to an as yet unspecified location. The two RCAF men and three RAF men formed an overseas draft which sailed from Liverpool to Halifax, took a train to San Francisco and caught the liner *Queen Elizabeth* for Sydney, Australia, arriving there on 6 April 1942. A more welcoming overseas posting would have been difficult to imagine, the warmth of the Australian people being exceeded only by the warmth exuded by the climatic conditions.

There is always someone, isn't there, who can't seem to let a person's life in the Services continue to run on its previously smooth course... Where Charlie and Doug were concerned, that 'someone' was the 'top brass' at their first station 'Down Under' [Bradfield Park]. This particular officer began querying the presence of a pair of Canadian airmen (however skilled, willing and able they may have appeared!) – when, at that time, no-one from the RCAF was supposed to have set foot in Australia. Fair's fair: so far as he was concerned, he knew that the land of 'Oz' wasn't a posting open to RCAF personnel.

Charlie recalls what occurred next:

'They signaled the RAF for an explanation, at the same time confining the two of us to barracks – maybe they reckoned we could have been impostors. For a week we heard nothing. Then an RAF Squadron Leader, wearing side arms and accompanied by two NCOs who were similarly armed, whisked us away to join his own unit, which was in the process of being established at Croydon, in Sydney, under the name of # 1 Radar Installation and Maintenance Unit. Our "rescuers" effectively answered *what* we'd do in Australia; the question as to *why* we were there took over two years to answer – and the explanation, when it did come, was a dandy!

'It seems that the radar mechanics' record cards in the UK were all filed together, irrespective of whether an individual was in the RAF or the RCAF. Those cards were all the same size; they were also the same in the way that the information was laid out on those cards, but for one significant variation. It was this: in the case of RCAF personnel, the surname appeared in the same box as the one which was used for the county of origin of RAF personnel. The cards themselves were a different color, being blue for RCAF personnel while those of the RAF were white. Now, add an RAF postings clerk who is color blind, give that person the job of picking five RAF radar mechanics and you'll see what happened. The guy correctly pulled out three radar mechs for the Australia draft whose cards were white and two more whose cards were in fact blue, supposedly radar mechs who came from the English counties of Cheshire and Wiltshire. So that's how Doug and myself ended up in Australia; and certainly from April 1942 to late 1943 we were the only RCAF personnel posted there. We weren't grumbling of course; Australia was a great place to spend a war! [1] '

Once that little problem about their posting and their credentials was sorted out, life at # 1 RIMU became even better when a Wing Commander who happened to be a buddy of the Canadian VC hero Billy Bishop took over from the Squadron Leader who had been in temporary charge while setting up the unit. On their first meeting with the Wing Commander, Charlie and Doug were shown a huge album which turned out to be more than anything a photographic record of the 25-years-plus friendship he had enjoyed with the WWI air ace, who was by then an RCAF Air Vice-Marshal. He offered the two 'Canucks' a 'deal': 'Do whatever you think is necessary to get this unit up and running in the shortest possible time, in the best manner possible, and I will see that you are excused all duties and all parades while you're at my Headquarters'. It was an offer too generous to miss so the two Corporals snapped smartly to attention and replied in unison: 'Yes, SIR!'

Charlie notes that he and they kept their word while based at Croydon. Both always attended CO's Parade but the rest of the time at HQ, which could amount to as much as one week in four while back 'home' from their far-ranging installation duties, 'we would report daily to the Adjutant, sometimes by phone, and we would put in radar stations like men possessed'.

At # 1 RIMU, Charlie and Doug were each in charge of a small (4-8 man) team of RAAF technicians, their assignment being to install these stations right around

Australia. Being mainly CHL stations from Britain, there were often delays or losses while at sea and this would mean components from an Australian unit, the AW, being patched-in for the missing parts of either the receiver or the transmitter. It was a mammoth task, Charlie's team alone installing 17 radar units from the tip of Cape York, west across the north coast to Broome, south along the east coast to Geelong, west on the south coast to Victoria Harbour and on the west coast from Albany to Geraldton. The first that Doug's team installed was near Port Moresby on the island of New Guinea, though the remainder of his dozen or so units were all on the Australian continent. The other NCO who had been drafted from the UK (he was a Sergeant) moved on later from installation work with # 1 RIMU to the development and improvement of radar equipment.

Charlie says of the work of the installation teams:

> 'If everything went according to plan, a radar station could be set up in a month, but it usually took six weeks from the time the equipment was landed on the beach until the unit was up, tuned in and ready for the hand-over to the operating personnel. Generally we had just one radar mechanic, who was the team leader, with an electrician, a motor mechanic, one to four tradesmen skilled in carpentry, concrete construction, sheet metal work, sometimes a cook and occasionally one or two "laborers". Almost without exception, one or more members of a team would be changed between assignments, which meant training the newcomers. The Aussies never seemed to mind that there was a Canadian in charge. By 1944, some of the equipment being installed was the American centimeter stuff; by now, though, the original network of radar stations around the Australian continent was virtually complete so our installation work was tapered off. In November 1944, Doug and I were posted home, arriving in Vancouver a fortnight before Christmas. And after four weeks' leave – our first home leave in four years – we were melded into Canadian units.'

For examples both of the spirit of international co-operation that was manifest in wartime radar and the globe-spanning travel that was the lot of so many radar personnel, the experiences of Charlie Mills would surely be hard to equal: an RCAF officer, he arrived in the UK in January 1942 and served on stations in Northern Ireland, England and Wales; then came a posting to New Zealand to help set up its defensive chain; on secondment he instructed members of the US Marine Corps in ground-controlled air interception; he installed radar sites in the jungle on a series of stepping-stone islands in the Pacific; he all but served in Australia (instead, a critical attack of malaria put him in hospital); and he finished his time in Europe, looking at enemy radar while with the occupying forces in Germany.

In some respects he was a comparative rarity: where most Servicemen crossed oceans on crowded troopships, Charlie's voyage from the UK to New Zealand in September/October of 1942 was on a freighter, the SS *Port Alma*, which had accommodation for just a dozen persons. Three were radar personnel, the others a mix of Royal Navy, Australian Army and one RNZAF aircrew member who was being invalided home accompanied by his wife. The radar group was Auckland-bound in response to an RNZAF request for personnel to develop a radar chain in case of Japanese attack; Charlie's experience included both CHL and GCI while with him was a fellow member of the RCAF specializing in CHL and an RAF member specializing in CH. Posted to RNZAF Headquarters, it would be Charlie's job to handle all GCI activities under their control as well as CHL stations southwards from New Plymouth.

With a 'roving commission' of sorts, Charlie made inspection and calibration visits to most of the operational sites in the south. Then, on secondment to the US Marine Corps, it was his job to train fighter controllers, mechanics and operators and to see them formed into units for shipment, the equipment in packing cases to be reassembled on site. He recalled that 'the personnel and technical equipment went by one ship, tents, kitchen etc in a second. All kit was American to keep up the US image. The only way we had of getting RNZAF markings was to liberate them from our last posting *en route*. This included borrowing the station flag from the base in Wellington' ₂ .

On Guadalcanal, by then liberated but in a hot-spot for aerial action, Charlie Mills first had to overcome problems resulting from the loss of equipment when one of the ships was sunk and then to find a way to put an end to interference which friendly radar systems was causing to the unit's GCI activities to combat enemy air attacks. Problem # 1 was solved by authority being given to scour US Army camps to obtain replacements. Solving Problem # 2, accomplished when Charlie was authorized to close down any station whose radar was interfering with the operation of his own unit, achieved a successful partnership between his ground station and the US Army Air Corps night fighters which were under its control.

The largest of the Soloman Islands in the western Pacific, Guadalcanal was the scene of the first major US offensive against the Japanese in August 1942, shortly before Charlie left the UK. After Guadalcanal, moving on to site and install radar stations on a succession of smaller and lesser-known islands (where in several cases the stations were sited prior to the US landing to secure the sites), Charlie and his team experienced other sorts of problems. One that came most readily to mind was the humidity in those jungle sites which created 'all kinds of troubles' in both the transmitter and receiver, particularly when starting up after power had been down. He recalled that…

> 'Unofficial modifications were introduced to overcome this, including such things as distributed soldering iron elements that came on when the set was switched off, which tended to keep the temperature above the condensation point. Fungus was common too – and this was only kept clear by elbow grease.'

Operations were also affected by climatic conditions. Normally radio waves travel in a straight line so that only aircraft and shipping above the horizon could be detected. However there were times when temperature inversion in the upper atmosphere caused the radio waves to follow the curvature of the earth and under these circumstances aircraft and shipping could be detected *below* the horizon. Charlie writes:

> 'For example, we found that temperature inversion allowed aircraft plotting and control at normally unheard of ranges and it was possible to plot the

movement of shipping, some 20 or 30 miles out to sea, from sea level sites. When using this extended range however, absolute height finding was impossible and relative heights were used once the fighter and target were in fairly close proximity [3].'

While serving in the Mediterranean in early 1944, Canadian radar technical officer Morris Olfman encountered this same phenomenon and recounted, later, how it had proved particularly helpful to the Allied cause.   Morris, fortunate indeed to have survived an incident the previous September when a wireless-controlled glide bomb hit a landing craft which his unit (AMES 8003) was unloading at Ajaccio, causing casualties and the loss of some of his unit's equipment, explains the outcome of that particular occurrence of what the scientists call 'anomalous propagation'.   Then with 501 AMES in Malta, Morris remembers that...

'In April 1944 a controller was assigned to 501 because of increasing numbers of hostile aircraft and in May one Junkers 88 was destroyed at 110 miles by a pair of Spitfires.   A few days later, a second aircraft of the same type was destroyed at 160 miles, again by a pair of Spitfires.   Apparently both "hostiles" were spotted when the pilots saw their shape against a wave on the water.   Nevertheless, had it not been for the beneficial (to us!) effects of anomalous propagation, 501's equipment would not have been able to pick up the presence of the enemy aircraft at such an extreme range [4].'

Unfortunately, Charlie Mills' time on those steaming Pacific islands had created an unwelcome legacy.   His work done, he was back in New Zealand in September 1943, the intention being a move to Australia to arrange the meeting of the radar nets of the naval and military commands on Bouganville.   But this was not to be: instead he was in hospital with malaria and in time resumed command of 61 Radar Squadron until being returned to the UK early in 1944 in anticipation of working with the Americans for the invasion of Normandy.   Again this wasn't to be: instead, having rejected repatriation back home to Canada, Charlie Mills remained in the UK until taking a posting to 8403 Air (RCAF) Disarmament Wing based at Oldenburg in Germany, investigating German radar and other anti-bomber equipment [*see page 163*].

With radar, there was an international aspect beyond its application in a particular country.   Within the Allied air forces in WWII, operational units comprising personnel of predominantly one country or a unit bearing the name of a particular country, invariably would have radar equipment in their aircraft.   Consequently this required specialist personnel to install, to maintain and to operate this equipment, though not always would those individuals be indigenous with the national identification associated with that particular unit – even where there was a common mother tongue.

It was on his last posting, towards the end of hostilities in Europe, that radar technician Lenny Palmer became embroiled for the first time in the problems of communication that arise when there is an inability among a group of people to speak a common language.   He explains:

'My final station was with a Polish squadron flying Mosquitoes out of Abingdon and we had 52 aircraft with GEE Mk II and IFF which was serviced every morning using a push cart with an APU [Auxiliary Power Unit]. A Polish Flight Sergeant in charge of the dispersal points was the only one who could speak English. I had to contact him every day to find out which aircraft was flying that night, as all the printing on the boards was in Polish [5] .'

Serving on a Rhodesian Air Force squadron at Dunholme Lodge, J Vic Davies would not have expected ever to be confronted with a language limitation. It was just as well – because one night there was a communications breakdown of a different sort. He was in a bomber, busy doing what he was supposed to be doing, his presence apparently unknown to the pilot. The outcome was that Vic 'nearly had a front row seat' to watch Bomber Command in action over Germany. This occurred when one of the squadron's Lancasters experienced both unserviceable radar equipment and an engine that quit while in the queue at the end of the runway and otherwise all set for take-off. Vic was duty radar mechanic that night so he and an aero-engine mechanic were dispatched to sort out the problems. He recalls:

'The aero-engine mechanic was able to get the motor going and hollered that it was OK. Then he jumped out of the kite. I was quite surprised when we went roaring down the runway as I was still trying to get the radar working. I went forward and asked where were they going; I was told we were heading for the city of Wesel in Germany.

'I explained that I hadn't signed the log book yet and they were not supposed to take off until I did. Further, I didn't have a flying suit or an oxygen mask – and I'd never flown before. I was very fortunate that time because the motor conked out again for good. Lancasters carried 14,000 lbs of bombs and with only three engines working we couldn't get much altitude. The navigator figured that if we put our wheels down we would hit the water, our location being over the Wash, near Skegness. Dropping the bombs didn't seem to be too good an idea, as they would go off right under our belly. Belly landing also was a bit of a problem.

'The pilot radioed Base for instructions and he was told to stooge around until he had used up as much fuel as possible, in hope that we could gain enough altitude to get over the trees along the coastline. We did as instructed and finally the pilot said that we "had to do, or die". He did a wonderful job; he landed that kite like a crate of eggs and never even blew a tire, though I figured that if that was flying, I wanted nothing more to do with it! I understand the RAF weren't too pleased with the pilot for taking me sightseeing but I never had any trouble over it [6] .'

Vic was at Dunholme Lodge for about a year, with # 44 Squadron and on detachment to 52 Base at Scampton, before being posted to a unit of the Royal Australian Air Force at Stoke Heath, near Market Drayton. Thus he was a Canadian who had been posted to England; who served with the RAF; and who experienced life both on a Rhodesian bomber squadron and with an RAAF Maintenance Unit.

Other radar mechs served with, or were associated with, training units and operational squadrons with personnel belonging to other Allied air forces, for example the Belgians, Dutch, Free French, Poles and Czechs whose competence in the English tongue ranged from the ability just to get by to accent-free fluency.

For a radar technician working on a squadron where most or many of its members had a mother tongue other than English, if there was a language barrier it would be an obvious one. But was there, in fact, a 'language barrier' when there was a Canadian (or an American for that matter) serving amid predominantly Britons? Gregory Biefer addressed this point in an article he wrote post-war for a Canadian publication, *Airforce*, explaining that generally a radar section would be billeted together in a Nissen hut holding up to 14 people; they formed a 'reasonably compatible group, despite a tendency towards long and fierce arguments in the evenings'. He continued:

> 'I was then, and remain, a patriotic Canadian, but under those crowded conditions I found the Brits easier to live with than the Canucks, because of their quieter and more orderly ways. I must admit that British accents and sentiments sometimes grated on me, though I never mentioned it, being overwhelmingly outnumbered. Some of the Brits were sufficiently uninhibited to let me know that the reverse was also true [7] .'

The RAF's needs being the greater, the vast majority of Canadians who answered Britain's call and received their initial training as radar technicians in their own country were shipped out to the UK; Bob Warner, though, remained to help satisfy the needs of the RCAF. Even so, he too arrived at his first radar station – it was at Ucluelet on Vancouver Island – during a time of high alert brought about by enemy action. The lighthouse at Estevan Point having been shelled a few days earlier by a Japanese submarine, 'those in the military services were required to carry rifles or sidearms at all times. However, we had to check them at the door when we went to the Wet Canteen – shades of the Old West days'. He recalls the Radar Building having 'a few Sten guns, hand grenades and a 200 lb bomb for use if it became necessary to destroy the radar equipment [*] .

A subsequent posting took him to Sea Island [*later to become Vancouver International Airport*], then the home of a GCI unit sited some two miles from an RCAF fighter base. Bob recalls there being a canine security guard named Renty, the story being that Renty had been taken on the unit roster under 'Personnel Other Than RCAF' and authorized to draw rations but no pay. The night that Renty arrived, Bob's friend and room mate Pete O'Neill missed the transport for the midnight shift so took a taxi as far as possible and then walked the rest of the way to the entry gate, only to find the bell was inoperative. O'Neill, having decided to climb over the fence, unfortunately was met by Renty, who kept him cornered against the fence until given an OK by the guard. As Bob remembers it, 'Renty was always

---

[*] After Clinton, Bob Warner joined other RCAF radar personnel at the Scarborough field station of a company manufacturing CHL and GCI equipment, their job being to carry out tests on the equipment located there and to install and test modifications to it. In June 1942 he was posted to # 13 Radio Detachment at Amphitrite Point, Canada's first operational radar station and the only one with CHL.

suspicious of O'Neill after that. The dog checked everyone who entered the compound and always stopped anyone who was new to him'.

After a few months at Sea Island, Bob answered a call for radar technicians to volunteer for service overseas. Yes, came the response, provided that he gave up his sergeant's stripes and reverted to LAC (a policy that was later changed). Instead of travelling to distant parts, therefore, he found himself posted to a detachment at Cape St James on a small island at the southern tip of the Queen Charlotte Islands, British Columbia. Its two humps of rock gave it a profile like a camel's back. There, sometimes the weather could be extremely harsh and he has since described the aftermath of one particular storm and its effect on this radar site:

> 'The weather anemometer was blown away but a reading of 100 mph had been obtained. We had an IFF antenna on top of a wooden tower that blew down, falling across the electric power lines. It was necessary to clear the tower to restore the power to the site so we could return to operations when the wind subsided sufficiently. The main antennae had been lashed down to prevent it from being damaged by swinging in the wind. There were three of us working on the fallen tower and we were completely soaked by salt water from the waves smashing against the rocks 325 feet or so below. Afterwards we had a hot bath and a liberal ration of Navy Rum (for medicinal purposes) [8].'

On Canada's east coast, the ground organization necessary to conduct fighter operations was created in 1942/43, using three types of radar station: early warning high flying, known as TRU, early warning low flying, known as CHL, with an approximate range of 100 miles, and ground control intercept, GCI, with a range of 50 miles [9]. Filter centres located at Command and Group Headquarters plotted information from the radar units, Aircraft Detection Corps detachments and other sources, feeding back this intelligence to sector control rooms at fighter airfields. In the event of an attack, personnel at those control rooms would direct aircraft to their target.

Unlike radar stations in the UK, those on Canada's west coast 'were few and rather distantly situated from each other'. Radar technician Les Dow has made mention of the fact that 'we poor mechanics and operators' were not in a position to recount such 'exciting stories' as their overseas counterparts. Writing in a commemorative brochure produced for the WWII Radar Reunion in London, Ontario, 21/23 September 1999, he indicated that the shelling of Ferrier Point 'by a supposedly Japanese submarine' was disclosed only post-war 'although the girls in the Victoria filter room knew it at the time'. Many of the stations on Canada's west coast were accessible only by sea, particularly those on the Queen Charlotte Islands. At one station, it was said, 'if you opened the front door during a storm, you had to open the back door to let the water out'!

In essence, East Coast radar operations monitored aircraft that were either shepherding convoys, taking part in submarine patrols or were lost; while the West Coast had a lot less activity and were mostly plotting coastal patrol and training aircraft, though 'a couple of Japanese submarine sightings were made, including shelling of a lighthouse' [10].

The Dominions were made aware of Britain's work on a radar-based air defense system before the start of WWII. An official history [*] recounts how, early in 1939, New Zealand was notified of the development of a 'secret device connected with air defense', which was sufficiently important to warrant the dispatch of a physicist to the UK to study it. The New Zealand government's representative, Dr E Marsden, Director of the Department of Scientific and Industrial Research (DSIR), arrived in London at the end of April 1939 and with Squadron Leader S Wallingford, RNZAF Liaison Officer at the Air Ministry, reported back to the New Zealand Chief of Air Staff on the technical and operational aspects of this 'secret device', which was of course radar.

In practical terms, the immediate outcome was the arrival of two radar sets ordered from the UK, one a ground unit, the other an airborne unit, plus drawings and specifications sufficient for the DSIR to make plans for production to commence in New Zealand, 20 sets being built. For much of the second half of 1940, an airborne radar set patterned on the one received from Britain and fitted to a Waco aircraft was used by the Electrical and Wireless School at Wigram for experimental work and to assist in the training of maintenance personnel.

A handwritten diary kept by Eric Morrin [11] provides historians with a useful insight into the manner in which these experiments were conducted during flights by day and by night, often using the inter-island ferry and other marine craft as targets to test the efficiency of this set and to make comparison between it and later equipment carried in an Oxford aircraft. For example, on one flight 'the tests indicated that the max distance for reliable indication when boat is broadside was five miles, while max for when boat is end-on is only two and a half miles', the next flight confirming those results. However, 'it was noted that when flying over the top of the boat, there was no indication at all, which is quite different from results in the Waco'. The diary continues: 'We then saw a larger ship than the ferry so transferred operations to this one, and results were practically identical with the previous ones except that the echoes were more distinct.' And on the following day, when there was no shipping in the area and the test was carried out using the shore line, 'the echoes appeared to be quite a bit better and apparently could be operated from a greater distance, 10 to 12 miles being the estimated distance for quite good echoes.' On that occasion 'there did not appear to be any increase in intensity when the plane was tilted over at an angle, but there was a decrease when it was tilted the other way'.

Latter-day radar technicians and others who are concerned with product design and development may be intrigued by the points that Eric Morrin, on 23 October 1940, noted for what he called 'improvement and alteration during flight': 1. Fit valve controller time base and calibrate with audio oscillator; 2. Reverse P.S. switch; 3. Make small cm scale with which to measure echo heights; 4. Make light shield; 5. Fit intensity control for night-day operation; 6. Ground test to compare relative efficiency of P.S. receiver aerials; and 7. Eliminate Near-Far switch. And by these 'particular tests': 1. Range check during experimental flights on ferry etc; 2. Polar diagram tests; 3. Daily flight on ferry; 4. Explore headlands etc for polar diagrams and range;

---

[*] *Royal New Zealand Air Force*, by Squadron Leader J M S Ross, one of the volumes comprising the Official History of New Zealand in the Second World War 1939-45, War History Branch, Department of Internal Affairs, Wellington, New Zealand, 1955.

5. Measurement tests; 6. Test for 4 hours flight; 7. Measure current; 8. Batteries low, half and fully charged; 9. Artificial load test; and 10. Examine generator bearings.

The official history previously quoted notes that in mid-1941, 'when the threat of war with Japan was becoming more evident, priority was switched to ground radar, and from then until the end of the war maximum effort was directed to the erection, maintenance and operation of air-warning systems, both in New Zealand and in the Pacific'. Dependence on New Zealand-built sets was 'not a practical proposition', consequently it was decided that complete units should be ordered from Britain.

By May 1943 there were 16 radar units operating round the coast of New Zealand, most of them in the North Island and 'nearly all in remote parts of the country, cut off from the amenities of civilization'. These units were small self-contained communities, each dependent on itself for its own well-being, and its personnel comprising RNZAF, including WAAF, and in some cases Navy. Although New Zealand was not subjected to air attack, these radar units 'did sterling work in other directions', their major commitment being to assist the Navy by plotting all ships round their respective areas of the coast. Especially in the Auckland and New Plymouth areas, they were 'often responsible for locating overseas aircraft which had lost themselves in bad weather and for guiding them in safely to a landing'. On record, however, there is a single instance of a hostile aircraft being plotted by radar units in the Auckland area though the plots were disbelieved until – its reconnaissance over – the plane had returned to its mother-ship, a Japanese submarine, and was safely out of harm's way. Also on record are 'one or two occasions' where radar stations at various points around the coast reported enemy submarines, 'but none was ever found'.

In the South Pacific, Fiji had the original CHL set obtained in the UK during Dr Marsden's visit and this was operated by RNZAF personnel until taken over by the Americans after a year of active service, during which time the tracks of numerous Japanese submarines were plotted round its sector of the coast. Further radar stations were positioned on the island of Tonga, Norfolk Island and on Guadalcanal, the New Zealand GCI set on this latter location being the first of its kind in the South Pacific. Subsequently a number of other radar units equipped with two additional GCI and four COL sets were formed and sent to the forward area, operating on Malaita, Munda, Rendova Island and Torokina, as well as on Guadalcanal. In the words of the official history, New Zealand technical officers in the forward area 'did excellent work in the face of very great difficulties. Sets had to be located in places which in almost every case offended all principles of radar siting, and their successful operation reflected great credit on the officers concerned [12] '.

In a talk post-war to the South African Military History Society, in which he reviewed that country's role in the development and use of radar in WWII, Dr F J Hewitt noted that 'as with all good inventions at least four countries claim the credit for it – the French, the British, the Americans and of course, the Russians' [13] .

Dr Hewitt, one of South Africa's radar pioneers, recalled that when the British government notified Commonwealth countries, in extreme secrecy, of the development of RDF, it had invited them to send senior scientists to the United Kingdom with a view to acquainting them to the principles, so that each country could build up a team who could in due course assist in the introduction of RDF systems as and when they became available. Dr Basil Schonland met the New Zealand government's representative, Dr Marsden, in Cape Town on his return from the UK to New Zealand, no-one having gone to the UK from South Africa. Schonland gathered a team without delay, the object being that they should design equipment themselves. This they did, said Dr Hewitt, and 'with such success that the first radio echo was "seen" on 16 December 1939'. This was achieved with none of the more advanced electronic components or test equipment that was available in the UK; the components they bought were what was available in Johannesburg on the amateur radio market; there was little in the way of test equipment and instruments; and they had to improvise for all measurements except the most conventional. Hewitt, a physicist by training and a radio enthusiast who had designed and built what he described as 'reasonably advanced radio receivers', joined that team on 2 January 1940. Without that radio experience, he told the S A Military History Society, 'I would have been lost'.

Within six months, equipment had been built which could be usable in the field, provided that specialist maintenance personnel were available, and in the summer of 1940, in Durban, 'we saw very few aircraft but we learnt quite a lot about detecting shipping – which at that time was not our object'.

He recalled being at Mombasa, attached to the 1st Anti-Aircraft Brigade, and moving some 100 miles north to establish a radar station. It was 'our job to detect possible Italian bombers proceeding down the coast to attack Mombasa. Theory had it that this would take place at dawn and dusk. Only once did we see Italian aircraft. They bombed the air strip at Malindi, 16 kilometers away. We did not see them coming in but we saw them going out to sea afterwards for 56 kilometers and then lost them because of our restrictive coverage arc of 180 degrees. So much for the theory of their flying along the coast. As a result of this we modified our aerials to cover the full 360 degrees – and thenceforth had endless trouble with breaking feeders'.

In April 1941 Hewitt went up to Egypt in preparation for the move of the East African stations to the Middle East. These were to be fully integrated with the RAF and sites were selected on the coast of Sinai. In South Africa during this time stations were established at the four ports using South African-built equipment initially, though with British CD/CHL sets introduced at Signal Hill, Cape Town and in Durban early on. The South African stations were used originally for the tracking of shipping but procedures were adopted for aircraft observations as well.

He went to the UK in 1942 to study microwave radar – 'a completely new development which made possible very narrow beams, freedom from the effects of ground and performance from small aerials never obtainable before'. For coastal defense purposes in South Africa, for the first two or three years of the war reliance was placed on locally designed and built equipment. Gradually larger and more sophisticated sets became available from the UK. By late 1943 there was 'a fairly extensive system for the detection of surfaced submarines, surface vessels, low- and high-flying aircraft'; in addition there were 'limited facilities for directing fighter aircraft to intercept unidentified aircraft detected by the radar system'. Other activities in which South Africa was involved were special types of radar for anti-aircraft fire control and for coastal artillery fire control. Hewitt said of one of those sets, known as the GL II [gun laying], that it was 'a relatively long wave length radar of British origin, somewhat outdated even then but excellently engineered to its maximum potential, which had borne the brunt of the anti-aircraft fire control for the defense of London during the early blitz'.

In Australia, although there were similarities with Britain in the manner in which radar was used, there were also some aspects in which significant differences existed, for example the dependence on air transportability because of the greater distances. As the war progressed, as well as the defense of vital areas on the Australian mainland, there was the advance against the Japanese on the New Guinea mainland and the islands of the associated mandated territories to require the increasing application of radar.

Radar production began in Australia early in 1942 with all three armed services taking a share: for the Army, shore defense equipment – adapted for the Navy to use for ship warning and gunnery purposes – and air warning and air-to-surface vessel equipment for the Air Force.   Subsequent production included equipment for searchlight control for the Army, beacons to go with ASV radar used by the Air Force and adaptations of ASV for the Navy to use as shipboard surface warning equipment.   During the latter part of 1942, production was commenced on a set operating in the 'S' band, together with the necessary magnetron and klystron electron tubes, those tubes being used by the Navy for its surface warning equipment and by the Army for its portable coast defense installations 14 .

The Royal Australian Air Force, with responsibility for the air defense of the Australian mainland, directed operations through an Air Officer Commanding each of five geographical areas – North West, North East, Eastern, Southern and Western. By the end of 1943 there were 113 ground radar stations operated by the RAAF and a further 35 planned to be brought into use in 1944.   The air defense of the Brisbane, Sydney and Perth districts was largely based on the receipt of adequate air warning from fixed radar stations, the system being organized in much the same way as the UK Fighter Sectors; however the air warning systems in the North West and North East areas were better suited to what were known as 'Mobile Fighter Sectors', utilizing a greater quantity of mobile equipment.   It emerged that in the Darwin area, where the Japanese usually approached from the north-west with bomber and fighter escort, 'more embarrassment was caused through unknown height than through their very rare low flying approaches'.   An RAAF report noted height measurement as being 'a facility markedly absent from Allied radar systems in the South West Pacific Area' though so far [that report was dated 12 February 1944] the Japanese 'have not exhibited any noticeable tendency to seek evasion by varying   altitude' 15 .   As for airborne radar work in the RAAF, general reconnaissance duties provided the main field with some 600 of its aircraft equipped with a locally-built equivalent to the British ASV Mk 2.   That same report carried a comment that 'the RAAF seeks better performance against all forms of shipping and would welcome a better navigational   aid', adding that it was 'imperative' to have airborne radar working on a frequency besides that of 'the well tried one and a half meter band'.

Training for the RAAF's radar officers, mechanics and operators was centred on # 1 Radar School at Richmond; in its peak year, 1943, some 640 RAAF radar mechanics and 40 US radar tradesmen passed through this establishment, together with 731 RAAF and 346 WAAF radar operators. There was a theoretical capacity for 600 'but it has never been necessary or possible to fill it to this extent' [16].

In the South West Pacific Area, where General Douglas MacArthur was the Allied Forces' Commander-in-Chief, air operations were in the hands of the US 5th Air Force, which was responsible primarily for those in New Guinea, and the RAAF with responsibility for those conducted from the Australian mainland. Under MacArthur, American and Australian forces would proceed to take back the islands that Japan had seized at the beginning of the war, his personal victory being the fulfillment of his famous vow to return to the Philippines, MacArthur having been ordered by President Roosevelt to leave for Australia before the islands were surrendered in the spring of 1942. In that campaign, the RAAF was 'particularly proud of the fact that the first radar station to go ashore during the American attack on New Britain was an Australian LW/AW Mk 1A with its RAAF crew', Allied Air Force policy allowing RAAF radar stations to operate as components of Air Forces otherwise entirely composed of American units [17].

The Australians' use of radar in the Allied advance in that theatre of operations may be compared to that in Europe. An LW/AW Mk 1A would be flown as close as possible to the desired site after an airstrip had been made or captured; if no airstrip was available, the equipment would be taken by sea, then to be put ashore and assembled as soon as possible. It was 'seldom, however, that a station reaches its site without considerable manhandling, usually in jungle and uphill' [18]. During 1944, however, the RAAF aimed to provide air transportable GCI stations to be brought up as soon as possible after the capture of an airstrip or beach-head so that fighter control might be incorporated quickly into the defense system.

With regard to airborne radar additional to ASV, Australian military thinking appears to have been markedly innovative with regard to the Rebecca/Eureka partnership. Conventionally, this was seen as a means of bringing aircraft within sight of visual signals to denote the dropping zones; more intriguing is the indication – and it comes in a report issued in early 1944 by the then Director of Radio Services in the Royal Australian Air Force – that the RAAF was 'most anxious' to develop that type of equipment as a 'close support aid' [19]. In this field, a research project was being set up in Australia to look into the single-seater use of Rebecca – one possibility being to install Rebecca in Vultee Vengeance dive bombers. Its potentiality appears not to have achieved support sufficient for it to have ripened into significance as an operational application of radar by any of the Allied air forces during WWII.

Countries involved in WWII, Allied and enemy alike, would naturally draw on their own competence in radar to strengthen their own defense capabilities; but what was the position in a neutral country, specifically Turkey, which kept out of the conflict until the final months when declaring war on Germany and Japan? While not necessarily meeting the levels that the Turks would have wished, Britain and the United States provided economic and military aid to Turkey from early on; then, towards the end of 1943, to meet that country's fear of air attack from the Luftwaffe's bases in Greece and on the Aegean islands now that the Allies no longer had a presence off the coast of Turkey, Britain decided to send in a radar screen. The first step: to choose where to locate the equipment.

Radar technical officer Herb Beall, having been posted to # 217 Group HQ in Egypt and at the same time promoted to Squadron Leader, entered Turkey on 29 November 1943 in civilian clothes, as protocol required when going into a neutral country. It was his assignment to select sites for a radar chain along the Aegean coast, in which he was accompanied by two Turkish officers 'who were my escorts and not supposed to let me out of their sight'. Herb picked out a dozen or so sites for various types of radar stations and on 29 January 1944 he was back in Egypt; it would be more than six months before he returned to Turkey, this time to set up Light Warning Units.

While Herb Beall was in Turkey on that first reconnaissance mission, another radar technical officer and coincidentally a fellow Canadian, Flight Lieutenant Cy Williamson, had left Aleppo in Syria for Turkey on Christmas Day, with six other radar specialists and their equipment [20]. All wore civilian clothes, naturally enough, but unnaturally all were dressed alike – save for their headgear. As Cy's widow, Ethel Williamson, would later explain, the officers wore felt hats and the men had caps. She continues:

> 'Due to poor facilities, all their gear, trucks and men had to be brought ashore in the port of Izmir, in full sight of the German, Italian and Japanese embassies. Everything had been carefully marked "Aid to Turkey" and all British markings had been removed; but there was no doubt that all of this was a ruse. While this was going on, Turkish police were assaulting the enemy bystanders with truncheons and smashing their cameras! On 6 October 1944, Cy was ordered to return to Port Said and issued with a collective passport, valid for 149 persons [predominantly Britons but including 6 Canadians and 3 South Africans, their units being Cy's own, which was AMES 515; AMES 633, 634, 636, 638, 6018 and 8037; # 17 Radar Detachment; and # 67 Line Section], for a single journey from Izmir to Syria, overland. All radio gear was to stay in Turkey. The airmen and officers were given shelter and food at various military camps *en route* to Egypt and arrived at their destination without incident [21].'

It is as well that this military-minded contingent, specialists in an advanced form of warfare, did reach their home territory 'without incident'. If all or any had been taken as prisoners-of-war while in a then neutral country – 'their uniforms in locked storage miles away in Cairo' [22] – none could have counted on protection under the Geneva Convention. In that situation it would not have been entirely inappropriate to have described radar as a Turkish delight that turned out to be somewhat less sweet for the British.

CHAPTER 15: THE LOST THANK-YOU

Aside from the consequences of enemy action, whether in South East Asia, the Middle East, Europe or wherever, the risk to life and limb was ever-present in a working environment where radio and radar equipment was dominant. Technicians had to contend with many inherent dangers such as losing one's footing while climbing a mast and a myriad other accidents waiting to happen when a site was under construction or a station in the process of dismantling. The obvious hazard was electrocution, which claimed one life early on when, apparently, a component in the transmitter failed and made the equipment alive [1] . There were incidents where others were more fortunate, for example one involving Clinton-trained Bob Warner at Ucluelet on Vancouver Island where, as he recalls it...

'The antenna for the radio transmitter was very close to the Mess Hall and the hot water heater in the kitchen reacted as a receiver so it was possible to distinguish what was being said. One time I was helping install a second transmitting antenna for a different frequency when I received a very painful RF [radio frequency] burn when someone transmitted a message – we should have deactivated the transmit function of the transmitter before installing the antenna. Another time I received a shock when adjusting the radar equipment after the scheduled maintenance time. I was thrown about three feet into the corner of the room and had to call the technician whom I had relieved to come back and complete the start-up procedure for the equipment. A shock from a 25,000-volt Cathode Ray Tube power supply certainly gave me the "shakes" for a few hours [2] .'

Related risks remained where a radar mech stayed on in the armed forces or, as some chose to do, put in a stint as a reservist.

Away from his homeland since 5 January 1941, Pacifico 'Puss' Valeriote joined RCAF Station, Debert, Nova Scotia, in April 1945 to spend the final few months of his service on a Radar Maintenance Unit looking after units along the east coast. For 'Puss' however, discharge (on 4 August 1945) was not the last that he would see of the paraphernalia of radar installations. He explains:

'In 1948, I was in business with my brothers Mike and Steve in Montreal and at this time Radar Reserve Units were being formed as additional defensive measures during the start of the Cold War. Wing Commander Ken Patrick was in charge of the newly formed # 1 Radar and Communication Unit in Montreal, so Mike met with Ken and discussed the idea of forming a detachment at Ste Anne de Bellevue, where we lived. This resulted in the recruitment of former RCAF personnel from this area to form one of these Reserve Units, with Mike as CO and myself as Technical Officer.

'We were given an airborne GCA radar unit, which was installed in a communications vehicle along with R/T equipment, and we used to spend many a weekend travelling throughout Quebec on single or combined maneuvers with Navy and Army reserve units. In 1951, an AMES 11 Radar Station was obtained by the Montreal Unit and we now became part of # 2451 Aircraft Control and Warning Unit. With this equipment we were able to hold joint operations with reserve units of the US Air Force as far away as New York City 3 .'

For the Canadians, if acted upon within a set time, discharge brought with it an opportunity to go to university; for many this was an opportunity not to be missed, perhaps because of a 13-week 'taster' when joining up or perhaps because this had been their intention before going into uniform.

Having held dual (Canadian/US) citizenship before enlisting in the RCAF in June 1942 at the age of 19, Jay Christensen first applied unsuccessfully to the Canadian authorities for university training, being turned down because he was two months beyond the 15-month limit after discharge. However, moving to the US in 1947 and taking up employment as a radar technician with the US Navy in Clearfield, Utah, he found that he qualified for education under a university training scheme for American war veterans. Consequently, Jay was able to spend four years at the University of Houston, graduating in 1952 with a BSc in petroleum engineering and going on to a lifetime career in the oil and gas industry which spanned 40 years in both the US and Canada.

He summarized his time in the RCAF in these words: 'My war years were brightened by an association with a great bunch of men. Some of the friendships have endured for over 50 years. I often felt we were a forgotten group by Canada but survived anyway. Most of our aggravations were broken promises and little things. The wonderful experiences, I still remember 4 .'

Forgotten group? Broken promises? Though feelings may have mellowed in subsequent years, some who entered the RCAF with youthful spirits and high hopes have not been able to brush aside, totally, the perception that more could have been done for them while serving their country.

While not exactly bitter about the treatment received by radar technicians, Dave Roumieu, on his return to civilian life in Canada, took the view that there should have been some provision for advancement in rank after the training period at # 31 Radio School, Clinton, if obtaining a commission at the time was not possible. He casts his mind back to the course he attended at Clinton where, among some 28 airmen, no more than 5 were commissioned, all of them four or five years older than his 21 years. He says that

'Whenever my children and my grandchildren have asked what I did during the war, I have always tried to give them some idea; but when I'm asked whether I was an officer I could only say that, as far as my exalted rank was concerned, I was an LAC [Leading Aircraftman]. I became an LAC within six months of joining in April 1942 and in my entire service, until my discharge in January 1946, I progressed no further than what I have seen described in some Air Force journals as 'the lowly rank of LAC'.   I am aware that in some cases 'shadow ranking' was implemented for some RCAF radar mechanics where their scale of pay was in accordance with their 'shadow rank', but wearing the NCO's stripes that aligned to this ranking was not part of the scheme.   I doubt if I'm alone in speaking-out about this lack of recognition of effort and knowledge by way of promotion. Strange, isn't it, when there has been so much publicity for the major part that radar had to play in helping the Allies win the war.

'I see that "Chubby" Power, telling Canada's House of Commons that our country had been asked for 5,000 radio personnel and supplied 5,000, had to concede to the House that these volunteers "did not get the advancement which one would expect people of that class to get; they are still LACs... they did not get much in the way of promotion" [5] .   There we were, beavering away doing jobs that we couldn't talk about – we were pledged to secrecy and, when a course was over where we had to assimilate still more highly technical information and put it into practice unfailingly, we had to surrender all the material that we had accumulated in the classroom.   When the matter of rank on discharge would occasionally crop up in post-war years, almost invariably I would learn that many of my friends, my business associates and my clients outranked me.   Is it surprising that so many of us, who were Canadian radar technicians of our own national air force but were attached to the Royal Air Force, have harboured for so long a deep and ingrained feeling of resentment that our promotion prospects were stifled? [6] '

The failure of some of Canada's radar technicians to go higher than Leading Aircraftman was indeed a subject of concern within that country's House of Commons.   As early as June 1943, Air Minister 'Chubby' Power – the man who had launched the recruitment drive more than two years earlier – answered criticism about the promotion and pay of those technicians, whose careers were 'dictated by the RAF' although serving in the RCAF.

It emerged that 'somehow or other we seem to have demanded too high qualifications' and the consequence was that 'we had lawyers, doctors, clergymen' answering the call.   He cited a clergyman 'up in the Hebrides' who was 'a private in the air force' and a Toronto headmaster 'somewhere in the Faroe Islands, holding the position of acting lance corporal without pay'.

The then Major Power recalled a discussion he had with Winston Churchill on the subject of radio mechanics and, he said, the British Prime Minister ascribed the victory in the Battle of Britain 'largely to radio mechanics or radio-locators, and the United Kingdom allotted the highest priority to them' [*] .   In a statement in answer to the evident dissatisfaction about the promotion and pay of such mechanics in the RCAF, Major Power told the House:

---

[*] Although the term 'radio mechanics' was used, because 'radar' was yet to come, both Power and Churchill were obviously referring to those technicians whose training and employment was in RDF.

'Evidently we exaggerated the required qualifications but the man who invented the apparatus thought, like most other inventors, that he needed the best possible men to handle it and he sold us the idea of obtaining the best educated men we could. We were asked for 5,000 and we supplied 5,000.

'These unfortunate fellows have been sent all over the world. Some of them went to West Africa, some to Singapore. Nearly all are of the class of university students, and, of course, they did not get the advancement which one would expect people of that class to get; they still are LACs.'

However their conditions had improved. Of the 5,000 required by the RAF all but 250 had been sent overseas and 638 had received their commissions and all had received trade pay. Ranks of sergeant or corporal were also given and the men were trade-tested by Canadian standards.

Before the matter reached the Canadian Parliament, aspects of that growing disquiet among Canadians over their treatment while serving on RAF units in the UK were being aired in the RAF itself. Group Captain G P H Carter, writing on behalf of the Director of Technical Training, informed the Air Officers Commanding-in-Chief of the operational commands that 'considerable concern is felt at the number of complaints which have been made of mis-employment or under-employment by Canadian RDF Mechanics (Air) [7] '. He asked that 'so far as is practicable', 50 per cent of the intake to any refresh or conversion course for RDF mechanics at # 7 Radio School be filled by Canadians.

Coastal Command countered that among the 160 RDF mechanics trained either at TRE Malvern, # 7 Radio School or under the Command's own training schemes, about 100 were Canadians; and 'every effort is made to reduce mis-employment or under-employment to a minimum'. The fault was due largely to delays in aircraft installation programs and 'a certain waiting period' with mis- or under-employment was sometimes unavoidable. In a similar stance, Bomber Command pointed out that the 'greatest care' was taken to post into establishments for RDF Mechanics (Air) only the number considered absolutely essential to maintain RDF equipment to the standard of efficiency required for the successful operation of its aircraft. The message was perfectly clear here: not only was Bomber Command unable to release any such personnel for transfer to other Commands, with H_2S coming along it would soon be calling on outside sources to make up its existing manpower deficiencies 'on a rate commensurate with the H_2S fitting program' [8] .

It may (or it may not!) have been useful, when fighting for one's corner in the numbers game, to be aware that in the UK at that time there were overall only some 3,000 RDF Mechanics (Air) yet the requirement was for some 4,000 – a contemporary manpower return showing the Home strength as being 3,017 on 1 April 1943 against a requirement for 3,936 [9] . For the record, the scales were balanced in the opposite direction relative to RDF Mechanics (Ground), with the Home strength showing 3,346 against a requirement of 2,797.

However, disquiet within the RCAF assumed a wider aspect than complaints about mis-employment and under-employment. At a top-level meeting on 30 March 1943 to discuss the position of RDF mechanics of the RCAF employed with the RAF, where the Air Member for Personnel, Air Marshal Sir Bertine Sutton, was in the chair and Air Marshal Harold Edwards, Air Officer Commanding-in-Chief, RCAF Overseas, among those attending, dissatisfaction over promotion prospects was to the fore [10].

Air Marshal Edwards contended that as 'a stimulant to recruiting RDF mechanics in Canada, a promise had been given by recruiting officers that these personnel should be treated generally on the lines of aircrew personnel'. Although he agreed that there was nothing in the pamphlets to justify potential recruits expecting 100 per cent promotion to NCO rank, 'it appeared that instructions to recruiting officers had preceded the issue of the pamphlets and there was no doubt that candidates felt that they had been misled'. There had been 'a good deal of dissatisfaction' among RDF mechanics with regard to promotion prospects; and he was 'most anxious that the obligations towards these airmen should be met'. In view of the weight of public opinion on this question in Canada, Air Marshal Edwards felt that there would be no difficulty in the Canadian Government sanctioning any financial outlay involved in meeting the obligations.

Making a comparison between the position of RDF mechanics in the two Air Forces, the Air Marshal stated that only one sixth of the Canadian RDF mechanics held NCO posts on the RAF roster, though 50 per cent held NCO rank on the Canadian roster. One of the Air Ministry representatives, Mr A E Slater, F11, felt that the upgrading of RDF mechanic establishments to provide NCO posts for RCAF personnel presented insuperable difficulties. RDF personnel worked in close contact with other tradesmen, and upgrading on the suggested lines would inevitably lead to repercussions. It was felt that it was impossible to meet the position by upgrading the RAF establishment and that the only course would be to rely on promotion on the Canadian roster, the grant of commissions and entry into aircrew training as going some way towards the solution of the difficulty. At the request of the Air Member for Personnel, it was agreed to undertake an examination of establishments to see whether upgradings could be made.

Before the meeting concluded, there was a comment that there had been 'a good deal of dissatisfaction on account of under-employment'; Air Marshal Edwards referred to an investigation having been carried out on 732 cases which revealed a certain amount of under-employment in 37 per cent of those cases. At that moment, the supply of personnel was ahead of the supply of certain types of equipment. The equipment position was improving, the consequence of which would largely solve the question of underemployment.

A forgotten group, abandoned once out of their own country... promotion prospects stonewalled because of broken promises... victims of mis-employment and under-employment... In different circumstances, such treatment might well have encouraged mutinous talk; here, with radar mechs being widely dispersed and this being something where some fared better than others, there were limited opportunities for like-minded complainants to meet and thus to discover the existence of common grievances.

Having served on a number of radar stations in Canada between initial training and being posted overseas, Bob Warner was a 'real' Sergeant, as distinct from shadow ranking, and in this he stood out among Canadian radar technicians serving on an RAF station. There were 'a few of us' who were unusual in that respect – 'Canadians who had been posted to RAF units were normally passed over for promotion,' he notes, hence the RCAF decision to adopt a 'Shadow' promotion list where personnel were promoted on paper and received the pay appropriate to the new rank but did not wear the rank badges until they returned to a Canadian unit. He explains:

> 'There was a report of one Canadian who had been with the RAF in the Far East and was returned to the UK with members of the RAF. Notification was sent to RCAF Headquarters in London – however they had no record of this individual as an LAC. He had been commissioned by the RCAF but notification of his promotions had not caught up to him while he was at various locations in Burma. It was finally figured out that he was now a Flight Lieutenant. Part of the problem was that RCAF personnel received new service numbers when they were granted a Commission [11].'

It seems that the Canadians were not alone in complaining that in going to Britain's help on the radar front there were sometimes lost promotion opportunities and other disadvantages. An American radar specialist, Jerry Stover, who was sent across to the UK towards the end of 1941, indicates that there was a parallel on his side of the Canada-US border. He points out that in late 1940 and early 1941, US Military Observers in Britain reported back to Washington on the vital role of electronics in warfare, especially air defense, and that the US Army Signal Corps and the US Navy, recognizing the need to have their own highly skilled radio and electronics specialists, launched major training programs. One of the first was the Signal Corps' Electronics Training Group (ETG), with which Jerry served in the US and in Europe. He explains what occurred to stimulate early recruitment and presents a balanced view of the reactions of those whose experiences he has become aware:

> 'In addition to combing Reserve ranks, a program of recruiting electrical engineers, ham operators and other "specialists" was initiated at colleges across the country. Over 700 received direct commissions as Second Lieutenants. Then, after three weeks of "military training" at Fort Monmouth, most were sent to England for radar training and duty with either the RAF or the British Army. Others were sent to Harvard and MIT. As early as August 1941, even before any of us in the ETG went to the UK, Signal Corps "regulars" and reservists set up and operated SCR 270s and 268s in Iceland and Hawaii. They were true radar pioneers!

> 'Based on discussions at a number of radar reunions and on seeing personal narratives, I would say that most felt that their service was personally and professionally rewarding. Some stayed on as regulars, one of them becoming Chief Signal Officer and retiring as a Lieutenant General, while others went into the Reserves.

> 'A few, with justification, did not share the good feeling toward ETG. Some were "lost" in the system and shorted on promotions. This was especially true of those serving (even commanding!) British units. Others, after qualifying and flying as Radar Observers with the RAF – several died while

doing so – failed to receive flight pay because they wore Signal Corps flags instead of Air Corps wings!

'Whether we complain or whether we don't, what we all share is the pride of knowing we contributed – and not in a small way – to the development and the operation of a major war-winning weapon. In these days of peace, that same "weapon" now provides safe passage for planes and ships all over the world. It guides spacecraft to the moon and to outer planets. Other veterans get the thrill of seeing their weapons – their tanks, their planes and their caissons – on parade two or three times a year. We can see ours (or at least a post-war development of our "weapon") every evening, displaying in full color the local, the national and the global weather! [12]'

No matter to which of the Allied air forces radar personnel belonged, no matter what was their place of work or its location around the world, a common thread brought together each and every radar mech: it was, of course, the bond of secrecy. Often, having joined an organization, advancement leads to the sharing of its secrets; with RDF (and with radar when thus known), once you enlisted you were introduced into what was effectively a 'secret society'. It was made plain from the outset that radar was something you didn't talk about, outside a workplace where all were party to those same secrets.

Where the Canadians are concerned, their long-lasting adherence to the ethos of secrecy may have its roots in their early days at the RDF School, Clinton. The 'top secret' security aspect was 'strictly enforced', according to Group Captain Adrian Cocks, its first CO; security surrounded those recruits, literally, with electrified barbed wire, floodlighting of the perimeter fence at night and armed RCAF guards maintaining surveillance from elevated security boxes. He recalls an occasion when, with John Martin, who would succeed him as CO on completion of two years in the post, he carried out his own security test.

'Alongside one stretch of the technical area perimeter wire was a strip of ground which was out of bounds after dark. We decided to try to walk along this bit of ground, which was floodlit. We were challenged by the sentry aloft. I said I was the Station Commander and he replied: "Nobody's allowed along there". I heard what sounded like a rifle bolt going into action, so I said to John: "I think this is where we do an about turn". And we did!' [13]

Ted Green remembers going there from the University of Toronto pre-Christmas 1942 when there was a couple of feet of snow on the ground. Clinton was, he says, 'a Stalag-like camp where our note books were super secret, the pages were numbered and each page had to be accounted for. Everything was so secret at Clinton. One note book got lost and was turned in by a railway station agent. I don't know what happened to the airman who lost it – maybe he's still in jail! [14] '

Is it any wonder that with such visible vigilance throughout the entire area and exhaustive enjoinders to keep everything to themselves in and out of the classrooms, Clinton trainees were a long time before opening-up about their wartime service to those who were not members of that rather special 'secret society' of radar personnel?

Post-war, sophisticated security systems such as magnetic cards and closed circuit television have become the norm. Not so in wartime, as 'Mac' McNarry remembers when casting his mind back to service at the Oboe ground station at Trimingham, which he joined in October 1943. In those days...

> 'The equipment for which I was to be responsible was in two Nissen huts joined end-to-end by a short corridor. The door was always kept locked and admission was by a password that was changed daily. Many an "admin" or aircrew officer would just "drop in" to see the station and we took a perverse pleasure in telling them to "hop it" if they didn't have the password. The only non-technical people allowed in the building were fire-protection personnel – and before they were allowed entrance we had to drape big sheets over the equipment. Civilian "boffins" from TRE were the only other people permitted into the building [15] .'

Maintaining the highest possible levels of secrecy at all times meant that often, when there were particularly stringent requirements to be observed, those who were privy to the level of secrecy involved were kept far away from those who were not so privileged, as occurred during a Royal visit to a bomber airfield. Jim Chisholm and Mike Burke, members of # 106 Squadron's Radar Section at the time, recall that occasion, which was when King George VI visited the squadron at their Syerston base to present Wing Commander Guy Gibson with his DSO. They note that...

> 'The ceremony took place in a hangar with all of the Squadron assembled except for the Radar Section. We were ordered to remove all the radar equipment from the aircraft and store it in the Radar Section where we were confined until the ceremony was over and the media and other visitors had left [16] .'

On a Pathfinder Force airfield and especially on one where there were aircraft equipped with the Oboe ground-controlled blind-bombing system, secrecy was paramount. It appears that PFF commander Don Bennett was 'extraordinarily strict' about where writers and cameramen could go and what they could see; and 'no-one but no-one was allowed close to the Oboe Mosquitoes. Before any visit, I had to spell out to Bennett what we would be doing – he was almost paranoid about secrecy', said Charles Harrold, veteran of 70 Oboe operations while serving as a navigator with # 109 Squadron, when recalling his time as a 'conducting officer' at PFF Headquarters where his job was to liaise with the media [17] .

Selected with others to provide technical 'know-how' at a radar school being established at Chivenor in Devon, Eric Coleman must have been wondering whether the requirements for secrecy had been somewhat overstretched in the past. There being 'no written documents', it was his task and that of his fellow technicians to produce instructions and descriptions covering all the airborne equipment with which they were acquainted. Working with a shorthand-typist, he began with Loran, meticulously putting down all he knew about it, in detail, with circuits, drawings of wave shapes and the functions of each circuit.   He would note later that 'I guess it was the most comprehensive description they had, probably the only one' [18].

Sometimes, without intent, an apparent secret would slip out...

Peter McCalla knows better than most the consequences of committing a breach of security, however accidental, however trivial.   He happened to have written a letter to a former neighbor then based, as he was, on an operational squadron in the UK; and he happened to have commented that he thought his new posting would be a lot more interesting than his previous as 'we even have Mark XXI Spitfires and a lot of Fleet Air Arm planes here'.   It seemed innocent enough at the time – after all, the planes were there for all to see.   Peter thought no more of this innocent transgression until, as much as a year later, there was an announcement on the station that security would be tightened.   Next day, sitting on an aircraft wing and trying to figure out a problem with an aerial, he is summoned to the telephone.   His reaction is immediate: it's the first time he has been called to the telephone since leaving Canada so 'they have finally recognized my worth and they are going to give me that promotion!'   Alas, he was way off beam... as he now explains:

> 'I rolled off the wing and rushed up to the squadron office [# 141 Squadron], where I saw Wing Commander 'Bob' Braham – a squadron commander and ace night-fighter pilot with more than a dozen confirmed "kills" before he reached 23 years of age – and he told me I was on a charge.   He started reading the letter I had sent to my friend; it was "very serious," he said.   The charge was a breach of security, too serious for him to handle, so I was just to carry on and go on trial before the Group Captain.   In a couple of weeks the trial came up and I got twenty-eight days in the glasshouse – the only one on the station of about 2,000 people to get into any trouble over this new security check [19].'

The passage of the years and the introduction of national and international reunions in more recent times have done something to foster an unraveling of some of the 'secrets' of WWII radar.   It is possible indeed that it is only because of the gradual uncloaking of wartime secrets in so many other fields that there have been these comparatively recent large-scale radar reunions – that coupled with the fact that, as radar mechs were generally individual specialists working alone or in two and threes, to try to make contact with sufficient like souls to warrant a reunion was close to an impossibility.

As much as 55 years on, Harold Wolverton, a radar technician on an RAF night fighter squadron for most of his time in the UK, learned for the first time why it was that a visiting Mosquito from # 109 Squadron in Pathfinder Force of Bomber Command was parked in a 'special' spot near his radar section.   The explanation, all those years later, came in a telephone conversation with someone he had met by chance at a radar reunion a few months earlier: Art Craig, an Oboe technical officer. Art worked on ground stations on the East Coast and on the Continent, some of this service in the UK being spent on attachment with 109 Squadron – the first to fly Oboe-equipped Mosquitoes.   Harold said that the information he gained so belatedly enabled him to solve 'one of the whispered Oboe secrets that none of us in the radar section was allowed even to share with our officer, who really tried hard to find out [20] '.   The purpose of that 'special' spot?   It was a survey marker over which the Oboe-equipped Mosquito would be parked, the Oboe ground station being able to direct its signal to the aircraft and – knowing the precise distance between that spot and their own location – to calibrate the Oboe equipment to the requisite accuracy. With this ground-controlled blind-bombing system, target ranges were determined to within one hundredth of a mile.   Another friend of Harold, a pilot flying bombers with the benefit of Oboe and also before its availability, said that while he was 'often scared witless on a bombing raid', Oboe meant that he could 'go right in and out again without dallying about as had previously been the case'.

It would be reasonable to expect the first major reunion of WWII air forces radar personnel to be held in the UK, since this was where the majority were based either permanently or temporarily at one time or another during their wartime service.   It took place in 1991, in Coventry, being followed by another in the same location a year later, 1992.   More ambitious still, there was one in Canada four years later, this one stemming from the two in the UK where Bob McNarry was present at the first and Les Card at the second [*].   Both had been attending a series of RCAF radar veterans' meetings in Calgary and during a chat afterwards, while walking to their cars, this sparked a wider discussion with others on 'the value and desirability of a radar reunion in Alberta, perhaps even in Calgary' [21] , Calgary being their home town.

A series of meetings developed and these continued into 1994, with increasing enthusiasm among those involved; but a call for volunteers to help organize such an event seemed first to fall on deaf ears – 'like true airmen, not a single person was going to volunteer for anything!'   Undaunted, the two men and their small band of enthusiasts persevered, determination and patience winning the day; now, nothing would stop them.   Les, a 'ham' radio operator, and Bob, a long-time computer user, drew heavily upon those hobby activities to keep spreading the message further afield and to handle the increasing amount of paperwork, eventually encouraging the formation of a 25-strong committee which then had to set budgets and find the initial cash.   The conclusion was that some 300 registrants were needed to break even – a modest figure, perhaps, when considering that 5,000 and more volunteers from the North American continent served the radar cause during WWII.   In the event the number of registrants was well in excess of twice the 'break even' figure, the total attendance of 792 comprising 490 radar veterans (including 9 deceased represented by family members) and 302 spouses and friends.   It could well have topped 800 since the restraints associated with advancing age, especially that of health, meant some registrants being unable to attend the gathering.   Nonetheless, at the time,

---

[*] Les Card, who was aged 26 when the war ended, worked for the Geodetic Survey of Canada, taught in high school for four years and in a career switch moved into geophysical and geological activities, continuing to answer calls for a trouble-shooter in oilfields across the prairies until he was well into his 70s. At the age of 80, Les is still an avid radio amateur. Bob McNarry, 29 when the war finished (during which time he had been known more often as 'Mac' than as Bob), made his career in scientific theory and research, working with the National Research Council in areas that included oxide cathode and ultra high vacuum reséarch, the IGY auroral programme and solar radio astronomy. A teacher, negotiator and instructor with a great sense of humor, Bob has a favorite admonition: 'I know you believe you understand what you think I said, but I am not sure you realise that what you heard is not what I meant!' [22]

the Calgary Radar Reunion '96 was undoubtedly the biggest of its kind anywhere in the world; it is likely that this distinction remains to this day.

As the event drew to its close, the unforgettable moment for many was when receiving a Certificate of Appreciation to acknowledge their 'selfless and devoted services' and their contribution to 'the development of this new branch of science, to the general benefit of the Allied cause'. It was, nonetheless, a long-deferred gesture of gratitude – for the record shows that the Air Ministry in London, on whose behalf this document was issued, intended its special 'thank you' message to RCAF radar personnel to have been issued back in 1946!

The astonishing half-century delay was attributed to 'bureaucratic secrecy covered by political timidity' [23] ; more's the pity, therefore, since so many individuals who earned that expression of gratitude had passed away in the meantime, oblivious to its existence. Remarkably, the fact that there was to have been any recognition of Canadian radar personnel's wartime service came to light purely by chance. It was a revelation spawning a campaign which was at times acrimonious and involved the governments of both Britain and Canada.

Les Card, chairman of the committee that organized that 1996 reunion, recalling how the crusade started and the pressure for long-overdue acknowledgement increased, said that...

> 'In 1993 there was a meeting of radar technical officers and radar technicians in the Calgary area when Bob Linden, an historian and a technical officer himself, came to speak to us about his plans to document the experiences of as many RCAF WWII radar technical personnel as possible. Some time later, he passed on to us a copy of what he described as being "the sole survivor" of some 5,000 Certificates of Appreciation that had apparently been issued at the request of the Director General of Signals in the British Air Ministry and forwarded, in March 1946, from RCAF Headquarters in London to the Department of National Defense for Air in Ottawa. Bob said that he had come across this document while researching in the National Archives in Ottawa and concluded that, inexplicably, none of those certificates was ever issued.

> 'All of us felt that it was high time action was taken to have the oversight acknowledged and the error corrected. Since we had already decided that there should be a big reunion in Canada, with Calgary hosting it, this seemed to be the appropriate time and place to start issuing those certificates [24] .'

Bob Linden, who was admittedly 'startled' by the discovery that he had made in his country's national archives, pursued his inquiries and extracted further intriguing information. He explains:

> 'It is clear that that the idea of a "Certificate of Appreciation" was in recognition of the valuable secret services given to the RAF and the other Allied air forces by Canadian radar personnel. The certificate was produced by Air Ministry to recognize those RCAF personnel who

volunteered for service with the RAF in response to the UK's special appeal for such personnel.   Some 5,800 of us were trained and served overseas as a result of that call, onwards from October 1940, though it does appear that only 5,000 certificates were produced for issue.   It is significant that no similar certificate was being issued to RAF radar personnel.   Eligibility for this Certificate of Appreciation was left entirely at the RCAF's discretion, though I did see a reference to RCAF Overseas HQ in London suggesting a minimum of six months' service in a ground radar posting overseas as being a basis for eligibility.

'The 5,000 "blanks" were forwarded from the RAF to the RCAF, with space for the name and number, and it would be the responsibility of the RCAF to insert those details and to issue the certificate.   Having found a copy of one such certificate, and as one of the eligible recipients, I wrote to the Department of Veterans Affairs in Ottawa, asking for one of those withheld certificates to be suitably inscribed and issued to me [25].'

What seemed a simple request turned out to be opening a 'can of worms'.   Lloyd Francis, a wartime radar technician himself and post-war a Liberal MP and Speaker of the House of Commons in Ottawa, took up the cudgels with the Minister of National Defense.   A reply from the Minister himself confirmed what Bob had discovered, that some 5,000 Certificates of Appreciation had indeed been forwarded to the Department of National Defense for Air in 1946.   That letter also made known the surprising and somewhat disturbing fact that 'the Department decided not to release the certificates'.   It continued:

'Neither the certificates nor any subsequent correspondence can be found. It would appear, therefore, that the certificates were not awarded because there was no way to ensure their fair and equitable issue.

'It is regrettable that the Royal Canadian Air Force radar personnel attached to the Royal Air Force were not issued the certificates of appreciation they so rightly deserved.   However, the rationale that seems to have been used in 1946 to withhold the certificates appears well founded.   Please be assured this response is by no means meant to undermine the obvious expression of gratitude that the certificates were intended to convey [26].'

It was the sort of governmental reaction that was bound to attract media attention. One newspaper columnist, Douglas Fisher, writing in *The Sunday Sun* on 21 April 1996, referred to 'stonewalling' by the Department of Veterans Affairs and the Department of National Defense and to the anger shown by Lloyd Francis at the 'brush-off'.   To put the matter in context for the lay reader, the writer recalled that RCAF radar personnel had 'worked in myriad scenarios, comparatively with short shrift on promotion, leave and extra pay because the RAF in many personnel provisions was less generous than the RCAF'.   He dismissed the governmental contention that, because many other Canadians also had served in the RAF, issuing those certificates 'would have unfairly singled out a particular group of individuals without specific reason, such as locality or duration of service'.   The Liberal government under Jean Chrétien, he observed, decided to award a decoration to each man who went to Dieppe's beaches 'although thousands of other Canadians landed under fire on other beachheads'.

Calgary Reunion Committee chairman Les Card explains what came next:

> 'By our action, in combination with Bob Linden and Lloyd Francis and others, agreement was reached with the Department of National Defense that the Certificate of Appreciation *could* be issued, provided the British Government agreed. This assent was obtained, the UK representative and our Minister of National Defense concurring that the Certificate of Appreciation *could and should* be issued. It seemed that it had all been "a misunderstanding that had gone on for 50 years", in the words of Minister of Defense David Collennette when one of our MPs, Marlene Catterall, the Member for Ottawa West, raised the matter in the House of Commons.

> 'I have no doubt in my own mind that what was accomplished was thanks to combined Calgary and Ottawa persistence and insistence. Nevertheless, it is an open secret that whether or not permission was forthcoming, the Calgary Reunion Committee had every intention of issuing, to all RCAF WWII radar technical officers and radar technicians attending the reunion, either an authorized replica of that certificate or, if it became necessary, a "mock-up" of the original which we had already produced in readiness $_{27}$.'

So it came about that, at the Calgary Radar Reunion on 7, 8 and 9 June 1996, WWII Canadian radar personnel attendees received their belated formal 'thank you' parchment at a climax ceremony which must have been for many *the* highspot of the entire reunion. Both the Department of National Defense and the Department of Veterans Affairs were represented, those officials of the Canadian government taking it in turn to announce the name of a recipient. In row upon row of seats there were some hundreds of ex-radar personnel, many wearing with pride the medals earned by their service around the world. It was a moving, eye-glistening occasion. As the names were called, one among a group of ten Calgary Air Cadets would find that person and, with a smart salute while standing in front of him, hand over the treasured certificate, generally to the individual himself but in some instances to a next-of-kin.

When making these arrangements, the Calgary Reunion Committee had themselves decided that both Bob Linden and Lloyd Francis should be honoured by the presentation of the first two Certificates of Appreciation in recognition of their respective roles in finding the certificate and in persuading the Federal Government to approve the issuing of a replica to all qualifying RCAF radar personnel who asked for them. Without Bob Linden's painstaking research and perseverance, the existence of that one remaining certificate would not have emerged; and without the political acumen of Lloyd Francis and intervention through Douglas Fisher, the Minister of National Defense would not have reversed his position and the Government would not have issued the certificates.

As many as 450 certificates were handed over to qualifying individuals or, in a number of cases, to a member of their family; for those present it was final recognition of their service, which many thought had been too long delayed.

Subsequently the Department of Veterans Affairs has assumed responsibility for issuing certificates to qualified recipients and compensated the Calgary Reunion Committee for the costs incurred in printing and preparing the replica certificates issued at the 1996 reunion. Thus a saga with its roots going back to 1946 became a saga without an end; because no-one who can establish eligibility need ever fear that there will not be a Certificate of Appreciation ready and waiting...

Radar reunions have been the means of renewing friendships and rekindling memories, the means of achieving a better understanding of life as it was for the radar mechs of WWII. There have been instances of long-lost chums being brought together... where quests to find a former friend have come to nothing... and where, in one particular case, an exhaustive and apparently unproductive search had an eventual happy ending...

Charlie Cheshire and Doug Wiltshire, having traveled together from the UK to Australia in what was perhaps the classic posting mix-up of all time [*see page 192*], served alongside each other from May 1942 to November 1944 and returned to Canada together in time for Christmas with their respective families (Charlie in Edmonton, Doug in Victoria). The two friends remained in close touch for a further 40-plus years, losing contact only in 1987. At that point all Charlie's inquiries to find Doug proved unsuccessful. Still more years passed until, in 1996, with the first reunion of their country's radar technicians taking place in Calgary, a unique opportunity seemed to present itself for the pair to meet again. Let Charlie take up the story...

> 'I saw Doug's name on the roster of attendees – in fact he had registered about 20 minutes ahead of me, at the very same table, so I guessed that this was going to be a simple matter. I had him paged, I put up notices; all were to no avail. Finally, when the Air Ministry recognition scrolls were being handed out, I spotted him. By the time I reached where he had been sitting, he was gone. It looked as if I'd muffed it...
>
> 'Nonetheless I had Doug's address, which was in Red Deer, Alberta, and next day I caught up with him. It was the first time we had seen each other in 22 years. He had gone to this reunion hoping that I would be there but, sadly, Doug had by then lost his sight so didn't see any of my notices. Doug did get his son, who was with him, to read off all the "C"s who had signed-on but unfortunately my name wasn't there... I was on another list of names as an "Addendum" [28] .'

Having joined the RCAF as Leading Aircraftmen, both men gained promotion in Australia from Corporal right through to the highest non-commissioned rank, that of Warrant Officer 1st Class, the progressive steps via Sergeant and Flight Sergeant being at the instigation of the Royal Australian Air Force – though neither of the last two ranks was accompanied by the expected increase in pay. On their return to Canada, the RCAF demoted both men to Sergeant and all requests for reinstatement came to nothing for more than six months. Justice prevailed in the end, reinstatement being achieved with the respective dates for promotion to Flight Sergeant and to Warrant Officer 1st Class being declared as effective from the dates promulgated in Australia.

Post-war, many radar mechanics have been back to see what (if anything) remained of their CH or CHL station. American James Farrior, who was at Scarlet on the Isle of Man for about a year and a half in 1942/43 – 'longer than most because RDF mechanics used to come and go' – reckoned that he spent as much time training new men as maintaining the equipment. Of the Manx people, he described them as 'wonderful'; they were 'very kind to me and often invited me into their homes. I corresponded with some of them for many years and returned to the island for visits in 1959, 1983 and again in 1994 [29] '. He said of those trips:

> 'Each time, I went out to the farm on Scarlet Point where the RDF station had been located and revisited each of the bunker-like concrete buildings that had housed the facility. The farmer was the grandson of the one I knew; strangely, he showed no desire to learn what had gone on in those buildings. In a pub in Castletown that I had frequented while stationed at Scarlet, I shared a table with some young men to whom WWII was ancient history. Two were descendants of people I had known and one said that the Scarlet facility was "so secret that even today nobody knows or talks about it". Another said he had been curious and searched around the buildings with a metal detector – and found mostly the discarded foil from old Players cigarette boxes. Someone told me that tourists show little interest in the very significant Manx contributions to the war effort. So much for history * .'

Just as there are now organizations which seek to reunite those with a common bond, for example The Yatesbury Association * , with members throughout the UK, Europe, Canada and Australia, there are others which seek to obtain and to retain information, memorabilia and so on relative to WWII radar and to those who worked on it. In Britain, the Historical Radar Archive * has as its objectives: To preserve radar history; to enhance (existing) museum facilities; the co-ordination of historical research and hardware preservation; and to promote interest in early radar via exhibitions and lectures. In Canada, the Canadian Radar History Project * is a non-profit organization which has been busy gathering material from individuals so that a detailed focus exists to cover all of the theatres of wartime operations and to demonstrate the role taken by Canadian radar personnel.

There is, however, one aspect of 'looking back' that is not necessarily of immediate or prime concern to any of those organizations: it is to recognize and to record the

---

* James Farrior joined the US Merchant Marine after serving at Scarlet, crossing the Atlantic 11 times and the Pacific 4 times. A 'hi-tech' specialist in those far off wartime days, he was 'higher-tech' still in the 1950s and 1960s: he was a member of Dr von Braun's guided missile team in Huntsville, Alabama, where his nine years' service included time in charge of guidance and control work on missiles and space projects.

* It has a web site accessible through http://www.g4ddm.force9.co.uk/ ya/yaindex.htm, the membership secretary being shown as Phil Tomaselli, 146 Stockwood Lane, Bristol, BS14 8TA, England.

* The HRA is an Associate Member of the British Aviation Preservation Council and the principal contact is Squadron Leader M S Dean MBE, Little Garth, High Street, Scampton, Lincoln LN1 2SD, England.

* The principal contact for the Canadian Radar History Project is its chairman, Robert F Linden, 2152 Calder Avenue, Ottawa, Ontario K2C 0X9, Canada (Telephone: 613-224-0640/Fax: 613-224-9681).

contribution that those pioneering technicians in radar have made to our daily life in the post-war world. It is appropriate to note that for many radar technical officers and radar technicians their training was their first exposure to disciplined education and learning at the university level. This, combined with courses taken during active service, resulted in a body of men with a knowledge of electronics both theoretical and practical which, post-war, was available to their country. For many, their training whetted their appetite for further education which resulted in university education in many fields such as engineering, geology, and sciences of various kinds. For those who chose to go immediately into the workforce, the electronics industry benefited in the design and manufacture, installation and repair of radar, radios, television and telephone equipment. National defense and international communication were key areas to profit from the skills of those wartime specialists, Canada's contribution to the DEW Line and that of the United States and Britain to telecommunications being paramount among such examples.

One who made a lifetime career in radar is Orv Marshall; he was posted out of # 205 Group in Italy in July 1945 for repatriation to Canada and the following summer joined a radio physics course where nearly all his classmates had been in the Services and a number of them in radar. On graduating, he joined General Electric, working first on AN/CPS-6B ground radar for the Pinetree radar line which was being established across Canada and later on airborne equipment in both Canada and the USA. Orv considers that he was very fortunate to be able to combine a lifelong interest in electronics and airplanes in one career – and he has no doubt whatever that his training and experience as a radar technical officer in WWII 'helped greatly' his civilian career.

There is a post-war quote from Sir Stafford Cripps, chairman of the British Radio Board, quoted in Wesley W Stout's book, *The Great Detective*, published in 1946 by the Chrysler Corporation, which puts the wartime achievements of radar in perspective. It reads as follows:

> ' "If radar had not prevented the enemy from getting by surprise over England", he said, after the war had ended, "I don't know where we would have been. It played a greater part in the war's outcome than did the atomic bomb itself. It contributed to the winning of the war more than any other single factor".'

Fifty-plus years on, the peacetime achievements of radar need someone to put this in perspective too. Has it, in fact, contributed more to the well-being of the great nations of the world than any other single factor? Perhaps even to make such a suggestion is to ignore, for example, the world of medicine; nonetheless radar has helped improve safety in the air and at sea, it is used in weather forecasting and in monitoring global land and sea resources. It may not have received universal acclaim as a device to check a motorist's speed but there are other uses for radar on the roads – for example by traffic engineers to measure the volume of traffic in their bid to ease congestion.

There can be no more fitting a tribute to each and every radar technician whose service benefited the Allied air forces in WWII than the words contained in a toast offered during what was then (and conceivably still remains so) the largest such reunion ever held anywhere in the world ₃₀ . That event was the Calgary Radar Reunion '96; and the fact that the message in that toast had the specific purpose of remembering those who were absent from that gathering in no way diminishes its relevance today; rather, its poignancy does much to make this a tribute equally appropriate to those still in the 'land of the living' as to those who passed on, either during or since the war.

Here is the text of that toast – and it matters not that the intention of those assembled in Calgary was in essence to salute primarily the radar technicians of their own country, Canada. In WWII, as has been shown in the preceding pages, there were radar technicians from throughout the Dominions who served, suffered and survived, just as there were radar technicians from the Mother Country herself who did the same. Accept these words, then, as a blanket tribute to all those volunteer comrades in radar in WWII, right around the world, who carried out their work selflessly and supremely, in the air, on the ground or at sea.

We were all volunteers.
We offered to go wherever we were posted.
To perform whatever duties were assigned to us.

Some fell to the ground or into the sea in the performance of those duties.
We remember them fondly tonight.
Most of us survived, to return to Canada.
In fifty years our ranks have thinned, our strengths have weakened.

Please raise your glasses and drink a toast to all those
radar mechanics who cannot join us here this evening –

To Absent Comrades

SOURCES

CHAPTER 1

1. *Globe and Mail* newspaper, published in Canada, running a CP dispatch with the dateline London, 14 August 1945. It was noted that 'these figures were released by the Air Ministry and the RCAF overseas as the lid was removed from what was one of the best-kept secrets of the war' when, for the first time, 'the public was given an official explanation of how radar works and what it has accomplished'.

2. Booklet produced for the WWII Radar Reunion in London, Ontario, 21/23 September 1999.

3. Souvenir Publication of Calgary Radar Reunion '96, prepared and written by A Wilson.

4. *A Radar History of World War II, Technical and Military Imperatives*, by Louis Brown, Institute of Physics Publishing, Bristol and Philadelphia, 1999.

5. Communication with author.

6. Article by WWII radar veteran Bruce Neale in Marconi Radar Systems' staff newspaper; it was one of a series first published in the 1980s.

7. Public Record Office (PRO) AIR 10/5485 *The Second World War, 1939-1945, Royal Air Force, Signals*, Volume 5, Fighter Control and Interception, Issued by the Air Ministry (AHB), 1952, Page 11.

8. PRO AIR 10/5485 *The Second World War, 1939-1945, Royal Air Force, Signals*, Volume 5, Fighter Control and Interception, Issued by the Air Ministry (AHB), 1952, Page 21.

9. PRO AIR 10/5485 *The Second World War, 1939-1945, Royal Air Force, Signals*, Volume 5, Fighter Control and Interception, Issued by the Air Ministry (AHB), 1952, Page 24.

10. *Brief History of # 60 (RDF) Group, Directorate of Signals, RAF, 1939-1945*, by J R Robinson, made available to author.

11. *Brief History of # 60 (RDF) Group, Directorate of Signals, RAF, 1939-1945*, by J R Robinson, made available to author.

12. PRO AIR 10/5485 *The Second World War, 1939-1945, Royal Air Force, Signals*, Volume 5, Fighter Control and Interception, Issued by the Air Ministry (AHB), 1952, Page 77.

13. J R Robinson in communication with author.

14. PRO AIR 2/5434 Radar and radio mechanics – Training, Encl 9A.

15. PRO AIR 2/5434 Radar and radio mechanics – Training, Encl 9A.

16. PRO AIR 2/5434 Radar and radio mechanics – Training, Encl 12A. Handwritten response from Group Captain Rodney, 18 August 1940.

17. Communication with author.

CHAPTER 2

1. PRO AIR 2/7439, Survey by AOC 60 Group of operational efficiency of RDF, Encl 1A, Survey dated 15 October 1940, para 8 (a) and (b).
2. PRO WO 219/4597 Report on 60 Group, produced by 2nd Lt Neal D Crane, Signals Corps, dated 23 May 1944, by which time 60 Group comprised Group HQ, 10 Signals Wings HQ, 140 operational stations in the chain and 35 GCI stations.
3. PRO AIR 2/7439, Survey by AOC 60 Group of operational efficiency of RDF, Encl 4B.
4. PRO AIR 2/7439, Survey by AOC 60 Group of operational efficiency of RDF, Encl 7A.
5. PRO AIR 2/3788, Recruitment in Canada for the RAF, Letter dated 24 October 1938.
6. National Archives, Ottawa, Call # RG 24, Volume 5282, File S34-5-1 Vol 1.
7. Paper by Bob Linden and Mel Goldberg which quotes RCAF Headquarters file S15-1-329 Vol 2, 4 June 1943.
8. PRO AIR 8/479 Overseas recruitment of radio personnel, Note of a discussion with Lord Hankey at the Air Ministry on 19 February 1941.
9. PRO AIR 8/479 Overseas recruitment of radio personnel, Note of a discussion with Lord Hankey at the Air Ministry on 19 February 1941.
10. PRO AIR 8/479 Overseas recruitment of radio personnel, Cypher telegram from the Air Attaché in Washington to Air Ministry, dated 5 March 1941.
11. PRO AIR 8/479 Overseas recruitment of radio personnel, Memorandum on Publicity, Overseas Recruitment of Radio Personnel, signed by Squadron Leader E W Russell, Signals 4, Air Ministry, and dated 13 January 1941.
12. *Bawdsey - Birth of the Beam*, by Gordon Kinsey, published by Terence Dalton Limited, Lavenham, 1983.
13. Communication with author.
14. Undated letter from Herbert C Bell to Bob Linden made available to author.
15. Undated letter from Francis J de Macedo to Bob Linden made available to author.
16. Communication with author.
17. Communication with author.
18. Communication with author.
19. Communication with author.
20. Communication with author.
21. *My Radar Service in WWII*, Fred B Grahame, Magra Publishing, 1993.
22. PRO AIR 2/5434 Radar and radio mechanics – Training, Encl 33A, Review of trade positions and training capacity in certain wireless and radio trades, dated 24 April 1941.
23. PRO AIR 2/5434 Radar and radio mechanics – Training, Encl 16C, Telegram from Acting UK High Commissioner in Canada, dated 25 February 1941.
24. PRO AIR 2/5434 Radar and radio mechanics – Training, Encl 40A, Note of 29 May 1941 re Dominion Radio Mechanics.
25. PRO AIR 2/5434 Radar and radio mechanics – Training, Encl 47A.
26. PRO AIR 2/5434 Radar and radio mechanics – Training, Encl 77A, Update by UK High Commissioner in Canada.
27. Communication with author.
28. Communication with author.
29. Communication with author.
30. *Globe and Mail*, Toronto, Metropolitan edition, Vol XCVIII Number 28,550, Wednesday, 18 June 1941. The headline: Radio Secret Dooms German raiders; the subhead: Ether waves warn defense of approach of hostile aircraft.
31. Communication with author.
32. Communication with author.

CHAPTER 3
1. Communication with author.
2. Communication with author.
3. Communication with author.
4. Communication with author.
5. Undated letter from Doug Gooderham to Bob Linden made available to author.
6. Communication with author.
7. *The Radar Mechanics' Secret War, 1940 – 1945*, a self-published manuscript by Dick Moule.
8. Communication with author.
9. Communication with author.
10. Communication with author.
11. Communication with author.
12. Communication with author.
13. Letter to Les Card, Chairman of the 1996 Radar Reunion in Calgary, dated 24 December 1995, made available to author.

CHAPTER 4
1. Communication with author.
2. *Beam Bombers: The Secret War of No 109 Squadron*, Michael Cumming, Sutton Publishing, 1998.
3. Communication with author.
4. Communication with author.
5. Communication with author.
6. Communication with author.
7. Communication with author.
8. Communication with author.
9. Communication with author.
10. Communication with author
11. Communication with author.
12. Communication with author.
13. *The Bruneval Raid: Flashpoint of the Radar War*, George Millar, The Bodley Head, London, 1974.
14. *The Bruneval Raid: Flashpoint of the Radar War*, George Millar, The Bodley Head, London, 1974.
15. Radar Intelligence and the Dieppe Raid, J R Robinson, *Canadian Defence Quarterly*, Vol 20, # 5, 1991.
16. Radar Intelligence and the Dieppe Raid, J R Robinson, *Canadian Defence Quarterly*, Vol 20, # 5, 1991.
17. *The March of the Prairie Men: a story of The South Saskatchewan Regiment*, G B Buchanan, Midwest Litho, Saskatoon, Canada, 1957.
18. Radar Intelligence and the Dieppe Raid, J R Robinson, *Canadian Defence Quarterly*, Vol 20, # 5, 1991.
19. Radar Intelligence and the Dieppe Raid, J R Robinson, *Canadian Defence Quarterly*, Vol 20, # 5, 1991,
20. Radar Intelligence and the Dieppe Raid, J R Robinson, *Canadian Defence Quarterly*, Vol 20, # 5, 1991.
21. Undated letter from L J Palmer, submitted to the Canadian Radar History Project and subsequently made available to author.

22. Communication with author.
23. Communication with author.
24. *WWII Radar, The Story of One Group, Royal Canadian Air Force, 1941-1945*, a privately produced compilation updated at 26 May 1999.
25. *Memories of a WWII Radar Mechanic*, unpublished manuscript by Robert G Warner, made available to author.
26. Communication with author.
27. Communication with author.
28. Communication with author.
29. Communication with author.
30. Communication with author.
31. Communication with author.
32. *Airforce*, January/February/March 1988.
33. Taped reminiscences, Calgary Radar Reunion 1996, made available to author.
34. Letter to Les Card, Chairman of the 1996 Radar Reunion in Calgary, made available to author.
35. *WWII Radar, The Story of One Group, Royal Canadian Air Force, 1941-1945*, a privately produced compilation updated at 26 May 1999.

CHAPTER 5
1. *The Radar Mechanics' Secret War, 1940 – 1945*, a self-published manuscript by Dick Moule.
2. *The Radar Mechanics' Secret War, 1940 – 1945*, a self-published manuscript by Dick Moule.
3. *Brief history of # 106 Squadron, Radar Section*, compiled by Jim Chisholm and Mike Burke, December 1993, made available to author.
4. Undated letter from L J Palmer, submitted to the Canadian Radar History Project and subsequently made available to author.
5. *Brief history of # 106 Squadron, Radar Section*, compiled by Jim Chisholm and Mike Burke, December 1993, made available to author.
6. *Brief history of # 106 Squadron, Radar Section*, compiled by Jim Chisholm and Mike Burke, December 1993, made available to author.
7. *The Silent Observer*, David W Acaster, Turner-Warwick Printers Inc, Saskatchewan, 1990.
8. *Brief history of # 106 Squadron, Radar Section*, compiled by Jim Chisholm and Mike Burke, December 1993, made available to author.
9. *Honours and Awards granted during the Second World War to RCAF Radar Personnel*, a limited private edition produced in 1996 by Hugh A Halliday, Douglas A Swanson and Robert F Linden.
10. PRO AIR 20/4776, Oboe and H_2S Results, see section relating to Oboe results prior to 29 May 1943.
11. *Beam Bombers: The Secret War of No 109 Squadron*, Michael Cumming, Sutton Publishing Limited, 1998.
12. Communication with author.
13. Communication with author.
14. Communication with author.
15. Communication with author.
16. Communication with author.
17. Communication with author.

18. Communication with author.
19. PRO AIR 2/5435 RDF Mechanics – Training, Encl 398A.
20. PRO AIR 2/5435 RDF Mechanics – Training, Encl 441A, HQ 60 Group letter, 31 March 1944.
21. PRO AIR 37/570 Radar Airborne Policy, Encl 10A, Minutes of a meeting held on 20 January 1944, quoting Squadron Leader H R Crowley, HQ AEAF, and Wing Commander L R Ridley, representing the Director of Radar.
22. Communication with author.
23. *WWII Radar, The Story of One Group, Royal Canadian Air Force, 1941-1945*, a privately produced compilation updated at 26 May 1999.

CHAPTER 6
1. Communication with author.
2. Communication with author.
3. Communication with author.
4. *WWII Radar, The Story of One Group, Royal Canadian Air Force, 1941-1945*, a privately produced compilation updated at 26 May 1999.
5. *WWII Radar, The Story of One Group, Royal Canadian Air Force, 1941-1945*, a privately produced compilation updated at 26 May 1999.
6. *WWII Radar, The Story of One Group, Royal Canadian Air Force, 1941-1945*, a privately produced compilation updated at 26 May 1999.
7. *WWII Radar, The Story of One Group, Royal Canadian Air Force, 1941-1945*, a privately produced compilation updated at 26 May 1999.
8. Letter from R Jay Christensen to Bob Linden, dated 27 September 1993, made available to author.
9. Letter from R Jay Christensen to Bob Linden, dated 27 September 1993, made available to author.
10. PRO AIR 27/2061, # 600 Squadron Operations Record Book.
11. PRO AIR 27/2062, # 600 Squadron Operations Record Book.
12. PRO AIR 27/2062, # 600 Squadron Operations Record Book.
13. PRO AIR 27/2062, # 600 Squadron Operations Record Book.
14. PRO AIR 27/2062, # 600 Squadron Operations Record Book.
15. *Honours and Awards granted during the Second World War to RCAF Radar Personnel*, a limited private edition produced in 1996 by Hugh A Halliday, Douglas A Swanson and Robert F Linden.
16. *Honours and Awards granted during the Second World War to RCAF Radar Personnel*, a limited private edition produced in 1996 by Hugh A Halliday, Douglas A Swanson and Robert F Linden.
17. PRO AIR 27/460, # 46 Squadron Operations Record Book.
18. *Honours and Awards granted during the Second World War to RCAF Radar Personnel*, a limited private edition produced in 1996 by Hugh A Halliday, Douglas A Swanson and Robert F Linden.
19. Undated letter from J O Camden to Bob Linden made available to author.
20. Communication with author.
21. Communication with author.
22. Communication with author.
23. Documentation gathered by one of his fellow Canadian radar technical officers, Al Revill, and made available to author.
24. Communication with author.

25. *Royal Air Force, 1939-1945,* Vol 2, Denis Richards and Hilary St George Saunders, HMSO, 1954.
26. *WWII Radar, The Story of One Group, Royal Canadian Air Force, 1941-1945,* a privately produced compilation updated at 26 May 1999.
27. *WWII Radar, The Story of One Group, Royal Canadian Air Force, 1941-1945,* a privately produced compilation updated at 26 May 1999.
28. Letter from J G Bishop to Bob McNarry, dated 17 July 1993, made available to author.
29. Document made available to author by Janet Macdonald, widow of the then CO of AMES 102.
30. PRO AIR 25/818 # 205 Group, Summary of Events.
31. Oral history by Robert F Linden, made available to author.
32. Oral history by Robert F Linden, made available to author.
33. Oral history by Robert F Linden, made available to author.
34. Communication with author.
35. Communication with author
36. Communication with author.
37. Unpublished manuscript by Bob Linden, made available to author.
38. PRO AIR 25/818 # 205 Group, Summary of Events.

CHAPTER 7

1. *Honours and Awards granted during the Second World War to RCAF Radar Personnel,* a limited private edition produced in 1996 by Hugh A Halliday, Douglas A Swanson and Robert F Linden.
2. *Honours and Awards granted during the Second World War to RCAF Radar Personnel,* a limited private edition produced in 1996 by Hugh A Halliday, Douglas A Swanson and Robert F Linden.
3. PRO AIR 10/5271 *The Second World War, 1939-1945, Royal Air Force, Signals,* Vol 4 – Radar in Raid Reporting, Chapter 24, Page 433.
4. *Honours and Awards granted during the Second World War to RCAF Radar Personnel,* a limited private edition produced in 1996 by Hugh A Halliday, Douglas A Swanson and Robert F Linden.
5. Document dated 23 May 1984 entitled '*D-Day, Normandy, 1944, Record of RAF 15083 GCI in training for, on and after 6th June 1944,* by R H McCall, Squadron Leader Commanding 15083'; submitted to the Canadian Radar History Project and subsequently made available to author.
6. Document dated 23 May 1984 entitled '*D-Day, Normandy, 1944, Record of RAF 15083 GCI in training for, on and after 6th June 1944,* by R H McCall, Squadron Leader Commanding 15083'; submitted to the Canadian Radar History Project and subsequently made available to author.
7. *World War II*, 50th Anniversary Commemorative Edition, Ivor Matale, Guild Publishing, London, 1989.
8. Communication with author.
9. PRO AIR 10/5271 *The Second World War, 1939-1945, Royal Air Force, Signals,* Vol 4 – Radar in Raid Reporting, Chapter 24, Page 433.
10. PRO AIR 10/5271 *The Second World War, 1939-1945, Royal Air Force Signals,* Vol 4 – Radar in Raid Reporting, Chapter 24, Page 433. This account refers to AMES 15082 personnel having 'the additional discomfort of being continually sniped at by Americans'; from a distance, faded RAF blue uniforms 'appeared very similar' to those of the Germany Army.
11. PRO AIR 2/8396, Controlled Interception from Fighter Direction Ships, Encl 98a.

12. PRO AIR 2/8396 Controlled Interception from Fighter Direction Ships, Encl 117, Operational Research Section A-3, NAAF Memorandum # 6 dated 5 September 1943.
13. PRO AIR 2/8396 Controlled Interception from Fighter Direction Ships, 6 November 1943, Encl 141A.
14. PRO AIR 2/8396 Controlled Interception from Fighter Direction Ships, Encl 157a, Note by CAS, 27 November 1943.
15. PRO AIR 2/8396 Controlled Interception from Fighter Direction Ships, Encl 160A, Note by DCAS, 4 Dec 1943.
16. Communication with author.
17. *The Forgotten Dead,* Ken Small, Bloomsbury, 1989.
18. PRO DEFE 2/421, A Report on the role and operation of British Headquarters Ships and Fighter Direction Tenders in the assault on the Continent of Europe, June 1944, Operation 'Neptune', HQ AEAF September 1945.
19. PRO ADM 1/29820 HM FDT 216 Lost during operations off Normandy, Report by Lieutenant Commander G Kelly, dated 9 July 1944.
20. PRO ADM 1/16095 Fighter Direction Tenders and Ships, Report by Staff FDO to NCETF on fighter direction in HM FDT 217 during the opening phase of Operation Neptune, dated 14 June 1944, Para 15.
21. PRO DEFE 2/421, A Report on the role and operation of British Headquarters Ships and Fighter Direction Tenders in the assault on the Continent of Europe, June 1944, Operation Neptune, HQ AEAF, September 1945, Para 75.
22. Communication with author.
23. Communication with author.
24. Communication with author.

CHAPTER 8
1. *Radar Days,* E G Bowen, Adam Hilger, 1987, which gives known production figures outside Great Britain and those of E K Cole and Pye Radio for 1940 and 1941.
2. Souvenir Publication of Calgary Radar Reunion '96, prepared and written by A Wilson.
3. Souvenir Publication of Calgary Radar Reunion '96, prepared and written by A Wilson.
4. *Radar Days,* E G Bowen, Adam Hilger, 1987.
5. Communication with author.
6. Communication with author.
7. *Radar Days,* by E G Bowen, Adam Hilger, 1987.
8. Fighting the U-boats: Technologies and Weapons; British ASV radars, prepared by Emmanuel Gustin – an Internet web page.
9. *The Squadrons of the RAF and Commonwealth 1918-88,* James J Halley, Air-Britain, 1988.
10. Interview on Calgary Reunion Video made available to author.
11. PRO AIR 27/1959, # 502 Squadron Operations Record Book.
12. PRO AIR 27/1959, # 502 Squadron Operations Record Book.
13. PRO AIR 27/436, # 42 Squadron Operations Record Book.
14. PRO AIR 27/436, # 42 Squadron Operations Record Book.
15. *Collins New Age Encyclopaedia,* William Collins, London and Glasgow, 1963.
16. Communication with author.
17. PRO AIR 27/436, # 42 Squadron Operations Record Book.
18. PRO AIR 27/436, # 42 Squadron Operations Record Book.
19. Communication with author.
20. Communication with author.

21. PRO AIR 27/436, # 42 Squadron Operations Record Book.
22. *World War II*, 50th Anniversary Commemorative Edition, Ivor Matale, Guild Publishing, London, 1989.
23. *Honours and Awards granted during the Second World War to RCAF Radar Personnel*, a limited private edition produced in 1996 by Hugh A Halliday, Douglas A Swanson and Robert F Linden.
24. *Honours and Awards granted during the Second World War to RCAF Radar Personnel*, a limited private edition produced in 1996 by Hugh A Halliday, Douglas A Swanson and Robert F Linden.
25. *Honours and Awards granted during the Second World War to RCAF Radar Personnel*, a limited private edition produced in 1996 by Hugh A Halliday, Douglas A Swanson and Robert F Linden.
26. *Honours and Awards granted during the Second World War to RCAF Radar Personnel*, a limited private edition produced in 1996 by Hugh A Halliday, Douglas A Swanson and Robert F Linden.
27. Undated letter from S N Flinders, submitted to the Canadian Radar History Project and subsequently made available to author.
28. *The Radar Mechanics' Secret War, 1940 – 1945*, a self-published manuscript by Dick Moule.
29. PRO AIR 27/1209, # 204 Squadron Operations Record Book.
30. *Honours and Awards granted during the Second World War to RCAF Radar Personnel*, a limited private edition produced in 1996 by Hugh A Halliday, Douglas A Swanson and Robert F Linden.
31. Letter from R Jay Christensen to Bob Linden, dated 27 September 1993, made available to author.
32. Communication with author.
33. Communication with author.
34. Communication with author.

CHAPTER 9
1. Angus Hamilton in communication with author.
2. Communication with author.
3. Angus Hamilton's book, *Canadians on Radar in South East Asia, 1941-1945*, ACH Publishing, New Brunswick, 1998.
4. Letter from RCAF Overseas Headquarters to AFHQ Ottawa, quoted in Angus Hamilton's book, *Canadians on Radar in South East Asia, 1941-1945*, ACH Publishing, New Brunswick, 1998.
5. *Oxford Interactive Encyclopedia*, TLC Properties Inc, 1997.
6. Article by Oss Luce in a special edition of the *Clinton News-Record* on 24 August 1994, commemorating the 60th Anniversary of the Air Force Telecom Association (AFTA).
7. Angus Hamilton's book, *Canadians on Radar in South East Asia*, 1941-1945, ACH Publishing, New Brunswick, 1998.
8. Canadians in Asia, 1941-1945, an historical document in the series The Second World War, which appears on the Internet web site of the Canadian Veterans' Affairs Department.
9. Canadians in Asia, 1941-1945, an historical document in the series The Second World War, which appears on the Internet web site of the Canadian Veterans' Affairs Department.

10. *WWII Radar, The Story of One Group, Royal Canadian Air Force, 1941-1945*, a privately produced compilation updated at 26 May 1999.
11. Angus Hamilton's book, *Canadians on Radar in South East Asia, 1941-1945*, ACH Publishing, New Brunswick, 1998.
12. Canadians in Asia, 1941-1945, an historical document in the series The Second World War, which appears on the Internet web site of the Canadian Veterans' Affairs Department.
13. Angus Hamilton's book, *Canadians on Radar in South East Asia, 1941-1945*, ACH Publishing, New Brunswick, 1998.
14. Angus Hamilton's book, *Canadians on Radar in South East Asia, 1941-1945*, ACH Publishing, New Brunswick, 1998.
15. Angus Hamilton's book, *Canadians on Radar in South East Asia, 1941-1945*, ACH Publishing, New Brunswick, 1998.
16. Communication with author.
17. *WWII Radar, The Story of One Group, Royal Canadian Air Force, 1941-1945*, a privately produced compilation updated at 26 May 1999.
18. Angus Hamilton's book, *Canadians on Radar in South East Asia, 1941-1945*, ACH Publishing, New Brunswick, 1998.
19. Angus Hamilton in correspondence with author.
20. Columnist writing in the RCAF newspaper *Wings Abroad*.
21. Angus Hamilton's book, *Canadians on Radar in South East Asia, 1941-1945*, ACH Publishing, New Brunswick, 1998.
22. *2194 Days of War, An illustrated chronology of the Second World War*, compiled by Cesare Salmaggi and Alfredo Pallavisini, Galley Press, 1988.
23. Angus Hamilton's book, *Canadians on Radar in South East Asia, 1941-1945*, ACH Publishing, New Brunswick, 1998.
24. Angus Hamilton's book, *Canadians on Radar in South East Asia, 1941-1945*, ACH Publishing, New Brunswick, 1998.
25. Angus Hamilton's book, *Canadians on Radar in South East Asia, 1941-1945*, ACH Publishing, New Brunswick, 1998.
26. Canadians in Asia, 1941-1945, an historical document in the series The Second World War, which appears on the Internet web site of the Canadian Veterans' Affairs Department.
27. Angus Hamilton's book, *Canadians on Radar in South East Asia, 1941-1945*, ACH Publishing, New Brunswick, 1998.
28. Angus Hamilton's book, *Canadians on Radar in South East Asia, 1941-1945*, ACH Publishing, New Brunswick, 1998.
29. Communication with author.
30. Angus Hamilton's book, *Canadians on Radar in South East Asia, 1941-1945*, ACH Publishing, New Brunswick, 1998.
31. Angus Hamilton's book, *Canadians on Radar in South East Asia, 1941-1945*, ACH Publishing, New Brunswick, 1998.
32. Angus Hamilton's book, *Canadians on Radar in South East Asia, 1941-1945*, ACH Publishing, New Brunswick, 1998.
33. Canadians in Asia, 1941-1945, an historical document in the series The Second World War, which appears on the Internet web site of the Canadian Veterans' Affairs Department.
34. Angus Hamilton in communication with author.
35. Angus Hamilton's book, *Canadians on Radar in South East Asia, 1941-1945*, ACH Publishing, New Brunswick, 1998.

36. *West Coast Radar News*, 1996.
37. *West Coast Radar News*, 1996.
38. Angus Hamilton in communication with author.

CHAPTER 10
1. PRO AIR 25/680 # 60 Group HQ Operations Record Book.
2. *Brief History of # 60 (RDF) Group, Directorate of Signals, RAF, 1939-1945*, by J R Robinson, made available to author.
3. PRO AIR 2/5436 Radar Mechanics – Training, Part III, Encl 49C.
4. PRO AIR 2/5436 Radar Mechanics – Training, Part III, Encl 1C gives the suggestions of J A Ratcliffe for the Chief Superintendent of TRE.
5. Communication with author.
6. Document made available to author by Janet Macdonald, widow of the then CO of AMES 102.
7. Communication with author.
8. Communication with author.
9. Communication with author.
10. Communication with author.
11. *WWII Radar, The Story of One Group, Royal Canadian Air Force, 1941-1945*, a privately produced compilation updated at 26 May 1999.
12. Document made available to author by Janet Macdonald, widow of the then CO of AMES 102.
13. Communication with author.
14. Communication with author.
15. *AMES 9442 Recollections*, by Tom Hatcher, Radar Operator, RAF, unpublished document made available to author.
16. *2194 Days of War, An illustrated chronology of the Second World War*, compiled by Cesare Salmaggi and Alfredo Pallavisini, Galley Press, 1988.
17. Communication with author.
18. Five-page Summary of RCAF Service, compiled by 'Pop' Pohoreski, made available to author.
19. *Beam Bombers: The Secret War of No 109 Squadron*, Michael Cumming, Sutton Publishing Limited, 1998.
20. Communication with author.
21. Communication with author.
22. Taped reminiscences, Calgary Radar Reunion 1996, made available to author.
23. *WWII Radar, The Story of One Group, Royal Canadian Air Force, 1941-1945*, a privately produced compilation updated at 26 May 1999.
24. Personal accounts by Fred Watters, 25 April 1991 and 1 September 1991, to 'Mac' McNarry, made available to author.
25. Communication with author.
26. AIR 29/169, Convoy # 1/9000 Operations Book.
27. C R Eastwood, writing in an issue of *Transmission Lines*, produced by the Centre for the History of Defence Electronics (CHiDE), based at Bournemouth University.
28. Communication with author.
29. *AMES 9442 Recollections*, by Tom Hatcher, Radar Operator, RAF, unpublished document made available to author.

30. *History of Concentration Camp Struthof Natzweile*, written by F J M Macdonald, submitted to the Canadian Radar History Project and subsequently made available to author.

CHAPTER 11
1. Communication with author.
2. PRO WO 219/4586 *Operation Overlord*, Draft account of Navigational Air Systems and Radar as employed by Allied Air Forces.
3. Communication with author.
4. PRO WO 219/2697, 1st Allied Airborne Army, Report on operations in Holland.
5. PRO WO 219/2697, 1st Allied Airborne Army, Report on operations in Holland.
6. Communication with author.
7. PRO WO 219/4586 *Operation Overlord*, Draft account of Navigational Air Systems and Radar as employed by Allied Air Forces.
8. PRO WO 219/4586 *Operation Overlord*, Draft account of Navigational Air Systems and Radar as employed by Allied Air Forces.
9. Communication with author.
10. Communication with author.
11. PRO AIR 2/5650 Rebecca Installation in Gliders, Encl 1A, Cipher Telegram from Air Ministry, Whitehall, to RAF Delegation, Washington, dated 16 June 1942.
12. PRO AIR 2/5650 Rebecca Installation in Gliders, Letter from HQACC to Under Secretary of State, Air Ministry, 13 June 1942.
13. PRO AIR 2/5650 Rebecca Installation in Gliders, Encl 6A dated 25 October 1942.
14. PRO AIR 2/5650 Rebecca Installation in Gliders, Encl 28A, para 10, document dated 9 March 1943.
15. PRO AIR 2/5650 Rebecca Installation in Gliders, Encls 39A and 52B.
16. PRO AIR 2/5650, Encl 61A dated 22 September 1943.
17. PRO AIR 37/570 Radar Airborne Policy, Encl 9A.
18. PRO AIR 2/5650 Rebecca Installation in Gliders, Encl 106A, document dated 8 September 1944.
19. PRO AIR 2/5650 Rebecca Installation in Gliders, Encl 109A.
20. PRO AIR 37/302 Reports on Allied airborne effort.
21. PRO AIR 37/302 Reports on Allied airborne effort, Report produced by the Assistant Adjutant General, Allied Force HQ, on 25 October 1944, para 6.
22. PRO AIR 37/302 Reports on Allied airborne effort, Encl 20A.
23. Communication with author.
24. Communication with author.
25. Document made available to author.
26. Communication with author.
27. Communication with author.
28. PRO AIR 20/10223, *34 Wing, An Unofficial Account*.
29. PRO AIR 20/10223, *34 Wing, An Unofficial Account*.
30. PRO AIR 20/10223, *34 Wing, An Unofficial Account*.

CHAPTER 12
1. PRO AIR 20/8970 V2 Rockets - Countermeasures Policy, Encl 3A.
2. PRO : AIR 20/8969 V2 Rockets - Countermeasures Policy, Encl 3A, Minute produced at the Telecommunications Research Establishment by R Cockburn, dated 12 July 1944, referring to the meeting which had taken place at the Air Ministry the previous day.

3. PRO AIR 20/8969 V2 Rockets - Countermeasures Policy, Encl 7A, Director General of Signals writing to the Deputy Chief of the Air Staff on 22 July 1944.

4. PRO AIR 20/8969 V2 Rockets - Countermeasures Policy, Encl 20A, TRE Memo D2432/5/DT dated 31 July 1944.

5. PRO AIR 20/8969 V2 Rockets - Countermeasures Policy, Encl 22A, Director General of Signals memo dated 3 August 1944, in which he proposed that immediate arrangements be made for two additional squadrons to be made available for fitting with the requisite jammer, which was already fitted on some aircraft in the one squadron currently engaged on radio countermeasures.

6. PRO AIR 20/8969 V2 Rockets - Countermeasures Policy, Encl 83A Cypher message from Air Ministry to the UK High Commissioner in Canada and the RAF Delegation in Washington dated 28 September 1944.

7. PRO AIR 20/8969 V2 Rockets - Countermeasures Policy, Encl 86A, DD of Tels 2, Message to D of Ops dated 7 October 1944; Encl 115A, DD of Tels 2, Message to D of Ops dated 16 December 1944; and Encl 127A, DD of Tels 2, Message to D of Ops, undated.

8. PRO AIR 20/8969 V2 Rockets - Countermeasures Policy, Encl 127A, DD of Tels 2, Message to D of Ops, undated.

9. *WWII Radar, The Story of One Group, Royal Canadian Air Force, 1941-1945*, a privately produced compilation updated at 26 May 1999.

10. Letter from Robert Jones to Janet Macdonald, dated 22 April 1996, included in the second issue of *West Coast Radar News*, edited by Janet Macdonald, made available to author.

11. Letter from Robert Jones to Janet Macdonald, dated 22 April 1996, included in the second issue of *West Coast Radar News*, edited by Janet Macdonald, made available to author.

12. Communication with author.

13. Communication with author.

14. Communication with author.

15. Communication with author.

16. Angus Hamilton's book, *Canadians on Radar in South East Asia, 1941-1945*, ACH Publishing, New Brunswick, 1998.

17. Angus Hamilton's book, *Canadians on Radar in South East Asia, 1941-1945*, ACH Publishing, New Brunswick, 1998.

18. Communication with author.

19. Communication with author.

20. Communication with author].

21. PRO WO 291/1331 Operational Research in North West Europe, June 1944 to July 1945, Report # 28, The use of mobile radar control posts for air support for the Army.

22. PRO WO 291/1331 Operational Research in North West Europe, June 1944 to July 1945, Report # 28, The use of mobile radar control posts for air support for the Army.

23. PRO WO 291/1331 Operational Research in North West Europe, June 1944 to July 1945, Report # 28, The use of mobile radar control posts for air support for the Army, Part II.

24. PRO WO 291/1331 Operational Research in North West Europe, June 1944 to July 1945, Report # 28, The use of mobile radar control posts for air support for the Army, Part II.

25. PRO AIR 37/570 Radar Airborne Policy, Encl 60A.

CHAPTER 13
1. Communication with author.
2. Communication with author.
3. Communication with author.
4. Communication with author.
5. Communication with author.
6. Angus Hamilton's book, *Canadians on Radar in South East Asia, 1941-1945*, ACH Publishing, New Brunswick, 1998.
7. Janet Macdonald, writing in the second issue of *West Coast Radar News*, October 1996, made available to author.
8. Communication with author.
9. Communication with author.
10. Communication with author.
11. Communication with author.
12. *WWII Radar, The Story of One Group, Royal Canadian Air Force, 1941-1945*, a privately produced compilation updated at 26 May 1999.
13. Don Tilley quoted this verse in a letter he wrote to Bob McNarry, dated 22 July 1991, which has been made available to author.
14. Taped reminiscences, Calgary Radar Reunion 1996, made available to author.
15. Communication with author.
16. Communication with author.
17. Communication with author.
18. Communication with author.
19. Communication with author.
20. Communication with author.
21. *WWII Radar, The Story of One Group, Royal Canadian Air Force, 1941-1945*, a privately produced compilation updated at 26 May 1999.
22. Communication with author.
23. Communication with author.
24. Communication with author.
25. Résumé prepared by J Victor Davies, 23 August 1993, and made available to author.
26. Communication with author.
27. *Memories of a WWII Radar Mechanic*, unpublished manuscript by Robert G Warner, made available to author.
28. Taped reminiscences, Calgary Radar Reunion 1996, made available to author.
29. Letter from G C Lee, dated 10 July 1993, submitted to the Canadian Radar History Project and subsequently made available to author.

CHAPTER 14
1. Communication with author.
2. *WWII Radar, The Story of One Group, Royal Canadian Air Force, 1941-1945*, a privately produced compilation updated at 26 May 1999.
3. *WWII Radar, The Story of One Group, Royal Canadian Air Force, 1941-1945*, a privately produced compilation updated at 26 May 1999.
4. *WWII Radar, The Story of One Group, Royal Canadian Air Force, 1941-1945*, a privately produced compilation updated at 26 May 1999.
5. Undated letter from L J Palmer, submitted to the Canadian Radar History Project and subsequently made available to author.

6. Résumé prepared by J Victor Davies, 23 August 1993, and made available to author.
7. *Airforce*, January/February/March 1988.
8. *Memories of a WWII Radar Mechanic*, unpublished manuscript by Robert G Warner, made available to author.
9. Commemorative brochure produced for the WWII Radar Reunion in London, Ontario, 21/23 September 1999.
10. Commemorative brochure produced for the WWII Radar Reunion in London, Ontario, 21/23 September 1999.
11. Made available to the author by the RNZAF Museum in Christchurch.
12. *Royal New Zealand Air Force*, by Squadron Leader J M S Ross, one of the volumes comprising the Official History of New Zealand in the Second World War 1939-45, War History Branch, Department of Internal Affairs, Wellington, New Zealand, 1955.
13. Text of Dr F J Hewitt's talk to the SA Military History Society on 9 May 1974, made available to author.
14. PRO AIR 20/6071 RAAF Radar situation in SW Pacific Area, A report by Group Captain G P Chamberlain, Director of Radio Services, RAAF, dated 12 February 1944.
15. PRO AIR 20/6071 RAAF Radar situation in SW Pacific Area, A report by Group Captain G P Chamberlain, Director of Radio Services, RAAF, dated 12 February 1944, Para 24.
16. PRO AIR 20/6071 RAAF Radar situation in SW Pacific Area, A report by Group Captain G P Chamberlain, Director of Radio Services, RAAF, dated 12 February 1944, Para 36.
17. PRO AIR 20/6071 RAAF Radar situation in SW Pacific Area, A report by Group Captain G P Chamberlain, Director of Radio Services, RAAF, dated 12 February 1944, Para 16.
18. PRO AIR 20/6071 RAAF Radar situation in SW Pacific Area, A report by Group Captain G P Chamberlain, Director of Radio Services, RAAF, dated 12 February 1944, Para 19.
19. PRO AIR 20/6071 RAAF Radar situation in SW Pacific Area, A report by Group Captain G P Chamberlain, Director of Radio Services, RAAF, dated 12 February 1944.
20. Submission by H W Beall to the Canadian Radar History Project and subsequently made available to author.
21. Undated letter from Ethel Williamson to Al Revill, in connection with the Canadian Radar History Project, made available to author.
22. Unpublished manuscript by Bob Linden, made available to author.

CHAPTER 15

1. Booklet produced for the WWII Radar Reunion in London, Ontario, 21/23 September 1999; it names Leading Aircraftman John Watson and gives the date as 28 August 1941, adding that he is buried in Cornwall, England.
2. *Memories of a WWII Radar Mechanic*, unpublished manuscript by Robert G Warner, made available to author.
3. Communication with author.
4. Letter from R Jay Christensen to Bob Linden, dated 27 September 1993, made available to author.
5. Paper by Bob Linden and Mel Goldberg which quotes Hansard 3376 Vol IV, 7 June 1943.
6. Communication with author.

7. PRO AIR 2/5435, RDF Mechanics – Training, Encl 214A, Group Captain Carter's letter was dated 30 March 1943.
8. PRO AIR 2/5435, RDF Mechanics – Training, Encl 230A.
9. PRO AIR 2/5435, RDF Mechanics – Training, Encl 221C.
10. PRO AIR 2/5435, RDF Mechanics – Training, Encl 4A within folder entitled 'Canadian and American personnel questions'.
11. *Memories of a WWII Radar Mechanic*, unpublished manuscript by Robert G Warner, made available to author.
12. Communication with author.
13. Article by Group Captain Adrian Cocks in a special edition of the *Clinton News-Record* on 24 August 1994, commemorating the 60th Anniversary of the Air Force Telecom Association (AFTA).
14. *The Radar Mechanics' Secret War, 1940 – 1945*, a self-published manuscript by Dick Moule.
15. Communication with author.
16. *Brief history of # 106 Squadron, Radar Section*, compiled by Jim Chisholm and Mike Burke, December 1993, made available to author.
17. *Beam Bombers: The Secret War of No 109 Squadron*, Michael Cumming, Sutton Publishing, 1998.
18. *Can You Keep A Secret*, Eric M Coleman, Nameloc Publishing, British Columbia, 1995.
19. *The Radar Mechanics' Secret War, 1940 – 1945*, a self-published manuscript by Dick Moule.
20. Communication with author.
21. Souvenir Publication of Calgary Radar Reunion '96, prepared and written by A Wilson.
22. Communication with author.
23. Douglas Fisher's column in *The Sunday Sun*, 21 April 1996.
24. Communication with author.
25. Communication with author.
26. Bob Linden's personal files, made available to author.
27. Communication with author.
28. Communication with author.
29. Letter to Les Card, Chairman of the 1996 Radar Reunion in Calgary, made available to author.
30. Souvenir Publication of Calgary Radar Reunion '96, prepared and written by A Wilson.

BIBLIOGRAPHY

2194 Days of War, An illustrated chronology of the Second World War, compiled by Cesare Salmaggi and Alfredo Pallavisini, Galley Press, 1988.

A Radar History of World War II, Technical and Military Imperatives, Louis Brown, Institute of Physics Publishing, Bristol and Philadelphia, 1999.

Bawdsey - Birth of the Beam, Gordon Kinsey, Terence Dalton Limited, Lavenham, 1983.

Beam Bombers: The Secret War of No 109 Squadron, Michael Cumming, Sutton, 1998.

Can You Keep A Secret, Eric M Coleman, Nameloc Publishing, British Columbia, 1995.

Canadians on Radar in South East Asia, 1941-1945, Angus Hamilton, ACH Publishing, New Brunswick, 1998.

Collins New Age Encyclopaedia, William Collins, London and Glasgow, 1963.

My Radar Service in WWII, Fred B Grahame, Magra Publishing, 1993.

Oxford Interactive Encyclopedia, TLC Properties Inc, 1997.

Radar Days, by E G Bowen, Adam Hilger, 1987.

Royal Air Force, 1939-1945, Vol 2, Denis Richards and Hilary St George Saunders, HMSO, 1954.

Royal New Zealand Air Force, by Squadron Leader J M S Ross, one of the volumes comprising the Official History of New Zealand in the Second World War 1939-45, War History Branch, Department of Internal Affairs, Wellington, New Zealand, 1955.

The Bruneval Raid: Flashpoint of the Radar War, George Millar, The Bodley Head, 1974.

The Forgotten Dead, Ken Small, Bloomsbury, 1989.

The March of the Prairie Men: a story of The South Saskatchewan Regiment, G B Buchanan, Midwest Litho, Saskatoon, Canada, 1957.

The Silent Observer, David W Acaster, Turner-Warwick Printers Inc, Saskatchewan, 1990.

The Squadrons of the RAF and Commonwealth 1918-88, James J Halley, Air-Britain, 1988.

World War II, 50th Anniversary Commemorative Edition, Ivor Matale, Guild Publishing, London, 1989.

Additional material

Honours and Awards granted during the Second World War to RCAF Radar Personnel, Limited private edition (1996), Hugh A Halliday, Douglas A Swanson and Robert F Linden.

WWII Radar, The Story of One Group, Royal Canadian Air Force, 1941-1945, a privately produced compilation updated at 26 May 1999.

Brief History of # 60 (RDF) Group, Directorate of Signals, RAF, 1939-1945, J R Robinson.

Brief history of # 106 Squadron, Radar Section, compiled by Jim Chisholm and Mike Burke.

The Radar Mechanics' Secret War, 1940 - 1945, a self-published manuscript by Dick Moule.

Memories of a WWII Radar Mechanic, unpublished manuscript by Robert G Warner.

D-Day, Normandy, 1944, Record of RAF 15083 GCI in training for, on and after 6th June 1944, by R H McCall, Squadron Leader Commanding 15083.

AMES 9442 Recollections, Tom Hatcher, Radar Operator, RAF.

WWII Radar Reunion souvenir publication, Calgary, 7/9 June 1996.

WWII Radar Reunion booklet, London, Ontario, 21/23 September 1999.

INDEX